Painting Dublin, 1886–1949

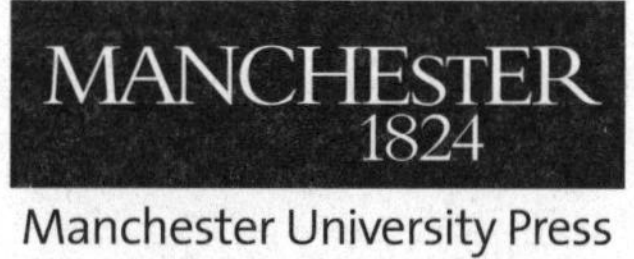MANCHESTER
1824

Manchester University Press

Painting Dublin, 1886–1949

Visualising a changing city

Kathryn Milligan

Manchester University Press

Published by Manchester University Press
Oxford Road, Manchester M13 9PL

www.manchesteruniversitypress.co.uk

British Library Cataloguing-in-Publication Data
A catalogue record for this book is available from the British Library

ISBN   978 1 5261 4410 2 hardback
ISBN   978 1 5261 6118 5 paperback

First published 2020

Typeset in 10/12 Apolline Std by
Servis Filmsetting Ltd, Stockport, Cheshire
Printed in Great Britain
by Bell and Bain Ltd, Glasgow

Contents

Plates

1.6 Walter Frederick Osborne, *The Fish Market, Patrick Street*, 1893, oil on canvas, 59.7 × 80 cm (unframed). Collection and image courtesy of Hugh Lane Gallery, Dublin (Reg. No. 23).

1.7 Walter Frederick Osborne, *Dublin Streets: A Vendor of Books*, 1889, oil on canvas, National Gallery of Ireland. Photo © National Gallery of Ireland.

1.8 Walter Frederick Osborne, *In a Dublin Park, Light and Shade*, c.1895, oil on canvas, National Gallery of Ireland. Photo © National Gallery of Ireland.

1.9 Walter Frederick Osborne, *The Four Courts, Dublin*, c. 1901, oil on board, National Gallery of Ireland. Photo © National Gallery of Ireland.

2.1 Rose Barton, *Relieving the Castle Guard*, 1891, watercolour on paper. Photograph by Davison & Associates, courtesy of the Office of Public Works.

2.2 Michael Angelo Hayes, *St Patrick's Day, Military Parade at Dublin Castle*, 1844, watercolour on paper. Photograph by Dennis Mortell, courtesy of the Office of Public Works.

2.3 Rose Barton, *Going to the Levée at Dublin Castle*, 1897, watercolour on paper, National Gallery of Ireland. Photo © National Gallery of Ireland.

2.4 Rose Barton, *Waterloo Bridge, London*, 1893, watercolour on paper, private collection. Image courtesy of Sotheby's, London.

2.5 Rose Barton, *South Kensington Station*, 1894, watercolour on paper, private collection. Image courtesy of Sotheby's, London.

2.6 Rose Barton, *The Rotunda Rooms*, 1900, watercolour on paper, private collection. Image courtesy of Sotheby's, London.

3.1 Jack Butler Yeats, *Rum Old Hairdressers near the Academy*, 1900, watercolour, ink and graphite on paper. Yeats Archive, National Gallery of Ireland. © Estate of Jack B. Yeats, DACS London / IVARO Dublin, 2019.

3.2 Jack Butler Yeats, *King Billy*, 1901, watercolour and ink on paper. Henry W. and Albert A. Berg Collection of English and American Literature, The New York Public Library. © Estate of Jack B. Yeats, DACS London / IVARO Dublin, 2019.

3.3 Jack Butler Yeats, *The DBC Café*, 1901, watercolour and ink on paper. Henry W. and Albert A. Berg Collection of English and American Literature, The New York Public Library. © Estate of Jack B. Yeats, DACS London / IVARO Dublin, 2019.

3.4 Jack Butler Yeats, *The Barcore*, 1908, watercolour, ink and graphite on paper. Yeats Archive, National Gallery of Ireland. © Estate of Jack B. Yeats, DACS London / IVARO Dublin, 2019.

3.5 Jack Butler Yeats, *A Westerly Wind*, 1921, oil on canvas. On private loan to the Collections of Trinity College Dublin. © Estate of Jack B. Yeats, DACS London / IVARO Dublin, 2019.

board, 67 × 97 cm (unframed). Collection and image courtesy of Hugh Lane Gallery, Dublin (Reg. No. 1824). © The Estate of Harry Kernoff.

4.4   Harry Kernoff, *Summer's Day at Leeson Bridge*, 1936, oil on paper, private collection. Image courtesy of Sotheby's, London. © The Estate of Harry Kernoff.

4.5   Harry Kernoff, *Boats at Anchor – Grand Canal Quay*, 1937, watercolour on paper, private collection. Image courtesy of Adam's, Dublin. © The Estate of Harry Kernoff.

4.6   Harry Kernoff, *Winetavern Street*, 1934, oil on panel, 37.8 × 58 cm (unframed). Collection and image courtesy of Hugh Lane Gallery, Dublin (Reg. No. 784). © The Estate of Harry Kernoff.

4.7   Harry Kernoff, *Self-Portrait*, 1929, oil on paper, private collection. Image courtesy of Sotheby's, London. © The Estate of Harry Kernoff.

4.8   Harry Kernoff, *Davy Byrne's Pub, Dublin, from the Bailey*, 1941, oil on board, National Gallery of Ireland. Photo © National Gallery of Ireland. © The Estate of Harry Kernoff.

Figures

Note: As there is no known copyright holder for Flora H. Mitchell, her works cannot be reproduced in this volume. However, the original watercolours for her *Vanishing Dublin* publication are available to view on the National Gallery of Ireland's website, and the relevant object numbers have been listed in the endnotes. The catalogue can be accessed at onlinecollection.nationalgallery.ie. It has not been possible to include reproductions of some private collection works, but many of these are available online through auction house records.

Acknowledgements

My first thanks go to those who have offered support, feedback, and mentorship at different stages of the research and writing of *Painting Dublin*: Yvonne Scott and Philip McEvansoneya, Department of History of Art and Architecture, Trinity College Dublin; Emily Mark Fitzgerald, UCD School of Art History and Cultural Policy; and Nicholas Allen, Willson Centre for the Humanities and Arts, University of Georgia.

An Irish Research Council Government of Ireland Postdoctoral Fellowship at the UCD School of Art History and Cultural Policy (2017–19) was crucial for bringing this book to completion. This fellowship enabled me to conduct further research abroad, travel to international conferences, and provided much needed funding to source images for publication. During this period, I was a Resident Scholar at the UCD Humanities Institute, and I offer sincere thanks to Anne Fuchs, Director of the HI, who ensures that the Institute is a sheltering and stimulating environment for early career researchers. The benefit of having a dedicated workspace, shared with other postdoctoral and postgraduate scholars cannot be underestimated, especially in these times of academic precarity. I am particularly grateful to the cohort of H105: Sarah Comyn, Stephan Ehrig, Sarah Galletly, Alison Garden, Scott Hamilton, Shonagh Hill, Britta Jung, Megan Kuster, Zosia Kuczyńska, Dan O'Brien, and Sarah Sharp. I would also like to thank Valerie Norton and Ricki Schoen, UCD Humanities Institute; Carla Briggs, Philip Cottrell, Kathleen James-Chakraborty, Conor Lucey, and Elizabeth Varley, UCD School of Art History and Cultural Policy, for making my time at UCD so fulfilling. I have frequently benefitted from the advice, knowledge, and support of Ewelina Bykuc, Marie Bourke, Nicola Figgis, Angela Griffith, Gearóid Hayes, Róisín Kennedy, Niamh McGuinne, Niamh McNally, Donal Maguire, Brendan Rooney, Ellen Rowley, and the committee members of the Dublin History Research Network.

I am grateful for the additional financial assistance offered by the National University of Ireland's Publication Grant Scheme. Emma Brennan and Alun

Richards at Manchester University Press have been a pleasure to work with; I would also like to thank the anonymous readers who gave insightful feedback on my proposal and manuscript.

The following people were instrumental in gathering together the images reproduced in this publication: Louise Morgan and Leah Benson, National Gallery of Ireland; Berni Metcalfe, James Harte, and Glenn Dunne, National Library of Ireland; Philip Roe, Dublin City Gallery the Hugh Lane; Anne Boddaert and Michael Waldron, Crawford Art Gallery; Johanne Mullen, Irish Museum of Modern Art; William Derham, OPW Dublin Castle; Antoinette Prout, Royal Irish Academy; Catherine Giltrap, Trinity College Art Collections; Phil Pound, Morgan O'Driscoll Fine Art Auctioneers and Valuers; James O'Halloran, Adams Auctioneers; Chris Sutherns, Tate; Órna Roche, UCD Digital Library; Sharon Sutton, Digital Resources and Imaging Service, Trinity College Dublin; Arabella Bishop and Beatrice Moller, Sotheby's; Stephen at the Picture Library of the National Museums of Northern Ireland; Mark at the Oriel Gallery; and staff of the British Museum Images Service, Getty Images, Harvard Art Museums, and the New York Public Library. Thanks also to Chris Walsh of IVARO – Irish Visual Artists Rights Organisation, and the representatives of the estates of Estella Solomons and Harry Kernoff.

I am immensely grateful to those at the National Gallery of Ireland who have continually supported my research and enabled me to share aspects of it with the public: Sarah Conroy, Joanne Drum, and Sinéad Rice deserve special thanks, as well as the wonderful voices of the National Gallery of Ireland Workplace Choir who provide a much needed respite from writing on Tuesday evenings. I have been blessed with a wonderful group of friends who have, in turn, offered good advice, cups of coffee, and pairs of keen eyes over the course of this process. My sincere thanks go to Myles Campbell, Catherine Coughlan, William Derham, Sarah Maguire, Caroline McGee, Niamh Nic Ghabhann, Fariha Shaikh, Colleen Thomas, and especially to Lisa Towell.

My final thanks go to my family: my parents, Lou and Henry; Jennie, Donal, and beloved goddaughters Rachel and Eleanor; Rick, Kate, and darling nephews Edward and Charles. This book is dedicated to Grace Madigan, my favourite *flâneuse* and Dubliner: thank you for being endlessly cheering, patient, questioning, and supportive.

Abbreviations

DCGHL	Dublin City Gallery the Hugh Lane
DMP	Dublin Metropolitan Police
DMSA	Dublin Metropolitan School of Art
DORA	Defence of the Realm Act
DSC	Dublin Sketching Club
FSR	Friends of Soviet Russia
GPO	General Post Office
IRA	Irish Republican Army
NGI	National Gallery of Ireland
NLI	National Library of Ireland
RA	Royal Academy of Arts
RDS	Royal Dublin Society
RHA	Royal Hibernian Academy
RIC	Royal Irish Constabulary
WCSI	Watercolour Society of Ireland

Introduction:
from Empire to Republic,
1886–1949

From the top of the steeple of St George's Church, Hardwicke Place, the city of Dublin stretches out across the canvas in a maze of streets and houses (Plate 0.1). Black, skeletal watercolour ships trace their way to-and-fro across the bay and up the river, carrying goods and people into the heart of the conurbation, while hazy blue mountains lie on the horizon, connecting land, sea, and sky. On close examination, the mass of rooftops and chimneys separate out into recognisable forms: the viewer of this painting can identify some of the city's eighteenth-century squares – Mountjoy, Parnell, and Merrion Square – the Rotunda Pleasure Gardens, the parkland of Trinity College and St Stephen's Green, the broad sweep of Sackville Street, and the curve of College Green. Looking closer still, sculptural and architectural features emerge: Nelson's Pillar rises beside the portico of the General Post Office on Sackville Street (renamed O'Connell Street in 1924); equestrian monuments of William III and George II are seen on Dame Street and in Stephen's Green, along with the campanile in Trinity College and the Rutland Memorial Fountain on Merrion Square. In addition to landmark buildings like the Custom House and Rotunda Hospital, the glass dome of the exhibition hall, constructed for the Irish Industrial Exhibition in 1853, extends along Leinster Lawn.

With the geography of the city mapped out, the artist draws our eye to the people of the city. Sackville Street is filled with carriages and outside-cars, a troop of red-coated soldiers march in formation, while people stroll in the Rotunda Pleasure Gardens. Smaller and narrower streets reveal people at work and leisure, with social demarcations made visible through the character of the street and the activities taking place within its environs. In parts of the composition, the dense warren of streets merges into abstract areas of ink and watercolour with simple geometric shapes giving a mere suggestion of windows and rooftops; chimneys emit gentle eddies of grey smoke. Painted by James Mahony, *Dublin from the Spire of St George's Church, Hardwicke Place* captures the geographical and physical life of nineteenth-century Dublin: a city of the

British Empire, replete with symbolic markers of its place within this global network of trade and military power. This painting, however, is also a record of a city on the brink of change. Although the architectural spine of the city was completed in the eighteenth century, by the 1850s it was rapidly expanding; both commercially, with new retail and banking districts, and physically, with the development of suburbs to the north and south. The statue of William III, for example, was a repeated flashpoint for political tensions; in 1916 the GPO became the headquarters of the Easter Rising; and in 1922, Sackville Street was largely destroyed by the Irish Civil War, having only just been rebuilt after its destruction in the earlier conflict. The artistic representation of this changing and evolving city lies at the heart of this book, explored through the paintings and prints of six artists spanning the late nineteenth and early twentieth century. Through their artworks we can glimpse at the experience of living in Dublin through these often-turbulent years and witness how the depiction of urban life connected artists in Ireland to an international artistic community and tradition.

Dublin in Irish cultural history

'To understand Dublin,' Oliva Robertson wrote, 'one must know its life in its fashionable squares and in its slums, in its suburbs and in its Georgian tenements; the life of its artists and students … the life of the old with their memories and the fresh hope that springs up with children; and the life that comes to us from airport and harbour.'[1] Writing in the 1950s, Robertson was taking stock of the changes that had been wrought in the city in the preceding decades, its characterisation in the writings of James Joyce and Seán O'Casey, and the challenges that still remained for Dublin to become a worthy capital of the young Irish Republic. Robertson's memoir of mid-century Dublin contributed to the considerable body of writing on the city (both real or imagined), creating a vivid textual picture of life in its houses, streets, and squares. To date, however, little attention has been paid to the equally varied visual representations of the city created by artists in Ireland during the late nineteenth and early twentieth centuries. Seeking to redress this imbalance, this volume will explore the representation of Dublin in visual art (chiefly painting and print), with a specific focus on the lives and artworks of Walter Frederick Osborne (1859–1903), Rose Mary Barton (1856–1929), Jack Butler Yeats (1871–1957), Harry Aaron Kernoff (1900–79), Estella Frances Solomons (1882–1968), and Flora Hippisley Mitchell (1890–1973). Presenting these artists as exemplars of urban painting in the Irish context, the text will take its lead from Robertson's suggestion, visiting the broad vistas and narrow courts of the city, outlining the social and political contexts which shaped the lives of these artists, and understanding how the ebb and flow of people, goods, and ideas has shaped the image of Dublin.

A well-established theme in the history of art, the depiction of the city has persistently adapted its form to reflect the concerns of the time and culture in which it was created. For example, when printed views of the city began to be produced by artists and publishers in the late fifteenth century, they 'provided some of the first widely available constructions of urban space that could serve as more than mere badges of a civic site'.[2] The increasing importance of the city as a place of work, industry, and leisure across Europe in the nineteenth century was noted by artists and writers who documented the changes wrought by the processes of commercialisation and industrialisation. As artists refocused on the subject of the city, the urban environment itself became an increasing support for artistic practice: as Theda Shapiro suggests, the city 'was the only acceptable place to live – because of its centrality to buyers and dealers, because of their need for continual dialogue with other artists, writers and critics, because of the unparalleled visual stimulation offered by the urban scene, and because of the privacy that the big city afforded'.[3] Conversely, from the middle of the nineteenth century, attitudes towards the city and urban identity in Ireland were indelibly influenced by the promotion of rural and agrarian life as the true marker of Irish identity, set against the view of cities generally, and Dublin in particular, as the opposite of this ideal, being colonial and largely commercial or industrial.[4] This position was further entrenched by the championing of landscape painting, particularly that of the Western seaboard, as being authentically Irish and forming a central part of an Irish national school of art. This book seeks to move beyond this position, demonstrating how the portrayal and experience of urban life played an important role in the art of the period. Depictions of the city were shaped by historical and social change, particularly as related to the shift from empire to independence, a formative and unavoidable aspect of life in Dublin in the period 1886–1949. Allied to this, a study of urban painting by artists in Ireland highlights their connection to a broader tradition in Western painting, inviting new readings outside of the realms of nationalism and national identity: a prevalent theme of the discipline to date.

Scholarship on Irish art in the nineteenth and early-mid twentieth century has tended to focus on a handful of themes: the relationship between art and national identity, the creation of a national school of painting (based largely, as already mentioned, on the representation of rural life in the west of Ireland), or the engagement of Irish artists with aspects of international modernism in European urban centres (chiefly Paris) and their subsequent difficulty in promoting modernist art in Ireland. Publication and exhibition practices have largely supported these key themes, tending towards biographical or broad survey approaches. More recently, the field has started to expand and take cognisance of more nuanced approaches to the study of the history of Irish art, notably in its connection to broader Western traditions through the circulation of art, artists, and ideas. For example, in volume two of the landmark *Art and Architecture of Ireland* series, Nicola Figgis recognised that despite being on the periphery of Europe, 'artistic ideas and artists flowed freely into and out of the country during the seventeenth, eighteenth and nineteenth centuries', a trend that carried through into the twentieth century, and which is clearly evident in much of the new research in that series.[5] Although the dominance of biography in writing on Irish art and artists has attracted criticism, the form does remain important and useful for elucidating themes within an artist's oeuvre and their approach to a subject. This text uses biography to illuminate aspects of an artist's life which inform their representation of Dublin, embracing their social background, access to education and training, political leanings, and other activities within the urban sphere.[6]

Although the country's national cultural institutions all have paintings and works on paper which represent Dublin and urban life in Ireland, these are rarely shown or presented in the context of the city in art history.[7] A recent publication astutely noted that 'Dublin's awareness and knowledge of her own portrait is weak … most Dubliners can call to mind few, if any, of the great paintings of Dublin'.[8] This is not because such paintings do not exist, but rather a result of these works being rarely shown, seldom reproduced, and, consequently, little discussed. Painting and other fine art media are not immediately associated with the city: from its development in the nineteenth century, photography (and later film) seemed to offer a more dynamic view of the Irish metropolis. Further to this, the role of the city itself as a centre for artistic practice, production, and exchange has been insufficiently examined in the extant history of artistic practice in Ireland. The social and professional networks active in Dublin and through which artists communicated and shared knowledge, along with the commercial businesses that supported the artistic community through provision of materials, framing, shipping, and for a time, special exhibitions; and the impact made by flow of art, artists, and ideas across the Irish Sea to Britain and beyond, played a crucial role in the development of Irish art. To understand the city that artists sought to represent on canvas, board, and paper, it is also important to understand how the environment of Dublin worked to support (or failed to support, as the case may be) its artists. By including this approach in an analysis of these urban painters, the specific nature of Dublin's artistic economy, and its transnational reach, can be fully integrated into the broader historical, social, and political context in which they painted.

Discussion of the cultural representation of Dublin has been dominated by literary studies, with the works of Joyce and other modernist writers providing a rich seam for scholarly research. Early studies of the city and its place in Irish literature written in English emerged from the late 1970s, with a collection of essays edited by Maurice Harmon being an important early foray in the field. In his introduction, Harmon noted that the city was a 'relatively recent subject in Irish writing', but that the approaches and critical perspectives offered in the volume mark it out as 'an increasingly important one'.[9] More recent texts build on the foundations laid by this collection, including Elizabeth Mannion's study of the urban plays of the early Abbey Theatre, and Liam Lanigan's consideration of Joyce, urban planning, and Irish modernism.[10] In 2010, a special issue of *Éire-Ireland* considered a variety of topics on Ireland and the urban, examining several locations in different disciplinary contexts but remaining chiefly focused on literature and history. The designation of Dublin as a UNESCO City of Literature in the same year further underpinned the importance of the written word in Dublin's cultural life, and the annual 'One City, One Book' programme has brought further attention to how the city has been represented by writers and poets over the centuries.[11]

While this scheme is to be lauded, it can only be equally lamented that a similar interest in the visual history of the city has not emerged. In both historical and literary publications, Irish artists' visions of the city have more often appeared as illustrations (if included at all), with no further exploration of the artist, the aspect of city life represented by the painter, or how this may relate to the broader history of urban depiction, causing, as Mary Jane Boland has noted, their place in 'a long tradition of painting urban life in European art history' to be overlooked.[12] Given the sustained interest in the city's history and culture, as shown by the continued appetite for new research on the city, a new awareness of the image of the city and the artists who created these works is long overdue. By examining these artworks in relation to the local context in which they were made and the art historical tradition in which they sit, we can gain a new understanding of the city in Irish art and Dublin's place in the history of urban painting.

Author Dermot Bolger has previously commented that Dublin was 'fortunate in not having been built on water, like Venice, or on sand, like Amsterdam. Otherwise its foundations would have sunk by now under the weight of the books written in recent years about aspects of its history.'[13] The city has indeed become the focus of many books, edited collections, and journal articles, as scholarly and general interest in Ireland's urban history spreads, with many focusing on topics related to political and social life in the city, as well as housing, planning, and commercial activity. Survey texts, such as David Dickson's *Dublin: The Making of a Capital City*, or *The Making of Dublin City* series, published by Four Courts Press and now numbering six volumes on different aspects of the city's history, encompass the broad sweep of Dublin's past, and build on several other studies completed at local and university level. As with literature, this flourishing of interest in Irish urban history is relatively recent: in 1986, Mary Daly noted that Irish historians had 'been rather slow to recognise that urban history constituted a valid area for research'; however, much ground has been covered in the interim.[14] Reassessing the field in a special issue of *Urban History* in 2018, Erika Hanna and Richard Butler also note that the dominant emphasis in Irish history has 'been on the field rather than the street', a phrase that could be equally applied to much of the scholarship on Irish art.[15] Aspects of this body of new research are particularly relevant for this study, notably the increasing focus on city politics, and the rise of the middle-classes, housing, and commercial life in Dublin through the period 1850–1950. In addition, Hanna and Butler emphasise that Irish cities 'have always operated as sites of movement', and as 'places of reception: of people, culture, and capital', factors that are important in relation to the movement of art, artists, and the development of an art market in Dublin.[16]

A focus on circulation and mobility, encompassing people, objects, or commodities, is useful in understanding the circumstances of art production in Dublin through the late nineteenth and early twentieth centuries. As a port city (referred to by David Dickson as 'the capital of the Irish sea'), Dublin was connected by travel and trade routes to a vast network of cities, bolstered in much of the period under discussion by its place within the British Empire.[17] Literary historians have started to trace how the flow of goods and commodities to and from Dublin can be traced in texts; for example, through Joyce's invocation of a 'sensorium of empire', through objects made from ivory, teak, or mahogany, or through goods such as tea and sugar.[18] For all of the artists considered in this volume, travel between Dublin, London, and other European cities was a formative aspect of their artistic development, while the display of international art in Dublin (often routed through dealers and galleries in Britain) offered opportunities to see contemporary art at home. This is mirrored in the broader social sphere: life in Dublin was enriched by a host of travelling cultural experiences, ranging from industrial exhibitions, theatre, music, and dance. A focus on these transnational connections further detaches the work of Irish artists from insular, nationalist readings, emphasising its relevance to a broader European cultural history. The conceptual frameworks around movement, mobility, and circulation (whether, for example, as related to the city itself or an artist's own journeys and travels through the city space) constitute an ever-expanding area of contemporary scholarship, particularly as related to urban life, migration, and diaspora. In addition to the scholarship of Nicholas Allen, Dickson, Figgis, Hanna, and Butler already mentioned, this text has been informed by the writings of Tim Cresswell, Alexandra Boutros, and Will Straw, as well as Ulrike Boskamp and Annette Kranen's exploration of the relationship between mobility studies and art history.[19]

Painting Dublin focuses exclusively on Dublin, rather than other urban centres on the island of Ireland, such as Cork, Limerick, Galway, or Belfast. While a future comparative study – for example, between Dublin and Belfast – would certainly be revealing, this book is concerned with laying a stronger foundation for such a study. Dickson has noted that 'Dublin has been the biggest urban place in a deeply contested island since towns first appeared west of the Irish sea', and its importance in Irish history cannot be disputed.[20] Other factors also guided the decision to focus solely on Dublin at this date: for example, its importance in Ireland's literary tradition, its centrality to political events in the first half of the twentieth century, as well as the city's transitory phases – from 'second city of the empire' in the eighteenth century, 'dear dirty Dublin' and its perceived decline following the Act of Union, and becoming the capital city of the Irish Free State in 1921 and of the Republic in 1949.[21] In contrast to Belfast, Dublin was (and to an extent remains), a commercial and administrative city rather than an industrial centre. This activity indelibly shaped the city's architecture, social calendar, and class structure: issues which all have an important role to play in how the artists considered in this text came to represent the city. As the later part of this introduction will outline, Dublin's importance as a national centre for the arts in Ireland must also be considered: students from around Ireland were attracted to the Dublin Metropolitan School of Art (DMSA); the main representative body for artists in Ireland, the Royal Hibernian Academy (RHA), was located there, and annual exhibitions for the other main societies and groups took place in various city centre venues.

Chapter organisation

Painting Dublin centres around five case study chapters, each of which explores the careers of one or two artists, locating their life and work in the city and delving into some of the key themes and issues which directed their representation of Dublin. Naturally some themes recur across the various chapters, such as identity, politics, and class, and these serve to draw connections between the artists discussed as we move through the late nineteenth and into the twentieth century. To locate the reader more fully in the changing context of Dublin in the period 1886–1949, the latter half of this Introduction will outline the key historical, political, and social events that shaped the city in these years, in addition to introducing the institutions which supported artistic life in the city as pertaining to artistic education, studio life, and artistic societies – as well as opportunities for exhibiting, viewing, and selling art, which will be developed further in subsequent chapters. The purpose of this contextual introduction to the city will be to highlight points of convergence and divergence in relation to the development of the modern city (particularly in the European context) and will argue that Dublin offers a unique example for the study of artists' depictions of the city.

Following this, Chapter 1, 'Poverty, parks, and painting', will focus on Walter Osborne. Although a prolific painter, Osborne's depictions of Dublin have never been fully explored either in relation to urban history or the history of painting the city. The transnational nature of Osborne's training and subsequent artistic career exemplifies themes of mobility and exchange. The chapter will explore Osborne's depictions of children and his practice of sourcing models from the city's tenements, his portrayal of the environs of Patrick Street and St Patrick's Cathedral, and his later paintings of St Stephen's Green. A close analysis of a key painting, *The Dublin Streets: A Vendor of Books*, will consider Osborne's practice of exhibiting works in multiple venues in Britain in relation to networks, circulation, and artistic mobility.

Continuing to focus on the late nineteenth and early twentieth century city, Chapter 2 centres on the watercolours and illustrations of Rose Barton. Like Osborne, Barton's artistic career was punctuated by periods of travel and training abroad, and by frequent movement between Dublin and London. In Dublin, Barton moved in upper-class circles: a persistent theme in her work is that of Dublin Castle and its ceremonies, which attracted viceregal patronage and support. A key section of this chapter will focus on Barton's contribution to *Picturesque Dublin: Old and New*, a descriptive guidebook to the city published in 1898. This text signals a then emerging narrative being spun around Dublin's Georgian past, largely emanating from Anglo-Irish figures, under the guise of recording the legacy and remains of the eighteenth-century city.

Chapter 3 'Dockers, swimmers, and dancers' will show how the depiction of Dublin city and urban life was a consistent theme in Jack B. Yeats's oeuvre, with paintings extending over a wide range of urban subjects and themes: from newspaper boys, flower sellers, and dock workers; to busy bridges, brightly lit streets, and the docks. Through a focus on Yeats's engagement with urban culture generally, and with Dublin in particular, this chapter will readdress this imbalance, demonstrating how his city paintings engage with themes of poverty, sexuality, and popular culture in the early to mid-twentieth century. Utilising the extensive holdings of the Yeats Archive at the National Gallery of Ireland (NGI), the artist's mobility within Dublin will also be illustrated, drawing on the collection of sketchbooks, scrapbooks, and ephemera collected from his routines of walking the city and observing daily life. Yeats's depiction of Dublin from the early 1920s through to the late 1930s will be examined in relation to comparable themes in American art, as well as considering recent scholarship on sexuality, dancing, and moral censorship in Ireland at this time.

Chapter 4, 'Radicals, workers, and drinkers', offers an exploration of the work of Harry Kernoff, a migrant artist working in Dublin from the early 1920s onwards. Although working in the same period as Yeats, Kernoff's artistic technique and choice of subject matter contrasts with his older peer, offering a different view of everyday life in twentieth-century Dublin. The chapter will consider Kernoff's leftist politics in relation to his depiction of Dublin's docks, labourers, and sites or figures associated with the left in Ireland, such as Liberty Hall and James Connolly. Moving into the later 1930s, the focus will shift from the political to the pastoral, examining the artist's cityscapes and urban landscape paintings, taking in a range of subjects, including Stephen's Green, the Grand Canal, and the Dublin literary pub.

The final chapter of *Painting Dublin* will return to the theme of 'old Dublin' (as explored in Chapter 2), but consider it in relation to two new artists, Estella Solomons and Flora Mitchell, and their contributions to publications on Dublin in the 1920s and 1960s respectively. By the time a selection of her Dublin etchings was included in *The Glamour of Dublin* in 1928, Solomons had already gathered a significant corpus of etchings depicting the Dublin streets. Examining these etchings, their subjects, and the publications they were reproduced in, the first part of this chapter will argue that Solomons's depiction of Dublin was more akin to the nineteenth-century city depicted by Osborne and Barton, rather than the times in which she lived and worked. The second part of this chapter will extend these themes, focusing on the art of Mitchell, largely produced, exhibited, and published in the 1960s. Mitchell's *Vanishing Dublin* watercolours will be examined in relation to the evolution of the depiction of Dublin as outlined over the course of the volume, as well as in relation to other contemporary visualisations – chiefly the photographs of Elinor Wiltshire from the Wiltshire Collection at the National Library of Ireland (NLI).

Empire to Republic: living in a changing city

On 17 April 1949, thousands of people gathered in Dublin city centre to mark, at midnight, the formal enactment of the Republic of Ireland Act (1948) (Figure 0.1). The act severed the formal link between the twenty-six county republic and the British state: by holding the ceremony on Easter Monday, it also sanctified the ambitions of the Proclamation of the Irish Republic which had been read by Patrick Pearse outside of the General Post Office some thirty-three years previous. There had been casualties, including the loss of the six counties which now constitute Northern Ireland, but the atmosphere of this photograph – the river illuminated by the brilliant neon signs scatted over the adjacent buildings – presents a scene of jovial urbanity, the capital of a modern Irish nation proclaiming its place in the world. For this book, this nocturnal scene marks the end point, and the beginning couldn't look more different. In April 1886, the British

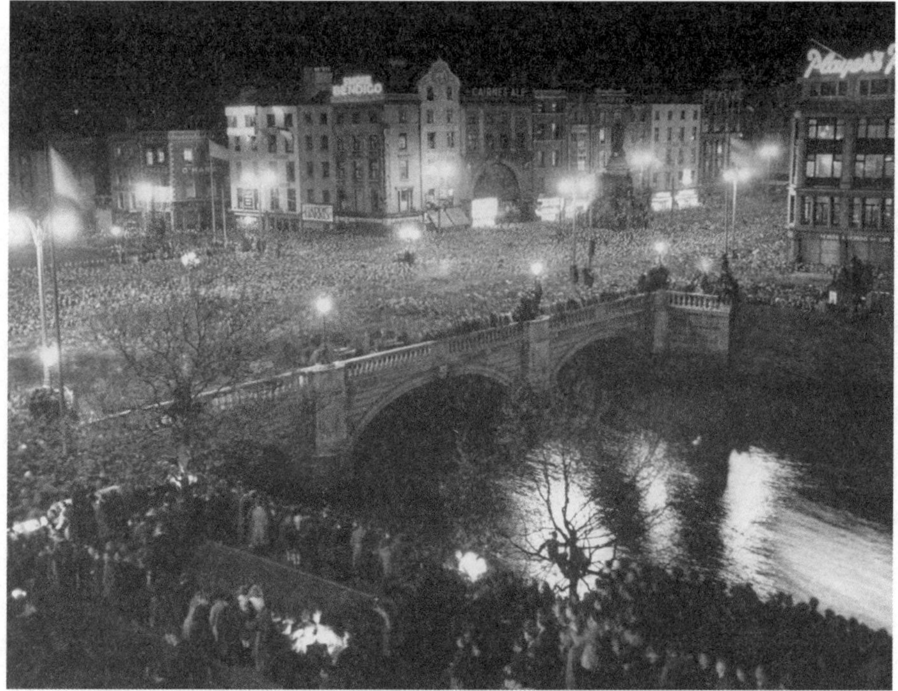

0.1   Larry Burrows, *People celebrating the independence of Ireland, 1949.*

Prime Minister William Gladstone introduced the Government of Ireland Bill (also known as the First Home Rule Bill) to parliament, following decades of campaigning by Irish politicians for a devolved government. Although the measures that the Bill proposed were imperfect, it was broadly supported by those who had been campaigning for it, yet, in June of the same year, it was roundly defeated. On the day following the Bill's defeat, the Dublin newspapers carried stories about jubilant Orangemen in Belfast and speculation on an imminent election. These two legislative moments bookend a crucial period in Irish modern history. In political, social, and cultural terms, Dublin became a central stage where the shift from city of empire to capital of a new republic was played out and where the confluence of different political and culture affiliation met.

By the 1880s, Dublin was among the most 'Anglicised' parts of Ireland, and as Gearóid Ó Tuathaigh has noted, was 'firmly embedded in an increasingly integrated UK economy, with a well-developed communications system, and with rising literacy'.[22] As the seat of the British administration in Ireland, Dublin Castle played an important role in both administrative and cultural terms both prior to and following the Act of Union in 1800. Overseeing this administration was the monarch's representative, the lord lieutenant or viceroy, who acted, as Peter Gray and Olwen Purdue have described, 'in theory if not always in practice' as both 'royal surrogate' and 'working head of a subordinate administration'.[23] By the late nineteenth century, much of the business of administering government in Ireland was undertaken by the Chief Secretary, rendering much of the viceroy's activities largely ceremonial. Like many other European cities at this time, Dublin was characterised by stark contrasts: signs of emergent modernity were evident in its public transportation system which connected the city and suburbs; the telegraph and postal system which connected it to America and Britain; as well as a thriving popular culture scene, replete with panoramas, theatres, and music halls (Figure 0.2). From the 1850s onwards, several large cultural institutions were established in the city. The NGI opened its doors to the public in 1864, followed by the National Museum (then called the Dublin Museum of Science and Art) and the NLI in the 1890s, all of which focused attention on Dublin as an artistic and cultural centre.[24] While national affairs were managed from Dublin Castle, the city was governed by Dublin Corporation and a City Council of eight elected aldermen presided over by the Lord Mayor of Dublin. Throughout the nineteenth and early twentieth centuries, the Council was the battleground between the city's main factions – nationalist and unionist – which often impacted on the municipal functions which lay under its remit.[25]

Reviewing the social composition of late nineteenth-century Dublin, David Dickson identified 'at least four distinct social layers across the greater urban area', comprised of 'a professions-centred layer, still mainly Protestant; a "respectable" world of the "shopocracy", mixed in its religious affiliations; a Dublin of the productive working classes, predominantly Catholic; and the city of the destitute'.[26] As the nineteenth century progressed, these social divisions

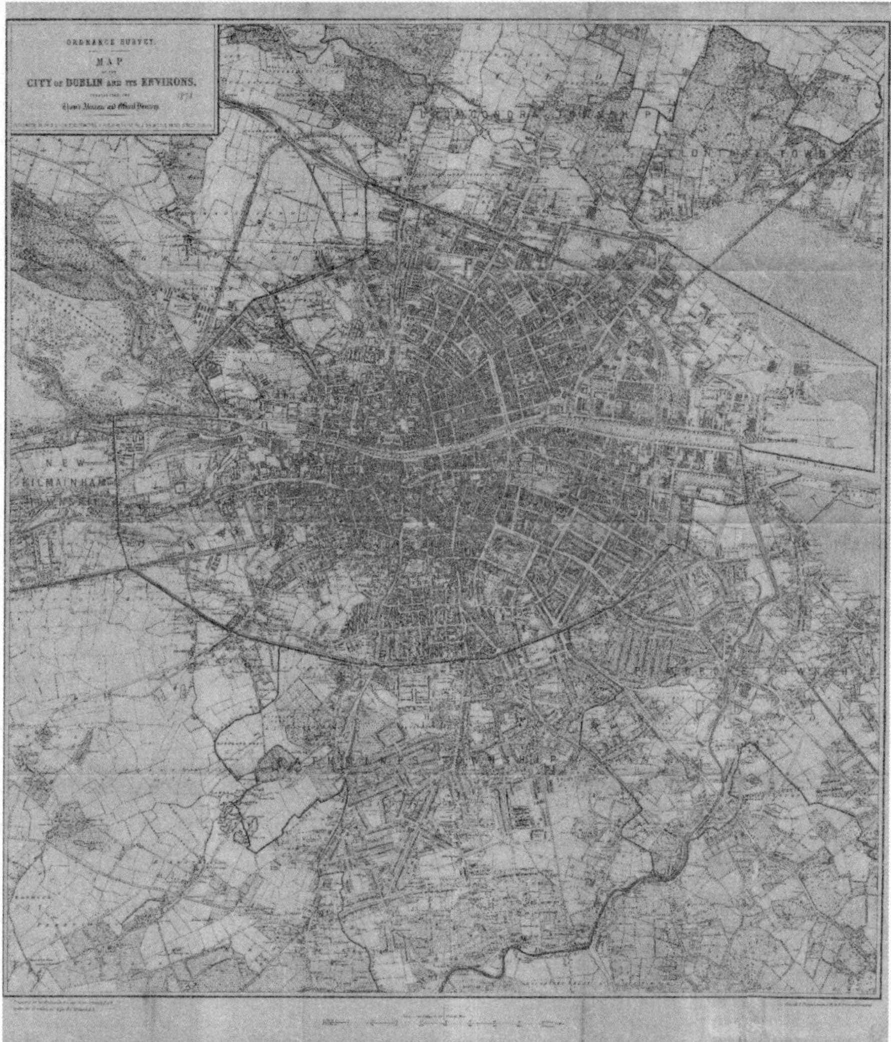

0.2   Map of the city of Dublin and its environs, constructed for *Thom's Dublin and County Street Directory*, c.1898.

were made evident through uneven urban development. As the professional and shopocracy classes increasingly moved to new towns in the suburbs (such as Rathmines and Rathgar to the south, and Phibsborough and Drumcondra to the north), the latter two categories foundered in the rapidly deteriorating housing stock of the city centre. For the purposes of governance, the city between the canals – the Grand and the Royal canals – was under the direct control of the Corporation, while the newer suburbs were independent and self-governing. As

Ciarán Wallace has outlined, this placed a stranglehold on the Corporation. As the city's population was largely lower-middle and working class, it could not expand its base of ratepayers, finance new housing, or tackle the slum problem.[27] Despite these difficulties, the late nineteenth century city was expanding and building: for example, the extensive development of Dame Street through the 1860s and 1870s speaks to the city as a growing financial centre, or the nearby South City Markets to small improvements in its commercial infrastructure.

Michael Angelo Hayes' *Sackville Street* expresses this commercial optimism and presents the city's main street as a centre of modernity and conspicuous consumption (Plate 0.2). The composition is framed by three key nineteenth-century architectural features: the General Post Office (1818), the Nelson Pillar (1808), and McSwiney and Delaney's 'New Mart', a palatial department store which opened to the public in 1853. Department stores across the city, such as the New Mart and Switzers, were often at the forefront of the city's modernity; consciously modelled on their French counterparts and providing access to luxury imported goods to those who could afford to shop there. At the *fin-de-siècle*, large-scale bazaars, fairs, and industrial exhibitions provided further venues for Dubliners to engage with consumerist trends.[28] There were commercial art repositories, such as Thomas Cranfield and J. D. Spence, which in addition to selling art and stationery supplies, occasionally hosted small or single painting exhibitions and sold a variety of engravings and other prints of popular and artistic subjects.[29]

The RHA occupied a central (if disputed) role in Dublin's artistic scene. Founded to provide a professional association for artists in Ireland, the remit of the Academy was broad, and included not only the annual exhibition of work by contemporary artists and the education and encouragement of art students at the Academy schools, but also the maintenance of the professional status of artists in Ireland through membership and association. Through its royal charter and its annual grant of three hundred pounds from Westminster, the RHA was strongly associated with the British administration – ties which were further strengthened by actions including the presentation of loyal addresses to visiting monarchs, the appointment of the lord lieutenant as vice-patron, and its association with its sister institutions – the Royal Scottish Academy, Edinburgh, and the Royal Academy, London (RA).

From the 1840s onwards, two central issues dogged the institution: first, it was broadly felt that a lack of patronage for the country's young and more established artists was detrimental to the development of an Irish school of painting and a stimulus was sought through the establishment of art unions, which purchased works and made engravings available to subscribers and prize winners. The issues around patronage intersected with the other key problem that the Academy faced, the flames of which were fanned by the nationalist press: that is, the inclusion, and in some respects, dominance, of work by English artists. As John Turpin has outlined, this discontent was expressed by artists themselves, who complained that English painters were hung in more prominent positions on the Academy's walls, an accusation that is both 'impossible to assess without more evidence but [which] is reasonable to assume'.[30] The inclusion of work by British artists at the RHA had been encouraged by the institution itself: from the 1830s, it invited artists from across Britain to submit to the exhibition and paid for the insurance and carriage of these works. Although expensive, the aim of this exercise was threefold, as Philip McEvansoneya has outlined: it was 'in order to make up the numbers, to increase the interest in the exhibitions and, unmistakably, to elevate the general standard of what was on display'.[31] While effectively sponsored by the RHA, this practice signals that there was an ongoing exchange of artworks travelling back and forth over the Irish Sea, a practice mirrored in many other parts of Dublin's cultural life.

In an attempt to further develop artistic life and opportunities for artists in Dublin outside of the RHA, the Dublin Sketching Club (DSC) had been founded in 1874 with the aim of uniting 'artists, amateurs and gentlemen interested in Art, in friendly and social intercourse promoting a taste for the fine arts in Dublin'.[32] The Club's activities centred around social gatherings and two-hour sketching sessions, as well as excursions to local beauty spots such as Ireland's Eye on Dublin's north coast.[33] Members included established artists, many of whom were members of the RHA, highlighting both the limited number of active artists, while also suggesting an indistinct boundary between amateur and professional. The sociable and open nature of the DSC was echoed in other nineteenth-century artists' clubs – such as the Dublin Art Club (1886–98), and to an extent the Watercolour Society of Ireland (WCSI) (discussed further in Chapter 2). The former of these was consciously modelled on the New English Art Club, formed in the same year, and sought to advance the work of British Impressionism in Dublin, making good use of the many artistic connections that its members (including Walter Osborne) had made with their contemporaries during their training in Belgium and France. While it attained some success in its lifetime and offers a further insight into the bourgeois cultural circles of the late-nineteenth century city, it ultimately failed, winding up before its tenth year. Of these clubs and societies, only the DSC and the WCSI would continue into the twentieth century and, indeed, to the present day.

The loyalty of the RHA to both the government that funded it, and the monarchy that provided its founding charter, was most publicly demonstrated through the presentations it made to visiting monarchs. The loyalty of some sections of Dublin society to the British crown was never more evident than on the occasion of a royal visit, several of which occurred in the period between the failure of the First Home Rule Bill and the outbreak of the First World War. On these occasions, many of Dublin's citizens expressed their loyalty to the monarchy through the display of illuminations placed on buildings or in windows, as well as reams of bunting, flags, and other ephemeral decorations. Although nationalist opposition to these visits increased (most notably by 1911 with the visit of George V and Queen Mary), the spectacle was enjoyed by many and was surely a boon to the city's many photographers and print sellers, who provided an ample selection of souvenirs. The city *en fête* was captured by painters, engravers, photographers, and filmmakers alike, creating some of the most enduring imagery of Dublin as a city of empire.[34] Following the death of Queen Victoria in 1901, the artist Richard Thomas Moynan attempted to capture a sense of the city's grief at her passing with *The Death of the Queen*, a large and somewhat sentimental canvas which displays a range of city-types gathered around a newspaper boy at College Green (Plate 0.3). The composition hinges on this impoverished character, who kneels beside a large poster for the *Mail* announcing the monarch's death, onto which he places a posy of violets, presumably purchased from the flower girl standing behind him. Moynan positions the group of mourners at the side of Trinity College, itself established by a royal charter in 1592, with the portico of the former House of Lords shoring up the left-hand side of the composition. This framing neatly encapsulates the political history and tension that was sown into Dublin's urban fabric, tempered by outwards signs of modernity such as a thriving print culture and an expanding public transport network.

In the early years of the twentieth century, the RHA's difficulties were highlighted by a number of official inquiries and reports: the 1901 Abney Report and a further government inquiry carried out in 1905, which produced two reports (reflecting the divided consensus of the committee) published in 1906. In addition to a range of other matters, these reports were united by their worries over the lack of patronage at the RHA, with Abney going as far as to say that unless significant action was taken to improve its fortunes, 'it would be better to revoke the Charter and let the Academy disappear rather than it should gradually sink to a position in which it would become an absolute discredit to the country through loss of influence'.[35] The later report had examined the RHA and the DMSA in tandem, and sought to establish whether both institutions were necessary. Artistic education in Dublin was available across several different levels, from private classes aimed at young women, to industrial and craft-based education, teaching training programmes, and specialised education in drawing and painting.[36] The DMSA operated under the South Kensington system, administered from London, while the RHA schools provided training in drawing and painting from life, taught by members of the Academy and at no cost to competent students. Both institutions struggled financially, and there was little additional monetary aid available for students, save for the two annual awards offered by the RHA and the Royal Dublin Society (RDS).[37]

The growing number of women in the visual arts had been noted in the reports and evidence of the 1905 Inquiry into the RHA and DMSA. The chief manifestation of this was the increase of women at the drawing and painting classes at the RHA schools, with the Secretary, Stephen Catterson Smith, also stating that 'after the admission of ladies the male students had begun to drop off'.[38] After expressing surprise at this, Mr Justice Madden (a member of the Committee) asked Catterson Smith if 'these women students' intended to become professional painters: the artist replied that 'that is made more or less a condition in the applicants for students, that they should be, at all events, in earnest, or desirous of making art their profession ... Most of them, I think, try to live by it, or, at all events, help themselves live by it. By teaching, for instance.'[39] Although Margaret Allen had been made an honorary member of the RHA in 1878, women were only elected to associate and full membership positions in the late 1920s, and of the three women artists discussed in this book, only Solomons was recognised by the RHA, being belatedly elected an honorary member in 1966.

The declining standard of housing in Dublin in the nineteenth century was one of the most pressing social issues of the period, and the crisis continued well into the twentieth century. In 1885, Sir Charles Cameron (the medical super-intendent officer of health for the city) gave evidence to a House of Commons commission on working-class housing in Ireland. When asked to comment on the number of families living in a single room, he replied that 'there are about 32,000 families out of about 54,000'.[40] From the late eighteenth century onwards, houses originally intended for single family occupancy had been converted into tenements, supplemented by the warren of old stable blocks and backstreet 'courts' converted into cheap and unsanitary domestic dwellings.[41] The inward migration of people from the countryside into Dublin during the famine years in the mid-century exacerbated an already acute problem, leading to more and more overcrowding. The uneven flow of people moving from the city centre to the new suburbs also intensified the problem in the city centre: very few working-class families moved to the new suburbs, and houses made vacant by the departing middle class were converted for either business use or subsumed into the tenement housing stock.[42] The extent of the crises for the working and artisan classes in Dublin were well documented and discussed. Between 1804 and 1900 twelve reports were published outlining the situation and possible remedies; however, no concerted and widespread effort was made to solve the situation until the 1930s. The report of the 1913 Dublin Housing Inquiry offered an update to Cameron's figures, revealing that on the eve of the First World War around 128,000 people were living in housing classified as tenements. The 1911 Census tallied the city's total population as being 304,802 people.[43] The inquiry also showed that many of the tenement houses in Dublin were, in fact, owned by members of the Corporation and that the law surrounding property inspection had not been strictly adhered to because of this.[44] The inquiry had come about following the collapse of two tenement houses on Church Street – killing seven people, injuring eight, and leaving eleven families homeless – on 2 September 1913.[45] The incident came just days after the beginning of one of the defining Dublin events of the pre-war years: the 1913 Lockout, which saw labour disputes, strikes, and riots unfurl across the city.[46] This bitter clash is surely unusual, and perhaps unique, for the way in which it brought together grievances over working conditions, housing, and the cause of modern painting.

Although those involved with the Celtic Revival may not have rated the city or urban life in terms of subject matter, the infrastructure provided by the urban environment was crucial to the movement's success. In the early 1900s, the seemingly opposing worlds of the artistic establishment and the Revival were joined in many ways through the charismatic figure of Hugh Lane, an art dealer and director of the NGI from 1914–15. Born in Cork but based in London, Lane's interest in furthering the cause of art in Ireland stemmed from his viewing of a joint exhibition by John Butler Yeats and Nathaniel Hone the Younger at 6 St Stephen's Green in 1901. Following this, Lane became more deeply involved in increasing Dubliners' opportunities to see historic and contemporary art from outside of Ireland for themselves. With the cooperation of the RHA, in December 1902 Lane arranged a winter exhibition of English and French Old Masters, followed by a selection of modern French paintings in 1904, including works from the J. Staats Forbes Collection, which he intended to purchase and donate as the nucleus for a new gallery of modern art in Dublin. This was the beginning of a long-running dispute between Lane and the Corporation over the formation, funding, and housing of a new art gallery. Although Lane opened the Municipal Gallery at a temporary premises on Harcourt Street in 1908, the debate continued through to 1913, with the proposition of the gallery (and the Council's funding of it) a key issue of public discussion.[47] The matter was further complicated in 1915, when Lane was among those who perished on the *Lusitania*, struck by a torpedo from a German U-Boat on its return from New York. The legal tangle caused by an unsigned codicil to Lane's will continued through to the 1950s, with several paintings still shared between Dublin and London as a result.[48]

Lane recorded the varied press responses to his Dublin endeavours, collecting reports and articles into a series of newspaper clippings books, now in the NLI. Reflected in these reports are the different political biases of the contemporary press, most notably in their attitudes towards the revival of art in Ireland and, to a lesser extent, modern art. The *Irish Daily Independent*, for example, noted that they did not agree with the current discussion about

> the advantages which would ensue from introducing the masses of our civic population, both by day and night, to a study of what are called the great masterpieces of Modern Art. The term in question is a wide one. If by it is meant some of the more recent productions of certain British, French, German, and Italian masters, we entertain no burning desire to see them exhibited in Dublin.[49]

Instead, they felt, art in Ireland would be better served if artists looked instead to the 'stories of Celtic legend and Celtic song, the dark, but sometimes lightsome, pages of the history of our country', which would lead to 'the creation of a genuine school of native art' based 'not on the wholesale importation of the works of alien painters, but the development of Irish artistic taste and skill on distinctly Celtic lines'.[50] The *Dublin Evening Herald* echoed this sentiment, questioning why 'while projects for the revival of the national language, the restoration of ancient music of Ireland … and the building up of national industries are now exciting so much enthusiasm, hardly any attention has been given to the question of the encouragement of native art'.[51] This criticism, however, did not deter those who sought to bring European art into Dublin's exhibition rooms: in addition to Lane's exhibition in 1904, further displays of modern painting took place in 1911 and 1912 – being iterations of Roger Fry's London exhibitions of post-impressionism, organised by Ellen Duncan at the United Arts Club.[52]

The formal declaration of war in August 1914 coincided with the establishment of a commission of inquiry into the events of the previous July, when a number of people had been killed on Bachelor's Walk by the British Army (see Chapter 3); as a result, Pádraig Yeates has written, the city 'barely reacted'.[53] However, as the war progressed, its effects were felt in Dublin – not only through the cancellation of public events and a decrease in news circulation, but also through rising prices for food and fuel, recruitment, and the arrival of injured soldiers on the docks, sent to various Dublin hospitals for treatment and convalescence. Recruitment posters pasted around the city appealed for men to join up, in one notable instance using the image of the former parliament building on College Green to appeal to men to 'come into the ranks and fight – don't stay in the crowd and stare' (Figure 0.3). In the first years of the conflict, recruitment across the city for the British Army was strong, with 21,187 men joining from the district by the end of 1916.[54] John Redmond, leader of the continuing Home Rule campaign, encouraged his followers to join up, certain that the promise of a devolved government would be made good after the conflict. As the war progressed, however, support for Redmond and his party dwindled, and as Dickson has outlined, support in Dublin turned increasingly to more militant nationalism.[55] In the years preceding 1916, support for more radical action had been building, organised through networks such as the Irish Citizen Army (led by James Connolly), Cumann na mBan, the Volunteers, and the Irish Republican Brotherhood, among others.[56] The fabric of the city had supported and even nurtured this movement, providing convenient places for covert meetings or for messages to be exchanged, such as Thomas Clarke's tobacconist and stationers shop on Amiens Street, or more daringly, when an unauthorised review of troops took place on St Patrick's Day, 1916 on College Green. The DMSA also acted as a meeting place for those with revolutionary politics, such as Willie Pearse (brother of Patrick Pearse), Constance Markiewicz, and Grace Gifford.

The Rising began on Easter Monday, 24 April 1916. A 'ragtag armed force of some 1,200' men and women gathered at various locations around the city, and at midday, the GPO was seized, followed by a number of other strategic buildings and areas in each corner of the city.[57] The use of the GPO, the centre of the island's communication system, was strategic and symbolic, with the 'proclamation of the republic planned to reverberate across the empire' (Plate 0.4).[58] Over the course of the week, fighting and looting spread throughout the city with the area around Sackville Street bearing the brunt of the destruction. On 27 April, a shell fired from the *Helga* set alight a barricade on Lower Abbey Street and the blaze spread along the street, engulfing the premises of the RHA,

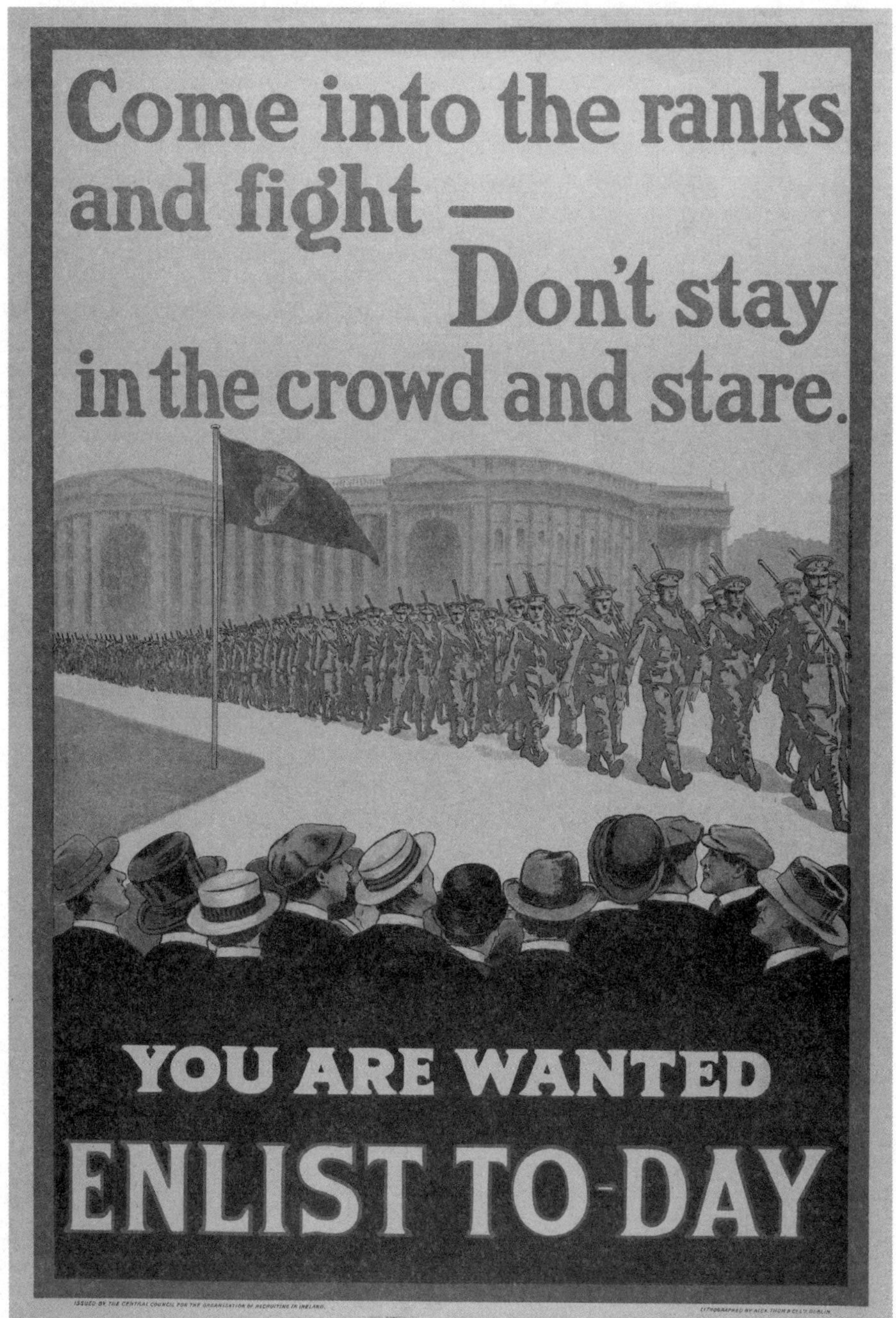

0.3   Central Council for the Organization of Recruiting in Ireland, *Come into the Ranks and Fight, Don't Stand in the Crowd and Stare!*, undated.

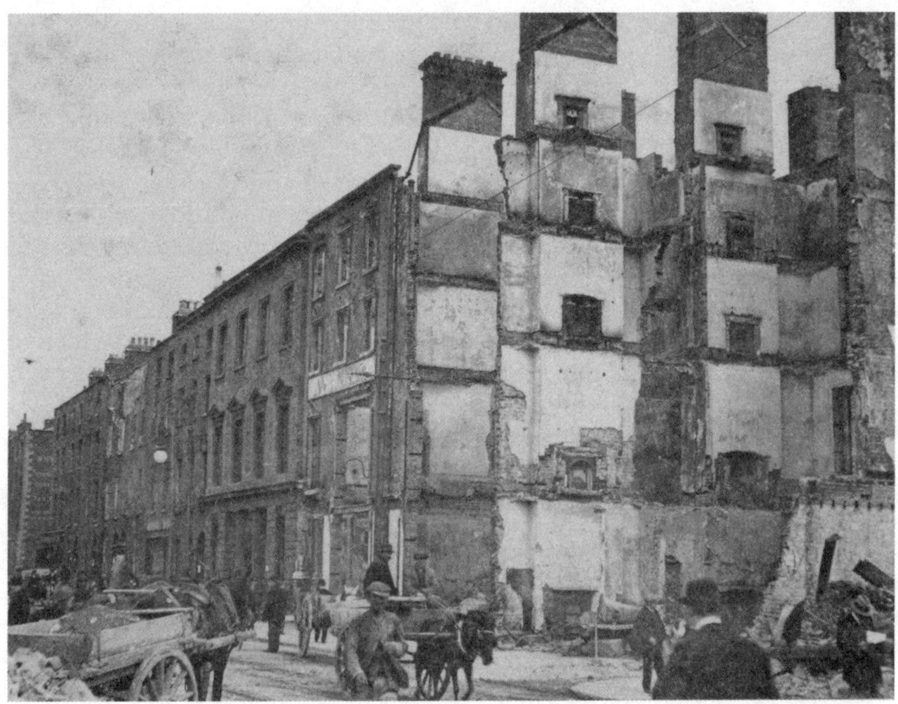

0.4   T. J. Westropp, *Royal Hibernian Academy, Wynne's Hotel and Abbey Street*, 17 May 1916.

which was then hosting its annual exhibition (Figure 0.4). Over five hundred works of art were on display, all of which were destroyed, along with the Academy's holdings of fine art prints, books, and other materials.[59] Claims by the institution and the individual artists who lost their work were submitted to the Property Losses (Ireland) Commission and reveal the multifaceted interests and lives of the exhibitors. While all broadly academic rather than modernist in artistic technique, the different claims show that artists connected to empire, to the nationalist movement, those displaced by the First World War, collectors and enthusiastic amateurs, were brought together in the broad church of the annual exhibition. The destruction caused by the Rising was ably captured by Edmund Delrenne (*fl.* 1916–18), a Belgian artist who had sought refuge in Ireland, only to find himself in the middle of another battle site.[60] Overall, artists did not embrace the representation of Dublin's difficulties in the years 1913–16, and the most lasting pictorial record of these years is photographic. Following the end of the Rising on 29 April, and the subsequent execution of many of its leaders, a thriving market for photographic souvenirs emerged.[61]

A vivid description of the city in the year immediately following the Rising comes from Frank Gallagher, a journalist and republican volunteer, who wrote in his memoir in 1917 that the 'life of the city went on outwardly as in any other city. Day and night ... there was the uninterrupted coming and going of the citizens, many shops were open in the late evening, the theatres and social gatherings drew their crowds, and that new invention, the cinema, was building up its great following'. Alongside this, however, 'there was an activity unbelievable in its intensity. Through the streets, with their sauntering couples, went a young lad here a there who, at some unpretentious doorway, melted away from the scene', disappearing into one of the many makeshift arms and explosive factories scattered across Dublin.[62] In November 1918, crowds gathered in College Green to mark the armistice and in December the country went to the polls. A landslide victory for Sinn Féin candidates, and the decimation of the Home Rule party, indicated that the political struggle for independence was not yet over.

On 21 January 1919, elected members of the Sinn Féin party assembled in Dublin to form the First Dáil, which would run concurrently to the British administration in Ireland until the latter's formal cessation in 1922. On the same day, an incident at Soldoheadbeg, Co. Tipperary in which two members of the Royal Irish Constabulary (RIC) were killed, marked the beginning of the War of Independence. In April 1919, Éamonn De Valera was elected President of Dáil Éireann and in the ensuing months a system of government and justice was established around the country. Parallel to this, the military campaign for independence escalated with attacks and reprisals being carried out both by the Irish Republican Army (IRA) and the RIC. Fighting in the War of Independence was geographically spread around Ireland with guerrilla warfare playing to the strengths and knowledge of the smaller IRA force. The city, however, remained a crucial environment for the planning, maintaining, and carrying out of military activities. Michael Hopkinson has noted that 'actions in Dublin gained the biggest publicity in the British and international press', and as such was important in keeping the Republican struggle in the news.[63] In addition, the presence of two large prisons in the city, Mountjoy and Kilmainham, gave rise to public demonstrations and key events, such as the hunger strikes in April 1920 and the execution of Kevin Barry in November 1920, when large crowds gathered at the gates to both protest and pray together. Significant attacks were carried out on public buildings and offices during this period; for example, the lunchtime attack on the Custom House by the IRA in May 1921. The role played by the built environment is revealed in the Bureau of Military History's Witness Statements, oral histories collected from those involved with the fighting in the 1950s. For example, Laurence Nugent (a member of 'K' Company, 3rd Battalion, Dublin Brigade), recalled how hotels, pubs, drapers, and outfitters were used to relay messages and conceal meetings.[64]

What is also clear from the Witness Statements is how the city facilitated the guerrilla tactics favoured by Republicans. Recollecting regular ambushes on Camden Street, Stephen Keys remembered how the Black and Tans 'never seemed to know from where they were being "hit up". I often noticed as they drove along looking up on roofs and upper windows … They never seemed to realise they were being attacked from the streets.'[65] Nugent confirmed the success of such tactics, saying that the 'enemy never knew where the next attack was coming from. They expected one from every corner.'[66] In an attempt to quell such attacks, one of the most constant enforcements through the War of Independence was a night-time curfew. The *Irish Times* reported that it was 'an effort to remedy a very disgraceful and dangerous state of affairs', hoping that 'giving military aid to the police' and 'keeping ruffians and criminal conspirators off the streets at night, may restore the ordinary decencies and securities of civilised society'.[67] It was also reported that the City Council 'forbade any of its servants to apply for "Curfew" permits; it instructed its night-watchmen to leave duty at eleven o'clock; [and] it had decreed that the streets shall be plunged into darkness after eleven-thirty p.m'.[68] This action by the Corporation was evocatively described the next evening in the *Freeman's Journal*, whose reporter noted that at the appointed hour, 'all the public lamps were extinguished … The darkness in which the city was enveloped was intensified by a fog … Save for the little light of the tramway poles all was in complete darkness.'[69] The effects of the curfew touched all aspects of everyday life in the city: there was a shortage of coal, as dock workers refused to oversee the berthing of vessels after the curfew commenced; visitors on the night time trains arrived to empty stations; and telegraphs remained uncollected at the offices. Again, the Witness Statements provide evocative accounts of the effect of the curfew. For instance, Sean Prendergast noted how the patrols disrupted the night with 'the continuous movement of British forces, the movement of men, motor convoys, armoured cars, the playing of huge searchlights on streets and houses … Sleep and quietude became for some hard to secure.'[70] It was not until 21 November 1920, after the events of 'Bloody Sunday' (when, in retaliation for a campaign against British intelligence agents that morning, the Auxiliaries entered Croke Park during a match, killing thirteen and injuring sixty others) that the Corporation began to light the street lamps again. The *Irish Times* reported that this 'was adopted as a precautionary measure, in view of what occurred during the day, and on the initiative of the Lord Mayor'.[71]

Artistic life in the city continued as normal and with only rare disruptions. In the years 1919–21, the RHA continued to hold its annual exhibitions (albeit at an alternative venue) and there was no disruption to the awarding of the annual Taylor Prizes. Nor does the ongoing political situation seem to have disturbed the running of the NGI: with the passing of the Government of Ireland Act in 1920 (which formalised partition, and created Northern Ireland), the Board of the NGI affirmed that the collection would stay in Ireland.[72] Disruption did come to the NGI, however, during the Civil War, when it closed for a prolonged period in 1922–23. Classes continued at the RHA Schools and at the DMSA, although evening classes were briefly disrupted between 8 March and 4 April 1921 due to curfew restrictions.[73] The Municipal Gallery continued to operate from its premises on Harcourt Street, while the ongoing dispute over the Hugh

Lane Bequest continued. Other notable activities during this period include the establishment of the Society of Dublin Painters in 1920 which held exhibitions at No. 7 St Stephen's Green. Founded by Grace and Paul Henry, the Society sought to be more self-consciously 'modernist' than the RHA and held both group and solo exhibitions at the city centre rooms. Other initiatives which sought to stimulate art production in the early years of the 1920s included the New Irish Salon, organised by J. Crampton Walker from 1923, the Daniel Egan Salon, and the Radical Club, which is discussed in more detail in Chapter 4.

When a truce was signed on 9 July 1921 and effected on 11 July, the celebrations were widespread throughout the city. The *Freeman's Journal* reported that 'as the bands marched through the city the citizens seemed to forget for the moment the years of agony through which they had scarcely passed, and gave themselves abandon to the exuberant joy of the occasion'.[74] The celebrations continued the following night, when 'round the blazing bonfires joyous crowds gathered and sang and danced to their hearts content. The streets were again profusely decorated with Republican and American flags.'[75] By 13 July, Slyne's Department Store was advertising a dress sale 'for days of truce', and by 14 July, questions were being asked as to how the depleted number of city hotels would cope with the influx of visitors for the first Dublin Horse Show since 1913.[76]

Following a period of negotiation in London, the Anglo–Irish Treaty was signed by Michael Collins and his team of plenipotentiaries on 6 December 1921. The Treaty established the Irish Free State, an autonomous, self-governing dominion of the British Empire. This, along with the requirement of elected representatives to pledge an Oath of Allegiance to the Crown, caused a split in the nationalist movement, despite the Treaty being narrowly accepted by Dáil Éireann. A provisional government, headed by Collins and Arthur Griffith, was formed to begin the transfer of power from Westminster to the Irish Free State, while those opposed to the Treaty mustered in opposition across the city and country. The cataclysmic effect of the split between the Treaty and anti-Treaty sides on Irish political history has been well documented, alongside the wider events of the Civil War throughout the island of Ireland.[77] On 28 June 1922, Dublin's streets once again became a site of war (Plate 0.5). Two incidents in the preceding months had perhaps hinted at what was to occur: on 31 January, Beggars Bush barracks had been taken over by a group of about fifty men known as the Dublin Guard, and on 14 April, an anti-Treaty group had successfully occupied the Four Courts. An instruction from the British Government for crown forces to return to the city and deal with this action was headed off at the last minute, and instead heavy artillery was loaned to the fledgling Free State Army remedy the situation. The shelling of the Four Courts began on 28 June 1922, and the next seven days marked the most intensive period of fighting in the capital, before the Civil War spread out across the country. Recounting the events of this battle, Liz Gillis has written how, 'at 4.10 a.m. on the morning of 28 June, the sound of rifle and machine-gun fire, followed by the thud of bombs exploding, reverberated throughout the city. The Civil War had begun, and there was no going back on either side.'[78] The fighting concentrated on the occupied Four Courts and the stronghold only surrendered on 30 July. Later that day a large explosion went off in the Public Record Office building at the Courts, destroying its contents and causing 'the works of a thousand years to waft slowly down'.[79]

When Civil War broke out in Dublin, many of the buildings on Sackville Street were still in the process of being rebuilt after the 1916 Rising: the task was reported to be nearly finished in May.[80] On 4 July, the *Irish Independent* published a list of 'Dublin's Destroyed Buildings', outlining what it termed to be 'the principal destroyed buildings', and excluded the 'large number … partially destroyed'.[81] On 23 May 1923, as the Civil War drew to a close, the *Freeman's Journal* dedicated several pages of the issue to the redevelopment of the capital, outlining plans for the reconstruction of the city in the Free State, as well as publishing aerial photographs of the city and others of 'Dublin Landmarks Past & Present'. Following the years of destruction, it was hoped that a new Dublin would emerge from the ashes and there was now an added desire for the city to become 'a fitting capital for the new State'.[82] Numerous challenges faced the government, not only in terms of rebuilding the civic and public buildings, but also in providing for the swathes of people still living in tenement conditions. On 4 May 1923, W. T. Cosgrave told the Dáil that 'the housing problem is, perhaps, the greatest of all problems we have got to tackle'.[83]

In contrast to the turbulent years of the revolutionary period, the later 1920s and 1930s saw a quieter period in the city's history emerge: the Council worked on building and housing projects, expanding the city outwards, as well as renaming several of the city's streets to better reflect the Free State's independence. In its cultural life, the offerings of the city continued to centre around established entertainments such as the theatre, cinema, and dance halls, which grew in abundance and variety, but which also came under increasing scrutiny (see Chapters 3 and 4). Economic stagnation was also a hallmark of the period, with growth severely impacted by the Anglo–Irish Economic War, 1932–38. Although new research reveals a more vibrant side to 1930s Ireland than previous historiography has suggested, it remains true that the decade saw a consolidation of 'Irish-Ireland': a society governed by the state's relationship with the Catholic Church (best exemplified by the spectacle of the 1932 Eucharistic Congress), and at least a seeming celebration of traditional, rural, and agricultural values over urban internationalism or cosmopolitanism, values which were inscribed into the 1937 Constitution.[84] Of course, given its status as a capital city, Dublin had some immunity to this, and the concentration of leisure activities and news outlets brought some of the wider world to the city's streets, newsstands, and cinemas. Listing some of the entertainment available to Dubliners on 31 May 1935, Anne Dolan notes that the range of films on offer included 'The Thin Man' starring Myrna Loy and '*Jew Süss*', which offered a critique of the Nazi regime. As Dolan comments, this range demonstrates how we 'package a period and people neatly up at our peril'.[85]

In contrast to its centrality to the artistic firmament of the city in the late nineteenth and early twentieth centuries, the RHA was increasingly sidelined; and while membership remained an appealing badge of professional status, the conservative nature of its exhibitions and outlook was questioned. In 1943, the formation of the Irish Exhibition of Living Art provided a new forum for artists to show their work, although as Riann Coulter has noted, the founders 'chose to embrace both the avant-garde and the academic and create an institution best described as pluralistic'.[86] In some respects, the Second World War brought an unexpected cultural flourishing to Dublin through the arrival of 'refugees, conscientious objectors, tourists, artists, musicians and others who contributed to a cosmopolitan atmosphere', although this was largely only experienced by the city's bourgeoise.[87] The influx was more than matched by outward migration from Dublin and other Irish ports – with people leaving either to find work in Britain's cities and munition factories, or to join the British Army. While Ireland's neutral stance largely protected it from any direct action in the conflict, it did experience aerial attacks in January and May 1941, most notably the North Strand bombing in which twenty-eight people died and around 300 homes were destroyed.[88] The experience of living in Dublin during the 1940s continued the strange contradictions that had been present since the 1880s: for those who could afford housing, had access to employment opportunities, and participated in high and popular culture, Dublin could provide a relatively engaging urban lifestyle – even among the deprivations of fuel shortages and food rationing. For many, however, this life was out of reach: many thousands of the city's citizens remained confined to decrepit and unsanitary tenement buildings, dependent on precarious casual labour, and without access to satisfactory healthcare. This divide was not unique to Dublin and was often characteristic of city life more broadly.

In comparison to the archetypal modern cities (for example Paris, London, Berlin, and New York) Dublin was smaller, less industrialised, and caught up in the struggle and negotiation of dual identities – between empire and independence. Among the ongoing political and social problems, artists in the city created work that engaged with the people and environment that surrounded them, as well as supporting and contributing to the wider art world of the city. As is evident through the writings of (for example) Jacinta Prunty, Stephanie Rains, and Wallace, Dublin in the nineteenth and early twentieth century was polarised between a range of concurrent issues. These included a growing divide between the working and middle classes, differing political allegiances, a crisis in housing, and poor governance. These tensions played out across the city, and were made visible (for example) through the continuing presence of crumbling and overcrowded tenement buildings, alongside the exodus of the middle class to the new suburbs, and the use of the urban fabric (through architecture and public sculpture) to signal and represent political ideas.

Writing in the introduction to *The Cambridge Companion to Modern Irish Culture*, Joe Cleary noted that modernity and modernisation in Ireland 'meant something quite different to what it did to its near neighbours in Europe', and certainly the experience of the 'modern city' in Dublin took a different course to many of the canonical cities associated with modernism.[89] Dublin was caught between competing ideas of what it meant to be modern: whether through engaging with imperial metropolitan culture, technological advances in communication, or the cultural or violent assertion of national identity. These competing cultures were played out in its streets, cinemas, cabarets, and news-agents, placing the city and its built environment at the heart of the country's journey towards a new political reality. While Dublin was not the only city which experienced near destruction on account of warfare in this period, the nature of its conflict sets it apart. Whether one views Ireland at this time as 'an integral part of the United Kingdom, a peripheral, backward sub-region, or a colony in all but name', the nature of its twentieth-century conflicts was inherently anti-colonial, with the Easter Rising and War of Independence fought against an imperial power, and the Civil War against the remaining vestiges of that power's influence and role within the new state.[90] Ireland's fight for self-determination in this period allied it with other small nations participating in a different type of modernity in the twentieth century. By exploring artists' depictions of Dublin 1886–1949 we see not only how modern life and modern subjects engaged artists in Ireland, but also how these visons were altered, and complicated, by contemporary political and social contexts. Through this mode of artistic expression, these artists engaged with a tradition and practice of urban representation that spanned Europe and North America, and through our engagement in turn, we can restore the representation of Dublin to the realm of urban painting in the late nineteenth and early twentieth centuries.

Notes

1   O. Robertson, *Dublin Phoenix* (London: Jonathan Cape, 1957), p. 15.
2   T. Cooper, *Paper Cities: Topography and Imagination in Urban Europe c.1490–1780* (London: UCL Art Collections, 2003), p. 1.
3   T. Shapiro, 'The metropolis in the visual arts: Paris, Berlin, New York, 1890–1940', in A. Sutcliffe (ed.), *Metropolis 1890–1940* (London: Mansell, 1984), p. 97. For more on the economic aspects of art production in the nineteenth century city, see A. Bermingham, 'Urbanity and the spectacle of art', in J. Chandler and K. Gilmartin (eds), *Romantic Metropolis: The Urban Scene and British Culture, 1780–1840* (Cambridge: Cambridge University Press, 2005) and P. Fletcher, 'Shopping for art: the rise of the commercial art gallery, 1850s–90s', in P. Fletcher and A. Helmreich (eds), *The Rise of the Modern Art Market in London, 1850–1939* (Manchester: Manchester University Press, 2011).
4   See L. Lanigan, 'The revival and the city in James Stephen's Dublin fiction', UCD Scholarcast Series 12, in G. Bruna and C. Wilsdon (eds), *Modalities of Revival*, 2015, pp. 2–4: www.ucd.ie/scholarcast/transcripts/Revival_and_the_city.pdf (accessed 21 April 2020).
5   N. Figgis, 'Introduction', in N. Figgis (ed.), *Painting 1600–1900, Art and Architecture of*

Ireland, vol II (London, New Haven and Dublin: Yale University Press in association with the Royal Irish Academy, 2014), p. 1.

6 See F. Cullen, 'Art and the post-Famine Irish diaspora in America', in E. Mark Fitzgerald, M. Corporaal, and O. Frawley (eds), *The Great Irish Famine: Visual and Material Culture* (Liverpool: Liverpool University Press, 2018), pp. 137–8, and N. O'Sullivan, 'History of art: the academic discipline', in C. Marshall and P. Murray (eds), *Twentieth Century, Art and Architecture of Ireland*, vol V (New Haven and Dublin: Yale University Press in association with the Royal Irish Academy, 2014), pp. 209–10.

7 A recent exception to this was 'Drawing Dublin', held at the National Gallery of Ireland (5 May–26 August 2018) and showing artworks of city and county Dublin from the Gallery's Prints and Drawings collection.

8 G. O'Brien and F. O'Kane, 'Portrait of the city: framing the significance of urban landscapes', in G. O'Brien and F. O'Kane (eds), *Portraits of the City: Dublin and the Wider World* (Dublin: Four Courts Press, 2012), p. 19.

9 M. Harmon, 'Introduction', in M. Harmon (ed.), *The Irish Writer and the City* (Totowa: Barnes and Noble Books, 1984), p. viii.

10 See E. Mannion, *The Urban Plays of the Early Abbey Theatre: Beyond O'Casey* (Syracuse: Syracuse University Press, 2014) and L. Lanigan, *James Joyce, Urban Planning and Irish Modernism: Dublins of the Future* (London: Palgrave Macmillan, 2014).

11 A particularly noteworthy example of the 'One City, One Book' programme is a volume of Dublin poems published for the event in April 2014: P. Boran and G. Smyth (eds), *If Ever You Go* (Dublin: Dedalus Press, 2014).

12 M. J. Boland, 'Visualizing the city: images of Ireland's urban world, c.1790–1820', in G. Laragy, O. Purdue, and J. J. Wright (eds), *Urban Spaces in Nineteenth-century Ireland* (Liverpool: Liverpool University Press, 2018), p. 162.

13 D. Bolger, 'Cornucopia of Dublin: Dublin: The Making of a Capital', review of *Dublin: The Making of a Capital City* by D. Dickson, *Irish Times* (21 June 2014), p. 11.

14 M. Daly, 'Irish urban history: a survey', *Urban History* 13 (1986), p. 61.

15 E. Hanna and R. Butler, 'Irish urban history: an agenda,' *Urban History* 1:8 (2018), 2. DOI 10.1017/S0963926818000196.

16 Ibid., 7.

17 D. Dickson, 'The state of Dublin's history', *Éire-Ireland* 45:1&2 (2010), 207.

18 N. Allen, 'Ireland, Empire and archipelago', UCD Scholarcast Series 7, in J. Branningan and P. J. Matthews (eds), 'The Literatures and Cultures of the Irish Sea', 2013, p. 3. www.ucd.ie/scholarcast/transcripts/Scholarcast28_transcript.pdf (accessed 21 April 2020). See also N. Allen, N. Groom, and J. Smith (eds), *Coastal Works: Cultures of the Atlantic Edge* (Oxford: Oxford University Press, 2017).

19 T. Cresswell, *On the Move: Mobility in the Modern Western World* (London: Routledge, 2006); A. Boutros and W. Straw (eds), *Circulation and the City: Essays on Urban Culture* (Ithaca: McGill-Queen's University Press, 2010); U. Boskamp and A. Kranen, 'Drawing the Dardanelles: art history and mobility studies' in A. A. Kjaerulff, S. Kesselring, P. Peters, and K. Hannam (eds), *Envisioning Networked Urban Mobilities: Art, Performances, Impacts* (Routledge eBook, 2019), pp. 109–22.

20 D. Dickson, *Dublin: The Making of a Capital City* (London: Profile Books, 2014), p. x.

21 The origin of the phrase 'dear, dirty Dublin' is attributed to the author, Lady Sidney

Morgan. It was also used by J. V. O'Brien for his text *Dear, Dirty Dublin: A City in Distress, 1899–1916* (Berkeley: University of California Press, 1982).

22 G. Ó Tuathaigh, 'Introduction: Ireland 1880–2016: negotiating sovereignty and freedom', in T. Bartlett (ed.), *The Cambridge History of Ireland, Vol. IV, 1800 to the Present* (Cambridge: Cambridge University Press, 2018), p. 1.

23 P. Gray and O. Purdue, 'Introduction: the Irish Lord Lieutenancy, c.1541–1922', in P. Gray and O. Purdue, *The Irish Lord Lieutenancy, c.1541–1922* (Dublin: UCD Press, 2012), p. 2.

24 See M. Bourke, *The Story of Irish Museums, 1790–2000: Culture, Identity and Education* (Cork: Cork University Press, 2011).

25 See C. Wallace, 'Fighting for Home Rule: competing identities in Dublin 1880–1929', *Journal of Urban History*, 38:5 (2012), 932–49. DOI 10.1177/0096144212449144.

26 Dickson, *Dublin: The Making of a Capital City*, p. 307.

27 Wallace, 'Fighting for Home Rule', p. 933.

28 See S. Rains, *Commodity Culture and Social Class in Dublin, 1850–1916* (Dublin: Irish Academic Press, 2011).

29 See W. Laffan, 'Buying, selling and exhibiting art in Ireland, c.1700–c.1900', in Figgis (ed.), *Painting 1600–1900*, pp. 17–22.

30 J. Turpin, *History of the Royal Hibernian Academy of Arts*, vol. 1 (Dublin: Lilliput Press, 2018), p. 112.

31 P. McEvansoneya, 'Ireland on show: art, union, and nationhood', *Irish Studies Review*, 21:2 (2013), 232.

32 Catalogue of the first Dublin Sketching Club exhibition, quoted in S. Armstrong Duffy, 'Late nineteenth century sketching clubs in Ireland' (BA Diss., Trinity College Dublin, 1984), p. 9.

33 Giving an account of a trip to Ireland's Eye, a correspondent reported that 'after some hours spent noting with brush and pencil … the members met again on the beach, and were immortalised in a group by the camera of a well-known member.' See 'Dublin Sketching Club', *Irish Times* (6 July 1886), p. 3.

34 See K. Milligan, 'Royal visits to Dublin, 1821–1911: pier, procession, Presence Chamber', in M. Campbell and W. Derham (eds), *Making Majesty: The Throne Room at Dublin Castle, A Cultural History* (Dublin: Irish Academic Press, 2018), pp. 200–35.

35 RHA Archive, RHA154(8)/5A, 1901, W. de Abney Report, 1901, included in the Minutes of the RHA General Assembly 1900–24.

36 For an in-depth account of art education in Dublin, see J. Turpin, *A School of Art in Dublin since the Eighteenth Century: A History of the National College of Art and Design* (Dublin: Gill & Macmillan, 1995).

37 See J. Turpin, 'Dublin art institutions', in Figgis (ed.), *Painting, 1600–1900*, p. 30.

38 'Minutes of Evidence', *Report by committee of inquiry into the work carried on by the Royal Hibernian Academy and the Metropolitan School of Art, Dublin*, pp. 9–10. According to Turpin, it was Walter Osborne who had proposed that women should be allowed to study at the RHA Schools in 1893. See J. Turpin, 'The RHA Schools 1826–1906', *Irish Arts Review Yearbook* (1991/1992), pp. 198–209.

39 'Minutes of Evidence', *Report by committee of inquiry into the work carried on by the Royal Hibernian Academy and the Metropolitan School of Art, Dublin*, p. 10.

40 *Third Report of Her Majesty's commissioners for inquiring into the housing of the working classes in Ireland* (London: Eyre and Spottiswoode, 1885).

41 J. Prunty, 'The town house as tenement in nineteenth- and early-twentieth century Dublin', in C. Casey (ed.), *The Eighteenth-century Dublin Town House* (Dublin: Four Courts Press, 2010), p. 153.

42 Ibid., p. 155. See also S. Galavan, *Dublin's Bourgeois Homes: Building the Victorian Suburbs, 1850–1901* (London: Routledge, 2017).

43 C. Corlett, *Darkest Dublin* (Dublin: Royal Society of Antiquaries, 2008), p. 53.

44 Ibid., p. 64.

45 P. Yeats, '1913 – a country and a city at the crossroads', in *Dublin Divided: September 1913* (Dublin: Dublin City Gallery the Hugh Lane, 2013), p. 14.

46 For a more thorough examination of the Lockout, see, F. Devine (ed.), *A Capital in Conflict: Dublin City and the 1913 Lockout* (Dublin: Dublin City Council, 2013).

47 See M. Cappock, 'Dublin divided: September 1913', in *Dublin Divided: September 1913*, pp. 23–55.

48 For a brief overview of this dispute, see R. Foster, 'How Ireland was robbed of Hugh Lane's great art collection, *Guardian* (30 May 2015), www.theguardian.com/artanddesign/2015/may/30/how-ireland-was-robbed-hugh-lanes-great-art-collection (accessed 21 April 2020).

49 NLI, BB242, A volume of newspaper cuttings relating to the proposal for a new site for the Academy and Gallery of Modern Art, cutting from the *Irish Daily Independent*, 16 January 1903.

50 Ibid.

51 NLI, BB242, A volume of newspaper cuttings relating to the proposal for a new site for the Academy and Gallery of Modern Art, cutting from the *Dublin Evening Herald*, 12 January 1903.

52 See R. Kennedy, 'Transmitting avant-garde Art: post-impressionism in a Dublin context', *Visual Resources* 31:1–2 (2015), 61–73. DOI 10.1080/01973762.2015.1004780.

53 P. Yeates, *A City in Wartime: Dublin 1914–1918* (Dublin: Gill and Macmillan, 2011), p. 26.

54 Dickson, *Dublin: The Making of a Capital City*, p. 444.

55 Ibid., p. 445.

56 See R. Foster, *Vivid Faces: The Revolutionary Generation in Ireland, 1890–1923* (London: Allen Lane, 2014), pp. 221–57.

57 Dickson, *Dublin: The Making of a Capital City*, p. 449.

58 N. Allen, *Modernism, Ireland, and Civil War* (Cambridge: Cambridge University Press, 2006), p. 1.

59 See K. Milligan, 'The cultural cost of 1916: The Property Losses (Ireland) Committee and the Royal Hibernian Academy', for Inspiring Ireland Project, Digital Repository of Ireland, May 2016: http://inspiring-ireland.ie/cultural-cost-of-1916-property-losses-ireland-committee-and-royal-hibernian-academy (accessed 21 April 2020).

60 See K. Milligan, 'Edmond Delrenne: witness to 1916', *Irish Arts Review* 32:4 (2015), 558–61. www.irishartsreview.com/edmond-delrenne-witness-to-1916/ (accessed 21 April 2020).

61 J. Carville, 'The city and the body in the archive: photography, history and the representation of Dublin 1860–1922' (PhD Diss., Dublin City University, 2005), pp. 304–59.

62 D. Hogan [*pseud.* F. Gallagher], *Four Glorious Years* (Dublin: Irish Press, 1953), p. 229.

63 M. Hopkinson, *The Irish War of Independence* (Dublin: Gill & Macmillan, 2002), p. 97.

64 Bureau of Military History Archives, Witness Statement Ref #907.

65 Bureau of Military History Archives, Witness Statement Ref #1209, p. 7.

66 Bureau of Military History Archives, Witness Statement Ref #907, p. 237.

67 'The Public Safety Order', *The Irish Times* (24 February 1920), p. 4.

68 Ibid.

69 'By Our Staff', *Freeman's Journal* (25 February 1920), p. 3.

70 Bureau of Military History Archives, Witness Statement Ref #755, p. 340.

71 'Lighting of Dublin Streets', *Irish Times* (22 November 1920), p. 5.

72 P. Somerville-Large, *1854–2004: The Story of the National Gallery of Ireland* (Dublin: National Gallery of Ireland, 2004), p. 286.

73 *Freeman's Journal* (8 March 1921), p. 1 and *Freeman's Journal* (4 April 1921), p. 2.

74 'Bonfires in Dublin', *Freeman's Journal* (12 July 1921), p. 5.

75 'Dublin Rejoices Again', *Freeman's Journal* (13 July 1921), p. 5.

76 *Irish Times* (13 July 1921), p. 6 and 'More Hotel Accommodation Needed', *Irish Times* (14 July 1921), p. 3.

77 See, for example, B. Kissane, *The Politics of the Irish Civil War* (Oxford: Oxford University Press, 2005).

78 L. Gillis, *The Fall of Dublin: 28 June to 5 July 1922* (Cork: Mercier Press, 2011), p. 50.

79 Allen, *Modernism, Ireland and Civil War*, p. 2.

80 R. McManus, *Dublin 1910–1940: Shaping the City & Suburbs* (Dublin: Four Courts Press, 2002), p. 72.

81 'Dublin's Destroyed Buildings', *Irish Independent* (4 July 1922), p. 18.

82 McManus, *Dublin 1910–1940*, p. 75.

83 Dáil Éireann, Friday 4 May 1923, in *Dáil Éireann Parliamentary Debates, 12 April 1923–2 July 1923* (Dublin: Stationery Office, 1923), p. 661.

84 See A. Dolan, 'Politics, economy and society in the Irish Free State, 1922–1939', in *Cambridge History of Ireland, Vol. IV*, pp. 323–48.

85 Ibid., p. 333.

86 R. Coulter, 'Irish exhibition of living art', in Marshall and Murray (eds), *Twentieth Century*, p. 236.

87 P. Ollerenshaw, 'Neutrality and belligerence: Ireland, 1939–1945', *Cambridge History of Ireland, Vol. IV*, pp. 354–5.

88 Dickson, *Dublin: The Making of a Capital City*, pp. 503–4.

89 J. Cleary, 'Introduction: Ireland and modernity', in J. Cleary and C. Connolly (eds) *Cambridge Companion to Modern Irish Culture* (Cambridge: Cambridge University Press, 2005), p. 9.

90 D. Fitzpatrick, 'Ireland and the Empire', in A. Porter and A. Low (eds), *The Oxford History of the British Empire, Vol. III, The Nineteenth Century* (Oxford: Oxford University Press, 1999), p. 494.

∿ I ∿

Poverty, parks, and painting

Reviewing the depiction of the urban scene in nineteenth-century British art, Caroline Arscott has noted that from the 1880s, the previous balance 'between celebration and despair' changed quite decisively to 'a bleak vision of urban alienation'.[1] Whereas previous generations of artists had sought to represent either 'a marked confidence in the achievements of urban development', or 'a growing middle-class awareness of social problems', this decade witnessed a marked 'gloom and anxiety about the state of urban life', occasionally offset by 'the emergence of utopian schemes of paternalistic or state-managed urban development'.[2] Allied to this, the influence of artistic training in France and Belgium – as well as realist and naturalist painting – filtered through, resulting in a shift towards subjects grounded in scenes of everyday life, without the moralising features of earlier narrative paintings. As Julian Treuherz has identified, from this time the 'artificially arranged subjects of social realism were rejected by the younger artists', although 'they retained a deep interest in the observation of the humble and commonplace'.[3] This approach to the depiction of the city can be seen in the work of Walter Frederick Osborne, whose paintings of Dublin invite the viewer into the nineteenth-century city, down crooked lanes, on to wide quays, and into leafy parks. If Osborne's urban vision tended more to the picturesque than the alienated, there is in these paintings, an underlying comment on living conditions in the city and class relationships.

Rooted in his observation of Dublin and its citizens and with the stylistic influence of his artistic training on the continent, Osborne's sketches, pastels, and paintings of the city have variously been considered as an important historical record of Dublin, as paintings of an imaginary 'any city', and as a visual precursor to the characters of James Joyce's *Dubliners*.[4] With these readings of the artist in mind, this chapter will focus on Osborne as an observer of his native city, as an astute businessman, and as an artist committed to raising the standard of artistic life in Dublin. Osborne approached the depiction of Dublin as an informed but detached observer: an approach which later led Thomas

Bodkin to state that the artist 'never saw Dublin with native eyes'.[5] Osborne brought the analytical skills he had learned at the Académie Royale des Beaux Arts in Antwerp to his representation of Dublin: an approach honed through a series of genre paintings of the English countryside and echoed in the urban paintings of his British and European peers.

While paintings of Dublin form only one aspect of Osborne's total oeuvre, they are arguably the most important collection of works showing the changing city from the 1880s to the opening years of the twentieth century. While noting the artistic context in which they were created, we can also look to Osborne's Dublin paintings to further understand the social conditions of the city in this period, as well as to track urban development and change, chiefly through the munificence of the Guinness brothers Lord Ardilaun and Lord Iveagh – which exemplified the 'paternalistic' schemes identified by Arscott. Many of Osborne's paintings reflect how Dublin was increasingly characterised in literary and other textual sources (as a place of deep social and architectural contrasts), but also as a city that was engaged in civic developments and modernisation projects, supported by a developing middle and upper class who also provided artistic patronage. As will be seen, Osborne's image of Dublin was often cultivated for British audiences, and his paintings of the Irish city present an interesting case of artistic regionalism and suggest how an Irish artist could operate within a British artistic system in the late nineteenth century.

Growing up in Dublin

Born in 1859, Osborne lived and worked at the Osborne family home at 5 Castlewood Avenue, Rathmines.[6] His father, William Osborne, was also an artist and was well known for his often-sentimental paintings of domestic and farm animals. Lying to the south of Dublin city centre, the independent township of Rathmines was one of the first suburbs to be developed outside of the traditional city boundary (Figure 1.1). Protestant and unionist in its government, Rathmines had been established in 1847 as a direct reaction to the Catholic-controlled municipal council and was largely home to well-to-do professionals and their families.[7] In 1870, Osborne was enrolled in Rathmines School under the tutelage of Dr Charles Benson, a clergyman who would remain part of the Osborne family's social circle through the closing decades of the century.[8] Teaching at the school was strongly influenced by Benson's faith, with prayer and religious study playing an important role in the school day, along with classics, mathematics, and modern languages. Religion does seem to have played an important role in Osborne's life: his brother Charles later became a clergyman, and the artist was a frequent attendee of services at St Patrick's Cathedral. The Osborne family's friends and acquaintances were largely drawn from the city's bourgeois (largely but not exclusively Protestant) intelligentsia – scholars, doctors, lawyers, and artists – with political opinions ranging from unionism, Home Rule supporters, and nationalists. In 1876,

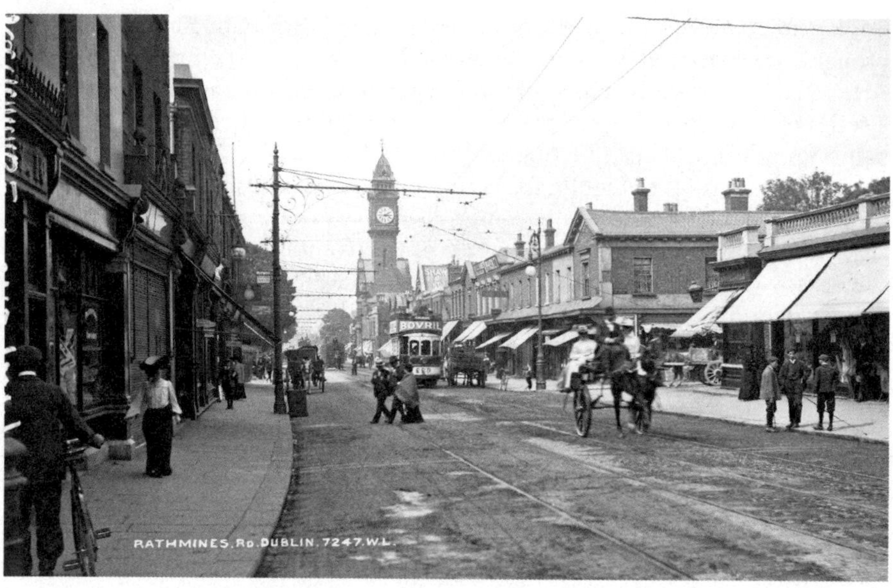

1.1   Robert French, *Rathmines Road*, c.1865–1914.

Osborne commenced his artistic training at the RHA schools. He achieved many successes in his early career, being awarded a Taylor Prize on four occasions, the RHA Albert Scholarship in 1880, and the Taylor Scholarship in 1881. Administered by the RDS, the Taylor Bequest awards enabled many Irish artists of the period to continue their education and training abroad, and in the winter of 1881, Osborne enrolled at the Académie Royale des Beaux Arts in Antwerp along with two fellow Irish artists: Nathaniel Hill and Joseph Malachy Kavanagh. Not only did this period of study strongly influence his painting style and technique, it also marked an important expansion of Osborne's broader network of artistic peers which would remain influential throughout his career.

The Académie Royale was popular with art students from across the Ireland and Britain, who saw it not only as an alternative to the South Kensington system, but also the studio system in Paris which was still strongly focused towards history painting and the annual Prix de Rome. At the Académie Royale 'strict discipline was enforced; most of the teachers spoke English; there were good museums; entry to the schools was free of charge; living in Antwerp was cheap and student life there was pleasant'.[9] Classes in Antwerp were divided into two categories: *antiek*, which focused on drawings from the antique, and *natuur*, drawing and painting from the living model. Perhaps more significant for Osborne was the use of clothed models (both as single figures and in groups) for the benefit of genre painters. The encouragement given to genre painters at the Académie, as well as the provision made for landscape and animal painting, made it a good alternative choice to a more restrictive classical training. Osborne entered the *natuur* class in the winter term of 1881. Students were expected to reach a certain level of proficiency in the *antiek* class before progressing to *natuur*, and of the three that had travelled from Dublin, Osborne was the only one to be promoted directly to the *natuur* class on arrival at the Académie.[10]

Osborne later travelled to Brittany, spending a year there in 1883, visiting Dinan, Quimperlé, and Pont Aven, an established route for artists visiting the region.[11] This period of travel in France brought Osborne into contact with a wide circle of artists, with Stanhope Forbes and Henry La Thangue among those whom Osborne met.[12] After his time in Belgium and France, Osborne established a base in Dublin, but continued to travel widely in England, capitalising on the friendships and connections made in Antwerp and Brittany. In 1884, he spent time in Walberswick, Lincoln, and Evesham with Hill and Edward Stott. Over the next seven years, Osborne also spent time in the predominantly rural environs of Wells-next-the-Sea, Southwold, Andover, Stratford-upon-Avon, Romsey, Winchester, Newbury, Uffington, Rye, and Hastings. Unusually, perhaps, Osborne does not seem to have visited the active and prolific colony at Newlyn, led by Forbes.[13]

The dominant influence on artists in Antwerp and Brittany during the 1880s was the work of French realist and naturalist artists – including, for example, Jules Bastien Lepage – with a predominant focus on rural and everyday settings and subjects. The result of this training was a detached, observational style of painting, characterised by a somewhat muted colour palette of grey-blues and muted greens, relieved by touches of pink and gold. Artists working in this method often embraced new technologies to enhance their academic training; for instance, using photography as a source and guide for compositions, as well as detailed pencil sketches and preparatory works. While the subject matter and colour palette of many of the finished paintings by Antwerp-trained artists may suggest that they were worked *en plein air*, they were more likely to have been completed in the studio using various source and preparatory materials. During his time on the continent, and while travelling in Britain, Osborne collected photographs, using them as *aides-memoir* for several early compositions, as seen for example in *A View in Antwerp* (c.1881, oil on panel, private collection), where the composition draws on a photograph of that city in an album now in the collection of the NGI.[14] The album shows his interest in recording his surroundings, with views of streetscapes and buildings often featuring among his photographs. In a small number of images of Brittany, the artist gathered portraits of the poor, including children in ragged clothing and an elderly man who sits with his work tools and holds rosary beads, while his hollow eyes look straight down the lens of the camera. Despite the potentially emotive nature of the subjects, the images captured by Osborne remain closely observant rather than sentimental, while also revealing more of his interest in depicting the rural and urban poor. These images established Osborne's concern for the built environment, and the concentration on picturesque urban scenes foreshadows his Dublin paintings.

Osborne's interest in observing the manners and behaviours of those around him is further revealed in a series of letters written to his father during his travels in England with Stott in 1884. While staying in the village of North Littleton, Osborne wrote that he had 'met with such quaint people here, some almost aboriginal in their ideas about painting'. The rural, backward nature of the area seems to have been a draw to the artist, and he continued in his letter that: 'it is great fun for me to go into the little inn … and sit by the fire an odd evening over a glass of beer and a pipe and listen to these old village oracles. The fireplace in this inn is really where all the wit and learning of North Littleton centres itself. The House of Lords receives little mercy at these meetings and would be dispatched in a rather summary manner if these old politicians had their way.' Osborne's writing reveals the artist's interest in the observation of everyday life, and the small events and arguments that contribute to it. This letter also suggests that this type of interaction and observation was something Osborne was unused to, suggesting that his freedom to frequent inns and public houses in Ireland was more limited, perhaps because of his middle-class background. While written tongue-in-cheek, the artist is careful to remind his father that 'you must tell Old Muddy … that I do not spend all my evenings drinking beer in a country inn but read until there is nothing more for me but sweet sleep and dreams'.[15]

Throughout the letter, the artist suggests a social gap between himself and the people around him. He cannot credit them with understanding or appreciating art, and although he is willing to observe and listen to their discussions in the inn, he declines an invitation to join in, stating that 'they sometimes appeal to me as a person of metropolitan experience … They seem to think painters even more mystical beings when I tell them they never talk about politics.' These details from Osborne's early career are revealing in relation to how the artist would later approach his depiction of Dublin. Through his education at the Académie Royale and the influence of the French realist tradition, Osborne developed his interest in observing the everyday and in the narrative opportunities of portraying this in paint. His working method was further informed by using photography in combination with more traditional preparatory drawings and oil sketches. Furthermore, Osborne's letter to his father reveals something of his detachment from his subject matter, a tendency to highlight differences of social class and outlook, and a reticence to be drawn on his political views.

Osborne and Dublin's 'town sparrows'

A photograph of the artist, likely taken in the mid-late 1880s, shows Osborne sitting in his studio at Castlewood Avenue (Figure 1.2). Seated in a Windsor-type chair and gazing directly at the lens, the tips of his full moustache finely pointed, Osborne presents himself as confident and self-assured. Behind him, a series of mounted and unmounted images fill the wall, perhaps the artists' own work, along with a collection of various *objets trouvés*. A similar backdrop

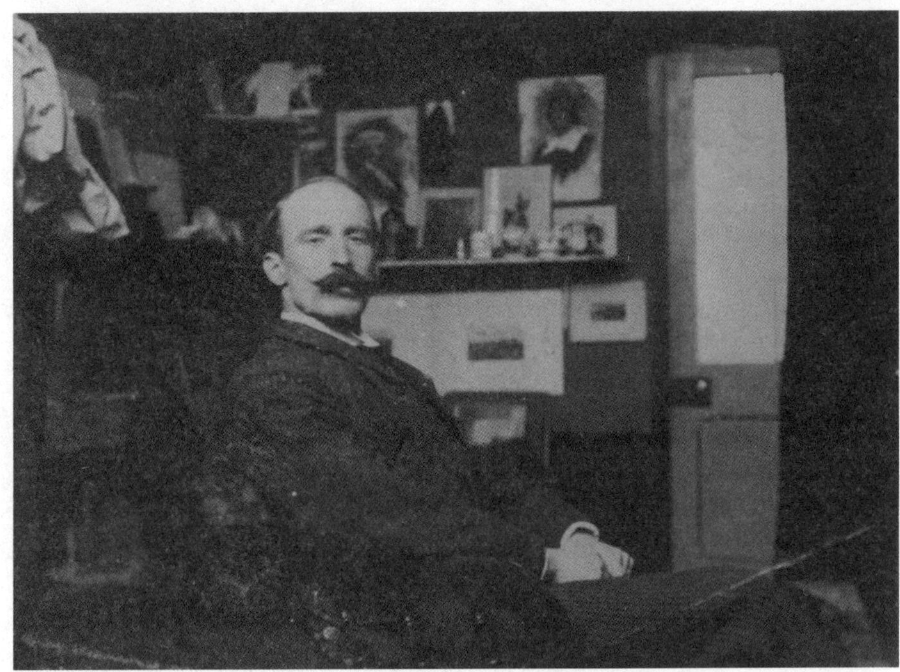

1.2   Anonymous, Photograph of Walter Osborne seated in his studio c. 1880s.

appears in *Portrait of Stephen Gwynn* (1885, oil on canvas, NGI), a writer and friend of Osborne's from the mid-1880s onwards, and these elements continually reappear throughout a series of paintings completed at this time. These works, however, do not depict Osborne's friends and colleagues; rather, they provide one of the earliest examples of Osborne's engagement with some of Dublin's most impoverished citizens in his artistic practice.

In 1886, Osborne contributed to the annual summer exhibition at the RA for the first time, exhibiting a painting titled *Tired Out* (1886, oil on canvas, private collection). The painting was also exhibited at the RHA and at the Walker Gallery, Liverpool the following year: an early example of the artist's practice of exhibiting works at multiple venues in Ireland and Britain, usually until they found a purchaser. *Tired Out* shows an injured and sickly-looking boy sitting in a chair, propped with a pillow, looking out to the right-hand side of the canvas, where light from an unseen window falls on his face and surroundings. On a table in front of the boy a fine tortoiseshell cat sits on a magazine with colour reproductions, along with a collection of loose sheets of additional colour images. A toy soldier, an apple, and an open wooden box also lie on the table, while a drawing or poster can be seen pinned to the wall, alongside a birdcage and a bunch of yellow daffodils. The *Art Journal* described the work as 'a pathetic rendering of a sick lad weary of his playthings', but, at the same time, the artist also uses the painting to demonstrate his skill in depicting both living and inanimate still-life subjects.[16] The tonal range of the painting suggests discrepancies between the boy's appearance and his surroundings: for example, shading around his hands and fingers suggest that his skin is dirty, along with similar markings on his clothes, while the items around him evoke a deeper purse.

The use of models from impoverished backgrounds was common at this time, as evidenced by the practices of Osborne's peers and contemporaries. For example, in France, Jules Adler 'took all his models from all sections of the vast working class of Paris'.[17] In London during the 1880s and 1890s, Edward Linley Sambourne used models who 'journeyed to Sambourne's home in Kensington from slum dwellings in Holloway, Euston and Fulham – a reminder of … their wretched existence beyond the studio'.[18] Dorothy Tennant (Mrs H. M. Stanley) also recounted her experiences of bringing children into her London studio and the challenges which that task presented, an account later echoed by Rose Barton in her *Familiar London* publication.[19] Like those travelling to Sambourne's studio, the models who travelled from the tenements in places like Gloucester Street and Chancery Lane to Osborne's studio in Castlewood Avenue or later to 6 St Stephen's Green, would have moved through the different spheres of life contained within the city. To date, only limited study of artist's models in the Irish context has been completed and little information on the employment of models has survived.[20] A rare and important source of information is contained in Osborne's diary for 1892. At the back of this pocket-sized notebook are the names and addresses of the models used by the artist. In that year, his models include two boys aged ten: Thomas Walsh and Louis Marc Antonio; and four other models: Michael O'Neill, Katie Kane, Maggie Kavanagh, and Mary Brophy.[21] The details of these models used by Osborne show that he sought out 'authentic' sitters for his paintings of the Dublin poor, but, unfortunately, no record exists to show how much, or even if, Osborne paid these models for their time.

The studio setting of *Tired Out* is repeated in several other works by Osborne, all showing children, for example in *Cupboard Love* (1886, oil on canvas, private collection), *A Boy Blowing Bubbles* (Plate 1.1), and *The Lazy Model* (or *Little Boy Asleep*, 1887, oil on canvas, private collection) which also include what must have been stock items in the artist's arsenal – such as the cat, bird cage, and the reproductions pinned to the wall.[22] Writing about her methods for portraying London's 'ragamuffins', Tennant noted that the artist should keep a supply of props in the studio, including 'a good supply of rags (carefully fumigated, camphored, and peppered)'.[23] While these paintings do not explicitly depict the urban landscape, the inclusion and probable use of models drawn from the city's population demonstrates the wider artistic economy that existed in Dublin, as well as showing clear similarities between Osborne's artistic practice and his naturalist contemporaries across Britain and France. Furthermore, it reveals a more practical element of Osborne's artistic practice, as representations of sickly children, waifs, or so-called 'street arabs', held popular appeal with the sentimental art-buying public of Victorian Britain. For the bourgeois attendee of the annual RA exhibition, such imagery 'could set in play a sentimental mode that stirred a self-congratulatory pity for the poor'.[24] These paintings are in stark contrast to Osborne's commissioned portraits of middle- and upper-class children, or of his niece, Violet, with her friends in the garden of Castlewood Avenue. Osborne's commercial nous is further exemplified by his reformulation of established poses: for example, John Everett Millais, *Boy Blowing Bubbles* (1886, oil on canvas, Lady Lever Art Gallery) and William Powell Frith, *The Sleeping Model* (1853, oil on canvas, Royal Academy).

Paintings of working-class children produced by British artists in this period tended to fall into one of two categories: that of children at play, or of suffering children, both of which 'converged to confirm and consolidate aspects of nineteenth-century bourgeois sensibility'.[25] A painting of a 'ragamuffin' could easily elide the very real poverty experienced by the child or children depicted. At the RHA in 1887, Osborne exhibited a work titled '*Who'll Buy?*' alongside *Tired Out*. Although the whereabouts of the painting is now unknown, it was described in the *Weekly Freeman's Journal*:

> The round rosy face of the little girl who is 'beginning to earn her own living,' though far from having the wan, pinched features and prematurely aged look of the children of the poorest class in London, has, nevertheless, an expression of care and anxiety that contrasts oddly with its natural curves. She stands near one of Landseer's lions in Trafalgar-square, her bundle of evening papers beside her, the pink-tinted *Globe* conspicuous among them, while she clasps a great placard of the *Evening Mail*. Her red muffler is drawn tightly round her throat to keep out the bitter wind, for her ragged jacket is but little protection.[26]

This painting may well be Osborne's sole depiction of London, and from the description at least would seem to bear close resemblance to works being exhibited by his contemporaries, such as Tennant and William Mulready, in that city.

The discourse around street children in the nineteenth and early twentieth century was shaped by two conflicting attitudes in contemporary society: that of the child as a victim of circumstance, and as a threat, with the 'potential to undermine public health, family cohesion, social stability and economic progress'.[27] In Dublin as in London, the sight of impoverished children on the city's streets was not unusual and was a key cause of the city's philanthropists from the mid-century onwards. As Maria Luddy has outlined, organised relief for Dublin's 'town sparrows' (a term used in the Dublin press in the 1880s to describe impoverished children), was heavily sectarian, with Catholic and Protestant groups as much engaged in a battle for souls as for providing shelter, sustenance, and education.[28] Shelters, refuges, and ragged schools were established by various groups in the city's most impoverished areas, a notable example being those run by Mrs Ellen Smyly in alliance with the Irish Church Missions, which had a strong evangelical ethos. Through his frequent attendance of services at St Patrick's Cathedral and his family's other religious connections, Osborne was surely aware of the philanthropic schemes in place to improve the lives of these children. Indeed, his representations of children in ecclesiastical settings seem to play on contemporary concerns around religion, poverty, and benevolence. For example, *A Children's Service* (1889, oil on canvas, private collection) exhibited at the Royal Birmingham Society of Artists in 1889 and at RHA in 1890, shows a group of listless children (and one mother and infant) in the cathedral interior. When the painting was exhibited in Dublin in the 1890s, the *Dublin Daily Express* noted that the viewer 'cannot but sympathize with the little prisoners who, condemned to listen, possibly, to the reading of a manuscript sermon, evidently are doing their best to shake off the too heavy burden'.[29] The setting of *A Children's Service* is reused in another painting, *Interior, St Patrick's Cathedral* (Plate 1.2), bequeathed by Charles Osborne to the Dublin City Gallery the Hugh Lane (DCGHL), but this second work shows children of a rather different type: two choristers sort through a chest of music, with an approximation of the Boyle Family monument behind them. Osborne's use of the cathedral interior as a setting for a type of sentimental genre scene arguably reaches an apotheosis in another canvas titled *Interior of St Patrick's Cathedral* (c.1887, oil on canvas, private collection), this time framed by the Captain Boyd monument and one of the cathedral's stained-glass windows. In the foreground, a boy and his grandmother take refuge in the quiet nave and both doze quietly, observed only by the young girl who sits behind them.

The presence of children on Dublin's streets was the subject of an inquiry in 1902, under the auspices of the Street Trading Committee (Ireland), which sought to find a means by which the state could 'monitor and regulate the lives of street children'.[30] The reports of the inquiry demonstrate the importance of clothing in assessing the conditions that these children lived in – as well as the middle-class attitudes and assumptions that shaped methods of relief and regulation. From these records, Gillian McIntosh notes that 'street trading children's clothing was considered a key indicator of the level of their impoverishment … Other witnesses cited the quality of street children's clothing as something that was so bad it distinguished them from other poor children on the street.'[31] Osborne's representation of impoverished children in Dublin can thus be understood with reference to several contemporary concerns: the public appetite for such imagery – shaped by middle-class viewers, the work of philanthropic groups in Dublin to ameliorate the lives of the city's 'ragged children', and not least of all, the very visible presence of these children of the city's streets. He was not alone in his depiction of Dublin's 'town sparrows': Richard Thomas Moynan was drawn to the subject in a number of works exhibited in the 1890s, and both John Butler Yeats and Sarah Purser completed paintings of urban tropes and subjects, such as the ragged child and the impoverished flower seller. In 1886, Yeats exhibited *The Bird Market* (Figure 1.3) at the RHA, showing a small boy in ragged clothes holding a small wooden cage. The *Dublin University Review* praised the painting as 'a remarkable piece of work, and we are inclined to think that in the whole exhibition there is no better instance of true

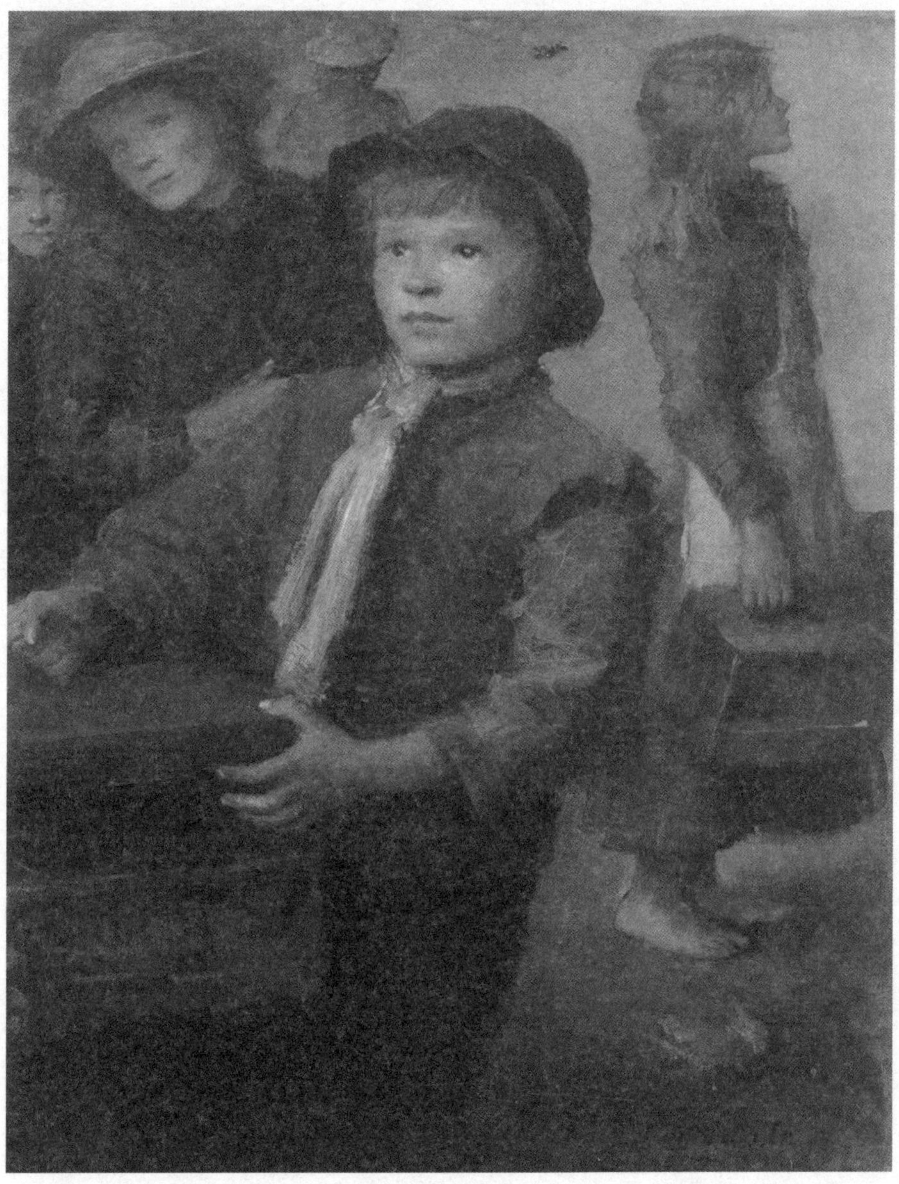

1.3   John Butler Yeats, *The Bird Market*, 1886.

art'.[32] The aestheticisation of poverty, transforming the pitiable existence of this young child into something to be valued for its pictorial qualities, speaks to the attitudes of the art-going public at this time.

The representation of impoverished children was by no means limited to visual art, and often correlations between text and image can be found. For example, in 1890, Moynan exhibited '*Jo*' (medium and location unknown), at the RHA, referencing the eponymous crossing-sweeper boy of Charles Dickens's *Bleak House*. More locally, in the 1870s and 1880s, May Laffan published a series of novels and short stories which often focused on impoverished children in Dublin and Edinburgh, most notably *Flitters, Tatters and the Counsellor: Three Waifs from the Dublin Streets*, first published as a short story in 1879. As Jill Brady Hampton has outlined, Laffan's depiction of these three destitute children draws on exemplars from British writing but responds to the conditions of colonisation rather than industrialisation.[33] The three protagonists are not siblings: Flitters, the oldest of the group, is alone after the death of her mother and her father's emigration to America; Tatters a foundling, 'whose nurse had turned him loose on the streets when she found no more money forthcoming for his maintenance'; while 'the Counsellor's antecedents were wrapped in complete obscurity'.[34] Through a description of their clothing, Laffan creates a textual image of the three children: Flitters wears, for example,

> a *princesse robe*, a cast-off perhaps of some dweller in the fashionable squares ... Viewed from a distance it seemed to have a great many pocket-holes, but on closer inspection these resolved themselves into holes without pockets; underneath this was another old dress, much more ancient and ragged.[35]

Church-based philanthropy is also a feature of the text through a hospital run by the Sisters of Mercy, where Tatters is induced by the Reverend Mother to attend Mass and say the Rosary.[36] At the RHA annual exhibition in 1890, Philip H. Miller exhibited a 'large painting of "Flitters, Tatters, and the Counsellor," street arabs under an archway'.[37] Although the painting is now unknown, Miller also produced an etching of the same subject as part of a portfolio produced at the Dublin Art Club (Figure 1.4). This was described as 'an imaginative study from the *brochure* [sic] by Miss Laffan'.[38] The composition shows the three children sheltering under a bridge, echoing the text's repeated use of the Liffey's bridges as landmarks and meeting points. While the three children are barefoot and ill-clad for anything but a warm summer's day, the background of Miller's etching relocates the children to a more pastoral rural setting. This change undoubtedly makes the scene more picturesque, further distancing the viewer from the challenges faced by children across rural and urban Ireland in this period.

Patrick Street and philanthropy: a changing streetscape

After visiting Dublin in 1853, Charles Dickens wrote about his experiences of the Irish city, eloquently describing its neighbourhoods in a series of short articles. His journeys through the Dublin streets led him to the Coombe and the area surrounding St Patrick's Cathedral, located in the south west of the city. He described Patrick Street:

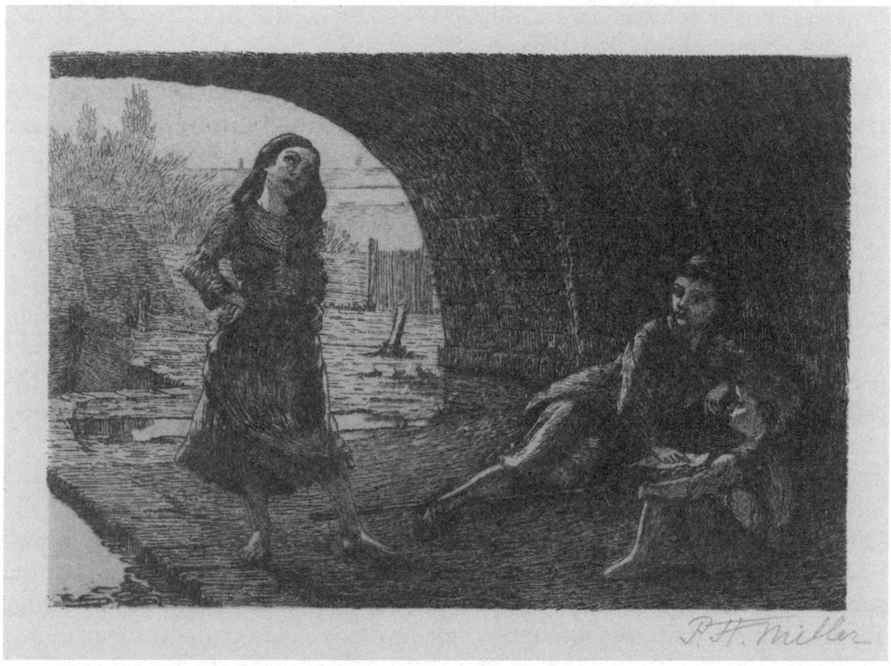

1.4   Philip H. Miller, *Flitters, Tatters and the Counsellor*, 1890.

one side is occupied by a manifestation of the old clothes interest, the other by a continuous line of stalls for the sale of butcher's meat and provisions in general – the stalls being overshadowed by projecting bulkheads prodigiously productive of *chiaro oscuro* [*sic*], picturesqueness, rottenness, and dinginess. This and the neighbourhood are the most ancient, raggedest, dirtiest, wretchedest part of Dublin's proud city.[39]

By 1887, the street was little changed. The listing for Patrick Street in *Thom's Official Directory* for that year offers a sense of the economic and social conditions of the area prior to its redevelopment: of the eighty-three buildings that made up the street, twenty-eight were classified as tenements, and one as 'ruins'.[40] The listing also offers a sense of the sights, sounds, and smells of the street: there were nine victuallers, nine spirit and wine dealers and merchants, a size and glue manufacturer, two tallow candle chandlers, as well as numerous grocery and provision dealers.[41] In addition to these, stalls and marketers would have added to the day-to-day bustle and atmosphere of the street. In *Picturesque Dublin: Old and New*, Frances Gerard described the street 'a squalid but picturesque ghetto', where

every conceivable article, from broken crockery to cast-off clothing, is for sale: the clothes indeed overflow; and the booths, which run along the hilly slope of the irregular street, not being sufficient to contain this collection of rags, the

41

overplus is flung in a promiscuous heap on to a carpeting of sacks, spread out to save the merchandise from the mire of the street.[42]

The large number of tenements on the street was not unusual for the less salubrious areas of the city. In the context of Dublin's housing crisis, the later redevelopment of the Patrick Street area was a notable exception, although it ultimately displaced more people than it rehoused.

Near St Patrick's Close, an Old Dublin Street (Plate 1.3) marks the beginning of Osborne's interest in the street and the surrounding area and incorporates themes and motifs that he would continue to use in later paintings. This initial painting takes in Patrick Street itself, looking down towards the tower and main façade of the eponymous cathedral. While a street called St Patrick's Close ran parallel to the side of the cathedral, here Osborne uses 'close' to refer to the cathedral precincts. Visually repeating Dickens's description, Osborne shows the narrow market street as framed by buildings in various states of dilapidation, housing various stalls and shops. While the young boy with a tin whistle in the foreground of the painting may initially attract the viewer's attention, along the left-hand side of the street the artist has included details of the fish stalls as well as other details such as a bundle of clothing, pots and baskets, which attract the eye. On the opposite side of the canvas, a horse and donkey wait outside various shops and meat stalls, the former attended by two children. Osborne exhibited the painting at the RA in 1887 and at the RHA the following year, where it did receive some critical attention. A reviewer for the *Dublin Daily Express* noted that the canvas 'proves satisfactorily that it is not only in the Upper Thames country that the painter can find inspiration'.[43]

In addition to diary entries which show that Osborne frequently attended services in the cathedral, three photographs of Patrick Street in the artist's archive each contain elements found in *Near St Patrick's Close* (Figure 1.5).

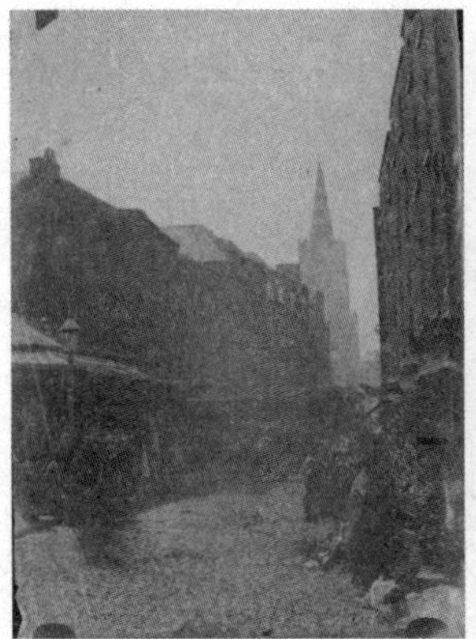
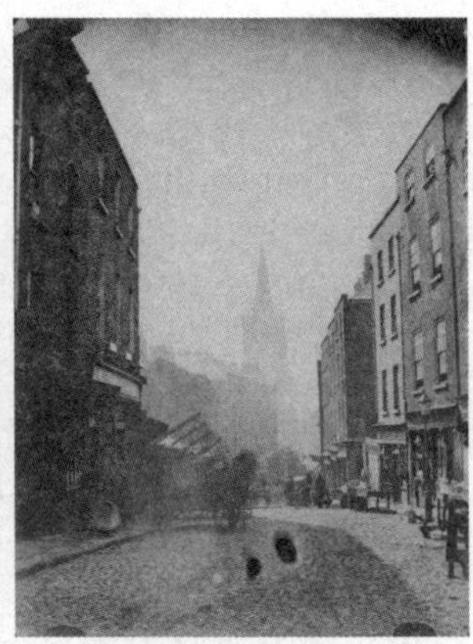
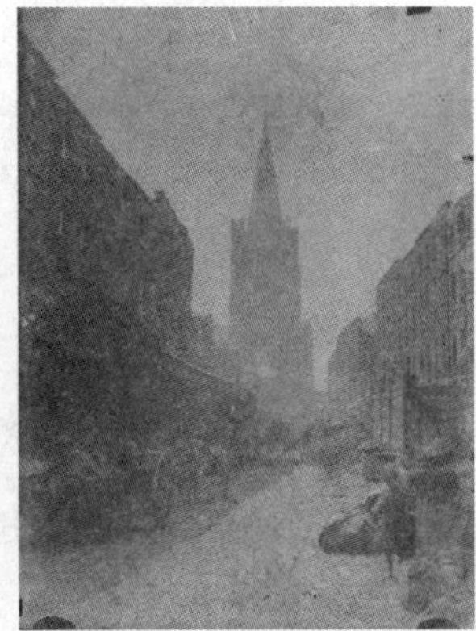

1.5   Anonymous, Three Photographs of Patrick Street looking towards St Patrick's Cathedral, c.1886.

These images are printed on thin brown paper and contain no stamps or marks to suggest that they were taken by a professional studio and were most likely taken by an amateur photographer, if not by the artist himself.[44] The last of these three photographs bears the strongest resemblance to *Near St Patrick's Close*, looking down a stretch of the street with the cathedral in the background on the left-hand side. It is clear that Osborne directly translated elements of the photograph into the composition: for instance, the horse, donkey, and carts on the left-hand side, and a bulging bag of rags, just visible on the right-hand side of the photograph behind the child, has been brought into the right-hand foreground of the painting. It is also clear that the artist altered part of the scene for the painting: the hoarding on the right-hand side of the photograph has been omitted and replaced instead with shop fronts more akin to those seen in the first photograph. In addition, Osborne has included two 'Dutch Billy' style houses, a clear change from the photograph. The shop fronts on the left-hand side correspond exactly with those seen in the third photograph, with distinctive uneven and overlapping wooden awnings.

While *Near St Patrick's Close* and its associated photographs looked towards St Patrick's Cathedral, two other works by Osborne turned northwards, taking in the busy street and the squat steeple of Christ Church: *Rags, Bones and Bottles* (Plate 1.4) and *Life in the Streets: Hard Times* (Plate 1.5). Osborne was not the only Irish artist drawn to this scene: Rose Barton produced a view of the street in 1881, albeit in a more open and colourful style to Osborne (Figure 1.6). The former of Osborne's paintings, exhibited in London and Liverpool in 1891, is a compact but powerful work: the white steeple and red brick of the street are bathed in strong sunlight, while in the foreground, a group of children gather around a fruit-seller. Behind this group, a wooden sign over the ramshackle shop front reads 'J Clarke, Rags, Bones, Bottles'. The distinctive wooden beam which supports the sign can also be seen in Barton's representation of the street, as well as in a photograph taken by Robert French for the Lawrence photography firm (Figure 1.7). However, the sign is absent, suggesting that Osborne incorporated it into the scene for artistic purposes.[45] When compared with the earlier, and larger, *Near St Patrick's Close*, this canvas shows how Osborne's sense of colour developed from the 1880s into the 1890s, leaving behind some of the restrictions of his Belgian training. An undated pen and ink sketch, titled *The Oyster Seller* (undated, pen and ink on paper, private collection), provides a more detailed study of the central figure of *Rags, Bones and Bottles*, while the motif of children engaging with a street seller is reminiscent of *Cherry Ripe* (1889, oil on canvas, Ulster Museum).

The sunlit atmosphere of *Rags, Bones and Bottles* is nowhere to be found in *Hard Times*, though there are other similarities between the two artworks. Situated a little further along Patrick Street, the central seated figure wears the same blue apron, brown coat, and bowler hat seen in the earlier oil, and again, the steeple of Christ Church is visible in the background. Even allowing for the damage caused during a flood in the Tate stores in the 1920s, the palette

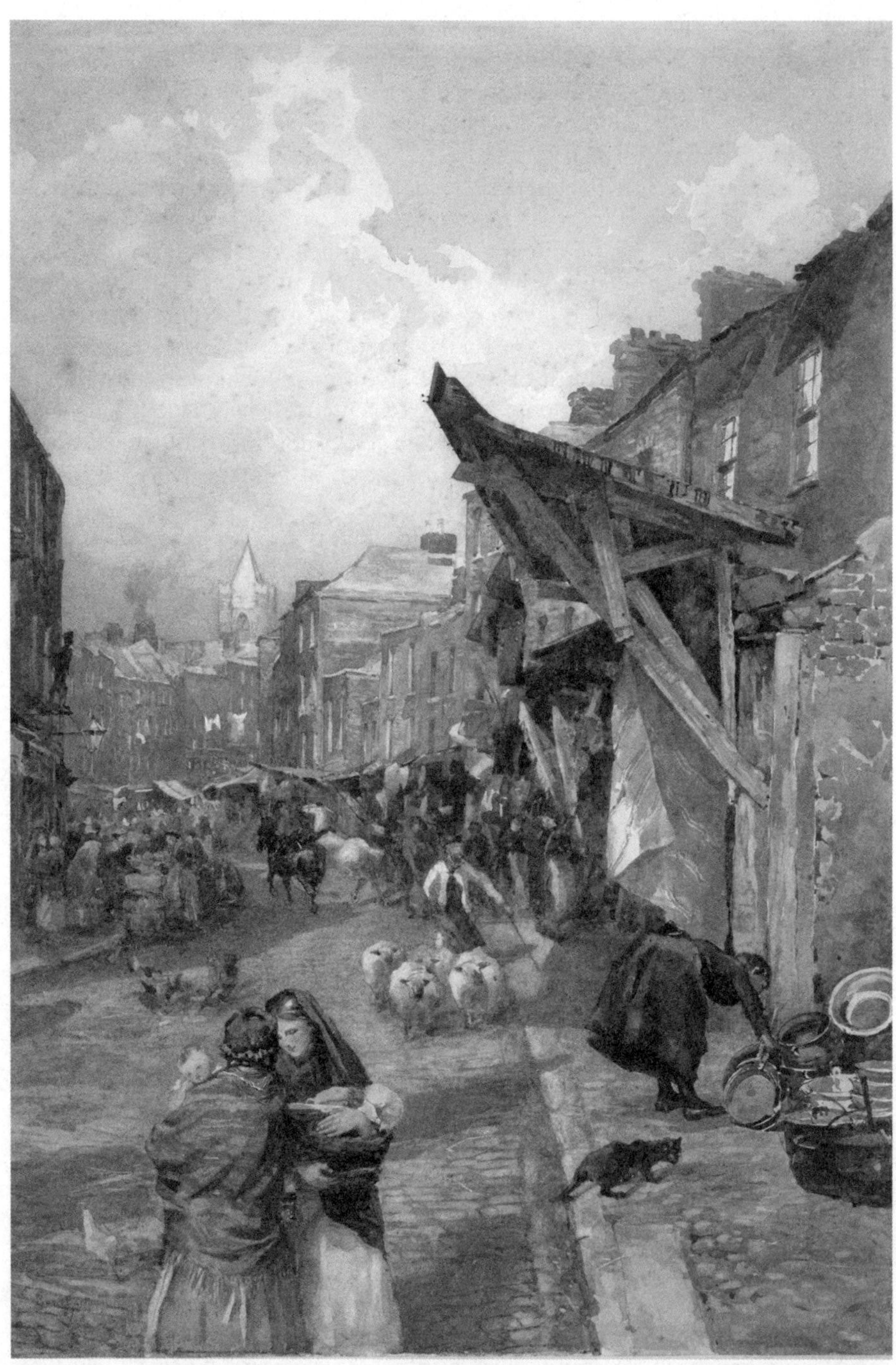

1.6   Rose Barton, *St Patrick's Close, Dublin*, 1881.

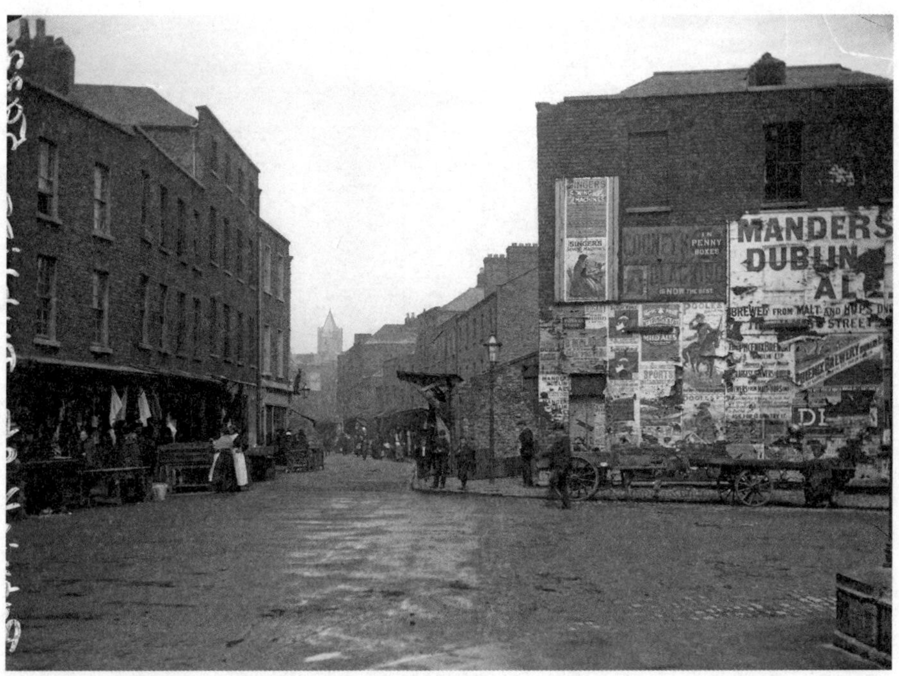

1.7   Robert French, *Patrick Street*, c.1880–1900.

reflects the pastel's title, filled with murky browns and grey, enlivened only by the cart of oranges and hints of pink in the clouds which surround the steeple. Two preparatory drawings for the pastel show the evolution of Osborne's idea: the first showing the outline of the street and shop fronts (Figure 1.8), and the second the placement of the main figures and market stalls.[46] A sketchbook dated February 1892 also contains preparatory sketches for aspects of the composition, including the fruit cart, drain, and wicker basket on the left-hand side, as well as notes in the artist's hand listing 'oranges and apples, stalls on the right, houses, windows and lamp, chimneys' (Figures 1.9, 1.10). Osborne's progression on this composition can also be traced though a series of diary entries: on 11 January 1892, the artist noted that he had 'made first sketch for a pastel of Patrick Street'. The next day, the artist returned to the street, this time ensuring that he 'brought a drawing board'. Work on the pastel continued until 17 March (appropriately, St Patrick's Day), when he recorded that the pastel was completed. The completed composition was submitted and accepted to the RA annual exhibition, and by 19 July 1892, Osborne had received a cheque from the Chantrey Bequest trustees for the purchase of *Hard Times*.[47] Established by the terms of the will of Sir Francis Leggatt Chantrey, the Bequest empowered the presidents or trustees of the RA to purchase art works for the benefit of the British nation. The fund came into effect in 1878, with selected works initially

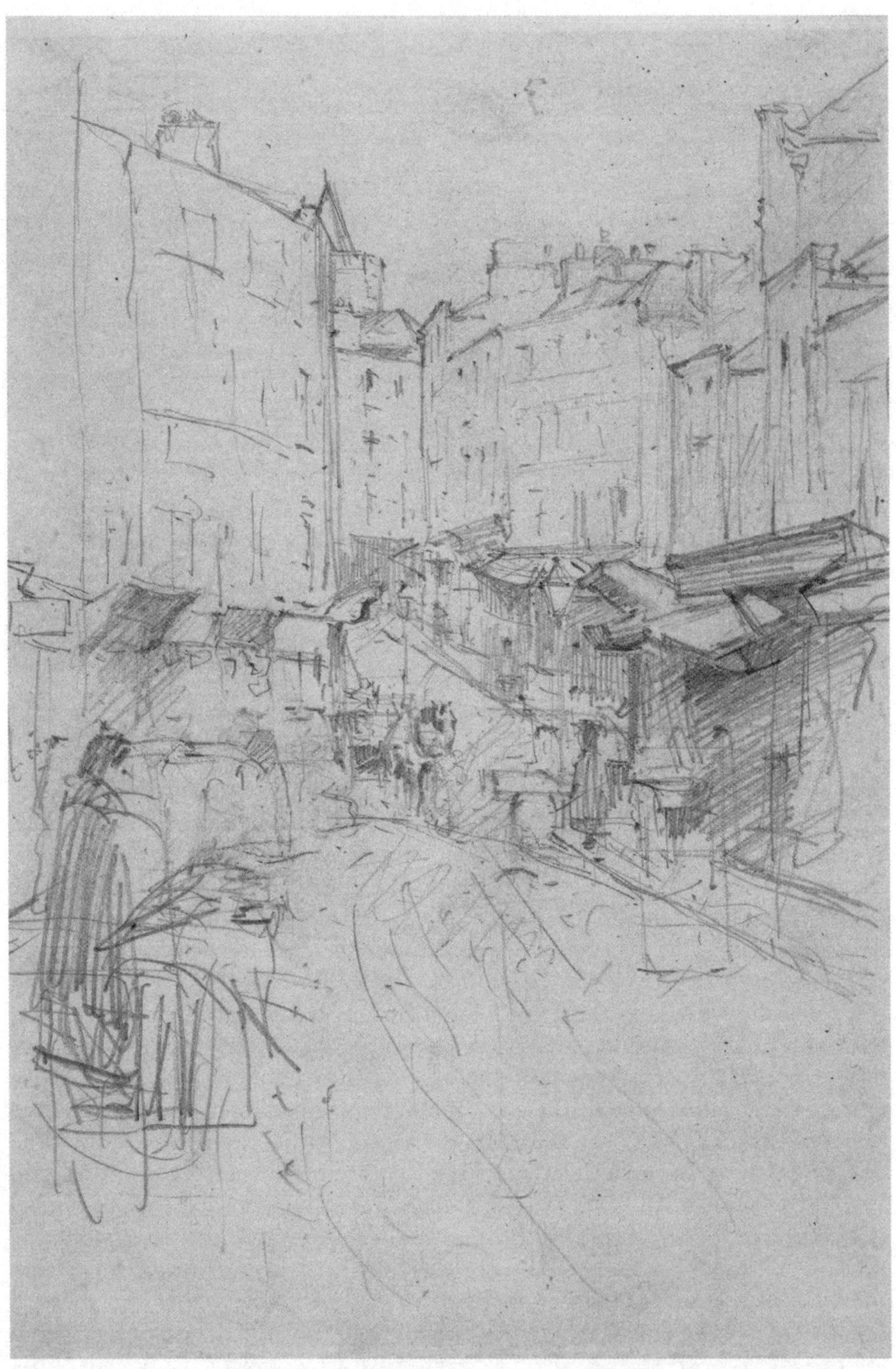

1.8   Walter Frederick Osborne, *Christ Church Cathedral, Dublin from Patrick Street*,
c.1892.

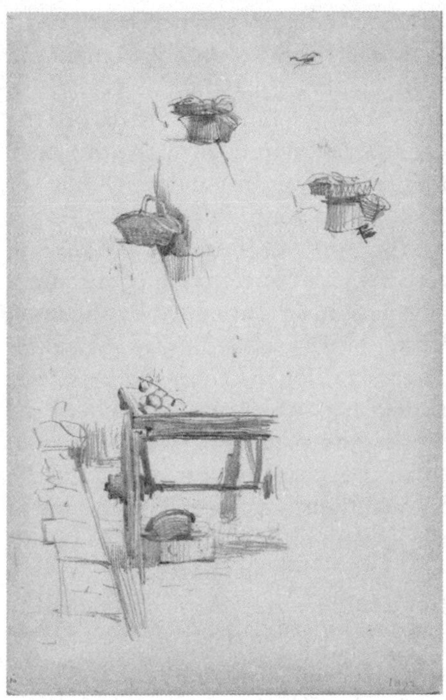 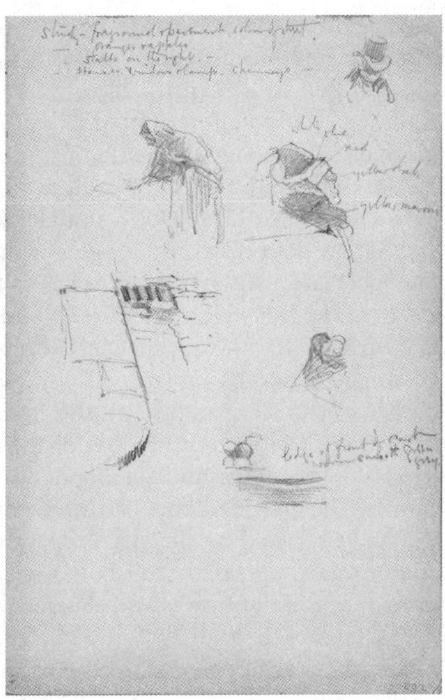

1.9 *Left.* Walter Frederick Osborne, preparatory sketches for *Life in the Streets: Hard Times*, 1892.

1.10 *Right.* Walter Frederick Osborne, preparatory sketches for *Life in the Streets: Hard Times*, 1892.

exhibited at the Victoria and Albert Museum, before their transfer to what is now Tate Britain in 1898. The terms of the Bequest stated that work could be purchased from British or foreign artists (dead or living), on the proviso that the work was executed in Britain. Not only was this the first time a work by Osborne was purchased by the RA, it was also the first work by an Irish artist purchased by the Chantrey trustees and would be the only such work for several years to come.

Following the success of *Life in the Streets: Hard Times*, Osborne returned to the area the next year, picturing its market stalls for *The Fish Market, Patrick Street*. Exhibited at the RA in 1894, Osborne initially titled the painting 'Life in the Streets: Musicians' which suggests he conceived of these works as part of a series, together with the variants *The Dublin Streets: A Vendor of Books* (and *In the Streets: A Touch of Winter* (1893, watercolour on paper, private collection).[48] Regardless of the title used, to those unfamiliar with Osborne's previous depictions of the street the connection to Dublin may not have been particularly obvious, a fact made apparent in a review in the *Globe* which described it as a painting of 'one of the poorest districts of London', in which the artist 'has depicted the fish stalls, the itinerant musicians, the slovenly women and the children in a manner showing keen observation of nature'.[49] While this comment could be interpreted as stemming from ignorance on the part of the journalist reviewing the exhibition, it also acts as a reminder of the universal nature of urban poverty: regardless of whether one was in London, Dublin, or even Glasgow or Liverpool, a similar scene could no doubt be found.

Rather than offering a long view down the length of the street, for *The Fish Market* (Plate 1.6) Osborne focuses in more detail on one section of the street market. The fish stall in the foreground of the painting is attended by a woman and young girl, who approaches with a basket of fish. As with *Near St Patrick's Close*, the canvas is replete with still-life details – for instance, the bowl and basket in the foreground and the baskets and hats which fill the stalls in the background. Close examination of the painting shows that the stall is rendered in an almost impressionistic manner, with areas of thick impasto applied to the canvas. The mix of colours used to convey the contents of the stall is repeated in the basket carried by the girl. Preparatory sketches for several elements of this composition suggest that Osborne spent some time on the street itself, taking note of its different stalls and characters: for example, the general outline of the fish seller and the stall are visible in 'A Fish Seller' (undated, graphite on paper, NGI) while the appearance of the woman is more fully realised in *A Dublin Fish Seller* (Figure 1.11). A sketch of the hat stall is also extant: the jumbled pile deftly depicted in graphite on paper (undated, graphite on paper, NGI).

The original title of the painting places more emphasis on the itinerant musician and the group gathered around to hear the barrel organ being played. Had Osborne exhibited the painting in Ireland during his lifetime, local audiences might have been aware of the significance of this inclusion: Chancery Lane, located just off Patrick Street, was home to a large proportion of the city's small Italian immigrant community, among them several organ grinders. The enclave attracted both good and bad press: the annual new year celebration, when organ grinders from across the city gathered on the Lane and played the instruments simultaneously, was noted in the press; while in 1887, the case of four Italian organ grinders charged with the assault of two men brought less-welcome attention to the area.[50]

In 1899, the passing of the Dublin Improvement (Bull Alley Area) Act brought sweeping changes to the environs of Patrick Street and St Patrick's Cathedral. The transformation of the area 'entailed the total demolition of one of the oldest and most historically significant areas of the city', with the 'warren of crooked lanes, alleys and yards' replaced with 'new straight, wide streets and a regular arrangement of compact blocks', in addition to clearing the way for a new public park and other civic amenities.[51] These substantial changes largely erased the streetscape that Osborne had depicted. The redevelopment of the area was championed and funded through the munificence of Arthur and Edward Guinness, heirs to the famous brewery and later styled Lord Ardilaun

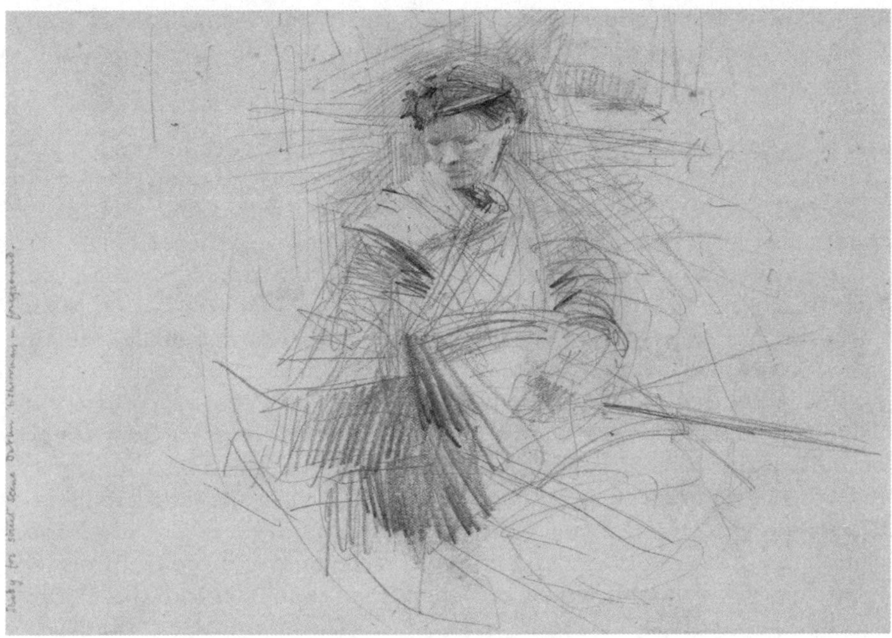

1.11   Walter Frederick Osborne, *A Dublin Fish Seller*, undated.

and Lord Iveagh respectively. The philanthropic association of the Guinness family with the Patrick Street area can be dated back to the 1850s, when Benjamin Lee Guinness undertook the restoration of the cathedral. This project was brought to fruition by his son, Arthur, who also oversaw the restoration of the adjacent Marsh's Library and the repurposing of St Stephen's Green as a public park. As employers, the Guinness family had been well regarded because they looked after their workers, including the provision of suitable housing. They were also singled out by the 1885 Commission as providing one of the few opportunities of employment for women in the city through the opening of a cloth and woollen factory.[52] In their efforts around Patrick Street there was also a secondary motive, particularly in the case of Edward Guinness who sought to 'expand and develop his philanthropic plans and social ambitions, which became increasingly inter-connected'.[53] In 1889, he formed the Guinness Trust to fund the development of working-class housing. Of the £250,000 available, 80 per cent was to be spent in London, and the remaining 20 per cent to be spent on housing in Dublin: as Andy Bielenberg notes, 'it was a matter of little surprise therefore that very shortly after … he was raised into the peerage as Lord Iveagh'.[54]

Archival evidence suggests that Osborne was interested in urban development and was concerned about the city's plight, although this was chiefly related to the fabric of the city itself, rather than the people who had to find shelter there. In an undated letter to his friend and fellow artist, Dermod O'Brien, Osborne invited O'Brien to become involved in 'a small committee being formed in Dublin with the object of protecting the old streets and buildings of the city and assisting in the improvement of [the] slums'.[55] The group was to be called the Dublin Protection Society, and although it does not seem to have evolved beyond early plans, this fragment provides a rare glimpse into Osborne's activities outside the art world. In the letter he detailed the aims of the planned society, and listed others who were being approached to join. This included society and artistic figures such as Sir Thornley Stoker, Lord Ardilaun, Lord Iveagh, and the Lord Mayor, as well as Laurence Waldron, George Moore, and artists Nathaniel Hone, John Hughes, Oliver Sheppard, John B. Yeats, and James Brenan. Finally, he concluded that 'we are anxious to exclude as far as possible the official and Departmental world here and of course the Society will be non-political'.[56] Osborne's letter demonstrates that there was an awareness of, and an admiration for, city planning in Europe, as well as a desire to improve the urban environment in Dublin. Given the disdain expressed for official channels, such as the Dublin Corporation, it is difficult to see how the Society would have made any impact on decisions made on city planning or planned improvements without deigning to cooperate on some level with these bodies. The listing of those also being asked to come on board is interesting: it clearly shows that the initial committee was aware of the philanthropic work carried out by Arthur and Edward Guinness (both of whom were staunch unionists), while also trying to keep a sense of balance: Laurence Waldron, for example, was a prominent business man and philanthropist, and was also later an MP for the Irish Parliamentary Party.[57] The other men mentioned by Osborne would also have been known to O'Brien, as they represent some of the main patrons of the arts in Ireland at this time. The idea for the Dublin Protection Society also resonates with the appetite for sociable activity in Dublin, often manifested through associations, clubs, and societies. The statement that the Society would be 'non-political' chimes with similar statements of such groups across the Anglophone world.[58]

Following Osborne's early death in 1903, the RHA held a memorial exhibition to mark the artist's contribution to the visual arts in Ireland. *The Fish Market* was lent to this exhibition by the trustees of his estate, and by 1904 the painting was owned by Hugh Lane, who included it in several subsequent shows, such as the Guildhall Exhibition of Works by Irish Painters in 1904, the Art Loan Exhibition, Belfast, 1906, and at the Franco-British Exhibition in 1908. When Lane opened the Municipal Gallery of Art on Dublin's Harcourt Street, the painting was transferred to that collection. While Osborne's original title for the painting was never revived, at the Franco-British Exhibition it was listed as '*The Old Fishmarket, Patrick Street (now demolished for Lord Iveagh's improvements)*'.[59] This third, temporary, title links Osborne's painting to the historical visual record of the Patrick Street area – as a depiction of a by-then lost cityscape – but also underlines the connection with the munificence of Iveagh and the Guinness family. Lane also, perhaps, wanted to draw Iveagh's attention to the collection of the Municipal Gallery: indeed, in September of the same year, the peer donated three paintings (by G. F. Watts, J. E. Millais, and James Holland) to Lane's gallery.[60]

Osborne and the urban scene

In 1889, Osborne exhibited *The Dublin Streets: A Vendor of Books* (Plate 1.7) in London and Liverpool, presenting an expansive and detailed view of Dublin city centre that is replete in its social and architectural detail. After the narrow confines of Patrick Street, a composition echoed in the artist's other exhibition piece of the same year, *Cherry Ripe*, the broad view of this painting offers a different sense of Osborne's home city. On the left-hand side, the viewer's gaze is drawn to the river, spanned by the recently widened and renamed O'Connell Bridge (previously Carlisle Bridge, widened between 1877–80), and down towards the Custom House, one of the main set pieces of Dublin's eighteenth-century architecture. Ship masts rise from the unseen water in front of this imposing building, evoking a sense of the busy port and docks, while the bustle of people crossing the bridge further suggests a sense of an industrious city centre. Osborne contrasts this with the scene of the painting's title: a group of older men sedately leaf through the jumbled pile of books and brightly coloured pamphlets, seemingly oblivious to the approach of a young flower seller, who proffers a bunch of daffodils. At the quay wall, another flower seller stands holding a young baby, a large basket of flowers at her feet. Towards the bridge, a soldier in the uniform of a Gordon Highlander walks along the quay, another book stall visible just behind him.[61] In contrast to the sharply cut Portland stone of the bridge and granite quay walls, the flagstones and cobbles of the street appear uneven and in bad repair, with areas of mud and straw suggesting the malodorous reality of horse-drawn transport.

The Dublin Streets: A Vendor of Books repeats motifs established by Osborne in *Near St Patrick's Close* and from the conventions of city paintings more generally, such as flower sellers, market stalls, carriages, and carts. Here, Osborne also includes a more literal repetition: the woman holding the baby also appears in *A Children's Service*, identical save for the infant's pose; and the open, illustrated magazine on the book stall is like that seen in *Tired Out*. No preparatory material for this painting is extant, although a rough sketch of a horse and carriage on the reverse of a William Lawrence photograph in the NGI's Osborne Archive is suggestive of that seen in the middle ground on the right-hand side. A line drawing of the composition, sold at auction in 2012 and described as 'a study for *The Dublin Streets: A Vendor of Books*', is more likely to be a drawing made after the completion of the painting given the exact copying of many of the painting's details.[62] It is likely that this drawing was meant for reproduction in an exhibition catalogue (such as the one produced by the Liverpool Corporation for the annual exhibition) or related press materials, such as *Academy Notes*.

The view from Carlisle or O'Connell Bridge towards the Custom House was frequently noted in nineteenth-century literature and guidebooks to the city. In 1842, J. Stirling Coyne wrote that 'the panorama of the river, and the city which encircles the spectator on this bridge, is un-equalled in grandeur and beauty, by the noblest prospects which could be obtained from any single point in any other European city'.[63] In 1853, Fraser's *Handbook for Dublin* noted that the

> best internal view of the city is unquestionably obtained from Carlisle-bridge ... Although it cannot for a moment be compared with the grandeur of the Thames, and the noble bridges which span that river, still there is a surpassing beauty arising from the numerous lines of wide streets that radiate from our feet as a centre; from the windings of the Liffey, with its quayed walls and ample avenues on either side ... by the various public buildings that from this point are more or less displayed; and the tapering masts of the vessels mingling with the ample outlines of the Custom House, the finest by far of Eblana's structures.[64]

The elevation of this prospect in text may have influenced Osborne's decision to commit the scene to canvas. The inclusion of an identifiable narrative scene appeals to the viewer and the scene conforms to the tropes that may have been familiar through texts, or from general contemporary conceptions of the city. As noted elsewhere in this chapter, textual representations of Dublin, whether by Dickens or Laffan, tended to focus on the simple dichotomies present in Dublin – for example, the gap between rich and poor, or between the past (as exemplified through eighteenth-century architecture) and the present state of the city. This trope was echoed in the (albeit limited) critical response to *The Vendor of Books* after it was exhibited in Liverpool: an article in the *Prescot Reporter and St Helen's General Advertiser* noted that the painting presented 'a view in the city of joviality and of discontent: of poverty and hospitality; of elegant brogue, pretty girls, devil-may-care men, and dirty windows', also noting that the 'familiar features of the capital city of Erin's Isle are to the fore, as is the sprightly jackeen, who may be chanting one of the wails of an oppressed people'.[65]

That Osborne did not exhibit *The Vendor of Books* in Dublin is telling of his commercial acumen in promoting and selling his paintings, often choosing only to exhibit his Dublin paintings in English venues, such as the RA, Royal Birmingham Society of Artists, and the Liverpool Corporation Autumn Exhibition of Pictures held annually at the Walker Art Gallery. This suggests Osborne's cognisance of the Irish picture market – and the meagre buyers' preference for rural landscape painting and portraiture, and the opportunity of accessing a wider audience with more varied tastes in Britain. Analysis of the exhibition catalogues of the regional exhibitions, such as those held in Birmingham and Manchester, reveal that Osborne was one of only a small number of Irish artists who persistently pursued this market, which is revealing of his ambition and doggedness in pursuing a successful artistic career. In considering the appeal of this painting to an English buyer (it was sold in Liverpool), several salient aspects might be considered: first, that it portrays one of the city's most celebrated viewpoints, and, second, that it visually supports the narrative of Dublin as a city of simple contrasts, as frequently portrayed in literary sources. Last, it is also possible that Osborne was aware of the success achieved by William Logsdail, a fellow Antwerp-trained artist, with the painting *St Martin-in-the-Fields* (1888, oil on canvas, Tate) which had been purchased by the Chantrey Trustees at the RA in 1888. Set against the backdrop of Trafalgar Square, Logsdail's painting depicts a child selling daffodils and other bouquets from a basket balanced by a thin string over her shoulders. Immediately to her left we see a well-dressed lady and her child, with the clothing of the two young girls contrasting strongly. Elsewhere in the painting, the artist has included a newspaper seller, a fruit stall, a mounted policeman, as well as other carriages and carts. As in Osborne's painting, a wide range of social classes are represented, showing the overlapping spheres and worlds that met in the social spaces of the city. For a British audience, *The Vendor of Books* underpinned the image of Dublin presented to them through a variety of other sources, and, through the inclusion of the Gordon Highlander and an additional red-coated soldier crossing the bridge on horseback, subtle reminders of Dublin's place as an imperial city are encoded into the composition. Through these symbols, and through the subject of the painting, Osborne creates an interesting series of 'gazes' between both the viewer and the painting, and between the figures themselves. For example, the group of men browsing the book stall studiously avoid each other's gaze, as well as the young flower seller. She, in turn, is observed by the woman by the quay wall, and by a man standing to the right-hand side of the canvas. The lack of physical or meaningful engagement between the figures turns the city street into a form of stage: each actor plays their part – vendor, purchaser, flower seller, observer – but remain isolated from one another in this urban play.

A year prior to Osborne's exhibition of *The Vendor of Books*, an article by 'C. J. H.' titled 'In and Out Among the Dublin Streets' appeared in *The Graphic* and offered a further example of how the city was characterised in the British press. The resonance between the title of the article and Osborne's painting is curious, suggesting that perhaps this phrasing was in common parlance at the time. In describing the city, the author notes that 'nowhere do we meet with more startling contrasts than in Dublin: contrasts between squalor and splendour, between squares and slums, velvet, rags, seal skin and sacking'.[66] The presence of beggars on the streets, both real and fictional (Flitters, Tatters, and the Counsellor are mentioned), feature in the article, contrasted with the finery of those attending the season at Dublin Castle and the city's new statuary and ecclesiastical buildings. Walking in the Coombe and the area around St Patrick's, the author takes the reader 'down Peter Street, with its clusters of girls and children sitting bare-headed on the steps of the doors to watch the well-dressed congregation streaming along towards St Patrick's; and going down York Street, we get into Stephen's Green, Lord Ardilaun's magnificent gift to the citizens of Dublin'.[67]

Further philanthropy: Osborne's move to St Stephen's Green

Around 1895, Osborne began to use a studio at 6 St Stephen's Green, where artists Bingham McGuiness and John B. Yeats had previously had their studios.[68] This brought a new focus to Osborne's depiction of Dublin city centre, away from the rundown market stalls and into the leafy environs of the Green itself. The relocation of his studio to this central address coincided with a general uplift in Osborne's professional reputation. Through the late 1880s and early 1890s, the artist had become more deeply involved in the Dublin art and social world; for example, through his involvement with the Dublin Art Club and his burgeoning portrait practice which gave him further introduction to viceregal and high-society circles.[69] In this setting, the artist could observe the city's residents at rest rather than at work. Both *In Stephen's Green* (c.1895, oil on canvas, private collection) and *In a Dublin Park, Light and Shade* (Plate 1.8), depict a group of people resting on a bench in the park's leafy surroundings from different viewpoints. These works visibly demonstrate changes within Osborne's painting style and technique from those employed in his representation of the Patrick Street market area: the artist was moving away from the muted colours of the naturalist palette, introducing vibrant blues and greens into his compositions. Additionally, these two paintings demonstrate Osborne's use of a looser technique combined with a thick application of paint, more suggestive of impressionism than naturalism.

In 1880, Stephen's Green opened to the public after being purchased, redeveloped, and presented to the Board of Works, through the sponsorship and generosity of Lord Ardilaun. Rather disappointingly, little fanfare heralded the occasion, with *The Graphic* noting that it 'was thrown open to the public on Tuesday without any inaugural ceremony'.[70] While a souvenir booklet was produced to mark the opening by Ardilaun, on the day the patron was 'unfortunately prevented attending, owing to sudden indisposition'.[71] The year 1880 was a difficult one for Ardilaun due mainly to his well-known unionist and conservative political views; and disagreements over tenancy rents on his estates in Galway caused him to leave Dublin for a period in that year. In describing the generous gift of the peer to the people of Dublin, the *Freeman's Journal* commented that 'we differ from Lord Ardilaun on the most public questions, and have never hesitated to express that difference in decided language'.[72] Despite this, however, the paper was willing to concede that the opening of Stephen's Green was not only beneficial from a 'sanitary and moral aspect', but also 'a boon to the wealthy classes' and

> a priceless gift to their poorer neighbours. No man could yesterday walk through the Green and see the hundreds of little children playing about, with a look of unaccustomed pleasure in their poor, pale, pinched little faces, without feeling his heart touched, or without realising how much the poor will benefit by having such a place of healthy, harmless recreation in their midst.[73]

This report of the opening of Stephen's Green intimates the different types of people who used the city centre park, ranging from the well-to-do to the down-at-heel, but also repeats the language of benevolence seen in relation to the city's impoverished children.

The creation of urban parks and green spaces for the public proliferated throughout nineteenth-century urban planning. In Paris in 1848, municipal parks totalled only 47 acres, but by 1870 this had grown to 4,500 acres.[74] In Britain, the growth of industrial cities and increasing urban populations led to concerns over the well-being of city dwellers, and thus the development of city centre parks. Many of the promoters of urban parks fervently believed in the power of green spaces to 'improve' the working-class populations: parks would be instrumental in removing other recreations enjoyed by the working classes, such as frequenting public houses, thus inducing them to 'become thrifty, industrious, docile and moral, in other words like the middle class themselves'.[75] America also followed a similar trend, and as Dorceta E. Taylor has discussed, these projects were guided by a complex set of social, moral, and class-related issues.[76] In addition to being a kind of sanctuary in the city's heart, the urban park was also a place for recreation – for example, if the park was large enough, it could host horse races, polo fields, or zoological gardens. In Dublin, the larger Phoenix Park provided these amenities to the urban populace, as well providing ample space for contrasting events such as military reviews and protest meetings. Artists across these cities responded to this new urban space, depicting parks as a kind of oasis at the heart of the city. While artists could merge the representation of these spaces with new artistic styles – for example, as seen in the work of Claude Monet – the portrayal of the different people in the park, concentrating perhaps on women or on different social classes, is a common feature.[77]

As noted already, Osborne's paintings of Stephen's Green show some adjustments in his painting style. *In Stephen's Green* shows this change most clearly, creating a richly coloured and textured canvas, capturing a sense of the light and atmosphere of the verdant park. Under the shade of the trees, Osborne shows people relaxing, observing the people around them, or engrossed in books or newspapers. In the bright sunlight on the left-hand side, two children play with a hoop, and another loosely painted figure suggests a woman in white carrying a pink parasol. Many of the figures seen sitting on the bench in this painting are repeated in *In a Dublin Park, Light and Shade*. Here, Osborne has used the brown tones found in his earlier works, alongside more vibrant green foliage. The figures are reminiscent of those found in Osborne's earlier depictions of the city. Like the resting figures in *In St Patrick's Cathedral*, this painting shows a range of different figures enjoying the park – a small boy, a mother with a young baby, and two sleeping men – and the boy is reminiscent of Osborne's earlier depictions of children, both in the studio and in his depiction of Patrick Street. The foliage in the upper ranges of the canvas shows how Osborne applied broad swathes of green and yellow in an impressionistic manner, similar to that seen

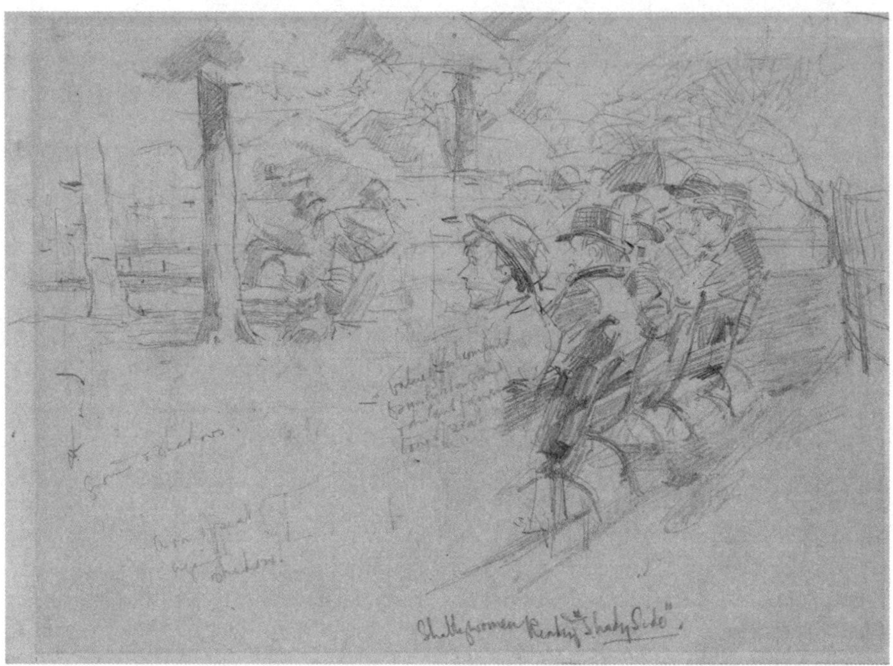

1.12   Walter Frederick Osborne, *Men Sitting in Saint Stephen's Green, Dublin*, c.1895.

in *Summertime* (1901, oil on canvas, Harris Museum and Gallery) and *Tea in the Garden* (c.1902, oil on canvas, DCGHL); there are also compositional similarities between these paintings, notably the bench and mossy wall in the background.

Two preparatory works relating to these paintings are extant: *Men Sitting in Saint Stephen's Green, Dublin* (Figure 1.12) and *Mother and Child* (1895, oil on canvas, DCGHL). The first, a pencil sketch with annotations in the artist's hand, shows a scene like that in *In Stephen's Green*. Here, Osborne has recorded the structure of the bench and the arrangement of the trees, along with details of some of the men sitting on the bench. When compared with the painting, we see that Osborne altered some of these figures, notably to include the mother and child and one of the men seen in *In a Dublin Park*. The second preparatory work relates directly to this mother and child, being a representation in oils of the woman and baby, shown in an interior setting. Loosely painted in weak browns with touches of moss green and pink, this painting captures a sense of the woman's sadness and weariness, particularly in her face and downcast eyes. While there is a soft edge to her features here, in *In a Dublin Park* this has been replaced with harder lines and tones, with dark shadows more suggestive of bruising running along her cheekbones. These preparatory works and the variations made to the painted versions of this scene demonstrate how Osborne carefully considered the different components of a composition. While aspects of both *In Stephen's Green* and *In a Dublin Park* suggest an awareness and interest in impressionist techniques, Osborne continued to work within traditional, studio-based practices.

The representation of the flower seller in paintings of the city was considered a way of bringing the rural and urban worlds together, while appealing to the social mores of the viewer or buyer. The representation of the poor within the natural space of the urban park also reflected this collision of worlds and sensibilities. The moral and social value of these new urban spaces was a key aspect of their creation, associated as they were with philanthropy, health, and hygiene, and the idea of providing an 'improving' space for a city's poorer inhabitants. With *In A Dublin Park*, Osborne makes manifest the feelings of contemporary observers who commented on how Lord Ardilaun's project would improve the lives of the poor, as he shows us in a forthright way how the park was used by the humble and lowly residents of Dublin. Although Osborne did not exhibit this work in his home city, the theme of the painting was understood by a contemporary (urban) audience in London. In the annual *Academy Notes* for 1895, a line drawing of the painting by Osborne was accompanied by the short description, '[a] group of poor city folk sitting on a bench'.[78] In addition to succinctly communicating what the painting represented, this description also reinforces the social difference between the subject and the viewer.

Conclusion: The Four Courts, Dublin

In 1901, Osborne exhibited his final paintings of Dublin: *In St Patrick's Cathedral* at the Belfast Art Society and *The Four Courts, Dublin* at the Society of Oil Painters, London. Although the former of these is now unknown, it was described in the *Belfast Telegraph* as showing 'light coming through a richly-coloured window', with 'a figure reading the inscription on a monument', tallying with themes seen in the artist's previous paintings of the cathedral's interior.[79] The latter painting is now in the NGI (Plate 1.9) and although it received no critical attention when first exhibited, it represents an important closing phase of Osborne's urban vision, and hints at how this might have progressed had the artist not died unexpectedly from pneumonia in 1903. On first glance, the composition of *The Four Courts* is reminiscent of *The Vendor of Books*: a broad expanse of the quayside leads the eye to an arched bridge (then known as Richmond Bridge in honour of the 4th Duke of Richmond, but later renamed after Fenian leader Jerimiah O'Donovan Rossa), and the large portico and dome of the Four Courts on the opposite river bank. Despite this compositional similarity, the technique of the later painting stands in stark contrast to Osborne's view of O'Connell Bridge and the Custom House. Painted using fluid, impressionistic brush strokes, the details of the scene are loosely rendered with the weave of the canvas clearly visible in places. A haze of blue smoke or fog blends with the thick clouds, the blue and purple tones echoed in the water, and in the far distance, the form of the Wellington monument in the Phoenix Park can just be made out.

Despite the evolution in style, archival sources suggest that Osborne had been considering the depiction of the Four Courts for some time. Among his surviving papers are two photographs of the imposing building, taking in its different aspects, the quayside balustrades, and the traffic of carriages passing along the quay. A third photograph is quite different: with no identifying studio marks, this large, atmospheric print was taken at street level – the photographer is among the figures who cross the bridge in front of the Courts.[80] As with the photographs of Patrick Street, the form of this print suggests that it was taken by an amateur photographer, and again we might consider that it was taken by the artist or one of his colleagues. Furthermore, a wood engraving bearing Osborne's signature, and the manuscript title 'The Old Four Courts', also in the collection of the NGI, takes its composition directly from this photograph, including the two female figures who cross the street arm-in-arm (Figure 1.13).[81] Others, including two uniformed men, are omitted. The squared form of the artist's signature, with the distinctive 'kicks' added to the letter 'r' suggest that Osborne created this scene in the late 1880s – making it roughly contemporary with *A Vendor of Books*.

By 1901, Osborne had replaced these sedate figures with the bustle of busy activity then taking place on the Dublin quays: the building of a central sewerage scheme running from Islandbridge to Ringsend. Taking ten years to

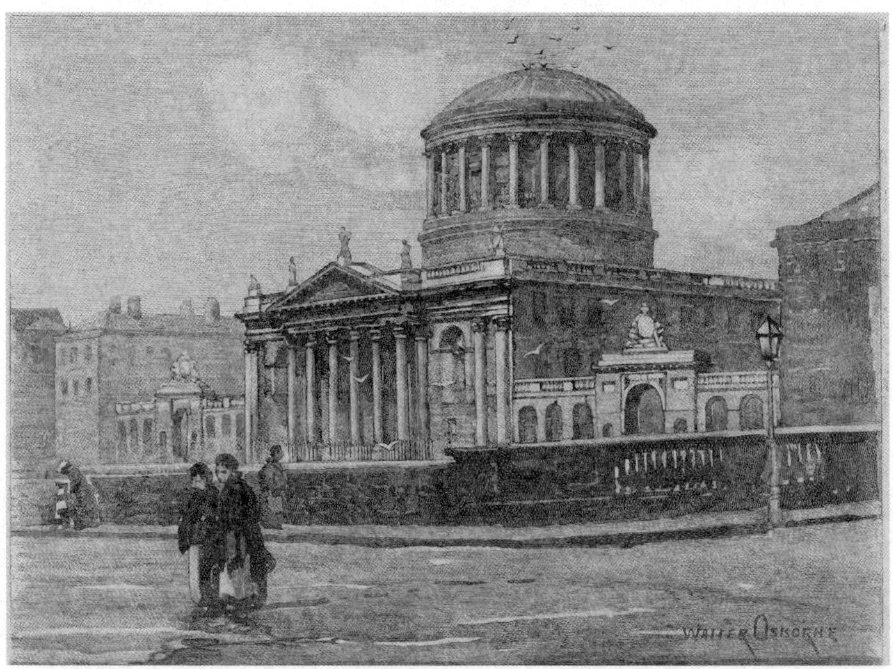

1.13   Walter Frederick Osborne, *The Old Four Courts*, undated.

construct (1896–1906), this was the largest infrastructural project undertaken by Dublin Corporation in the period: the sewers running along the north and south quays were contracted to Messrs. H. & J. Martin, Limited, and work commenced in early 1896. By September 1901, the work was largely completed, despite a report that the contractors 'unexpectedly encountered a great deal of rock' on the south quays.[82] A rare representation of the works in progress, Osborne shows several labourers clearing stone from the trench being created, overseen by a green-suited figure in the left-hand foreground. Although previously described as a 'purely topographical urban view', this painting clearly offers a more informative and nuanced view of Dublin in the opening years of the twentieth century: it suggests the possibility that Osborne was moving away from the narrative or pathos driven works of the 1880s and 1890s towards a more expansive view of the city.[83]

Returning to Arscott's comments noted at the opening of this chapter, however, we can see how, from the 1880s onwards, Osborne engaged with the shifting nature of urban representation – finding links with his British and other European contemporaries, whether through his style and palette, or through his choice of subject matter – such as the impoverished child, changing streetscape, or leisure activities. His view of the changing city was shaped by his engagement and pursuit of patronage, whether by British exhibition-goers, or aristocratic patrons such as the Guinness family, and through these paintings he created a distinctive typology of urban life in Ireland in this period. This was, however, heavily mediated, and Osborne sought to draw on how Dublin was characterised in other art forms and how it was understood by a British audience. As previously mentioned, in 1920 Thomas Bodkin noted that Osborne's paintings of Dublin 'show careful detached observance: but it is the trained, detached observance of an intelligent foreigner. For all his interest in humanity, he never seems to see Dublin with native eyes.'[84] Yet, as this chapter has shown, Osborne's depiction of the city where he lived for the duration of his life was shaped by his upbringing there, by the opportunities the artistic establishment in Dublin provided for him in terms of education (including, through the Taylor Scholarship, the means to advance his artistic training in Europe), and the subjects and views offered by the life of the city's streets. Furthermore, this collection of paintings offers an engaging counterpoint to the characterisation of the city in literature, inviting a closer examination of the tropes and motifs used to describe Dublin to audiences in Ireland and beyond. By simultaneously viewing these artworks alongside contemporary debates around religion, society, and urban development, a more nuanced view of Osborne's urban paintings emerges, acknowledging the complex context in which he was working. Returning to Bodkin's reading of Osborne's paintings, we might ask what exactly it means to view a city 'with native eyes': certainly, Osborne could not have been more closely connected to the city, either through birth or professional activity. Underlying Bodkin's comments is a thinly veiled criticism of the artist's middle-class background, his close association to English painting, and his choice of urban subject matter: all of which to some extent railed against the ideal of what constituted Irish painting when Bodkin was writing in the 1920s.

On several occasions after his death, Osborne was referred to as an English artist. After such an incident, the artist's brother felt compelled to write to the *Magazine of Art* to correct their description of the artist as 'an Englishman resident in Ireland'. He was, Charles Osborne wrote, 'an Irishman in the fullest sense of the word ... The family to which my late father belonged has been resident in Dublin for generations past, being descended from an Osborne who was a Cromwellian settler.' Although they apologised unreservedly, the *Magazine of Art* also stated that 'we understood – or rather, it is now evident, we misunderstood – from the late artist's own lips ... that he was English'.[85] This exchange points to the (still) live issue over the claiming of artists for one nation over another, and elides what was a more complex reality over identity and affiliation, which, like Osborne's depiction of Dublin, needs to be understood in a more nuanced fashion: without doubting the artist's 'Irishness', we must understand that here was an artist who moved with ease between the two islands, and who, perhaps, envisaged Ireland as a constituent part of a larger British art world. Like the goods that moved between Ireland and the wider world on ships from Dublin port, Osborne's paintings engaged in a network of circulation that was assisted by Dublin's imperial status. Rather than something to be fought against, the union between Ireland and Britain could be used to an artist's commercial advantage and absorbed into their professional identity. As will be seen in the following chapter, Osborne was not alone in this, and the work of Rose Barton drew the cities of Dublin and London even more closely together.

Notes

1   C. Arscott, 'The representation of the city in the visual arts' in M. Daunton (ed.), *The Cambridge Urban History of Britain, Volume III, 1850–1950* (Cambridge: Cambridge University Press, 1989), p. 813.

2   Ibid.

3   Julian Treuherz, *Hard Times: Social Realism in Victorian Art* (London: Lund Humphries with Manchester City Art Galleries), pp. 109–10.

4   See, for example, C. MacGonigal, 'Walter Osborne RHA 1850–1903', *Irish Times* (16 June 1978), p. 10 and K. McConkey, 'Walter Frederick Osborne RHA (1859–1903), *Rags, Bones and Bottles*', in Morgan O'Driscoll Fine Art Auctioneers and Valuers, Irish and International Art Auction, 4 December 2016, p. 48.

5   T. Bodkin, *Four Irish Landscape Painters* (Dublin: The Talbot Press, 1920), pp. 43–4.

6   Details for occupancy of 5 Castlewood Avenue can be found in *Thom's Dublin and County Street Directory, 1864–1904*.

7   See C. Wallace, 'Fighting for Unionist Home Rule: competing identities in Dublin 1880–1929', *Journal of Urban History* 38:5 (2012), 932–49. DOI 10.1177/0096144212449144.

8   *Rathmines School: The School Roll from the Beginning of the School in 1858 till its Close in 1899* (Dublin: The University Press, 1932), p. 30.

9   J. Sheehy, 'The flight from South Kensington: British artists at the Antwerp Academy 1877–1885', *Art History* 20:1 (1997), 126.

10   Ibid.

11   J. Sheehy, 'Walter Osborne' (M.Litt Diss., Trinity College Dublin, 1971), p. 38.

12   Ibid., p. 39.

13   Ibid.

14   NGI, Walter Osborne Photograph Album, Walter Osborne Archive, p. 3. This album is available online: doras.nationalgallery.ie. For a further discussion of Osborne's photographs of Brittany, see J. Campbell, 'Postcards from Brittany: Walter Osborne's wallet of photographs', *Irish Arts Review Yearbook* 17 (2010), 150–5.

15   NGI, CSIA/OSB/3/1/1, letter from Walter Osborne to William Osborne, 12 October 1884.

16   'Exhibitions and Art Notes', *Art Journal, 1839–1912* (1887), pp. 255–6.

17   G. Weisberg, *Beyond Impressionism: Naturalist Impulse in European Art 1860–1905* (London: Thames and Hudson, 1992), p. 92.

18   M. Postle, 'Behind the screen: the studio model', in M. Postle and W. Vaughan (eds), *The Artist's Model from Etty to Spencer* (London: Merell and Holborton, 1999), p. 62.

19   Mrs H. M. Stanley (Dorothy Tennant), *London Street Arabs* (London: Cassell and Co., 1890); R. Barton, *Familiar London* (London: Adam and Charles Black, 1904), p. 80, p. 83.

20   See I. Evangelisti, 'The nude in modern Irish art: tradition and transgression' (PhD Diss., Trinity College Dublin, 2013).

21   NGI, CSIA/NGI/311/5, Walter Osborne's Diary for 1892. In the case of the two younger models, a comparison between the addresses given for the models and *Thom's Official Directory* for the same year shows that both lived in tenements. It is interesting to note that Chancery Lane was noted at the time for being home to several Italian immigrant families. Given his name, it is possible that Louis Marc Antonio came from such a background. The address given for Michael O'Neill was John Long & Co, a family grocer and wine merchants on Bride Street, which was flanked by tenement buildings. Osborne lists Kane as living at '13 Angelsea St' and this could either refer to South Angelsea Street on the south side of the city, or Angelsea Fruit Market (from Little Green Street – Angelsea Row) on the north side. It is more likely that the model's address was the latter of these, where a 'Mrs. Kane, fruit dealer' is listed as living at number 13. Both Kavanagh and Brophy were resident in the suburbs and neither is listed in the directory. In Upper Milltown, Kavanagh's address, there are two entries for a Michael Kavanagh and one for Thomas Kavanagh, so perhaps Maggie was connected to one of these. There is no record for Lawlor's Cottages, Milltown, the address of Mary Brophy. See *Thom's Official Directory*, 1892, p. 1419, p. 1372, p. 1360, p. 1344.

22   Both *Cupboard Love* and *Little Boy Asleep* are illustrated in *Lavery and Osborne: Observing Life* (Limerick: The Hunt Museum, 2018), exhibition catalogue, p. 97, p. 103.

23   Stanley, *London Street Arabs*, p. 7. Tennant exhibited two works at the RHA in 1886, but also may have visited Dublin on other occasions. In his biography, historian G. M. Trevelyan recalls how she helped him with his homework and drew 'lifelike sepia sketches of street arabs' during his father's tenure as Chief Secretary, when

the artist was a guest of the family the Phoenix Park. See G. M. Trevelyan, *An Autobiography and Other Essays* (London: Longmans, Green and Co., 1949), p. 8.

24 N. R. Marshall, *City of Gold and Mud: Painting Victorian London* (New Haven: Yale University Press, 2012), p. 146.

25 Ibid.

26 'The Royal Hibernian Academy by A Peripatetic', *Weekly Freeman's Journal* (28 May 1887), p. 5.

27 V. Crossman, 'Cribbed, contained and confined? The care of children under the Irish Poor Law, 1850–1920', in M. Luddy and J. Smith (eds), *Children, Childhood and Irish Society, 1500–Present* (Dublin: Four Courts Press, 2014), p. 83.

28 M. Luddy, *Women and Philanthropy in Nineteenth Century Ireland* (Cambridge: Cambridge University Press, 1995), pp. 68–96.

29 'The Royal Hibernian Academy Exhibition – Third Notice', *Dublin Daily Express* (17 February 1890), p. 5.

30 G. McIntosh, 'Children, street trading and the representation of public space in Edwardian Ireland', in Luddy and Smith (eds), *Children, Childhood and Irish Society*, p. 47.

31 Ibid., p. 48.

32 *The Dublin University Review Illustrated Art Supplement* (March 1886), p. 28.

33 J. B. Hampton, 'Ambivalent Realism: May Laffan's "Flitters, Tatters, and the Counsellor"', *New Hibernia Review* 12:2 (2008), 131.

34 M. Laffan, *Flitters, Tatters and the Counsellor* (London: Macmillan and Co., 1881), p. 6.

35 Ibid., pp. 3–4.

36 Ibid., p. 76.

37 'The Royal Hibernian Academy Exhibition (Second Notice)', *Dublin Daily Express* (10 February 1890), p. 5.

38 'A Dublin Portfolio of Etchings', *Dublin Daily Express* (20 January 1890), p. 5.

39 C. Dickens, 'An Irish Stew', *Household Words*, vol. VII (27 August 1853), p. 619.

40 *Thom's Official Directory*, 1887, pp. 1463–4.

41 Ibid.

42 Frances Gerard, *Picturesque Dublin: Old and New* (London: Hutchinson and Company, 1898), pp. 91–2.

43 'The Royal Hibernian Academy – First Notice', *Dublin Daily Express* (20 February 1888), p. 5.

44 P. Slattery, 'The uses of photography in Ireland, 1839–1900' (PhD Diss., Trinity College Dublin, 1992), p. 134.

45 See R. French, *Patrick Street, Dublin*, c.1880 – 1900, Lawrence Photograph Collection, NLI, L_ROY_05933. This has been digitised and is available to view online through the NLI catalogue: catalogue.nli.ie.

46 See W. Osborne, *A Street with Figures*, c.1892, graphite on paper, NGI 2995.

47 NGI, CSIA/NGI/311/5, Walter Osborne's Diary, 1892.

48 *In the Streets: Wintry Weather* was purchased from the RHA in 1895 by the then Lord Lieutenant, Lord Haughton, later styled as the first Marquess of Crewe. It passed by descent to Crewe's daughter, Mary Evelyn Hungford Crewe-Milnes, later Duchess of Roxburgh, and was sold from her estate at Sotheby's in 2015 under the title *A Backstreet in the Snow* (Lot 170, 25 May 2015). As of September 2018, it is in the collection of the Jorgensen Gallery, Dublin.

49 'The Royal Academy – Fourth and Final Notice', *Globe* (31 May 1894), p. 3.

50 See C. Ó Gráda, "Because she never let them in': Irish immigration a century ago and today', UCD Centre for Economic Research Working Paper Series: WP/13/19: www.ucd.ie/t4cms/WP13_19.pdf (accessed 21 April 2020).

51 F. H. A. Aalan, 'The working-class housing movement in Dublin, 1850–1920', in M. J. Bannon (ed.), *The Emergence of Irish Planning 1880–1920* (Dublin: Turoe Press, 1985), p. 158.

52 Third report of Her Majesty's commissioners for inquiring into the housing of the working classes in Ireland.

53 A. Bielenberg, 'Later Victorian elite formation and philanthropy: the making of Edward Guinness', *Studia Hibernica* 32:3 (2002), 142.

54 Ibid., 144.

55 NLI, Ms 36, 870/5, papers of the Family of O'Brien of Cahirmoyle, Co. Limerick, letter from Walter Osborne to Dermod O'Brien, 24 September [no year].

56 Ibid.

57 See D. Murphy, 'Waldron, Laurence Ambrose,' in *Dictionary of Irish Biography*, http://dib.cambridge.org/viewReadPage.do?articleId=a8841 (accessed 21 April 2020). Waldron later became an important patron of the arts, most notably encouraging and commissioning work from Harry Clarke in the early years of his career.

58 See S. Comyn, 'Literary sociability on the Goldfields: the Mechanics' Institute in the colony of Victoria, 1854–1870', *Journal of Victorian Culture* 23:4 (2018), 447–62; S. J. M. M. Alberti, 'Conversaziones and the experience of science in Victorian England', *Journal of Victorian Culture* 8:2 (2003), 208–30.

59 A. M. Stewart, *Irish Art Loan Exhibitions 1765–1927: Index of Artists*, vol. II (Dublin: Manton Publishing, 1990), p. 533.

60 'Famous Pictures for Dublin', *Irish Times* (29 September 1908), p. 5.

61 The soldier's uniform was identified by R. Brown, 'Painting the military – art into history, Ireland 1780–1930' (MPhil Diss., Trinity College Dublin, 2008) p. 68.

62 See W. Osborne, *A Bookseller by the Liffey*, pen and ink, private collection, Adam and Sons, Important Irish Art Sale, 30 May 2012, Lot 38.

63 J. Stirling Coyne, *The Scenery and Antiquities of Ireland, Drawings by W.H. Bartlett* (London: Mercury Press, 2002), pp. 399–400.

64 J. Fraser, *Hand Book for Dublin and its Environs with Map of the City, and Street-maps on an Entirely New Plan* (Dublin: James McGlashan, 50 Upper Sackville Street, 1853), pp. 59–60.

65 'Liverpool Corporation Exhibition of Pictures', *Prescot Reporter and St Helen's General Advertiser* (5 October 1889), p. 3.

66 C. J. H., 'In and Out Among the Dublin Streets', *The Graphic* (18 August 1888), p. 23.

67 Ibid.

68 Snoddy notes that Osborne went to this studio in 1895, having taken it over from John B. Yeats. See T. Snoddy, *Dictionary of Irish Artists: 20th Century*, 2nd Edn (Dublin: Merlin Publishing, 2006), p. 506. However, *Thom's Official Directory* shows that Yeats did not use the studio after 1887, and Osborne is only listed as an occupant from 1897.

69 For a recent assessment of Osborne's portraiture see: G. A. Hayes, 'The portraits of Walter Frederick Osborne (1859–1903): a critical analysis' (MPhil Diss., Trinity College Dublin, 2018).

70 'A New Park for Dublin', *The Graphic* (31 July 1880), pp. 8–9.

71 'Opening of St Stephen's Green', *Irish Times* (31 July 1880), p. 5.

72 'Stephen's Green', *Freeman's Journal* (28 July 1880), p. 5.

73 Ibid.

74 R. L. Herbert, *Impressionism: Art, Leisure, and Parisian Society* (New Haven: Yale University Press, 1988), p. 142.

75 H. Conway, *People's Parks: The Design and Development of Victorian Parks in Britain* (Cambridge: Cambridge University Press, 1991), p. 34.

76 See D. E. Taylor, 'Central park as a model for social control: urban parks, social class and leisure behaviour in nineteenth century America', *Journal of Leisure Research* 3:4 (1999), 420–77.

77 The representation of women, and by implication, their social class, in urban parks has been a focus for scholarship to date. See, for example, G. M. Thomas, 'Women in public in the parks of Paris', in A. D'Souza and T. McDonough (eds), *The Invisible Flâneuse? Gender, Public Space, and Visual Culture in Nineteenth Century Paris* (Manchester: Manchester University Press, 2006), pp. 32–48.

78 H. Blackburn (ed.), *Academy Notes 1895, with Facsimiles of Sketches by the Artists* (London: Chatto and Windus, 1895), p. 22.

79 'Belfast Art Society Annual Exhibition', *Belfast News-Letter* (9 October 1901), p. 5.

80 NGI, Walter Osborne Archive, photograph of the Four Courts from Wood Quay, undated, CSIA/OSB/1/11. These photographs are available to view on doras.nationalgallery.ie.

81 Two etchings by Osborne are in the collection of the British Museum (BM. 1902,0107.22 and 1902,0107.23); however, no other wood engravings have been connected to the artist to date. The medium of this print was identified by the Paper Conservation team at the National Gallery of Ireland.

82 *Dublin Main Drainage Scheme Souvenir Handbook 1906* (Dublin: Sealy, Bryers and Walker, 1906), pp. 54– 156. The connection between Osborne's painting and the drainage scheme was made by a student of the UCD School of Art History Cities MA programme during a visit to the NGI led by the author in February 2018.

83 J. Sheehy, *Walter Osborne* (Dublin: National Gallery of Ireland, 1983), p. 116.

84 Bodkin, *Four Irish Landscape Painters*, pp. 43–4.

85 'Chronicle of Art', *Magazine of Art*, 1 (1903), p. 524.

∮ **2** ∮

Fog, gas, and the picturesque

Arscott's comments on the changing nature of urban representation in the 1880s (as outlined at the beginning of the previous chapter), draw on a variety of sensory emotions to describe how artists were imagining the city on canvas and paper. Capturing both the feelings evoked by the scene depicted (for example, the bleakness of an industrial or ramshackle urban environment) of the effects of living in this environment (alienation), or individual emotions (gloom, anxiety), these characteristics speak to the sensory worlds contained within the nineteenth-century city. The urban environment was frequently characterised by the sensations it could evoke in its citizens or visitors; the barrage of the crowd, the noise of transport or cries of street sellers, or the smells arising from various deficiencies in cleansing and sanitation. Through texts and images, this world was codified into a broad understanding of what constituted a city, creating, as James Duncan has argued, 'an imagined environment', which 'embraces not just the cities created by … architects, planners and builders, sociologists and novelists, poets and politicians, but also the translation they have made into the imaginary reality of our mental life'.[1] This 'archive' of the imagined city, Duncan states, has 'been learned as much from novels, pictures and half-remembered films as from diligent walks round the capital cities of Europe'.[2] Whether in textual accounts of the nineteenth-century city – think, for example, of the opening pages of Charles Dickens's *Bleak House* – or visual representations (ranging from J. M. W. Turner to James Abbott McNeill Whistler), the evocation of fog and mist became a dominant trope – evoking a particular kind of sensory aesthetic.

This association was parodied by Oscar Wilde in 'The Decay of Lying', a short essay in which the character of Vivien declares that

> where, if not from the Impressionists do we get those wonderful brown fogs that come creeping down our streets, blurring the gas-lamps and changing the houses into monstrous shadows? To whom, if not to them and their master, do

65

> we owe the lovely silver mists that brood over our river, and turn to faint forms
> of fading grace curved bridge and swaying barge?

He continues that, 'At present, people see fogs, not because there are fogs, but because poets and painters have taught them the mysterious loveliness of such effects.'[3] This view aligns with Duncan's notion of the 'imagined environment', and the circular nature of how the modern city was characterised and understood. Reviewing a selection of Rose Barton's work exhibited with the Irish Fine Art Society in 1884, the critic for the *Dublin Daily Express* cautioned the artist 'not to get too misty and grey'.[4] If Walter Osborne's depictions of Dublin drew on his naturalist training in Antwerp and Brittany, Barton represented the more ethereal evocation of the city as suggested by Wilde, with compositions filled with sun and gaslight filtered through fogs, smog, and mists, strongly influenced by Whistler and other urban impressionists. Quite prolific in her output and exhibition career, urban scenes (of both Dublin and London) form a key part of Barton's oeuvre, which also included scenes of rural and family life and, in her early career, still life and flower studies. The use of watercolour to depict urban life enabled visual artists to chime with the characterisation of the city in other artistic genres; for example, in fiction or early urban photography. The medium's malleability could produce effects of both light and dark – to ominously shroud buildings in haze or to show the lights of an omnibus moving through a dark street – reducing cities, almost regardless of their actual geographical location, to a series of tropes, themes, and motifs.

By using Barton as an exemplar of this type of urban painting, contemporary discussions around the place of women within the urban public sphere can also be considered. While the figure of the *flâneur* has played a central role in analyses of the modern city, modernity, modernism, and the work of the Impressionists, it has also been widely criticised for limiting the existence and potential of other kinds of urban observer or viewer of everyday life. This urban observer also connects the sensory experience of the body in the city: while vision and the act of seeing or observing has been central to studies of the *flâneur*, scholars have increasingly drawn attention to the embodied experience of moving through and observing in the city.[5] While there has been little study of women in the urban sphere in an Irish context, exhibition catalogues certainly suggest that they had access to an expanse of the city – bearing in mind that, in a similar manner to Osborne, these artists made use of photographic and print resources for their urban scenes. Feminist critiques of the *flâneur* have also been particularly strong; for example, Griselda Pollock argued that Charles Baudelaire's text, through its structured opposition between the freedom and space of the city and the domestic confines of the home, reduces women to the status of an object to be observed, rather than an active urban agent, or observer herself.[6] Exploring the Parisian context more recently, Aruna D'Souza and Tom McDonough have considered the relationship between gender and the *flâneur* or *flâneuse* and the perceived limitation on women in the public sphere; however, none of the essays in the collection pertain to women as creators of urban visions – focusing instead on their role as subjects.

Literary studies provide a more useful framework to consider Barton's urban paintings, several recent studies have focused on Irish women writers and the city at the *fin-de-siècle*. Marking Dublin's provincialism, Ciaran O'Neill and Mai Yatani note that a 'common theme' in novels of the period was 'the metropole (usually London) as a site of greater personal liberty and freedom for young female characters'.[7] London, and indeed Paris (as Matthew Reznicek has explored), offered Irish women both the physical and imaginative space to explore modernity through an urban lens – whether reflecting on Ireland from these cities, or utilising their new locations for literary inspiration.[8] Barton was part of a cohort of notable women who championed and professionalised watercolour painting in Ireland, and these women should be considered alongside their literary counterparts in a broader conception of female agency and artistic production in late nineteenth-century Ireland, intersecting with studies of the elite (many artists and writers came from a privileged background) and the cultural politics of the period. These artists and writers often, though not exclusively, shared similar social backgrounds, and this has undoubtedly led to some reticence to engage with their work, especially if it did not adhere to particularly 'Irish' themes, or if their politics veered more towards unionism than nationalism.

Painting and patronage at Dublin Castle

Previous biographies of Barton suggest that she was born in Rochestown, Co. Tipperary, the home and birthplace of her father, Augustine Hugh Barton. However, recently digitised newspaper and genealogical records show that this wasn't in fact the case, and rather, on 21 April 1856, Rose Mary Anne Barton was born at 6 Fitzwilliam Square, and later baptised in the Parish of St Peter, City of Dublin.[9] Her sister, Emily Alma Barton, had been born at this address in 1854, and the artist also had two half-brothers, Hugh McCalmont and James Martin McCalmont, from her mother's first marriage, and who later became well known in British military and unionist political circles.[10] On either side of the family tree, Barton was connected to many notable landed families across Ireland and this social setting would inherently shape the outline and progress of her professional artistic career.[11] It is likely that Barton and her sister were educated at home by a governess, with a curriculum including modern languages, drawing, and elementary watercolour painting. Although no dates were indicated, an article in *Lady of the House* noted that Barton 'took her first instruction in art from Miss Jane Underwood, of Herbert Place, a well-known teacher in Dublin circles'.[12] In 1875, both Alma and Rose were successful in achieving the 'second grade of examination' at the RDS's School of Art, with further honours being awarded to Rose when her work was awarded first prize in the still life category at the Dublin Amateur Artists Society in the same year.[13]

It is possible that around this time, Barton undertook further artistic training in Brussels: following her father's death in 1874, she travelled with her mother and sister on the continent, where she would return in 1880 with Mildred Anne Butler to study at the atelier of Henri Gervex in Paris and Paul Jacob Naftel in London. Evidence of further formal artistic education dates to 1877, when Barton was enrolled at the DMSA.[14]

As Barton's artistic profile developed through the aegis of the Amateur Drawing Society (renamed the Irish Fine Art Society in 1878, before becoming the WCSI in 1887), and later the RHA, so too did her social profile. A glimpse of the Bartons's milieu can be gained from newspaper reports of an amateur dramatic performance organised by her mother during the Dublin season in 1870. Aged just 14, Rose joined her sister, half-brothers, and cousins in performances of 'The Little Sentinel' and 'Orange Blossoms', both of which were attended by notable members of the landed and aristocratic society circles.[15] Rose and her sister were presented at court in Dublin Castle in 1876, where, the *Freeman's Journal* reported, they wore matching gowns of white silk and tulle, a headdress of court plume and feathers, and pearl jewellery.[16] From this date, the society pages of the Dublin papers and magazines frequently carried descriptions of Barton's appearances at state balls, levées, and drawing-rooms at Dublin Castle, as well as at other functions across the city. Her fashionable clothing was of frequent interest, to the extent that on one occasion an illustration of her attending the Fitzwilliam Lawn Tennis Tournament was reproduced in *Irish Society*.[17]

While not to diminish Barton's talent as an artist, her visibility within the upper echelons of Dublin society was undoubtedly beneficial as it offered an assembly of potential patrons for her work. On four occasions paintings by Barton were purchased by the families of the various viceroys, a fact circulated in the press, largely with the intention of stimulating further sales for the exhibition, but which also placed weight behind the artist's name. The diplomacy around securing and maintaining viceregal patronage is illustrated in correspondence from 1892 between Philip Chenevix Trench, treasurer of the WCSI, and Lord Longford, who complained that he and his wife, along with 'Their Excellencies', were unable to purchase the paintings they desired at the exhibition opening. Longford stated that as much 'is made of their name and of their presence for furthering the ends of the exhibition', the viceroy should have the first opportunity to purchase works.[18] After a somewhat heated debate, Trench could only reply that 'I am sorry now that I did not act on an idea which did occur to me of purchasing "Haste to the Levée" myself in case his Ex. [*sic*] might fancy it, as I felt sure that, even if not bought in the morning, someone would have purchased it before he reached it.'[19] Not only does this illuminate relations between one of Ireland's artistic societies and the viceregal court, it further shows that Barton's work (the painting referred to by Longford) was at the centre of the tussle. Given the centrality of the Castle to Barton's family and social life, it is unsurprising that she sought artistic inspiration from within its precincts.

During the Castle season, which ran for six weeks from the beginning of February until the week of St Patrick's Day, several state balls, levées, and drawing rooms were held at Dublin Castle, making full use of the suite of lavishly decorated rooms in the State Apartments, such as the throne room and St Patrick's Hall. Among the ceremonies that attended these functions was the routine of changing or 'relieving' the guard, which took place at the opening and close of the season. For example, on 20 January 1888, the *Dublin Evening Mail* reported that 'the inauguration of the Castle season was marked by the military ceremony of the relief of the guard, which was carried out at eleven o'clock'.[20] A similar ceremony was utilised for St Patrick's Day, accompanied by military bands playing patriotic airs, and the presence of the viceregal family and entourage at the windows or balcony of the throne room, located on the south side of the Upper Castle Yard. Despite the popularity of the spectacle, it was suspended for a short time in the mid-late 1880s and, when revived, efforts were made to avoid 'the scenes of horseplay and rowdyism which the roughs in former years considered to be the most fitting manner of celebrating the occasion'.[21]

Barton painted two representations of this ceremony, dating to 1891 and 1894 respectively, with the former of these being exhibited at the Watercolour Society of Ireland exhibition in 1895 (Plate 2.1).[22] In the year that the artist first painted the scene, the ceremony was carried out before the Earl and Countess of Zetland, and formed by troops of the 1st Battalion Grenadier Guards and the 4th Dragoon Guards, each accompanied by their band. A report for the *Freeman's Journal* offers a sense of the atmosphere in the yard, describing how 'with the gay coats of the soldiers, the number of fair faces in the windows, and along the borders of the yard, the contagious warmth of the people who assembled, and the capital band performances, the scene was really interesting to an ordinary onlooker'.[23] This genial atmosphere is ably captured by Barton. The troops, both on foot and horseback, along with their bands, form the central focus of the composition, framed by the imposing architecture of the Upper Castle Yard, the Bedford Tower to the left, and the castellated Record Tower replete with a union flag to the right, with the state apartments below. To the left of the painting, a small crowd of onlookers observe the ongoing ceremony. Barton was not the first artist to record this ceremony in watercolour, a notable predecessor being Michael Angelo Hayes' *St Patrick's Day, Military Parade at Dublin Castle* (Plate 2.2). In contrast to Barton's softly coloured and ordered scene, Hayes's version is crowded and bustling with activity and spectators.

By 1894, there seemed to be a renewed excitement around the annual ceremony, matched by an increase in the number of troops involved with the handover of the guard. As the *Dublin Daily Express* reported, the 'outgoing guard was furnished by the Munster Fusiliers, and the arriving of the relieving guard was heralded shortly before eleven o'clock by the playing of "St Patrick's Day" by the drum and fife band of the Grenadiers'.[24] The spectacle was observed by the viceroy, Lord Houghton, along with his family and entourage. As many accounts mentioned, the weather was unseasonably fine, and perhaps well-suited to Barton's artistic medium: the *Weekly Irish Times* later reported that 'over the square [the Upper Castle Yard] hung a slight fog, not an obstinate fog, but rather kindly, such as on an early summer morning be-tokens mid-day heat, a fog that yielded gracefully to the warm beams of the sun'.[25] This is reflected in Barton's depiction of the scene: the blue sky and sun-lit yard are seen through a thin film of atmospheric mist, complemented by a darker twist of smoke which curls from the chimney stack close to the Record Tower. There is no extant evidence to suggest that this later version of the guard scene was publicly exhibited; however, when reproduced as the frontispiece to *Picturesque Dublin: Old and New* in 1898, it was listed as being in the possession of Field-Marshall Lord Wolseley, who had received the salute during the 1894 ceremonial.[26] At some point in the painting's history, it passed into the family of Lord Houghton (who served as Viceroy from August 1892–June 1895), who had previously expressed his admiration for Barton's paintings, noting that her work 'has shown what genius can do to make interesting the apparently dull aspects of the nineteenth century city'.[27] In both of these paintings, Barton gives the impression of observing the ceremony from the yard itself, placing the viewer on the level of the other spectators. It is quite possible, however, that Barton, along with other women of the gentry and aristocracy, observed the pageant from the windows of the state apartments, a practice amply described in the contemporary reports. The works may have been composed from memory, aided by sketches and coloured by newspaper accounts. A pencil sketch of the Bedford Tower (Figure 2.1) in the NGI offers a rare suggestion of Barton's preparatory materials.

The distinctive tower and gate in the sketch are seen from the rear in another of Barton's Dublin Castle works. *Going to the Levée* (Plate 2.3) depicts a train of carriages entering the Upper Castle Yard through the Cork Hill gate, topped by the often-scorned statue of Iustitia (Lady Justice), who turns to face the Castle authorities rather than the citizens.[28] Crowds of onlookers flank the carriages: to the right, a huddled mass of brown and black is relieved only by touches of light blue, while to the left, a more sparse crowd includes a scarlet coat (perhaps indicating a soldier) and brightly dressed children. The muted sky and foggy atmosphere created by Barton's loose application of paint perfectly evokes the early afternoon in winter (the levée usually started between 11:30 and 12:00), as well as capturing the class relations of the city, succinctly suggesting the distinction between the 'haves' and the 'have nots', as well as the centrality of the Castle in Dublin high society. Disappointed by the limited formalist analysis of this painting, Vera Kreilkamp has argued that in this work, Barton reveals a 'funereal depiction of a social class and an empire', and connects the painting to various historical and literary sources including those pertaining to social and economic conditions in the city.[29] Among these, Kreilkamp draws a connection with George Moore's novel, *A Drama in Muslin*, published in 1886, which follows the travails of the Barton family through a social season at Dublin Castle. The naming of the family at the centre of the book was surely coincidental but is certainly evocative when placed alongside the artist's work. Although the main

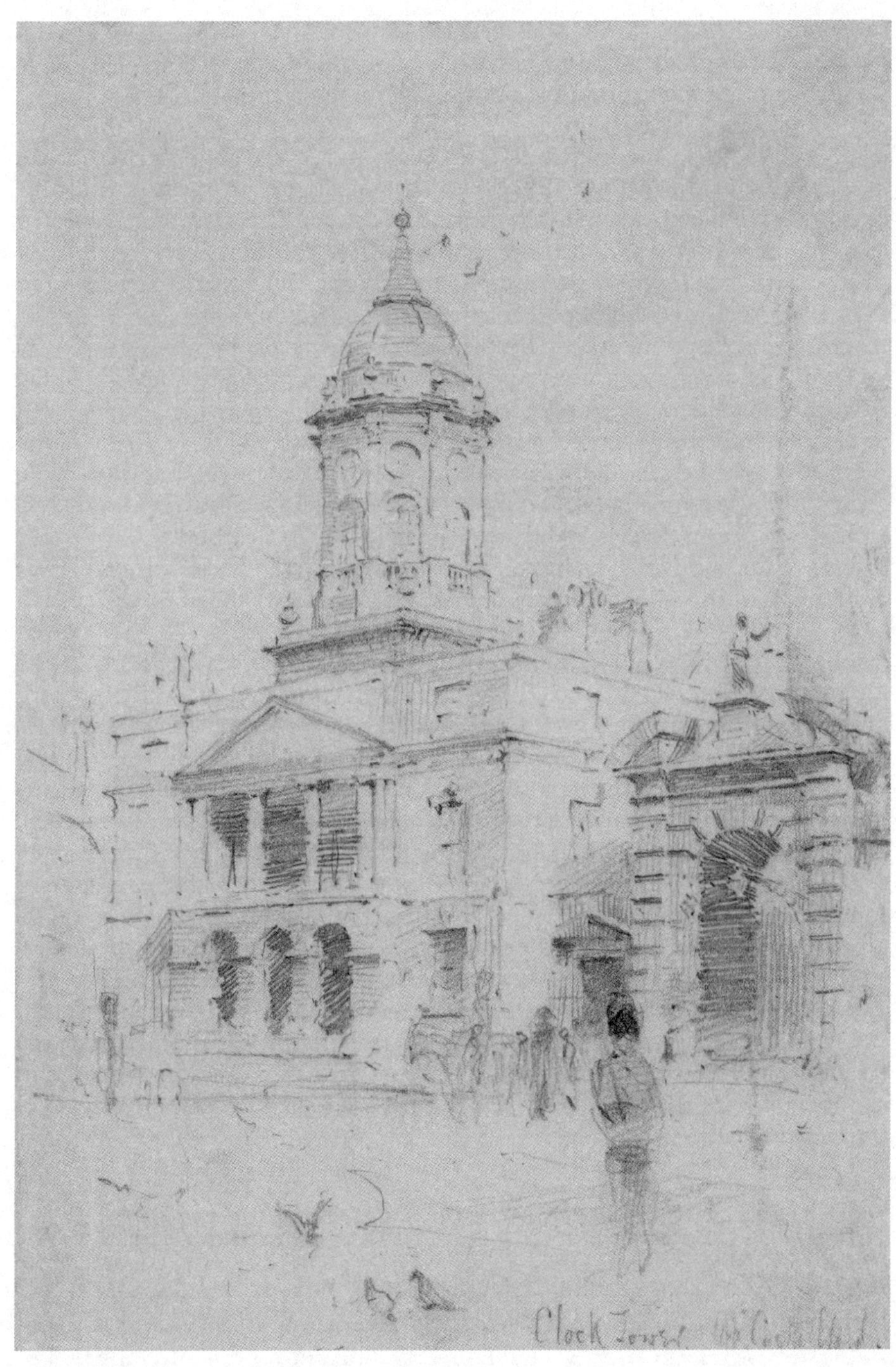

2.1   Rose Barton, *The Bedford Tower, Upper Castle Yard, Dublin,* undated.

ceremonial of Moore's text is an evening drawing-room rather than a levée, his description of the city and atmosphere share an aesthetic with Barton's watercolour. On the night of the drawing-room, the fictional Bartons leave the Shelbourne hotel as 'the rain rushed along the streets – and it could be heard wildly splashing on the flagstones'.[30] As they crossed the city, 'carriages came from every side: the night was alive with flashing lamps; a glimpse of white-fur or silk, the red-breast of a uniform, the gold of an epaulette, were seen, and then lost a moment after in the devouring darkness'.[31] As the line of carriages formed to enter into the Upper Castle Yard, Moore described how 'sometimes no more than a foot separated their occupants from the crowd on the pavement's edge. Never were poverty and wealth brought into plainer proximity.'[32]

Although it cannot be ascertained whether Barton read *A Drama in Muslin*, as already alluded to, the painting and novel have a shared aesthetic, influenced in part by both their creators' shared interest in impressionism. This was the third work on the theme of the levée that Barton had exhibited: the others being shown at the Irish Amateur Drawing Society and at the WCSI as *Haste to the Levée* and *Levée at Dublin Castle* respectively; a final version of *Going to the Levée*, dated to 1924, was exhibited in the Barton retrospective in 1987, suggesting that it was a composition that she repeatedly returned to, even after the event it depicted had ceased to occur. In the NGI watercolour, the line of carriages is viewed from a slight elevation, placing the viewer above both the participants in the carriages and the onlookers to either side. When compared to a contemporary photographic rendering (Figure 2.2) of the scene, it is evident that Barton has altered the streetscape to enhance the grandeur of the gate and surrounding buildings, and reduced the imposing black railings and granite pillars to negligible notes of light black on the left-hand side. These alterations to the perspective and scale of the street and buildings further broaden the possibility that Barton at least partly conceived of this composition from other visual and literary sources, and perhaps drawing on her own experience of attending the levée. As a participant in the rituals of the Castle, and coming from a generally unionist-leaning family, it seems unlikely that Barton would have shared Krielkamp's view of this painting as 'funereal', but rather as an important ritual within the Dublin society season, and therefore eminently worthy of representation. As with Moore's impressionist text, Barton evokes the fogginess and haze of continental watercolourists, and connects the scene to an established mode of urban representation.

The city guidebook and *Picturesque Dublin: Old and New*

In the introduction to *Picturesque Dublin: Old and New*, Frances Gerard wrote that when in Dublin 'we move amidst traditions; the past is everything, the present has a small place'.[33] This nostalgic tone is found throughout the text as the author grieves over what she sees as different aspects of Dublin's lost past, from the decline of the Liberties to the waning and deterioration of the

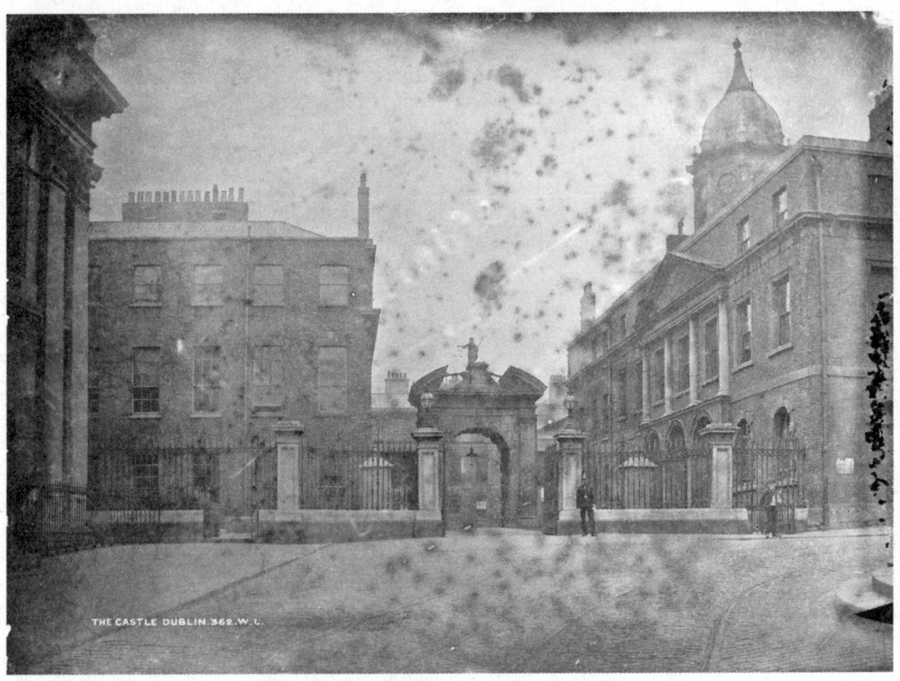

2.2   Robert French, *The Castle, Dublin City*, c.1865–1914.

squares and houses on the north side of the city. For Gerard, the past glories of Dublin lay in the years prior to the Act of Union, stretching back to the vibrant communities of Dutch and Huguenot settlers in the seventeenth century who were influential on 'mercantile as well as intellectual matters'.[34] Written in the form of an extended travelogue, *Picturesque Dublin* is part guidebook, part history, delivered in a light, conversational tone. Along with reproductions of old engravings and photographs, the text includes ninety-one illustrations, with thirty reproductions of watercolours by Barton.

Gerard's interest in the history of Dublin in the seventeenth and eighteenth centuries speaks to what was then a growing interest in 'old Dublin', a nostalgia-heavy term frequently used to refer to the city's history prior to the Act of Union. It was used, for example, by Walter Osborne as part of painting titles, as seen in Chapter 1. On a far larger scale, in 1892, the bazaar organised in aid of the Masonic Female Orphan School recreated 'old Dublin' across two large halls, complete with replicas and representations of St Patrick's and Christ Church cathedrals, St Audeon's Arch, St Nicholas Street, and 'the quaint old gables, mullioned windows, picturesque towers and romantic looking gates of Dublin in 1792'.[35] This type of 'recreated' city had become popular at fairs and bazaars across Europe through the nineteenth century.[36] Within the buildings of 'old Dublin', the stalls and offerings from the Lodges of the Dublin District were displayed, while visitors could find refreshment in a replica of Daly's Coffee House or the other cafés housed in 'Bride's Lane'. A further example of the interest in these areas can be found in the pages of *Lady of the House* in a series of articles written by Etta Catterson Smith (possibly the wife or daughter of portrait painter Stephen Catterson Smith Jnr,) through the 1890s – for example, on 'Handle's Dublin' (October 1891) and 'Huguenot Dublin' (June 1894); while readers of the *Evening Telegraph* could enjoy W. F. Wakeman's 'rambles' in 'old Dublin', later reproduced as a series of pamphlets.[37]

While 'old Dublin' referred to a particular area of the city (the oldest parts of medieval Dublin, containing the walled city and its suburbs which included the Liberties and the area around St Patrick's Cathedral), it also enabled people like Osborne, Gerard, and Barton to further insulate themselves from the social realities then affecting many of the city's citizens. Much like the modes of viewing and depicting impoverished children described in the previous chapter, 'old Dublin' is best understood in terms of the picturesque, a nebulous aesthetic category which shaped the view of poverty and the social order across many cultural forms. While the roots of the term and concept are rooted in the eighteenth century, its meaning has been outlined, questioned, and redefined on several occasions, with key texts produced by William Gilpin, Richard Payne Knight, and John Ruskin. For Gilpin, the 'irregularity, roughness and variety' of the natural landscape could evoke the 'picturesque', producing a feeling of aesthetic pleasure in the viewer.[38] Later in the nineteenth century, Ruskin considered the ethical implications of the picturesque in relation to the social conditions which often produced its aesthetic, asking, after seeing a rural cottage and its inhabitants, 'how many suffering persons must pay for my picturesque subject and happy walk'.[39] Emily Mark Fitzgerald has recently considered Ruskin's 'ethical picturesque' in relation to the visualisation of the Irish Famine, noting that while he 'is troubled by the suffering he views', it 'does not lead to subsequent action; [his reflections] inspire a sympathetic eye that momentarily reaches outward towards the subject, but cannot supersede the aesthetic eye'.[40] Looking more specifically at the picturesque in an urban setting, Malcolm Andrews further explores the criticism of the category in the nineteenth century, when its preponderance to dwell largely on 'poverty, neglect and decay', were questioned, but not entirely erased, by the period's social mores.[41]

As Andrews shows, the picturesque found new expression in photography and the conservation movement: a trend which manifested itself in Ireland through the activities of the Irish Georgian Society, which, from 1909–13, produced three large volumes documenting Dublin's eighteenth-century architecture and interiors. Evaluating these, Mark Crinson has noted that they were 'the product of an attempt to wrench history away from the living present of the houses that it represents towards the golden age of a leisured and fashionable Dublin represented by James Malton's sketches and John Roque's map', a description which could be equally applied to *Picturesque Dublin*.[42] This detachment from contemporary reality echoes with the notion of 'reflective nostalgia' as defined by Svetlana Boym as being concerned with 'ruins, the patina of time and history, in the dreams of another place and time'.[43] This is quite distinct from 'restorative nostalgia', which 'characterizes national and nationalist revivals all over the world which engage in the antimodern myth-making of history by means of a return to national symbols and myths': a theme which was at the heart of the Celtic Revival and running concurrently with this interest in 'old Dublin'.[44] Considered comparatively, the joint categories of the picturesque and reflective nostalgia speak to an attempt to find continuation and stability in an environment that was rapidly changing. Dublin was not unique in this regard: a concurrent interest can be seen in 'old Paris' and 'old London' in this period, with publications on 'old London' and 'vieux Paris' flourishing through later decades of the nineteenth century.[45]

While the history of travel guides extends long into antiquity, the nineteenth century witnessed a boom in their production, supported not only in the advance of transportation but also in printing processes. Dublin, like many other European and American cities, was amply furnished with guides – particularly in the years of large industrial exhibitions in the later part of the century – but even prior to this, the novelist John Banim provided an engaging example of their use in his three-volume novel, *The Anglo-Irish of the Nineteenth Century*, when the protagonist, the Honourable Gerald Blount, discovers the beauty of the city by following the suggested routes of a guidebook. Standing on Carlisle Bridge with the Custom House before him, Gerald could finally see how 'Dublin and her public buildings, though so inferior to London and hers, *seem* [sic] superior, or at least more interesting. They group together and make pictures together. In London they stand widely separated or hide themselves amid mazy streets and dusky houses.'[46] This type of embodied understanding of the cityscape, gained through walking its streets and lanes, foreshadows the characteristic nineteenth-century *flâneur*, as alluded to at the outset of this chapter. Alongside this type of prescriptive guidebook, David Michalski has also identified what he terms the 'belle-lettres' guide in which the reader is 'treated to longer, more elaborate descriptions, and more picturesque images'.[47] It is to this latter category that *Picturesque Dublin: Old and New* belongs, adding to a corpus of city literature that stretched back to James Malton's *Picturesque and Descriptive View of the City of Dublin*, produced in 1799.[48]

Published in the early months of 1898, the concept of *Picturesque Dublin: Old and New* had been in the ether for considerably longer. In the autumn of 1896, Gerard published two articles in the *Art Journal* under the title 'Picturesque Dublin', accompanied by reproductions of several photographs, engravings from the Brocas family, and a pencil sketch by Barton of Patrick Street. An analysis of the text shows that much of what was printed in 1896 made its way into the expanded and enlarged publication, suggesting that Gerard was at an advanced stage of the writing at that point, and may also have been collaborating with Barton on the illustrations. Published by a London house, Hutchinson & Co., the text was likely aimed at a British audience with some pre-existing knowledge of Ireland. Drawing a firm social or professional connection between the two women is hampered by confusion over the exact identity of Gerard, but suffice to say, she may well have been aware of Barton's reputation as an artist specialising in urban scenes, and those of Dublin and London in particular.[49] Barton's contribution to the volume was not insignificant: in total, thirty lithographic reproductions of original works by the artist were included in the text, along with several other reproductions of photographs, old engravings, and artworks bringing the number of illustrations to ninety-six. In 1955, Barton's nephew, Raymond Brooke, gifted a set of works by Barton to the Dublin Civic Museum, which are now in the collection of Dublin City Archives. Among these are ten of the original artworks produced by the artist for Gerard's book. Painted in black and grey watercolour (highlighted with touches of white gouache) these works confirm that Barton created bespoke illustrations for *Picturesque Dublin*, and it is only lamentable that a full set is not extant.

From the outset of the text, Gerard invoked the nostalgic narrative of 'old Dublin', and teamed it with an evocation of a city that is largely quiet. She writes that 'when we come to Dublin from the busy activity … which is a salient feature of provincial towns such as Manchester, Birmingham, and Liverpool, we are struck with the *dolce far niente* [*sic*] that pervades the Irish capital'.[50] This description places Dublin within the archipelago of regional British cities, a position further underlined by her statement that in the eighteenth century 'this cheerful city was the second capital in the British dominions. It gave itself all the airs of a centre of fashion and gaiety.'[51] In this vein, Gerard frames the text as an exploration of a city that to some extent has already died, and whose best days are certainly behind it. This echoes with Moore's description in *A Drama in Muslin* of 'the weary, the woebegone, the threadbare streets', which 'stare the vacant and helpless stare of a beggar selling matches on a doorstep'.[52] However, while this fall in status is central to Moore's criticism of the city, it is essential to Gerard's understanding of it as a site for the picturesque, a view shared by Barton, who the author states is 'equally enthusiastic in her appreciation, and I think has imparted to her sketches a melancholic air which gives such a tinge of romance to the scenes of the long-vanished glories of Ireland'.[53] By the close of the introduction, it is clear that Gerard, while an admirer of Dublin, leans towards unionism in her politics – she notes that 'there are some who, like myself, cling to the past, and look with distaste upon the levelling of all old-world associations', a statement which seems not only to refer to the modernisation of the city's infrastructure, but to the growing strength of nationalist politics.[54]

Fealty to the Castle, its occupants and ceremonies is prominent in *Picturesque Dublin*. Dedicated to the vicereine of the day, Countess Cadagon, the first two chapters of the book are devoted to the history of the Castle, a description of its festivities (particularly those on St Patrick's Day), concluding with a further simper to the present lord lieutenant, described as popular ('[he] seems to win golden opinions'), and whose 'hospitality is likewise unbounded; and better still, he seems to have the real interest of the country at heart'.[55] In addition to the frontispiece mentioned above and some photographs of different locations within the Castle complex, Barton contributed three additional illustrations showing the Record Tower and Chapel Royal, the Palace Street entrance to the Lower Yard, and finally *Going to the Levée up Cork Hill* (Figure 2.3), a version of the previously discussed painting, this time worked in black and grey watercolour and reproduced in greyscale.

Immediately following these chapters, Gerard turns to the area of the city identified as the heart of 'old Dublin' – the Liberties – which included Hoey's Court, the birthplace of Jonathan Swift, St Patrick's and Christ Church cathedrals, and mercantile areas associated with the city's seventeenth- and eighteenth-century history. Illustrated with twelve works by Barton (in addition to other reproductions), the chapter takes in the development of this area of the city (by 'the English settlers, who generally sought protection from the attacks of the native Irish'), the activities of Robert Emmet, Theobald Wolfe-Tone, and Lord Edward Fitzgerald, as well as the history of George Friederic Handel's visits to Fishamble Street and St Werburgh's Church in 1742.[56] As already mentioned in Chapter 1, Gerard described in some detail the outdoor market stalls that filled Patrick Street, describing the malodorous collection of clothing and crockery that lined the pavement. As it continues, her account of the area becomes almost Orientalist in its description, the accents of the people who live there are 'to a stranger … altogether incomprehensible', but present 'an almost endless variety of pictures: boys, like street arabs with hardly a shred of clothing, yet with faces Murillo would have loved to paint; girls with all the grace of girlhood gone; old women, veritable hags, horrible to look at, disfigured as they are by drink; mothers with babies; babies without mothers, sprawling on the pavement'.[57] To accompany this, a view by Barton of the street market was reproduced – similar to the figure that had appeared in the *Art Journal*, but taking in a different aspect to that seen in the Ulster Museum *St Patrick's Close*. Rather, here we see Barton echo Osborne's view in *Near St Patrick's Close*, looking down the street towards the cathedral, with the series of uneven roofs and awnings along the left-hand side (Figure 2.4).

In the latter half of the seventeenth century, the Liberties became strongly associated with the trades and guilds which furnished the city's burgeoning upper classes with luxury goods. As David Dickson writes, while there was naturally an uptake in 'artisanal employment in traditional fields', new work was being created for those who could fulfil the market for 'new lines in fine cloth-making, cloth-finishing and glass-making', with these new artisans being 'immigrant masters, Dutch, Italian, English and French'.[58] The production of silk was of key importance to the city's weavers, and many shop-owners and aristocratic ladies promoted the wearing of Irish-made silks and poplins: deviation from this could spark trouble, as demonstrated in the summer of 1763, when a silk mercer on Dame Street imported silk from Lyon – a black flag was hung above Weaver's Hall (which was among the buildings depicted by

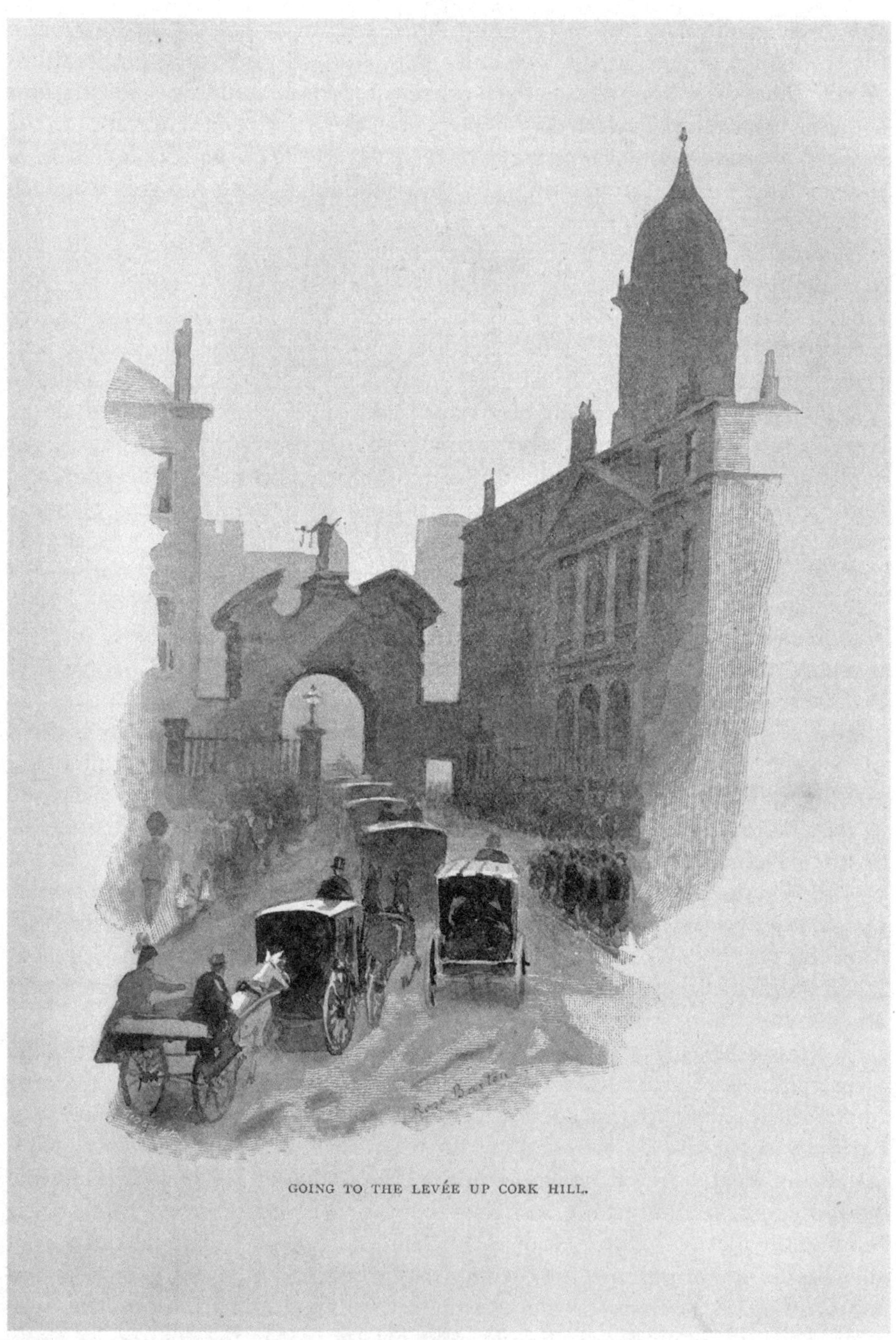

2.3   Rose Barton, *Going to the Levée up Cork Hill*, from F. Gerard, *Picturesque Dublin: Old and New* (London: Hutchinson and Co., 1898).

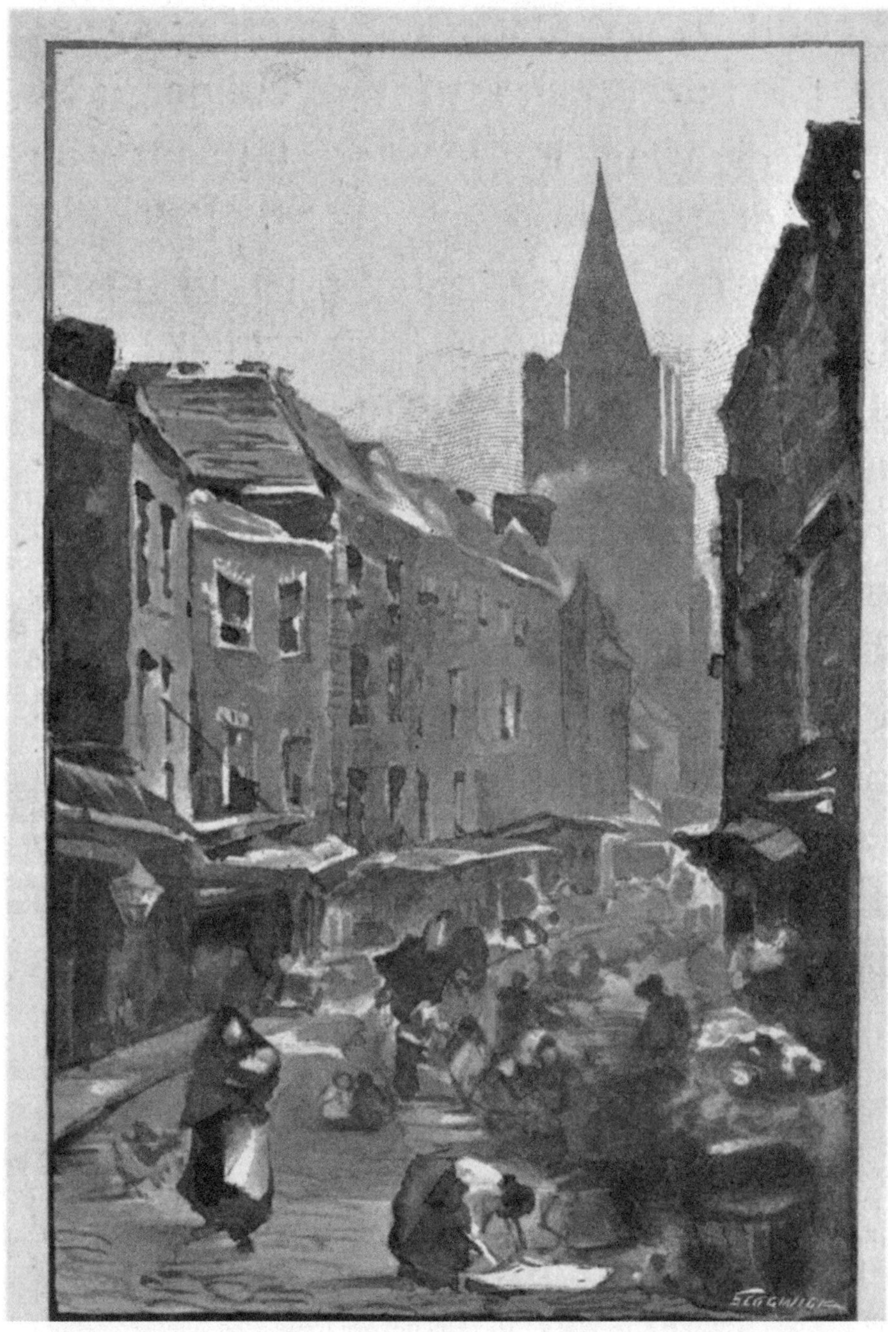

2.4   Rose Barton, *Patrick Street*, from F. Gerard, *Picturesque Dublin: Old and New* (London: Hutchinson and Co., 1898).

Barton) (Figure 2.5) and a crowd of men caused havoc and destruction in the workshops.[59]

The Hall had been built in 1745 and was a testament to the strength of the industry in the area: as can be seen in Barton's representation, it was a handsome building with a prominent statue of George II placed in a niche over the door. This bronze portrait of the monarch had been completed by John van Nost II in 1750, and showed the king adorned by tools associated with the weaving trade: it was removed in the 1930s. Although little record of the interior decoration of the Hall remains, one of its more splendid decorative items was a tapestry portrait of George II made by a Dublin weaver, John van Beaver, complete with a highly ornate frame, which is now in the collection of the Metropolitan Museum of Art.[60] This choice of decoration reflected the political and religious beliefs of the predominantly Protestant artisans then living in the locality. The deep connections between the weaving tradition in Dublin and Protestantism may also have been appealing to Gerard as she compiled her volume.

The book's focus on the Coombe was further augmented by two illustrations by Barton showing the distinctive housing of the area, notable for its distinctive triangular gables (Figures 2.6 and 2.7). Known as 'Dutch Billies' (after William III), these houses were intimately connected to the weaving trade, providing both industrial and domestic space for those involved with the trade. The first of these illustrations depicts a row of these distinctive houses in Weaver's Square; however, it is evident that they are no longer the homes of prosperous artisans. With the textile industry in decline from the early 1800s (Kenneth Milne notes that the economic downturn of 1827 was particularly devastating), the previously prosperous area became increasingly deprived, and its distinctive buildings were transformed into tenements with high occupancy rates. The noted travel writers, Mr and Mrs S. C. Hall, noted in 1840, that in this 'once flourishing region: large houses of costly structure [were] now the abode of the most miserable'.[61] Barton alludes to this decline through the depiction of the dilapidated buildings: in several of the windows panes of glass are missing, while others are partially shuttered. Sheets hang from the window of one dwelling, and children wander unsupervised on the pavement. While it is certainly possible that Barton visited Weavers' Square to view the Hall and houses, she may also have drawn on contemporary photographs such as those produced by Robert French. The photographer's representations of the square contain some distinctive features, such as the squat water hydrant and the three-quarter window shuttering held in place by a diagonal bar (Figure 2.8). The location of the row of houses in the second illustration is not listed, with the caption simply reading 'Huguenot Houses in the Liberties', and so could refer to several other streets in the vicinity of Weaver's Square. However, it is possible that Barton turned to one of the most distinctive of these: Chamber Street (Figure 2.9), also known as Chambré Street, after the Huguenot family who financed its development. In her illustration, Barton depicts a pair of gabled houses, which in addition to a shop front also has doorways with distinctive architraves: these can

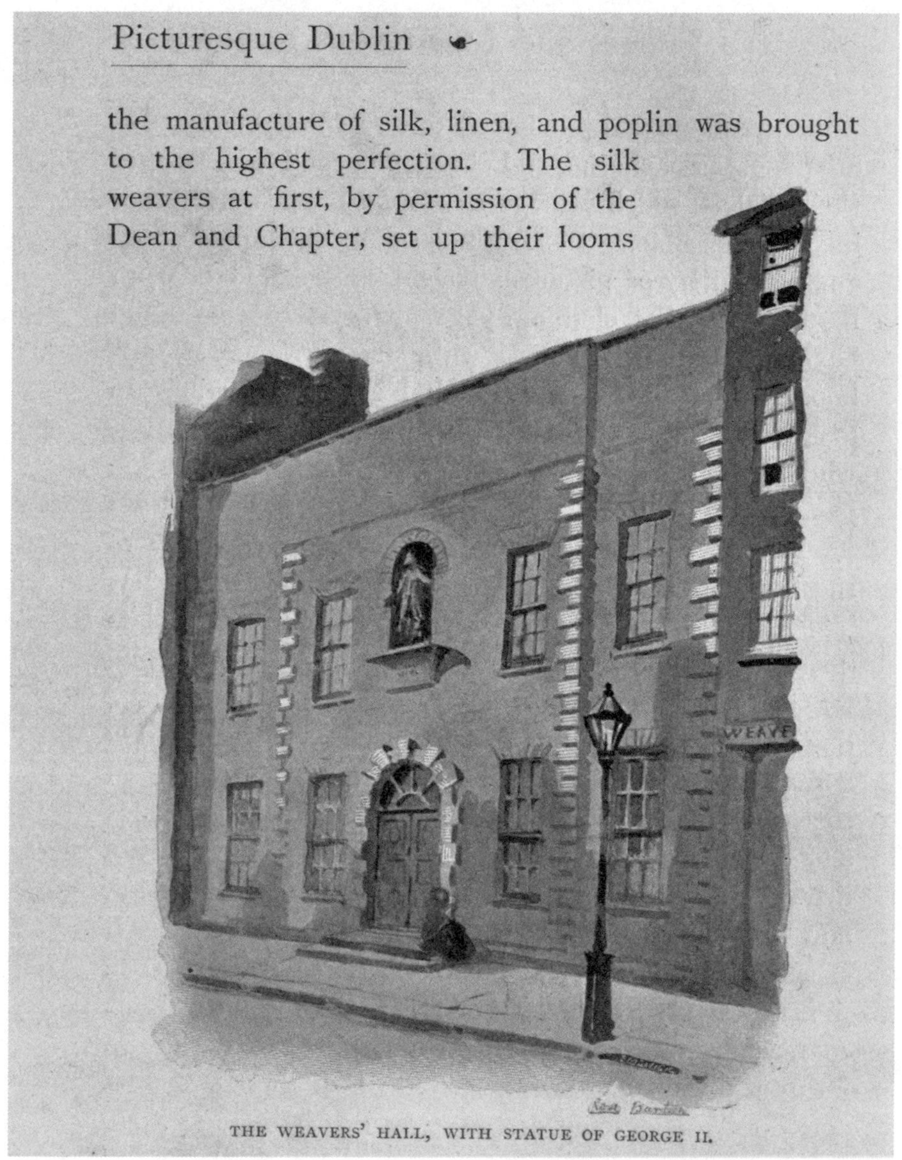

2.5   Rose Barton, *Weaver's Hall*, from F. Gerard, *Picturesque Dublin: Old and New* (London: Hutchinson and Co., 1898).

also be found in photographs of the street in sources dating from Barton's own time, right through to the decades immediately prior to the street's demolition in 1964. Remaining in the vicinity of Weaver's Square, the social reality experienced by many in the area is emphasised, although again not discussed, by a

☙ The Fringes and Liberties of Dublin City

had fought under Caillemote for William III. at the Battle of the Boyne), established a manufactory in High Street, where his countrymen could carry on

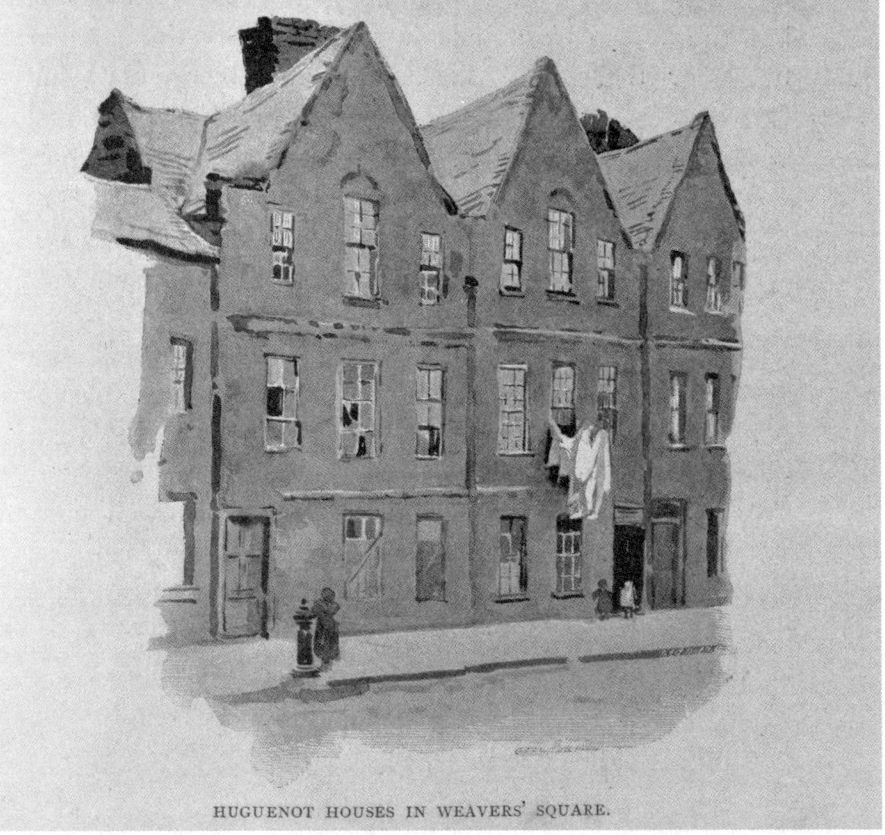

2.6   Rose Barton, *Houses in Weaver's Square*, from F. Gerard, *Picturesque Dublin: Old and New* (London: Hutchinson and Co., 1898).

reference to the night refuge at the former Tenter House. Founded in 1861 and administered by the Sisters of Mercy from about 1890, the refuge provided food and shelter for women and children of all denominations. In 1892, an article in the *Irish Times* noted that 'over 120 destitute women and children apply to the

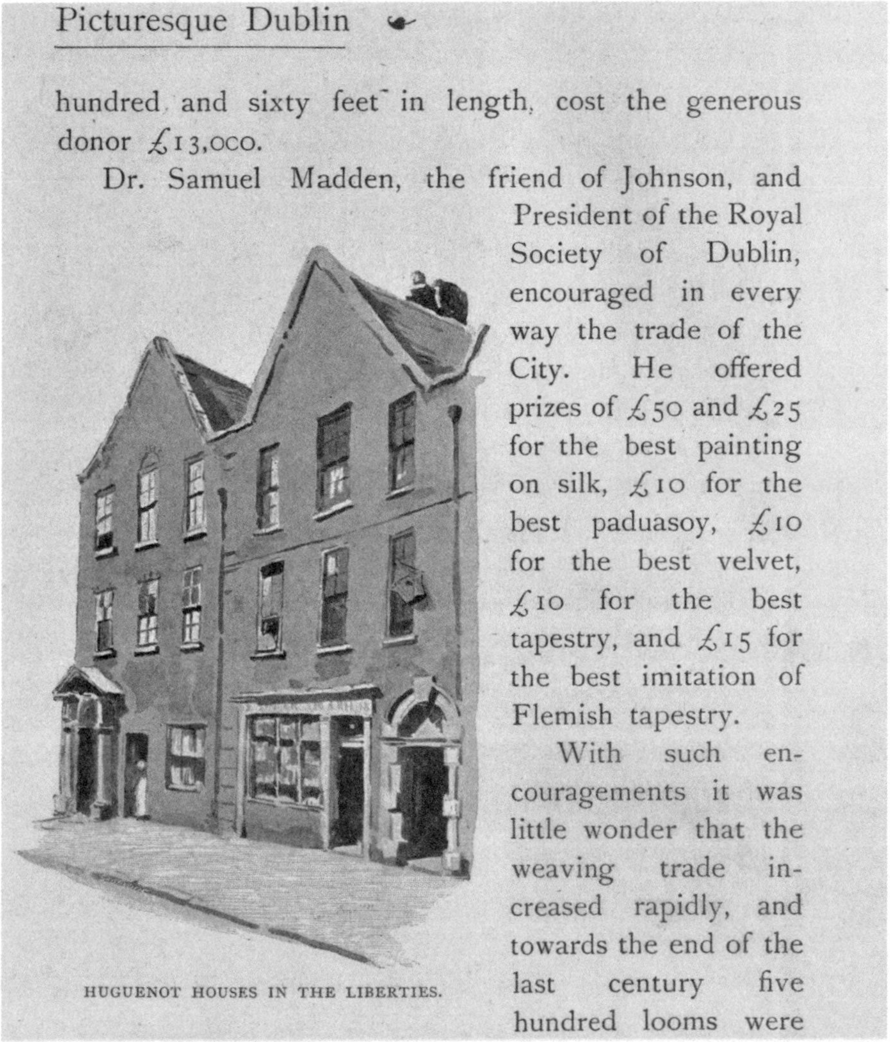

Picturesque Dublin

hundred and sixty feet in length, cost the generous donor £13,0co.

Dr. Samuel Madden, the friend of Johnson, and President of the Royal Society of Dublin, encouraged in every way the trade of the City. He offered prizes of £50 and £25 for the best painting on silk, £10 for the best paduasoy, £10 for the best velvet, £10 for the best tapestry, and £15 for the best imitation of Flemish tapestry.

With such encouragements it was little wonder that the weaving trade increased rapidly, and towards the end of the last century five hundred looms were

HUGUENOT HOUSES IN THE LIBERTIES.

2.7 Rose Barton, *Huguenot Houses, Dublin*, from F. Gerard, *Picturesque Dublin: Old and New* (London: Hutchinson and Co., 1898).

Refuge every night' suggesting that for some, even the lowest rates for tenement accommodation were unaffordable.[62]

Following this journey through the Liberties, the text returns the reader to the centre of the city with chapters on 'The Bank and College Green' and 'The Quays, Bridges, and the Four Courts'. As with the preceding chapters, the city's history presented here concentrates on the history of William III in Ireland, the Irish Parliament before the Act of Union, and the importance

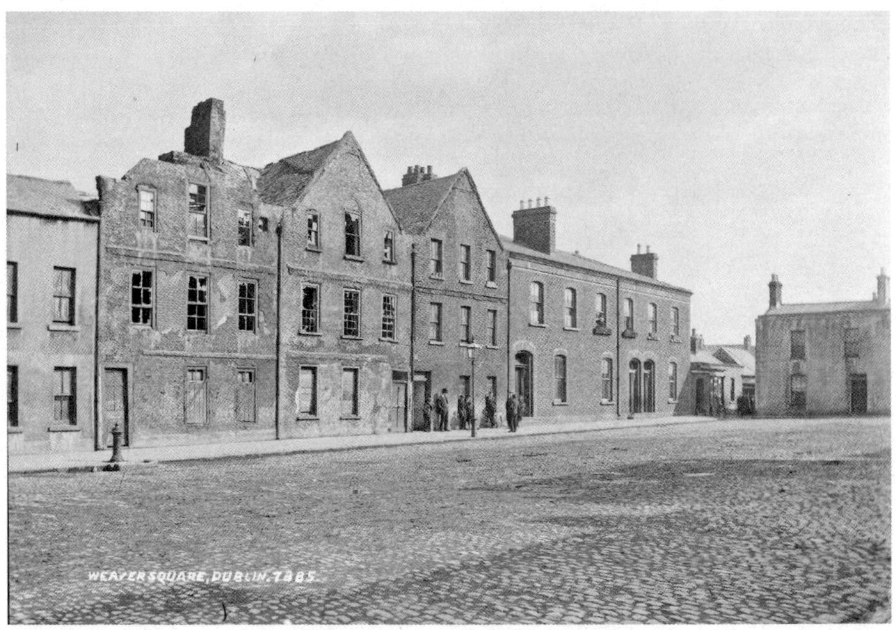

2.8   Robert French, *Weaver's Square*, c.1865–1914.

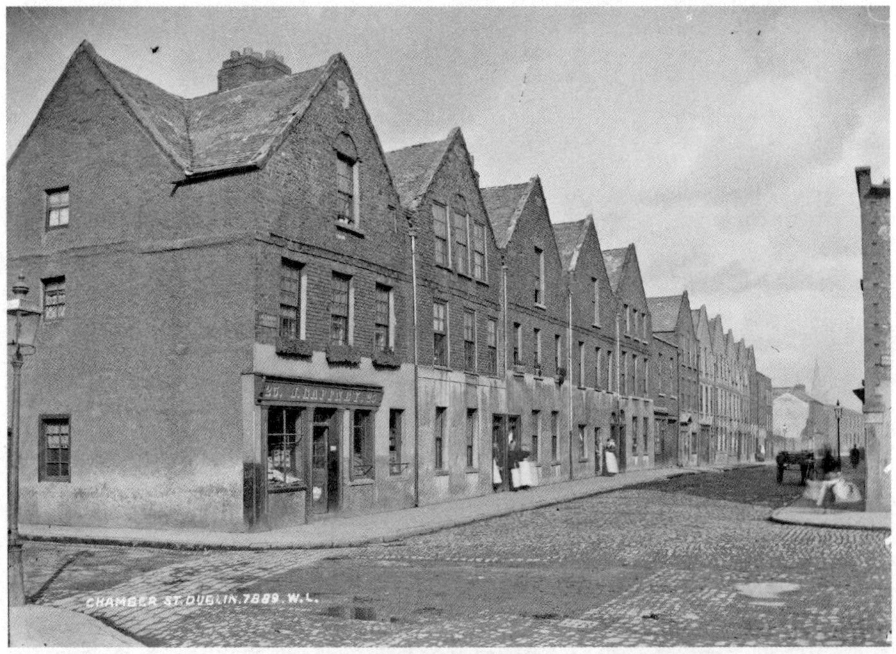

2.9   Robert French, *Chamber Street*, c.1865–1914.

of the legal business to the city's economy, of which the 'leading members … do duty for the absentee nobility, who have long ceased to reside in the capital'.[63] The former of these is visually represented through a reproduction of John van Beaver's tapestry of the monarch at the Battle of the Boyne, which is still in situ in the former House of Lords, as well as a full-page illustration by Barton showing the imposing, and often controversial, statue of the king on College Green (Figure 2.10). Made by Grinling Gibbons and erected in 1701 to mark the ten-year anniversary of the Battle of the Boyne, Gerard described the monument: 'Nearly opposite to where Daly's Club stood is the statue erected to the pious, glorious, and immortal memory of William of Orange.'[64] The author outlined some of the statue's controversial history, including an attempt at its destruction in 1836: writing at the close of the 1890s, Gerard could hardly have supposed that the cycle of damage and reconstruction would continue long into the twentieth century.

The 'old Dublin' atmosphere which pervades *Picturesque Dublin* also prevails in another text by an Irish author published in 1898: George Egerton's novel, *The Wheel of God*. In the second chapter of the novel, the young protagonist – Mary – traverses the Liberties, beginning in Meath Street, which 'was at its worst this soft, grey, Irish forenoon; squalor and sordid poverty; slatternly, bedrabbled women; neglected filthy children'.[65] She is familiar with the history of the area, 'gleaned out of old numbers of the *Dublin Penny Magazine*, or old books skimmed at the bookstalls in Drury Court', and 'knew the houses and courts where the Huguenots had lived – silk weavers and carvers in ivory and wood; knew the names of the long-vanished tenants of mansions rich with superb panelling and ornate carving, now given over to humanity and vermin'. A curious evocation of Gerard's text comes with Egerton's reference to a child being like 'a little Murillo'.[66] Mary's first journey through the city leads her to the Marshalsea, a debtors prison where her father was resident: following this, she travels 'downhill towards the quays, through narrow alleys and cobble-stoned streets', arriving at the 'malodorous Liffey' and Aston quay with its many curio and antique shops.[67] Later in the novel, after a lapse of five years, the reader again joins Mary as she runs errands in the city: on Dame Street 'she looked up at the figure of King Billy. She had a dislike, quite unmotivated, perhaps racial, to that equestrian statue.' The text then marks the Castle, Smock Alley, Golden Lane, Hoey's Court, and figures such as James Clarence Mangan and Lord Edward Fitzgerald – sites all associated with the city's eighteenth-century and imperial history.[68] While Whitney Standlee has highlighted the connections between Egerton's descriptions of Dublin as a form of precursor to James Joyce's later novels, *Portrait of the Artist* and *Ulysses*, Mary's journey through the city should also be understood in the context of other contemporary characterisations of the Irish city – be it in a guidebook or artwork.[69]

The advance publicity for *Picturesque Dublin* made clear that the aim of the publication was to provide an overview of the city's traditions and that 'no attempt has been made to give a history of Dublin'.[70] Indeed, several of the

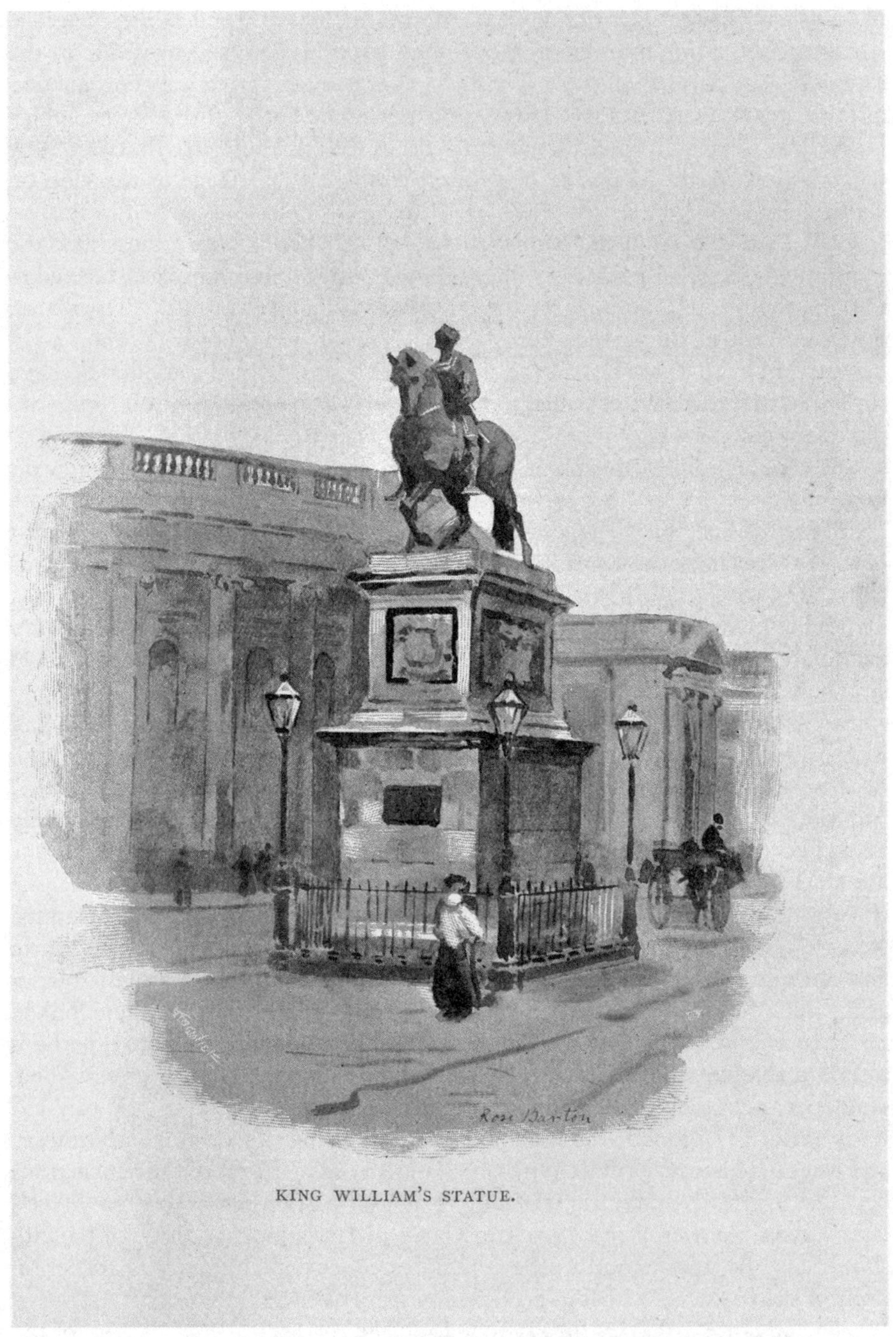

2.10   Rose Barton, *College Green*, from F. Gerard, *Picturesque Dublin: old and new* (London: Hutchinson and Co., 1898).

reviews made clear that Gerard's texts contained many historical errors, but Barton's illustrations were largely well received. Reviews appeared in newspapers across Britain and Ireland: for example, *The Scotsman* praised Barton's pictures 'whether of the fresher or more decayed specimens of Dublin streets and dwellings'.[71] Noting the book's introductory comments, a critic for the *Freeman's Journal* remarked that 'Miss Gerard must have overlooked on the one hand the rent-lists of our local house agents and on the other the congested tenements of the very poor'.[72] Furthermore, the reviewer noted that 'the volume is liberally sprinkled with errors that will make most Dubliners smile'.[73] The *Pall Mall Gazette* also noted such deficiencies, although as they noted 'it is quite clear that the study of Old Dublin had much charm for their minds, and they have not by any means failed to produce a bright, chatty volume which, within its limits, is attractive and readable'.[74] The reviewer devoted considerably more space to Barton's contributions to the publication than other critics, noting that 'her pencil has shown itself most happy in catching, with rare skill in many instances a number of picturesque out-of-the-way nooks and corners', and that the:

> part of her work which is the outcome of her rambles in and about the Old Liberties, and up and down the decayed streets around the Castle and Christ Church, will have more than a passing value, as she here fixed for the guidance of future students the outlines and characteristics of old houses and landmarks which have been part and parcel of Dublin's history, and which are now falling rapidly into ruins. We would cite the Weavers' Hall, the "Tenter House", the Huguenot house in Weavers'-square, and the Huguenot houses in the Liberties as cases in point.[75]

Despite its historical failings, *Picturesque Dublin: Old and New* offers an engaging insight into how the city was viewed, painted, and presented in the closing years of the nineteenth century. The unionist-inflected lens of Gerard (and perhaps of Barton, too) presents a version of the city that overlooks nationalist developments in the same period – for example, the introduction of new public sculpture or the introduction of new bridge or street names. At the close of the text, Gerard notes that the publication had 'been compiled by an Irishwoman, illustrated by an Irishwoman, and dedicated to one of Ireland's kindest friends'.[76] This confident assertion of nationality is striking, and acts as an important reminder of the complexity of nationhood and identity in this period. As will be seen in Chapter 5, the characterisation of parts of the city with the nostalgia-driven label of 'old Dublin' would cast a shadow well into the twentieth century, coming to the fore in both the work of Estella Solomons and Flora Mitchell.

Dublin, London: representing the nineteenth-century city

As noted at the opening of this chapter, the cultural trope of London as a smog-filled, gas-lighted, pea-souper city was well-established through various cultural representations of the city in the nineteenth century, ranging from Dickens's novels to Claude Monet's hazy views of the Palace of Westminster and Waterloo Bridge, created in the late 1890s. Writing of mid-Victorian London, Linda Nead has identified a 'poetics of gas', with gaslight being notable for creating 'patches of light interspersed with pools of darkness. Gas seemed to have the power equally to create illumination and to cast shadow.'[77] In 1890, *Irish Society* wrote satirically of the campaign for electric street lighting to be introduced across Dublin, suggesting that the city's citizens 'have been cautiously feeling our way around the night all these years, and we are not going to favour any new-fangled process of illumination. If our fathers were contented with the darkness of Dublin gaslight we could not grumble.'[78] In *The Wheel of God*, Egerton frequently refers to light in the city, using it to describe the effect of the evening drawing in and evoke a sense of danger through the darkness: for example, on Mary's first journey through the city, we read that 'The lamps were lit as she reached Carlisle Bridge, and the oil lamps of the stall keeper … flared against the black background, in which the Custom House loomed.'[79] Later, as she walks from the tram stop to her home along the South Circular Road, she 'hurried, because there were lonely patches of building ground, and a long way between the lamp-posts'.[80]

In 1895, a review of the annual Royal Society of Painters in Watercolour (now the Royal Watercolour Society/RWS), noted that one 'ought perhaps, to deplore that Miss Rose Barton should remain too consistently faithfully to her dove-grey mists touched with pink, blurring the contours of the great city; and yet it is difficult to do so, or to resist the charm of poeticised truth which she throws over her subjects'. Noting her view of Chelsea in particular, the reviewer noted that to 'succeed in a subject such as this without calling up memories of one of Mr Whistler's lovely "nocturnes" is in itself a remarkable achievement'.[81] If viewers of the painting, which although unidentified may be similar to *The Last Lamp, Thames Embankment* (1886, watercolour, private collection), had not already conjured the visual connection between the two artists, the reviewer's comments would certainly have brought it to mind. A passage in *Familiar London* (1904), a publication like *Picturesque Dublin: Old and New*, written and illustrated by Barton suggests her familiarity with the American artist's work, as well as a further shared influence, that of J. M. W. Turner. In a chapter on Chelsea, she wrote that 'if one wanders past Battersea Bridge … and it happens to be an autumn evening, with a brilliant sunset flooding the river with light, who can help thinking of Turner?' Furthermore, Barton noted that when walking along the Chelsea Embankment on a November evening at dusk, she 'meditated on how truly Whistler had interpreted the scene', and quoted a passage from the artist's *Ten O'Clock* lecture which described how 'when the evening mist clothes the riverside with poetry', 'the whole city hangs in the heavens, and fairy-land is before us'.[82] In addition to ample opportunities to see Whistler's work in several London galleries, Barton may also have seen the loan collection of his work at the Dublin Sketching Club in December 1884: among the twenty-six works exhibited by the American artist were four watercolours, including *Nocturne in Grey and Gold – Piccadilly* (1881–83, watercolour on paper, NGI), which had been exhibited in the artist's one-man exhibition in London earlier that year.[83]

Despite frequent assertions of Whistler's influence on Barton in previous accounts of the artist's work, this has seldom if ever gone further than a general invocation of artistic style. What, however, can be ascertained about the nature of this influence by looking specifically at both artists' urban watercolours? A comparison of Barton's paintings of Dublin and London show that the artist repeatedly returned to a number of compositional frameworks; for example, using and reusing the natural perspective of a long street, framed by notable buildings or park railings, and filled with a variety of figures, trams, and carriages which are almost interchangeable. Four works in particular demonstrate this working style, as well as the artist's embrace of fog and mist: *Waterloo Bridge, London* (Plate 2.4); *South Kensington Station* (Plate 2.5); *The Rotunda Rooms* (Plate 2.6); and *Evening on the Liffey* (1905, watercolour on paper, private collection). In addition to their compositional similarities, these works also show Barton's clear embrace of Whistlerian colour and form: dominated by greys and light indigos, enlivened by touches of yellow and white lamp light.

Waterloo Bridge, London, dating to 1893, may have been included in the artist's London exhibition of the same year. Viewed from a low vantage point, the bridge looms over the tugboats that pass through the arches. While evidently on a different scale to *Nocturne: Blue and Gold – Old Battersea Bridge* (c.1872–75, oil on canvas, Tate) there is an echo of the earlier artwork in Barton's river view. The influence of Whistler is not only evident in the perspective of Barton's composition, but also in the blue grey tones and the effect of the gas or electric light which shines from the lamp posts across the bridge and from the industrial buildings on the far bank. Furthermore, the framing of the painting, with a gold mount and simply reeded frame, is in keeping with Whistler's own method for presenting works.[84] The greys and soft blues of this work were repeated by Barton in another London scene from the following year: *South Kensington Station, London*, where not only has the 'evening mist' descended, but a heavy shower of rain, suggested by raised umbrellas and the shimmering reflection of illuminated water on the street and pavement. As loosely painted figures move into the bright interior of the station, a horse and cab travels down the street, perhaps to collect the lady standing with her furled umbrella outstretched on the right-hand side. Another version of both works appeared in *Familiar London*, but show a radically different painting style, perhaps either a reflection on Barton's malleability as an artist or reworked in a less ethereal or aesthetic fashion in order to be better reproduced.

The composition and weather effects of *South Kensington Station* were mirrored by Barton in *The Rotunda Rooms*, the curved wall of the station transformed into the arcaded façade of the eighteenth-century assembly rooms. The hansom cab has been replaced by a horse-drawn tram, and two women, ill-equipped for the sudden downpour, bustle down the street – a bright pink skirt gleams from under a black-brown coat, and is reflected in the wet street along with a burst of lamp light that seems to hover behind the tram. In contrast to the limited grey palette of the London scenes, here Barton has introduced notes of heather-purple and blue, reminiscent of those seen in *Going to the Levée*. This palette is further utilised in *Evening on the Liffey*, created by the artist in 1905. Although the colouring of this work makes a clear departure from the limited tonal palette of Whistler's early watercolours, the silver-purple mist rising over the Whitworth Bridge (renamed in 1938 after the temperance leader, Father Mathew), is reminiscent of the effect in *Waterloo Bridge*.

These examples demonstrate how Barton applied the formal qualities of Whistler's urban watercolours to both Dublin and London, which of course were replicated across many of the artist's other city scenes. However, a further comparison may be drawn between the two artists by looking more generally at the way in which they viewed the city as a subject which could be interpreted as 'picturesque': as Kathleen Pyne has written, Whistler 'began schooling himself in the picturesque early ... by 1859 he was in command of the idiom that would provide him with a definitive strategy in portraying London'.[85] Pyne continues that 'The codes of the late-eighteenth century picturesque allowed Whistler to aestheticize the tragic historical conditions of his human subjects': through a selective vision of the riverside, he could overlook the chronic poverty endured by those who lived there, and by repeating the 'stock motifs' of the picturesque tradition, respond 'to a current nostalgia for an era of stability and order that was fast disappearing'.[86] This, of course, echoes with the picturesque view of 'old Dublin' as portrayed in image and text by Barton and Gerard: the stability of the union between Ireland and Britain increasingly threatened by social and political change; as well as with how the social conditions of, say, the Liberties, were carefully placed at a distance from the reader and viewer.

Conclusion: a sense of the city

Considering Duncan's notion of the 'imagined environment' of the city in relation to Barton's depiction of Dublin, we can see how her watercolours evoke the world of the imperial city, which, as nationalist sentiment began to rise, was fading to the realm of the imagination. Allied to a nostalgia for the city's historical past – notably as related to its seventeenth- and eighteenth-century past – her record of the city addresses the concerns of her social class around the changing nature of Ireland's relationship with Britain. By mediating this through the aesthetics of urban impressionism and the picturesque, Barton participated in a wider visual conversation around the representation of the city.

Like Osborne, she consciously sought to establish her reputation outside of Ireland – chiefly through a series of successful exhibitions in fashionable London galleries (such as the Dudley and Grosvenor) and through exhibition societies such as the RWS (to which she was elected an associate in 1893) and the Society of Lady Artists (later the Society of Women Artists). Among her most successful exhibitions there were displays of London street scenes: for example, in 1893 she exhibited sixty views of that city at the Japanese Gallery on Bond Street. *Lady of the House* reported that all of the works sold, netting the artist £1000, while also 'receiving commissions for twenty pictures', which were 'to be treated on the lines of her successful speciality – familiar thoroughfares, with the crowd of figures and activity of incident common to them'. Among the purchasers of Barton's works on this occasion, the magazine reported, was Lord Iveagh, said to have purchased twenty paintings in total, including *Parliament Street*.[87] Unlike Osborne, Barton did not exhibit her Dublin paintings in the English city, choosing instead to only display them in Irish venues.

After moving with some frequency between Dublin and London throughout the 1880s and 1890s, Barton made London her permanent residence around 1904. Her interest in Ireland was maintained through family and friends, as well as through her connection with Hugh Lane. In 1904, Lane included four works by Barton in his exhibition of Irish Art at the Guildhall and the following year, Barton led the campaign to raise funds to purchase Camille Corot's *View of Rome from the Pincio* from the collection of James Staats Forbes for Lane's Dublin Gallery.[88] Correspondence between Barton and Lane in the NLI also shows that Barton called on the dealer for advice regarding the sale of some family pictures, and she later painted two scenes of the garden at Lindsey House, Lane's home in Cheyne Walk, Chelsea. Her involvement with Lane's project to establish a gallery of modern art in Dublin speaks to the changing circumstances in Dublin and Lane's move towards the categorisation and promotion of an Irish school of painting. The Barton works that Lane included in the 1904 exhibition received little (if any) critical attention; rather, it was the next generation of painters – particularly Jack B. Yeats – who garnered the critics' notice, with his depictions of life in the west of Ireland hailed as being 'authentically' Irish and fully representative of this 'new' school. Lane's project exemplified the continuing artistic connections between Dublin and London, and the movement of art, artists, and artworks between the two cities. This connection would continue and played an equally important role in Yeats's career through the twentieth century as it had for Barton (and indeed, Osborne) in the previous one.

Notes

1 J. Duncan, *Imagining the Modern City* (London: The Athlone Press, 1999), p. 8.
2 Ibid., p. 7.
3 O. Wilde, 'The decay of lying: an observation', in G. Brandreth (ed.), *Beautiful and Impossible Things: Selected Essays of Oscar Wilde* (London: Notting Hill Editions, 2015), p. 107.
4 'Irish Fine Art Society's Exhibition', *Dublin Daily Express* (11 March 1884), p. 5.
5 See, for example: J. Crary 'Techniques of the observer', *October* 45 (1988), 3–35 www.jstor.org/stable/779041; A. Boutin, 'Rethinking the flânuer: Flânerie and the senses', *Dix-Neuf: Journal of the Society of Dix-Neuviémistes* 16:2 (2012), 124–32. DOI 10.1179/dix.2012.16.2.01; E. Maurail, 'A body passes by: the *flâneur* and the senses

in nineteenth-century London and Paris', *The Senses and Society* 12:2 (2017), 162–76. DOI 10.1080/17458927.2017.1310454.

6   G. Pollock, *Vision and Difference: Feminism, Femininity and the Histories of Art* (London: Routledge, 1988), pp. 70–1.

7   C. O'Neill and M. Yatani, 'Women, ambition, and the city, 1890–1910', in A. Pilz and W. Standlee (eds), *Irish Women's Writing, 1878–1922: Advancing the Cause of Liberty* (Manchester: Manchester University Press, 2016), p. 101.

8   See M. Reznicek, *The European Metropolis: Paris and Nineteenth-Century Irish Women Novelists* (Clemson: Clemson University Press, 2017).

9   'Births', *Warder and Dublin Weekly Mail* (26 April 1856); Irishgenealogy.ie, DU-CI-BA-203890, d-45-2–11–020, published digital record, Baptismal Record for Rose Mary Anne Barton, 5 June 1856.

10   Emily Anne Martin (d. 1907) married James McCalmont (1819–49) on 27 April 1843. Following McCalmont's death, Emily married Augustine Hugh Barton in Dublin on 12 October 1853. Emily Anne was one of five daughters of James Martin of Ross, Co Galway (b. 1804) and Anne Higinbotham (m. 1824): after Anne's early death, Martin married Anna Selina Fox (m. 1844) and the couple had eleven children. Their youngest child was Violet Florence Martin (*pseud.* Martin Ross, 1862–1915). See entries of 'Barton of Grove', 'Martin of Ross', and 'McCalmont of Abbeylands', in B. Burke, *A Genealogical and Heraldic History of the Landed Gentry of Great Britain and Ireland*, 9th Edn (London: Harrison and Sons, 1898). In an account of her family history, Martin Ross noted that her stepsiblings (including Barton's mother), 'grew up, very good-looking and agreeable, and were married when still in their teens. Their husbands all came from the County Antrim, and two of them were brothers. Barklie, Callwell, McCalmont, Barton, are well-known names in Ireland to-day.' See O. E. Somerville and Martin Ross, *Irish Memories* (New York: Longmans, Green and Co., 1918), pp. 10–11.

11   Previous sources have stated that Barton was a cousin of Martin Ross's co-author, Edith Somerville (1858–1949); however, there was a much closer familial connection between Barton and Ross. See A. Crookshank and the Knight of Glin, *The Watercolours of Ireland: Works on Paper in Pencil, Pastel and Paint* (London: Barrie and Jenkins, 1994); N. Figgis, 'Barton, Rose Mary (1856–1929)', in Figgis (ed.), *Painting, 1600–1900*, p. 173.

12   'Distinguished Irishwomen: The Professions, Pleasures, and Pursuits', *Lady of the House* (15 January 1896), p. 4.

13   'Royal Dublin Society's School of Art, 1875', *Irish Times* (22 October 1875), p. 3 and 'Dublin Amateur Artists Society', *Dublin Daily Express* (6 December 1875), p. 3.

14   NIVAL-National Irish Visual Arts Library, College Student Registers, October 1877–July 1978, IE/NIVAL CR/CR01/45.

15   'Grand Amateur Performance at the Rotundo', *Dublin Evening Mail* (22 January 1870), p. 3 and 'Private Theatricals at the Rotundo', *Saunders's News-Letter* (16 December 1870), p. 3.

16   'The Drawing Room – Last Night', *Freeman's Journal* (3 January 1876), p. 7.

17   'The Fitzwilliam Lawn Tennis Tournament', *Irish Society* (4 June 1892), p. 26.

18   NGI, Watercolour Society of Ireland Archive, Box 3, letter from Lord Longford to Philip Chenevix Trench, 14 March 1892.

19   NGI, Watercolour Society of Ireland Archive, Box 3, letter from Philip Chenevix Trench to Lord Longford, 20 March 1892.

20 'The Castle Season', *Dublin Evening Mail* (30 January 1888), p. 2.

21 'St Patrick's Day', *Dublin Daily Express* (18 March 1890), p. 5.

22 Although this is the smaller and more loosely painted of these two works, an original label for the 1895 exhibition is extant on the reverse of the frame. See Whyte's, Irish Art, 18 May 2009, Lot 82.

23 'The Festival: St Patrick's Day in Dublin', *Freeman's Journal* (18 March 1891), p. 6.

24 'Trooping of the Colours', *Dublin Daily Express* (19 March 1894), p. 5.

25 'St Patrick's Day. Trooping the Colours in the Castle Yard', *Weekly Irish Times* (24 March 1894), p. 6.

26 Garnet Joseph Wolseley (1833–1913), Viscount Wolseley, served as commander-in-chief in Ireland from 1890–95. A distinguished military strategist, Wolseley was thought to be the inspiration for the 'Modern Major General' in Gilbert & Sullivan's *Pirates of Penzance*.

27 'Metropolitan School of Art – Speech by the Lord Lieutenant', *Freeman's Journal* (19 January 1894), p. 6. Three works by Barton were included in the sale of 'Property & Precious Objects from the Estate of Mary, Duchess of Roxburgh', Sotheby's, 25–28 May 2015, Lots. 6, 292, and 294.

28 J. Hill, *Irish Public Sculpture: A History* (Dublin: Four Courts Press, 1998), pp. 51–2.

29 V. Kreilkamp, '*Going to the Levée* as ascendency spectacle: alternative narratives in Irish painting', in A. Dalsimer (ed.), *Visualizing Ireland: National Identity and the Pictorial Tradition* (Winchester, MA: Faber and Faber, 1993), p. 52.

30 G. Moore, *A Drama in Muslin* (Gerrards Cross: Colin Smythe, 1981), p. 166.

31 Ibid., p. 170.

32 Ibid., p. 171.

33 F. Gerard, *Picturesque Dublin: Old and New* (London: Hutchinson and Company, 1898), p. vii.

34 Ibid., p. 93.

35 'The Masonic Bazaar,' *Irish Times* (18 May 1892), p. 5.

36 E. Emery, 'Protecting the past: Albert Robida and the *Vieux Paris* exhibit at the 1900 World's Fair', *Journal of European Studies* 35:1 (2005), 70. DOI 10.1177/0047244105051155.

37 W. F. Wakeman, *Old Dublin* (Dublin: Evening Telegraph Office, 1887).

38 J. Dixon Hunt, 'Picturesque', *Grove Dictionary of Art/Oxford Art Online*, 10.1093/gao/9781884446054.article.T067408 (accessed 21 April 2020).

39 John Ruskin, quoted in M. Andrews, *The Picturesque: Sources and Documents*, vol. 1 (Mountfield: Helm Information, 1994), p. 35.

40 E. Mark Fitzgerald, *Commemorating the Irish Famine: Memory and the Monument* (Liverpool: Liverpool University Press, 2013), p. 18.

41 M. Andrews, 'The metropolitan picturesque', in S. Copley and P. Garside (eds), *The Politics of the Picturesque: Literature, Language and Aesthetics since 1770* (Cambridge: Cambridge University Press, 1994), p. 288.

42 M. Crinson, 'Georgianism and the tenements, Dublin 1908–1926', *Art History* 29:4 (2006), 633.

43 S. Boym, *The Future of Nostalgia* (New York: Basic Books, 2001), p. 41.

44 Ibid.

45 For an overview of 'vieux Paris', see R. Fiori, *L'Invention du vieux Paris: naissance d'une conscience patrimoniale dans la capitale* (Wavre: Mardaga, 2012).

46 J. Banim, *The Anglo-Irish of the Nineteenth Century*, vol. 1 (London: H. Colburn, 1828), p. 183.

47 D. Michalski, 'Portals to metropolis: 19th-century guidebooks and the assemblage of urban experience', *Tourist Studies* 4 (2004), 95.

48 See E. McParland, 'Malton's views of Dublin: too good to be true?', in R. Gillespie and B. P. Kennedy (eds), *Ireland: Art into History* (Dublin: Town House & Country House, 1994), pp. 15–25.

49 The *Wellesley Index to Victorian Periodicals* records that Geraldine Penrose Fitzgerald (*fl.* 1870–1903) wrote under the name of 'Frances A. Gerard', contributing articles to *The Temple Bar* at the close of the nineteenth century; Snoddy suggests that Fitzgerald was the sister of the lawyer, writer, and sculptor Percy Fitzgerald (1830–1925), while the *Database of Victorian Fiction* contains details of five novels written by a Geraldine Penrose Fitzgerald (dates given 1846–1939), written under the pseudonym 'Naseby'. One source does suggest that Gerard, Naseby, and Penrose Fitzgerald are one and the same, and the themes of Naseby's novels do echo the later publications of Gerard. See: 'Fitzgerald, Geraldine Penrose', in W. Edwards Houghton and J. I. Slingerland (eds), *The Wellesley Index to Victorian Periodicals, 1824–1900*, vol. V (Toronto: University of Toronto Press, 1989), p. 265; T. J. Bassett, *At the Circulating Library: A Database of Victorian Fiction, 1837–1901*. Victorian Research Web. www.victorianresearch.org/atcl (accessed 21 April 2020); and 'Editor's Note', in B. Tyson (ed.), *Bernard Shaw's Book Reviews*, vol. I, (University Park: Pennsylvania State University Press, 2008), p. 85.

50 Gerard, *Picturesque Dublin: Old and New*, p. vii. 'Dolce far niente' is an Italian phrase which translates as 'pleasant relaxation in carefree idleness'. Merriam-Webster, www.merriam-webster.com/dictionary/dolce%20far%20oniente (accessed 10 July 2019).

51 Ibid.

52 Moore, *A Drama in Muslin*, p. 158.

53 Gerard, *Picturesque Dublin: Old and New*, p. xii.

54 Ibid., p. xiii.

55 Ibid., p. 60.

56 Ibid., p. 66.

57 Ibid., p. 93.

58 Dickson, *Dublin: The Making of a Capital City*, pp. 93–4.

59 Ibid., p. 186.

60 Weaver John van Beaver (*fl.* 1727–50), *Portrait of George II*, 1732–37, wool and silk, Metropolitan Museum of Art, New York, Accession No. 64.101.1331a.b.

61 Mr and Mrs S. C. Hall, quoted in K. Milne, *The Dublin Liberties, 1600–1850* (Dublin: Four Courts Press, 2009), p. 16.

62 'St Joseph's Night Refuge,' *Irish Times* (12 December 1892), p. 5.

63 Gerard, *Picturesque Dublin: Old and New*, p. 135.

64 Ibid., p. 113.

65 G. Egerton, *The Wheel of God* (London: G. P. Putnam's Sons, 1898), p. 12.

66 Ibid., p. 13.

67 Ibid., pp. 22–3.

68 Ibid., pp. 49–50, pp. 55–6.

69 See W. Standlee, 'George Egerton, James Joyce and the Irish *Küstlerroman*', *Irish Studies Review* 18 (2010), 439–52.

70 'Publishers' Column', *Dundee Courier* (17 November 1897), p. 6.

71 'New Books', *The Scotsman* (23 December 1897), p. 9.

72 'Literature', *Freeman's Journal* (14 January 1898), p. 2.

73 Ibid.

74 'Dublin', *The Pall Mall Gazette* (26 March 1898), p. 10.

75 Ibid.

76 Gerard, *Picturesque Dublin: Old and New*, p. 419.

77 L. Nead, *Victorian Babylon: People, Streets and Images in Nineteenth Century London* (New Haven: Yale University Press, 2005), p. 83.

78 'Old Monopolies', *Irish Society* (12 April 1890), p. 238.

79 Egerton, *The Wheel of God*, p. 24.

80 Ibid., p. 30.

81 'The Royal Society of Painters in Watercolours', *Daily Telegraph and Courier* (30 November 1895), p. 8.

82 Barton, *Familiar London*, pp. 91–2. See also *Mr Whistler's "Ten O'Clock"* (London: Chatto and Windus, 1888), p. 15.

83 R. Anderson, 'Whistler in Dublin, 1884', *Irish Arts Review* 3:3 (1986), 48.

84 For a thorough analysis of Whistler's framing technique (and its history), see: 'How Pre-Raphaelite frames influenced Degas and the Impressionists', The Frame Blog, 25 July 2017, https://theframeblog.com/2017/07/25/how-pre-raphaelite-frames-influenced-degas-and-the-impressionists/ (accessed 21 April 2020).

85 K. Pyne, 'Whistler and the politics of the urban picturesque', *American Art* 8:3/4 (1994), 61.

86 Ibid., p. 61, p. 73.

87 'Vanity Fair', *Lady of the House* (15 April 1893), p. 1.

88 'A Modern Art Gallery', *Irish Independent* (20 January 1905), p. 4. The painting referred to is: Jean-Baptiste-Camille Corot, *Rome from the Pincio* (1827, oil on canvas, Dublin City Gallery the Hugh Lane), Reg. 550.

3

Dockers, swimmers, and dancers

While the quintessential *flâneur* might be associated with the nineteenth-century city, the trope of the urban observer continued to evolve after the turn of the century, tracking and tracing life in a variety of urban spaces across the globe. For example, the Ashcan painters in New York based their observations of the teeming city on an intimate knowledge gained from consistent travel through streets, parks, and suburbs, creating a gritty view of the daily grind of the city, while Expressionists such as Max Beckmann and Ernst Ludwig Kirchner captured the colour and movement of the city at night. While previous scholars have suggested that the comparative scale of Dublin 'prevented or severely compromised any possibility of [Yeats] attaining the status of a true *flâneur*', this seems unduly limiting, particularly in light of recent and ongoing reappraisals of the trope, and the expanded field in which the urban observer is now understood.[1] As Rebecca Zurier has noted, a restriction of 'the concept of the *flâneur* as defined by Baudelaire and later elaborated by Walter Benjamin actually limits our understanding of the varied personalities and attitudes towards urban visions such figures could embody'.[2] The characterisation of the city as a place of alienation and despair was augmented by the embrace of new artistic styles which emphasised difference and fragmentation, and by the social upheaval of conflict and economic crises.

In 1928, the *Irish Times* 'Quidnunc' columnist described how Jack B. Yeats:

> dressed in his unfailing Donegal tweeds, with a carnation in his coat lapel, may be seen walking in our streets, his loose, spare frame swinging along with a rhythm of its own. Sometimes … the artist strides forward at a rapid pace, unconscious probably of the onlookers, but keenly alive to his surroundings.[3]

A review of his 1919 exhibition at the Mill's Hall, Merrion Row in which several Dublin paintings were shown, noted how these works showed an 'arresting glimpse of that seamy side of life which is to be found in all large cities, and in few cities more commonly than in Dublin'.[4] Despite the artist's focus on urban themes throughout his career, Yeats is more often thought of for his representations of rural and coastal life. In addition, and as Bruce Arnold has outlined, Yeats's 'undoubted commitment to the representation of life in Ireland in an overwhelming number of works' has led to 'the understandable identification of him as both a national and a nationalist cultural figure', and that as a result of this, the 'normal influences on Yeats – social, political, sexual and artistic – have either been ignored or played down because of an obsession with the homogeneity of his perceived nationalism'.[5] Immersed in Revivalist circles through his family connections, and living to see the formation and formative years of the newly independent Ireland, Yeats's experience of Dublin was remarkably different to that of Osborne and Barton. Through sketchbooks, illustrations, and paintings, Yeats introduces the viewer to the river, trams, theatres, and nightlife of Dublin in the twentieth century, building on the repertoire of the city's earlier painters, but imbuing them with a new sense of an emerging capital city.

City life: the early sketchbooks

On 17 August 1925, Lady Gregory recorded a conversation she had with Jack and his wife, Mary Cottenham Yeats, about James Joyce. The artist, she noted, thought 'some parts of Joyce very fine indeed, though some revolting. I [Gregory] thought a selection might be made and he says that is what he wanted. Dublin he thinks was what absorbed him, his enemy, his obsession.'[6] Perhaps Yeats recognised a kindred spirit: in 1929 Joyce purchased two paintings by the artist from his exhibition at the Alpine Club, London, one of which was a depiction of Guinness barges on the Liffey, and later commented that 'Jack Yeats and I have the same method'.[7] The exact whereabouts of Joyce's Liffey painting is now unknown: it may well have drawn on a sketch from 1905, showing one of the brewery's laden barges travelling down the river towards the docklands.[8] It has also been suggested that a painting which passed through a French auction house, titled *Barges Guinness sur la rivière Liffey, Dublin*, may have been that which belonged to the author.[9] While the notion of a shared method between the artist and writer might conjure connections between the fluid prose of *Finnegans Wake* and Yeats's later paintings of the 1940s and 1950s (Nicholas Allen, for example, has suggested that Yeats's depiction of Dublin in the 1920s changes as 'much as the Liffey splits and fragments from *Ulysses* to *Finnegans Wake*') a closer parallel can be found between the early work of both men.[10] Through their focus on the ordinary, daily routines of the city, Yeats's early sketches of Dublin offer a visual companion to the different episodes of *Dubliners*, Joyce's series of twelve short stories, published as a collection in 1914, as well as the later novels, *Portrait of the Artist as a Young Man* and *Ulysses*. Written for the most part in 1904 and 1905, *Dubliners* was not well received: the author had previously noted to his publisher that 'it is not my fault that the odour of ashpits and old weeds and offal hangs around my stories'.[11] The sense of the quotidian, perhaps even mundane, life in Dublin presented in Joyce's stories has a visual counterpoint in Yeats's sketches and illustrations created from the turn of the century onwards.

The artist's interest in depicting everyday urban life was not born in Dublin, however, and these early sketches and illustrations have a precedent in the artist's earlier and ongoing depiction of other cities, chiefly London, from the 1890s onwards, and New York, which he and Cottie visited in 1904. These sketchbooks make clear that from his early days as a young artist in London, urban life and culture fascinated Yeats. Born in that city, Yeats cut his artistic teeth there, working as an illustrator while sporadically tending to his formal artistic training. Early urban sketches show Yeats's interest in the boxing rings of the East End; for example, a sketch in black ink captures the atmosphere of a bout in Earls Court, with the closely hatched lines suggesting that the artist was working at speed as he watched the contest unfold. Also included in the sketchbook is the handbill produced for the event, which took placed on 20 January 1900.[12] This is one of many instances where Yeats pasted a piece of ephemera into a sketchbook, thus adding additional details to the scenes he was depicting. A further example is a 1901 sketchbook, where the programme for the London Hippodrome, Leicester Square precedes a selection of sketches from the night's entertainment, including 'The Lady Juggler' and a black saxophone player.[13] A general view of the theatre's interior places Yeats in the upper circle, viewing the performance from behind a row of hats and caps. This vantage point is like that taken by Walter Sickert in his views of the Bedford Theatre, some of which are contemporary with Yeats's own theatre views. Other sketches from this period show Yeats's interest in the migrant communities of the city. A sketch of a Chinese man counting on an abacus was completed in Limehouse Causeway, an area of east London known as the original Chinatown.[14] Sketchbooks from the artist's visit to New York in 1904 further reveal his interest in Chinese and Japanese immigrant communities, with sketches encompassing a Chinese laundry and restaurant, and visual notes from an evening spent at a Japanese theatre. Along with other members of the Yeats family, the artist seems to have had a strong interest in eastern art and culture, creating, for example, two watercolours of Japanese pirates in 1901.[15] During his visit to New York, Yeats also visited Ellis Island, sketching the area where immigrants waited for their papers to be cleared before entering the United States. These sketches intimate Yeats's interest, from the very beginning of his artistic career, in and identification with those on the margins of society, a theme that would be later developed in his circus and Traveller paintings.[16]

In addition to the ample subject matter the city provided for the emerging artist, London was also central to Yeats's early exhibiting career: he first exhibited watercolours there in 1897, and oils in 1912 at the Walker Art Gallery. From 1909, he contributed on several occasions to the Allied Artists Exhibition, a venture spearheaded by the critic Frank Rutter in 1908 and supported by an impressive group of founding members which included Sickert, Paul Henry, and William Orpen. The exhibition aimed to be akin to the Salon des Indépendents or Salon d'Automne, and submissions were not subject to a hanging committee or jury. This connection to the British art market was maintained throughout his career through exhibitions at a range of commercial London galleries, including Arthur Tooth and Son, the Goupil, and the Gieves Gallery.[17] A similar course was followed on the other side of the Atlantic. Following an exhibition in New York organised by John Quinn in 1904, Yeats contributed to the landmark Armory Show in 1913, as well as to later group exhibitions such as the New York based Society of Independent Artists and at the Helen Hackett Gallery.[18]

Even before his relocation to Ireland in 1910, Yeats frequently recorded Dublin scenes and streets, with the inscriptions and shared pages suggesting that these were made as the artist passed through the city on his way to the west of Ireland, or, indeed, returning home to London or Strete, Devon. For example, in a sketchbook from 1900, labelled by the artist 'London and Strete. March and April 1900. Timber measure. Dublin', an image in crayon, ink, and graphite shows a 'rum old hairdressers near Academy (Hibernian). Very dusty and musty' (Plate 3.1). The sketch shows posters of boxers and boxing bouts lining the walls, echoing Yeats's own sketches of the Wonderland and other venues in London. A sketchbook from the following year (1901) exemplifies Yeats's sketching practice around this time, leading the viewer of its pages on a journey through the city's streets and into its theatres and cafés. Here we see the ill-fated monument of William III (Plate 3.2) on College Green, the curve of the former parliament house visible in the background, and a number of pages later, an illustration of a phonograph flanked by American and Irish flags, noted as being 'opposite King Billy's Tatoo'.[19] At the Gaiety Theatre, Douglas Hyde appears in a Gaelic League Amateur Dramatic Society of his own play, *The Twisting of the Rope*, while the audience intently watches the stage of the Mechanic Theatre, Abbey Street (later the Abbey Theatre). Advertising hoarding (Figure 3.1), an outdoor clothing market on Little Mary Street, and a funeral passing over Grattan Bridge all speak to the daily rhythms of the city, the continuing cycles of commercial and human life all viewed by the artist as he moved through the city's streets. Some sense of quiet contemplation is found in a charming interior scene of the 'DBC' (the Dublin Bread Company) café on Dame Street (Plate 3.3), while the trams and traps pass by on the street below. Located on Dame Street, the DBC appears frequently in Joyce's *Ulysses*: the scene of chess games, 'damn bad cakes', and start of the love affair between Molly Bloom and Blazes Boylan.[20]

These early sketches later served as sources for the illustrations Yeats would produce for *A Broadside*, a collaboration between the artist and his sister, Elizabeth Corbet Yeats, founder of the Cuala Press. In 1913, *The Tatooer's* [sic] *Shop on the Quays of Dublin* (Figure 3.2) appeared in the August issue of *A Broadside*, showing a man inspecting a range of tattoo designs on display in the paned window. The origins of this illustration can be found in two earlier sketchbooks dating to 1901 and 1903.[21] Little is known about the history of tattooing in Dublin, although the presence of tattoo establishments in the city is not surprising given its connections to maritime history. In 1901, a small advertisement in

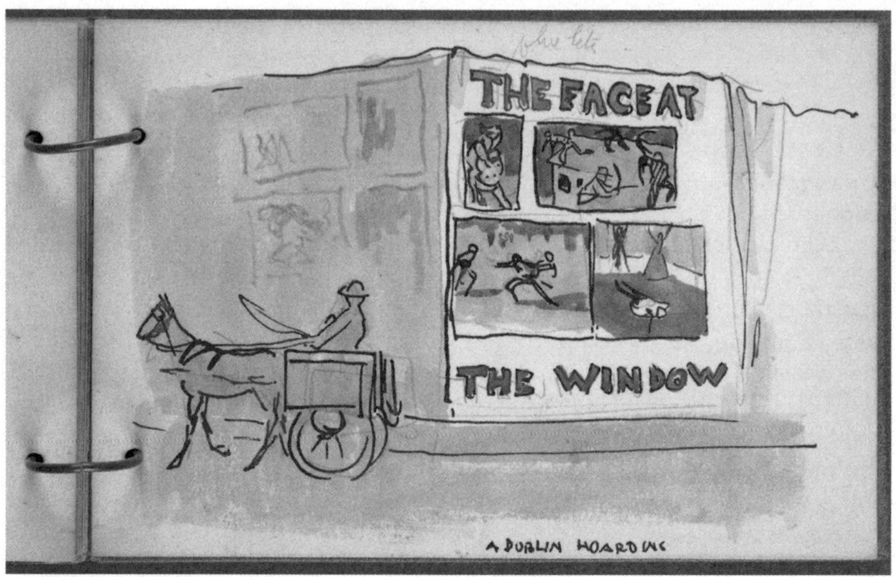

3.1   Jack Butler Yeats, *A Dublin Hoarding*, 1901.

the *Dublin Evening Herald* invited 'Gentlemen, wishing to be Tattooed in all shades would find it worth a visit to Prof. Kilbride, 27 Lower Ormond quay'.[22] The range of tattoo designs depicted in Yeats's sketches is quite extensive, with designs for dragons and examples of leg sleeve and full back tattoos. The images seen in the shop window also include a desert island, a matador in action, and a woman holding a fan. In the *Broadside* illustration, the expression and stance of the onlooker, although he his encumbered with newspapers and other items, suggests some satisfaction with the contents of the tattoo parlour's window. In the 1901 sketch of a 'tattoing [*sic*] saloon' on the quays, an image of a ship has been placed in the centre of the window, alongside a notice proclaiming the shop 'open on Sundays': this image and the flexible opening hours underline the trade's connection to the busy port, and the dockers who worked there.

The relationship between the city, its port, and the wider world is also suggested in another of Yeats's illustrations for *A Broadside*. Published in October 1914, *The Dublin Quays* (Figure 3.3) shows a docker on the quay. Beside him, a ship with a large figurehead of a South Asian man offers an exotic contrast to the sparse background of houses and a lone industrial chimney. Once again, the origin of this image can be found among the artist's sketchbooks. In 1908, two graphite and watercolour drawings show the ship 'Barcore' moored at the dockside, with the second drawing focusing on the figurehead (Plate 3.4). Partially coloured, the artist also noted details such as the gold star placed on the figure's turban, the gold dagger tucked into his red sash, and the green pistol placed in his hand. Although the *Broadside* drawing captures a quiet moment

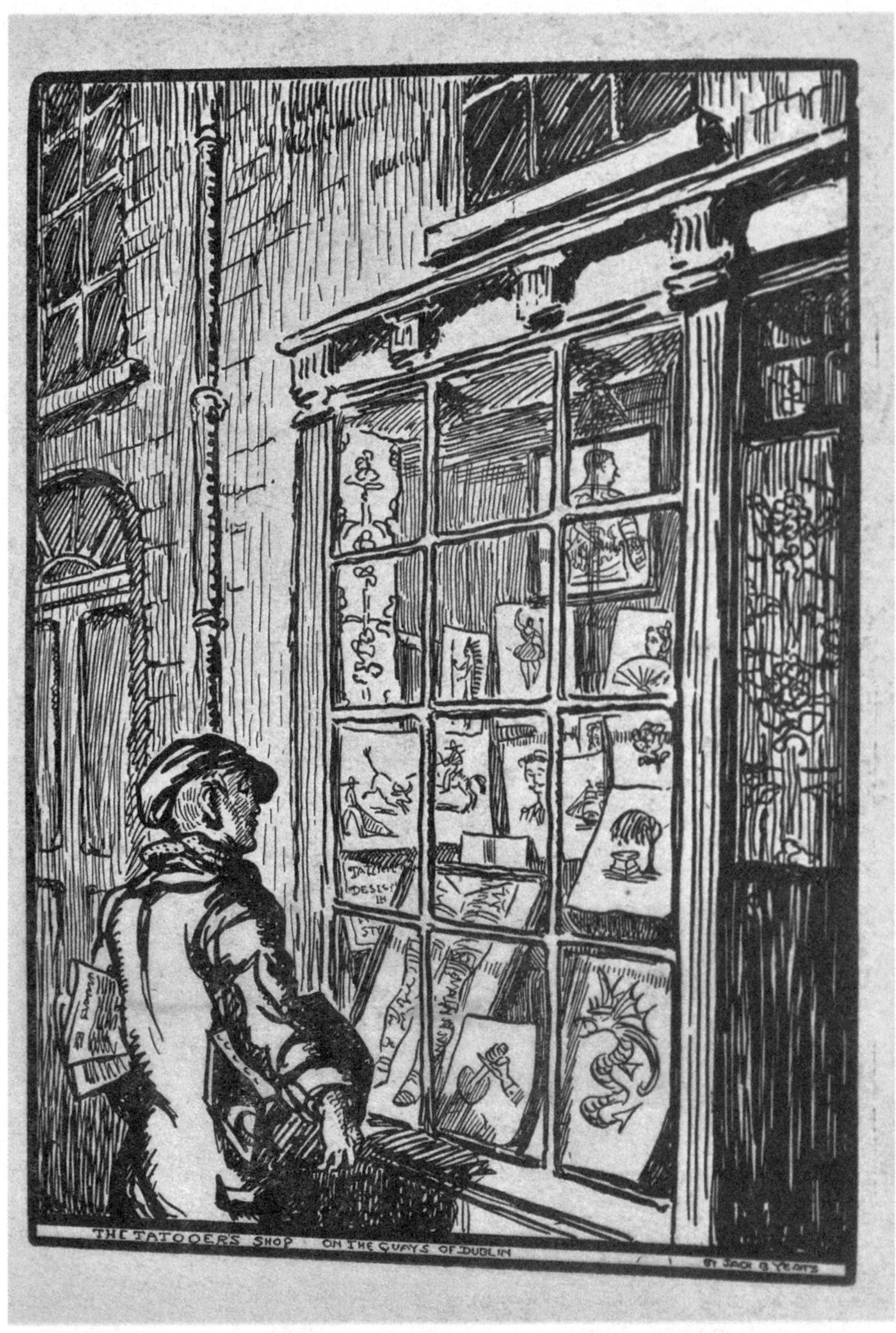

3.2   Jack Butler Yeats, *The Tatooer's Shop on the Quays of Dublin*, from *A Broadside*, August 1913.

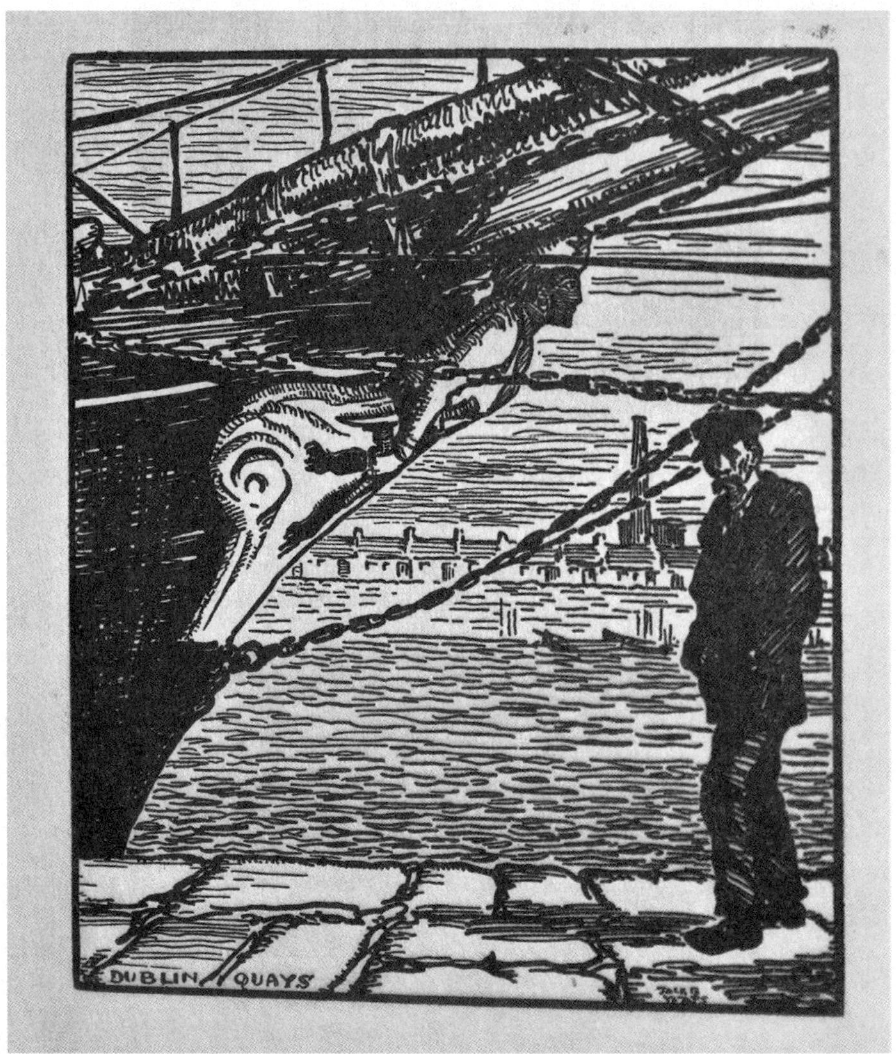

3.3   Jack Butler Yeats, *The Dublin Quays*, from *A Broadside*, October 1914.

on the usually busy quays, the figurehead acts as a cipher for the shipping trade which connected Dublin to the world. The excitement and bustle of the port was captured by Joyce in 'An Encounter', when the narrator and his friends sit and watch a vessel being unloaded, and imagine how 'it would be a right skit to run away to sea on one of those big ships and even I, looking at the high masts, saw or imagined the geography which had been scantily dosed to me at school gradually taking substance under my eyes'.[23] In this story, this sense of the world outside of Ireland's shores is also evoked through reference to the 'wild west' and the boys' re-enactments of battles in Joe Dillon's back garden. Here again we find a thematic chime between Yeats and Joyce: the artist's sketchbooks and library reveal his longstanding interest in stories of indigenous Americans, their depiction in advertising in Ireland, Britain, and America and in the touring Buffalo Bill entertainment. Through these early sketchbooks and prints, Yeats offers the viewer a glimpse into a city of possibilities, of colliding worlds, and everyday activities and routines. Their illustrative nature reflected his interest in that format, but also pre-figure his early oil paintings of Dublin.

'Life above everything': quotidian Dublin

In 1924, Walter Sickert wrote a short note to Yeats following his visit to the younger artist's exhibition at the Gieves Art Gallery, London: 'Forgive me for saying that I think your exhibition superb,' he wrote, 'It fulfils my theory that there can be modern paintings. Life above everything.'[24] The older artist was so taken with Yeats's work that he further expounded on it at a lecture at the Royal Institution, focusing on *A Westerly Wind* (Plate 3.5). He noted that:

> there is a jaunting car with a child in it. The centre of the focus is the child's inspired little face and golden hair, its eyes full of wonder. Behind it, and seen though one were looking at the child, is a luminous street scene, and integral part of the whole composition.[25]

This painting returns to the setting of Osborne's *Dublin Streets: A Vendor of Books*, although in his composition Yeats turns towards the Ha'penny Bridge and the Four Courts, rather than O'Connell Bridge and the Custom House. Completed in the early 1920s, the streetscape has changed significantly since the 1880s. The uneven, dirty cobblestones and paving have been replaced or repaired; a tramline and a row of new saplings now run along the quay. Osborne's top-hatted coachman has been replaced by an idle jarvey, and instead of browsing a stall of second-hand books, city-dwellers gaze into smart shop windows. The dress of a woman just beyond the jarvey shows the changes that have taken place in women's fashion, with the hem length rising to mid-calf and a loose silhouette, unrestricted by corsetry or a heavy shawl. Overall, this painting gives an impression of a quietly urbane city space – the blue grey tones lend a calm atmosphere to the composition, and the long shadows suggest evening summer sunlight. The promenading couples and the jarvey's interaction with a passing dog further imply a gentle and relaxed pace of life. *A Westerly Wind* suggests that even among the social issues and political upheaval of the time, everyday urban life continued and there was space for quiet contemplation and enjoyment of the city in early 1920s Dublin. However, Sickert's emphasis on the figure of the child once again returns us to the repeated use of this figure in urban paintings. While the golden-haired figure atop the jaunting car has a dreamlike quality, several other depictions of Dublin's children by Yeats return to and develop the motif of the 'ragged child', as seen in nineteenth-century depictions of the city.

By 1924, Yeats had largely moved away from the watercolour sketches previously discussed, although many oil paintings from this time retain an illustrative style. From the 1910s, watercolour largely disappears from the sketchbooks, replaced only with quick graphite notations and compositional outlines. Yeats continued to use these books as sources to develop new artworks long after he first made the initial sketch: for example, *Bachelor's Walk, In Memory* (Plate 3.6) continued a subject first sketched by the artist in July 1914 and that of an illustration published in *A Broadside* in February 1915. The sketch depicts a gateway, with several flowers lying at its base. The headline inscription reads, 'where the people were shot on Sunday', with a longer notion recording that 'a few paces further towards O'Connell Bridge, flower girls had thrown flowers. I suppose one of those killed fell there.'[26] The subject of the sketch, and the later iterations, relates to the events of the previous day when a detachment of the King's Own Scottish Borderers, intercepting a group of Volunteers transporting arms from Howth, opened fire on the crowd gathered on the quay, killing three people and injuring over thirty. The painting, created in 1915 but not exhibited until 1922, is characteristic of Yeats's early work in the medium: the colours are muted, reminiscent of Sickert, and the thick black outlines recall his graphic illustrations. The central subject of the painting is a young woman, a flower seller wrapped in a thick woollen shawl, who lays flowers at a gateway – transposed from Yeats's initial sketch of the scene. Beside this ordinary yet elegant figure, a barefoot boy gazes out of the canvas. The artist later recalled the instance of witnessing this scene in a newspaper interview, saying: 'some of our fellows had been shot along the quay here. A common flower woman, passing with a basket of carnations, dropped one or two of them as a memory-offering on the spot where one fell. They were her stock-in-trade, and I thought it a noble action.'[27]

Given the subject on which *Bachelor's Walk* is based, it is understandable that to date, the painting has largely been interpreted as a deeply political painting: used as a 'nationalist ikon [*sic*]', and understood as Yeats's 'first major contemporary historical painting'.[28] Similarly, historian Roy Foster described the depiction of the boy and woman as symbolic of the 'future and renewal after sacrificial death: unconsciously predicting the aftermath of the Easter Rising a year later'.[29] Yet Yeats's own comments suggest that he did not see it in these terms, focusing instead on the actions of the flower seller and his observation of the scene. An alternative reading of this painting can also be proposed: namely that it is a painting of the city which draws on established tropes of urban representation. As Sickert would later note in relation to *A Westerly Wind*, Yeats presents active figures within the urban landscape. Behind the boy and flower seller, two further figures populate and add movement to the composition. Alongside them, a horse and trap make their way out of the city, with the bright sunlight casting a strong shadow on the cobbled street while on the right-hand side of the canvas a hodgepodge of notices and advertisements cover the wall, with their gaudy colours reflected on the damp pavement. As previously discussed in relation to Osborne's urban paintings, the figure of the flower seller in an urban context has a long history, being seen, for example, as a representation of pastoralism or understood in terms of a clear class binary. Similarly, the motif of the ragged child also pervades urban imagery, and in addition to its perceived allegorical meaning, the barefoot boy in *Bachelor's Walk* connects Yeats to a strand of the urban picturesque, visualising the pervasive attitude towards impoverished children that focused more on morality and aesthetics than practical help for the city's poor. By bringing these elements together (that is, the flower seller and ragged child, fellow travellers in the city, and the advertisements), Yeats offers the viewer a panoply of urban themes that link the painting to a wider tradition: for every reading of the painting as a political comment, or as having a particular relevance to the visualisation of Irish national identity, it can also be seen as a snapshot of the concerns of urban painting in the early twentieth century.

While the Democratic Programme for the First Dáil enshrined a child's right to food, clothing, shelter, and education, the reality of childhood in the revolutionary period and subsequent Irish Free State was radically different, particularly for children trapped in poverty. In most respects, the arrival of political independence did nothing to improve the lot of Dublin's impoverished children: rates of poverty remained high, and the lack of adequate housing for the city's poor and working classes had yet to be properly addressed.[30] Viewed together, *Dublin Newsboys* (1923, oil on panel, private collection) and *In Capel Street* (Plate 3.7) make for an interesting study. Both paintings are small in scale, measuring just 23 × 35.5 cm, and were shown together in an exhibition at the Stephen's Green Gallery in 1923.[31] In the 1920s, Dublin's newspaper sellers were a sizable working-class presence and played their own role in the social and political strife in the city during the revolutionary period.[32] Depictions of news sellers appear in Yeats's sketchbooks from the early 1900s, with the artist's notations often drawing attention to the children's lack of appropriate clothing given the fact that they were expected to be out in all weather. *Dublin Newsboys* depicts the interior of one of the city's public houses, and two boys are seen in their characteristic caps. The four men at the bar appear to ignore the children, continuing with their conversations, like the men browsing in Osborne's *Vendor of Books*. The boy in the foreground, who appears older than the barefoot child leaving through the door behind, looks out past the viewer, perhaps to a potential customer elsewhere in the bar. While first exhibited by Yeats in 1923, the painting has its origin in a sketch made by the artist some twenty years earlier. Worked in graphite and lightly coloured with brown watercolour, Yeats notes that the scene depicts 'barefoot news boy [sic] in the swell lounge': two boys proffer newspapers to the lounge's customers, with the attitude of the man at the bar anticipating that seen in the oil painting.[33] *In Capel Street* is a more poignant imaging of childhood in the city, showing a young girl sitting in a doorway, holding a baby. She is placed between a basket of flowers (suggesting that she also finds work as a flower seller) and the window of a sweetshop – a site often associated with children or used to evoke memories of a happy childhood. Around her, the street is strewn with litter, a fact almost emphasised by her proximity to it. The relationship between the girl and the baby is ambiguous: is she a young mother, or an older sibling tasked with the care of the infant?

Reviews of the exhibition were included in the main Irish newspapers in circulation at the time; however, only the *Irish Independent* commented on these two paintings.[34] Noting *Dublin Newsboys*, the author of the piece described it as showing 'a couple of youthful followers of that occupation … pursuing their operations in a drinking parlour. The triumphant strut of the boy who is leaving would seem to suggest that he had got there first and had left very little trade for the other newspaper sellers.'[35] While the genre and narrative element of *Dublin Newsboys* was praised, it was the colour and technique of *In Capel Street* that drew comment: 'on the opposite wall is a small picture in which the artist shows his power of manipulating colour. It represents a flower seller seated on a doorstep in Capel Street, Dublin, with a baby on her lap and a basket of flowers beside her. It is excellently painted.'[36] These reviews suggest that Yeats's depiction of children continued to be seen in similar terms as those by Osborne were in the nineteenth century, with the visual enjoyment and pathos of the scenes praised over the lived reality which they depicted. The familiarity of the reviewers and members of the public with newspaper sellers and other impoverished children cannot be denied. A further interesting correlation between Yeats's sketches and paintings can now be found in the recently digitised footage of British Pathé newsreels. For example, a reel from 1922 showing crowds of people waiting to attend the lying-in-state of Michael Collins includes several shots of newspaper sellers and other children moving through the crowds, often making direct eye contact with the camera as it takes in the spectacle.[37]

In addition to linking Yeats to the preceding generation of urban painters, we can also view his depiction of Dublin in the late 1910s and into the 1920s alongside a group of American artists who also made the city their subject. During the Progressive Era (1895–1917) urban culture had flourished in America, as Yeats himself had witnessed during his stay in New York in 1904. A group of artists based in that city, now known as the Ashcan School, epitomised the type of urban painting being produced through the early decades of the twentieth century. The Ashcan painters came to prominence in 1908, although their work was seen by some critics as conservative and derived from French Impressionism.[38] For Zurier, the Ashcan artists 'sought to locate beauty in the everyday and among the working classes', and their paintings show urban scenes that resonate with Yeats's depictions of Dublin, representing, for instance, streets, parks, shops and stalls, and urban entertainments such as boxing matches, cinemas, and theatres.[39] Like Yeats, many of the painters associated with the Ashcan School, such as George Bellows, Robert Henri, John Sloan, George Luks, and William J. Glackens, had begun their careers as illustrators working for newspapers and other publications, with several based in Philadelphia. Henri brought the group together in New York in 1907–08, when they exhibited together as 'The Eight'.[40] The connection with illustration not only illuminates the link between Yeats and the Ashcan artists, but also finds a correlation with artists such as Luke Fildes and Frank Holl in nineteenth-century Britain.[41] When Yeats's father, John B. Yeats, relocated to New York in 1908, he became friendly with both Henri and Sloan. In 1910, Sloan painted himself alongside John Yeats in the garden of the Petitpas' boarding house in a work simply titled *Yeats at Petitpas'* (oil on canvas, 1910/c.1914, National Gallery of Art, Washington). From their extant letters, Sloan was particularly close to John, a curious friendship given that Sloan was so much younger than the elder Yeats: in fact, he was an exact contemporary of Jack's – the two younger artists being born within twenty days of each other in August 1871. While it is unclear whether Jack met any of the artists that would go on to form the Ashcan School, it is possible that he maintained some contact with them due to his father's personal friendship: their contact details also appear in his address book.[42]

Molly S. Hutton has further explored the relationship between Sloan's journeys through New York, his diaries and sketchbooks, and his paintings of the city. Sloan's paintings, Hutton argues, represent both the artist's personal need to 'continually locate himself within the urban fabric' and to represent a more general urban experience.[43] The artist achieved this by placing the viewer at street level, inviting them to observe the scene from the same perspective of the artist, but also maintaining a sense of distance between the viewer and subject. An impetus to walk, to map, and to represent the city came from the artists' late arrival in New York from their hometowns, making them both tourist and local, and seeking a way to better understand their new surroundings. The *flânerie* of Sloan and the other Ashcan painters, Hutton suggests, enabled them to create a 'modern painting that somehow managed to eschew Modernist style', and this resonates particularly well with Yeats's painting in the early 1920s.[44] Movement, or circulation, through the city was at the heart of the Ashcan painters' urban vision, a theme further explored by Yeats in his representation of the River Liffey and Dublin's public transport network.

Circulation: the river

Undoubtedly Yeats's best-known painting of Dublin from the 1920s is *The Liffey Swim* (Plate 3.8), painted and exhibited in 1923, and which came to public prominence in 1924 when it was awarded a silver medal at the Paris Olympics. When exhibited at the RHA in 1925, the *Irish Times* commented that the 'charm of the picture is in the people, those men and women of ordinary life to whom Mr Yeats gives life on canvas'.[45] Previously described as 'a significant attempt to represent a new kind of capital city, one that is willing to move on from the division of previous years, and indeed, previous centuries', the colourful depiction of the crowds enjoying the spectacle of the race contrasts strongly to the black and white photographs of the destroyed city which had circulated during the revolutionary period.[46] Among the crowd, a newspaper boy in a green cap leans forward to catch a glimpse of the swimmers, with his bundle of papers depicted in broad strokes of off-white and grey. Through this figure, Yeats represents once more one of the more mobile types of the Dublin citizenry and one that was immediately recognisable to any urban viewer, regardless of location.

Looking at the composition of this painting more broadly, we see that mobility and movement are encoded into its very fabric: the swimmers themselves move against the motion of the tide; the raised leg and moving skirt of the woman in a yellow hat suggest that she has rushed to the scene, while beside her a bicycle attempts to push through the crowd. Another form of transport is more conspicuous: dotted along Bachelor's Walk and O'Connell Bridge are three double-decker trams, with the trolley on the left-hand side of the painting shown in some detail. Filled on both levels with passengers, the tram has been transformed into a mobile viewing platform for the race, replete with hats, furs, and faces pressed against glass, as well as the suggestion of advertising along the sideboard. A similar sense of immersion within a fast-paced urban environment is found in *Dublin Night* (1925, oil on panel, Birmingham Museums Trust). Once more, the viewer of the painting is placed among those walking on the street: standing behind two onlookers, we see a newspaper boy, with his distinctive cap and armful of papers, and a non-descript man in black. Beyond these figures, three modes of transport move through the city: to the left, a figure in brown-grey clothing boards a full tram filled with yellow light; in the centre, a horse-drawn carriage appears to be in full movement, while to the right, a woman sits on an open jaunting car.

Returning to the river, Tricia Cusack has noted that throughout history, these bodies of water have 'been associated with fertility and regeneration and also with destructiveness when they transgress their edges'.[47] While Cusack has also considered Yeats's depiction of the River Shannon, little attention has been paid to the representation of the Liffey.[48] In Dublin's landscape, as in many other cities, the river is a defining feature, dividing the city's core but also providing employment and industry through its docks and port. Elsewhere, Cusack further notes that as they are 'often the site of social-cultural as well as a geographical divide', rivers can be considered as liminal, allied to the notion of a 'boundaried interstitial space and time in which subjects slough off their habitual identity but have not yet acquired one marking entry to a new social status'.[49] This conceptual reading of the river offers a useful context for a number of Yeats's Liffey paintings, opening them up to a more symbolic and nuanced reading; moving away from the depiction of particular events or spaces, to think more broadly about how the river shapes the geography of the city and the internal world of Dublin's citizens. In nineteenth-century urban painting, particularly in depictions of London, the river was often seen as a site of danger, the last refuge of the desperate, as in George Frederic Watts's *Found Drowned* (oil on canvas, 1848–50, Watts Gallery), or as an industrial, imperial space; for example, in George Vicat Cole's *The Pool of London* (1888, oil on canvas, Tate). In contrast to the might of the Thames, the Liffey was generally characterised as foul-smelling and meandering in nineteenth and twentieth century texts: Egerton described it as 'malodorous … [running] in a sluggish stream in the middle, with stretches of slime on each side'.[50] Yet, as discussed elsewhere in this chapter, it was also the gateway to a world of trade and adventure.

Yeats frequently turned to the bridges which crossed the water, presenting Dubliners in the act of crossing the river; being quite literally 'in-between' the formalised spaces of the city. As with the series of tram paintings discussed later in this chapter, these works also engage with the themes of mobility and movement, of being part of an urban crowd, even if feelings of loneliness and isolation pervade. In *O'Connell Bridge* (1925, oil on canvas, Pyms Gallery), the artist reverses the scene portrayed in *The Liffey Swim* and presents the view facing back towards the Ha'penny Bridge. The arch of this landmark structure can be seen in the distance: the thickly painted blue water, conveyed through broad strokes of rich blue and black seems to rise threateningly between the bridges and the quay walls. A surrealist note is added to the painting through the disparity between the inky black water, quays, and touches of yellow light – all of which suggest an evening setting – and the white and blue sky. On both sides of the river, patches of red and gold suggest brightly lit shop fronts, while in the foreground several figures cross the bridge. The eye is immediately drawn to the face of the woman on the left-hand side, worked in vivid yellow, further suggestive of electric illumination. The yellow light also stretches over the hat of the man beside her, while to his left a more unusual figure appears, dressed in a similar hat and coat but with his face rendered in black paint. Turning slightly, this figure looks directly into the face of the other man: Yeats's depiction of this figure is ambiguous, and it is unclear to the viewer whether this man is black, or whether the difference in skin tone is due to the surreal lighting of the composition more broadly. If the former, this painting stands as a rare suggestion of racial diversity in 1920s Dublin.

The surging force of the ink-blue river in *O'Connell Bridge* pre-empts the richly worked surface of *Crossing the Metal Bridge* (Plate 3.9). Mirroring Yeats's repetition and reuse of scenes recorded in sketchbooks, this painting reworks an earlier composition in oils exhibited by the artist in both Dublin and London. When *From the Metal Bridge* (1923, oil on panel, private collection) was shown at 7 Stephen's Green in 1923, the *Irish Independent* described the work as giving 'a realistic view of the Liffey',[51] while the following year the *Freeman's Journal* praised the artist's 'discovery of the pictorial qualities of life in Dublin', and admired 'the dark river seen from the railings of the Metal Bridge at night with the glare of lamps'. Together with *A Westerly Wind*, the reviewer felt that these paintings revealed 'a character in Dublin that no other city possesses'.[52] The reworking of the composition to include a lone woman invites a more symbolic interpretation of the work instead of a more straightforward cityscape. Looking out over the dark railings towards the water and O'Connell Bridge, her pose suggests sorrow or wistfulness, and while her bobbed hair again references contemporary styles, her black coat or cloak gives no further suggestion of her personal circumstances. The sense of introspection and loneliness which surrounds the figure calls to mind Thomas Graham's earlier painting, *Alone in London* (c.1904, oil on canvas, Perth Museum and Art Gallery), which shows a lone woman leaning on the quay wall, contemplating Waterloo Bridge: a scene which suggested a fate 'which would have been obvious to contemporary viewers, long accustomed to Waterloo Bridge … as a symbol for the suicide of tainted women'.[53] Roughly contemporary with *Flower Girl, Dublin*, with both figures depicted in similar fashions, this painting invites the viewer to consider the fate of women who found themselves in difficult circumstances in 1920s Dublin: for many viewers of the painting, the further reference to a specific urban trope may also have been evident.

Crossing the Metal Bridge was included in an exhibition of Yeats's work in London in 1928, but the *Irish Times* London correspondent singled out another Liffey painting for praise in their review. Describing *Lingering Sun, O'Connell Bridge* (1926, oil on canvas, private collection) they wrote that it 'charmingly depicts the evening skies, with the faint blues, greys and yellows'.[54] Indeed, the sky is easily the most charming and colourful section of the painting, as the city beneath it is shown in grey and black, with only occasional dabs of white and yellow. In this painting, Yeats returns to Aston Quay, a setting discussed earlier in relation to *A Westerly Wind*. In this painting, Yeats includes O'Connell Bridge, and depicts people, a tram, and a horse and cart moving through the city. Figures rest against the quay wall and at the corner of the quay and the bridge, a flower seller is suggested through the inclusion of a seated figure and yellow flowers to one side. Perhaps the most striking inclusion in the painting is the woman in the foreground on the right-hand side. Wrapped in a black shawl, the woman's face is gaunt, and her blue eyes evade the viewer, looking instead towards the quayside shops. The contrast between light and dark in this painting is also striking in a similar manner to *O'Connell Bridge*: the sky suggests a daytime setting, yet the streetlight shines brightly.

If the Shannon, and Yeats's depiction of it, was representative of the forging of national identity, how then should we understand the artist's depiction of the Liffey? Like its western sister, the Liffey is not without its own mythology, but its purpose and presence were more strongly connected to the maritime connections between the city and its trading partners – as shown by Joyce in 'An Encounter'. For Dubliners, the river was a site of employment and occasional leisure, but also the site of tragic accidents and death. It is notable that in his depiction of Dublin, Yeats rarely strayed beyond the quays which flanked the river, save for the occasional visit to Croke Park, yet the thoroughfares of O'Connell or Henry Street, or the tenements of Mountjoy Square, Henrietta Street, or Dominick Street do not feature in his urban oeuvre. Over the course of the 1920s, Yeats's view of the Liffey was transformed from the largely positive view depicted in *The Liffey Swim*, with its sense of momentum and community, to the isolated and murky canvases of *Crossing the Metal Bridge* and *Lingering Sun*. Returning to Cusack's identification of the river as a place where subjects could

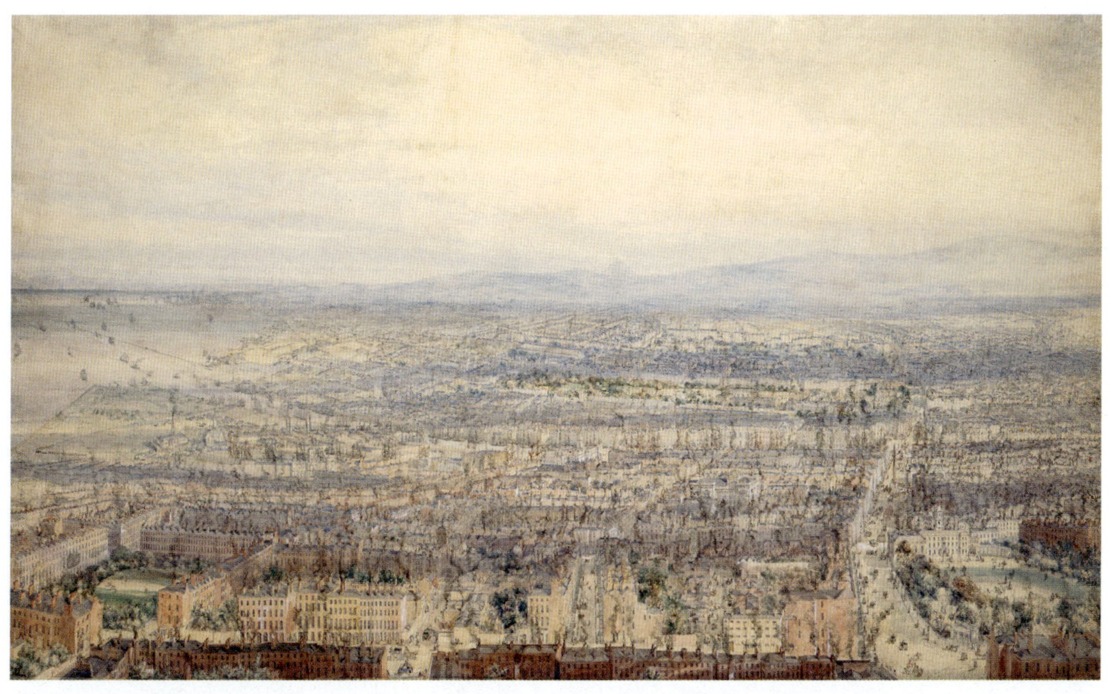

0.1   James Mahony, *Dublin from the Spire of Saint George's Church, Hardwicke Place*, 1854

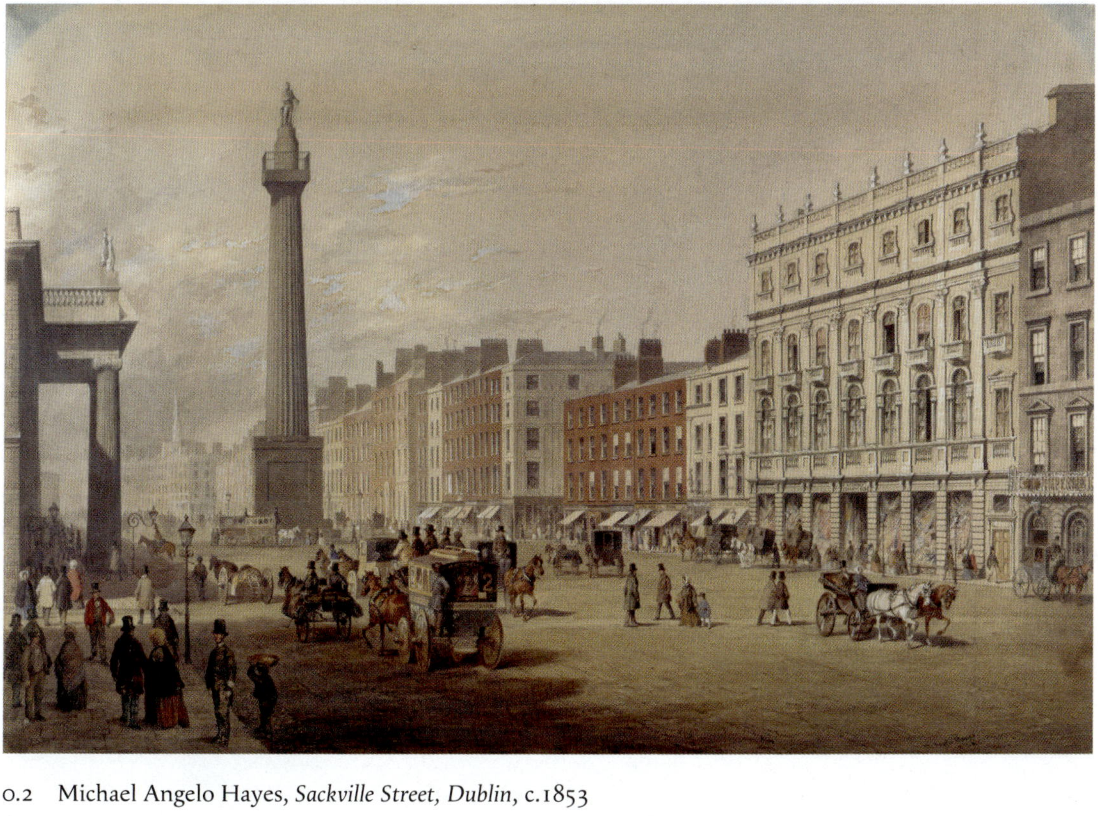

0.2   Michael Angelo Hayes, *Sackville Street, Dublin*, c.1853

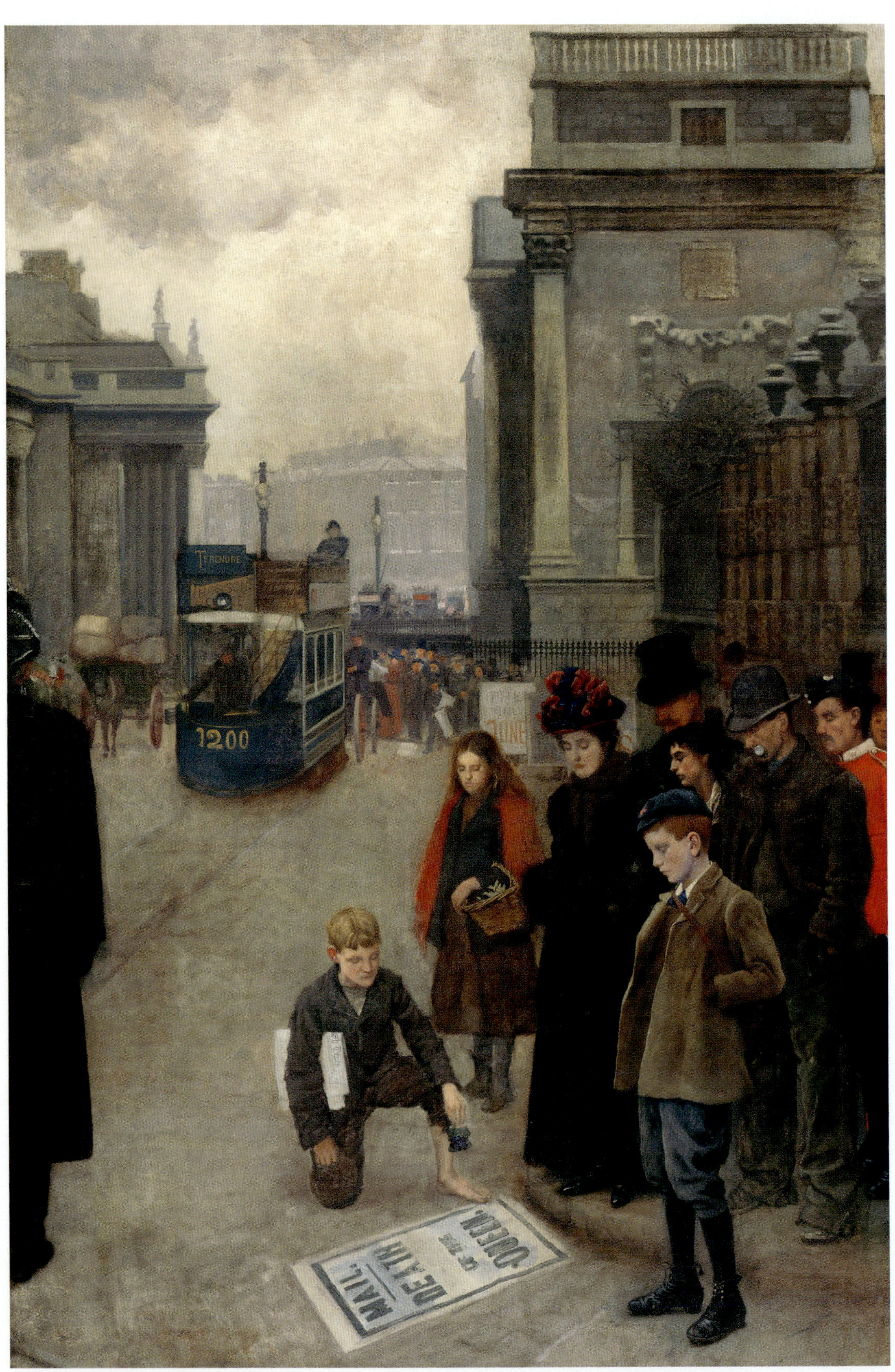

0.3   Richard Thomas Moynan, *The Death of the Queen*, c.1901

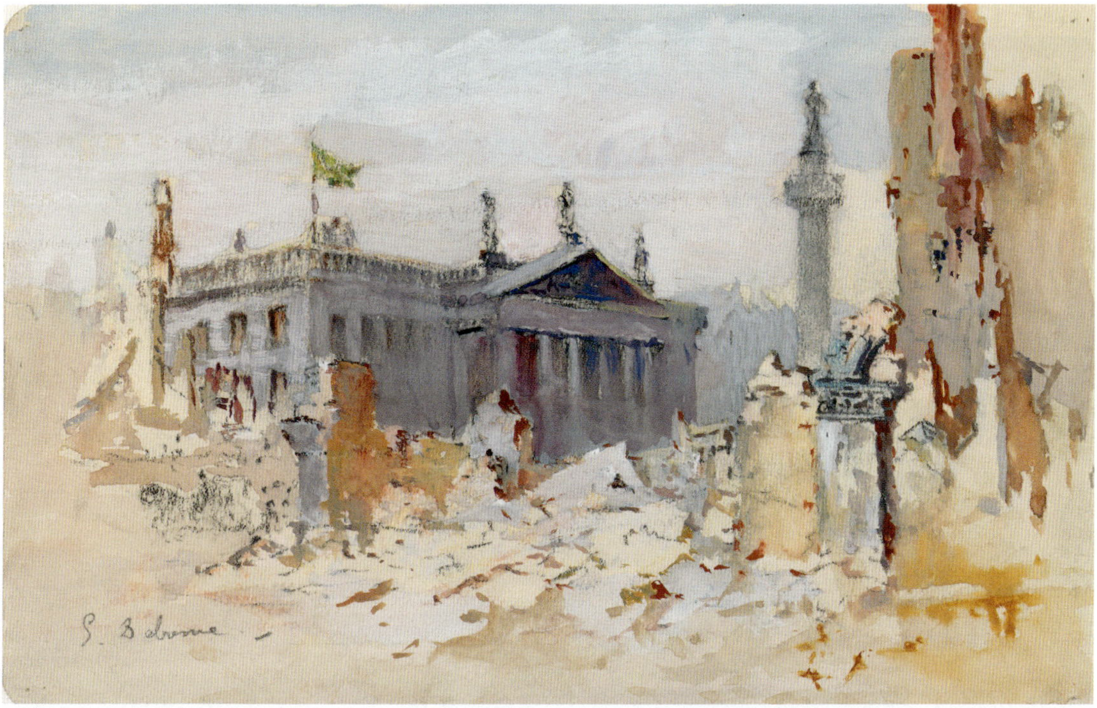

0.4   Edmond Delrenne, *Sackville Street in Ruins*, 1916

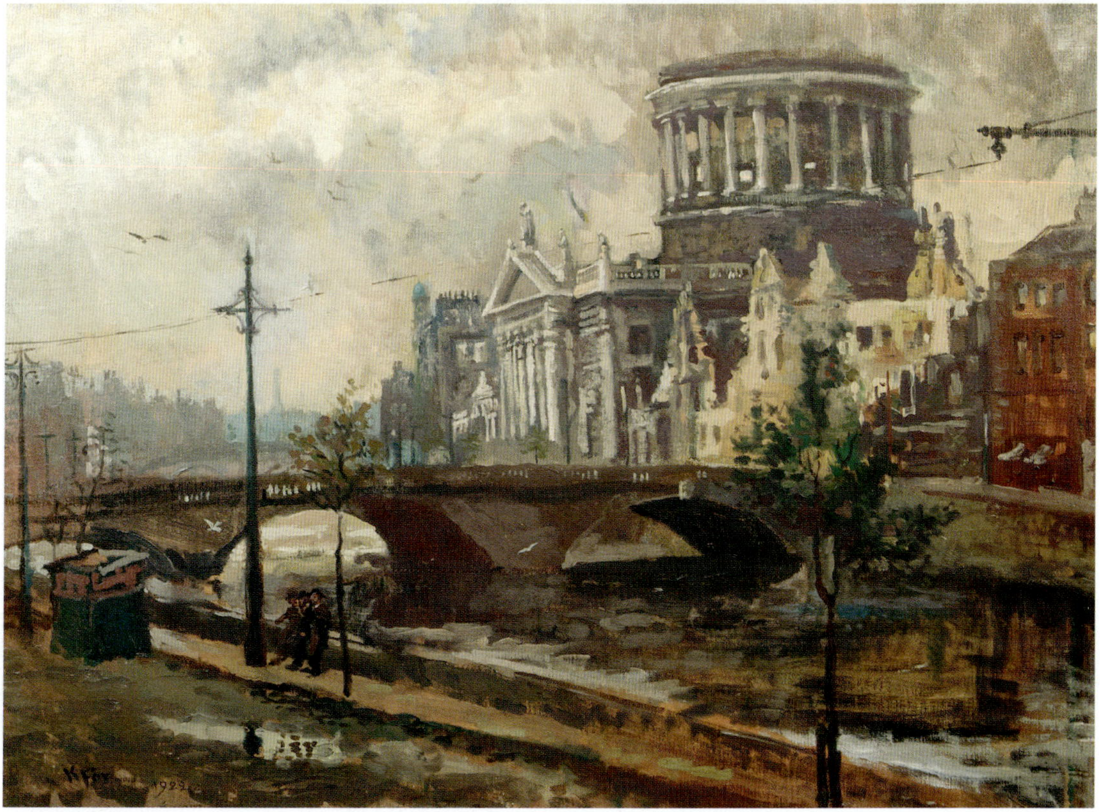

0.5   Kathleen Fox, *The Ruins of the Four Courts*, 1922

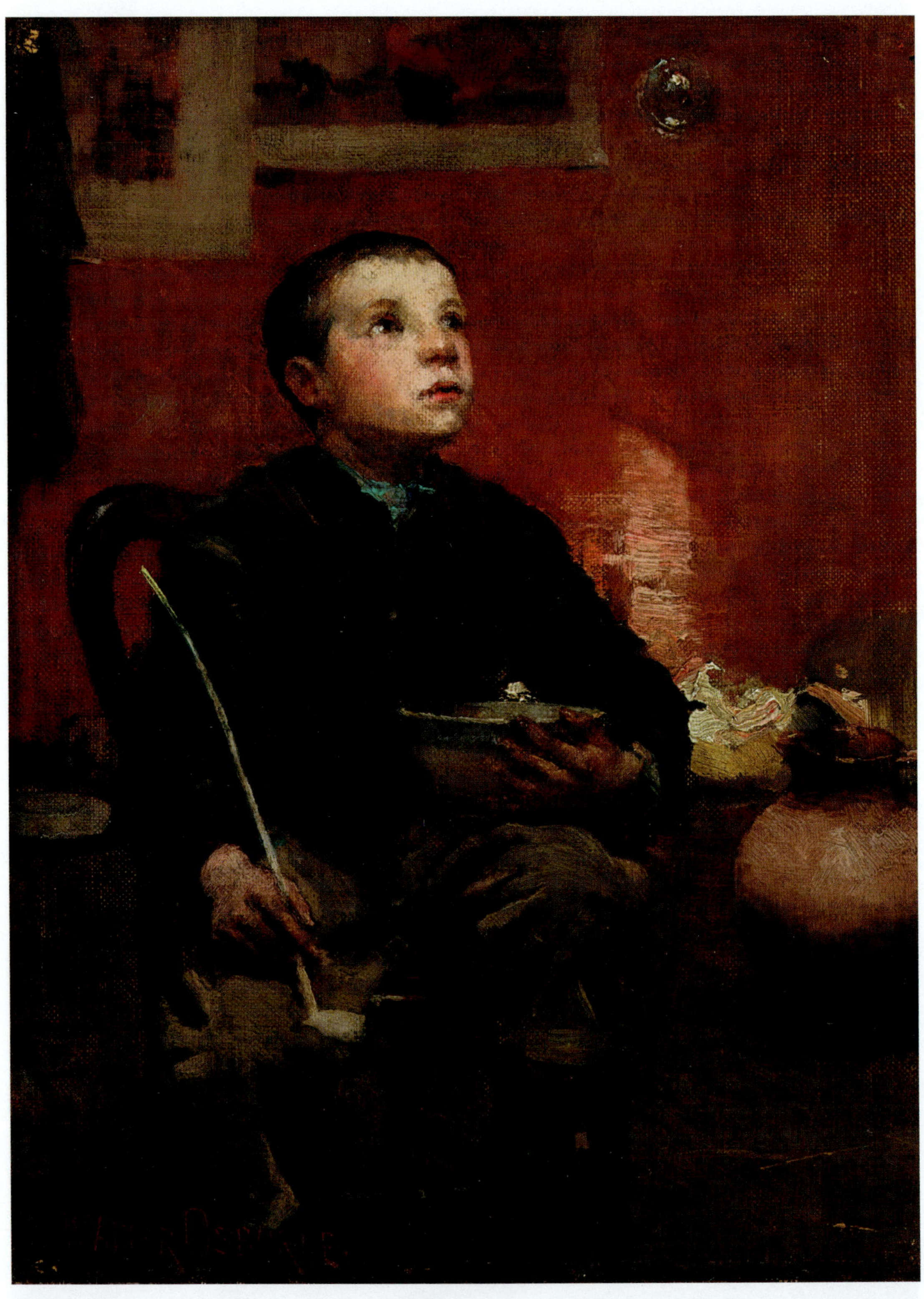

1.1   Walter Frederick Osborne, *A Boy Blowing Bubbles*

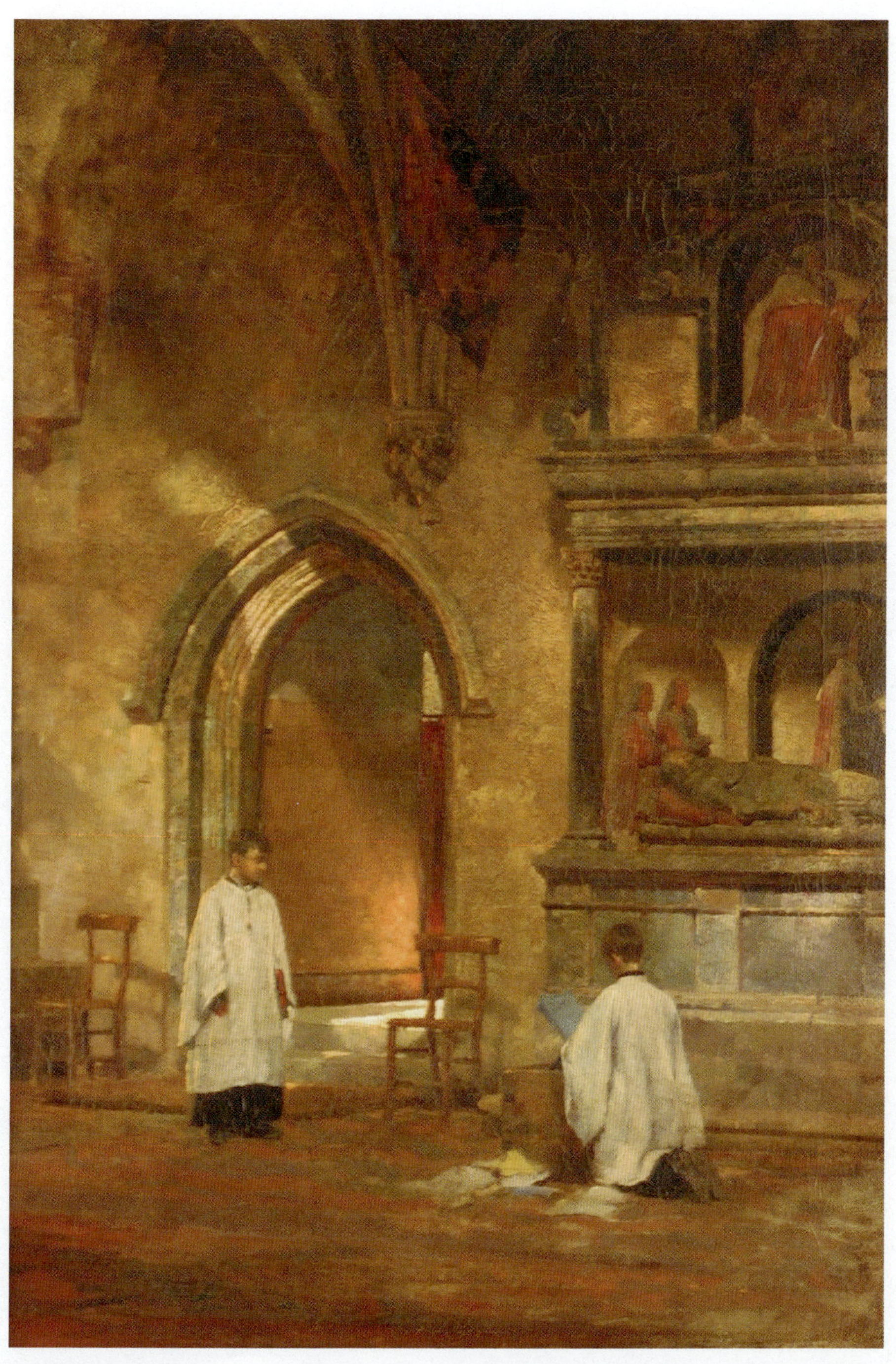

1.2   Walter Frederick Osborne, *Interior, St Patrick's Cathedral, Dublin*

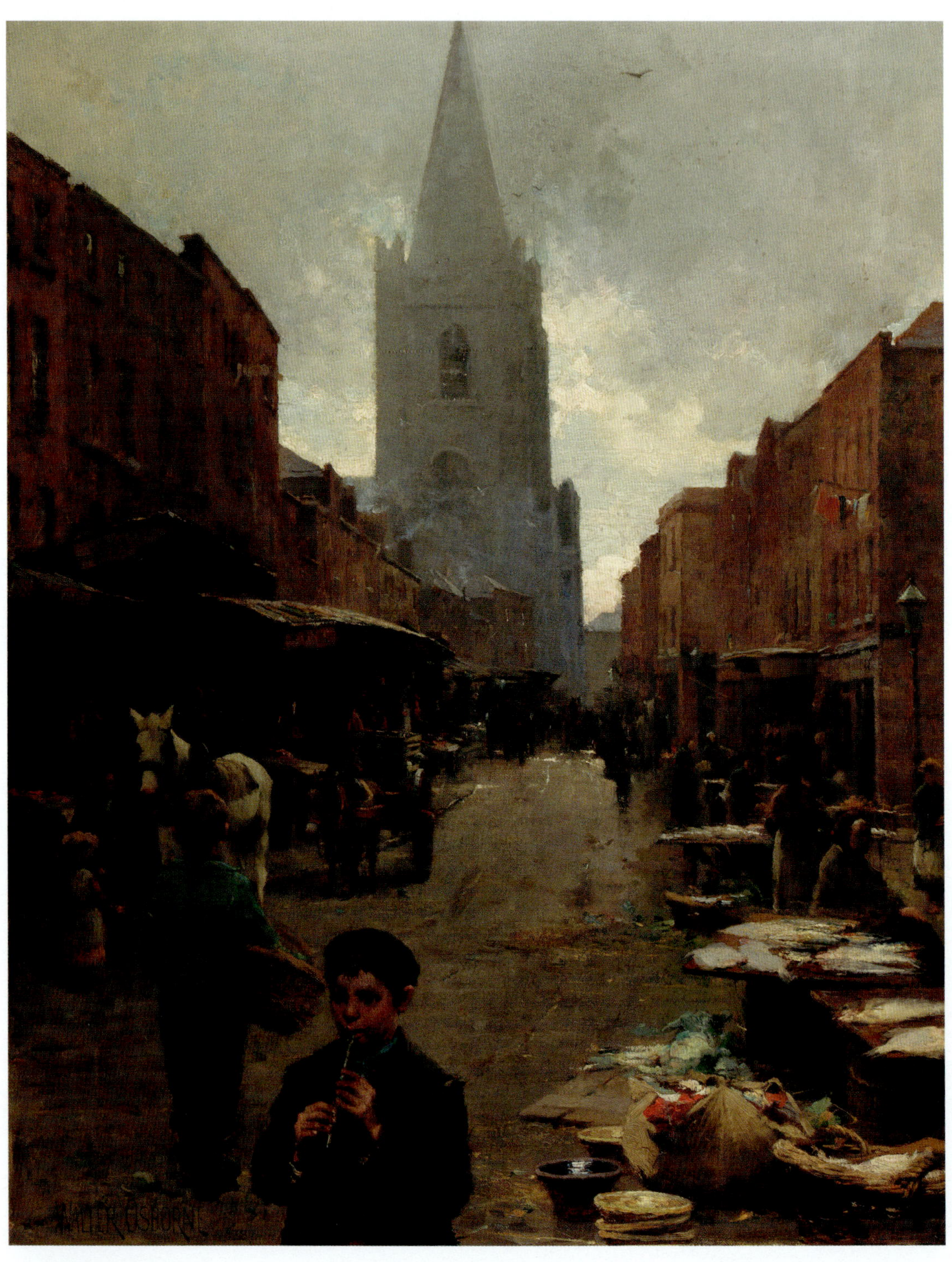

1.3   Walter Frederick Osborne, *Saint Patrick's Close, Dublin*, 1887

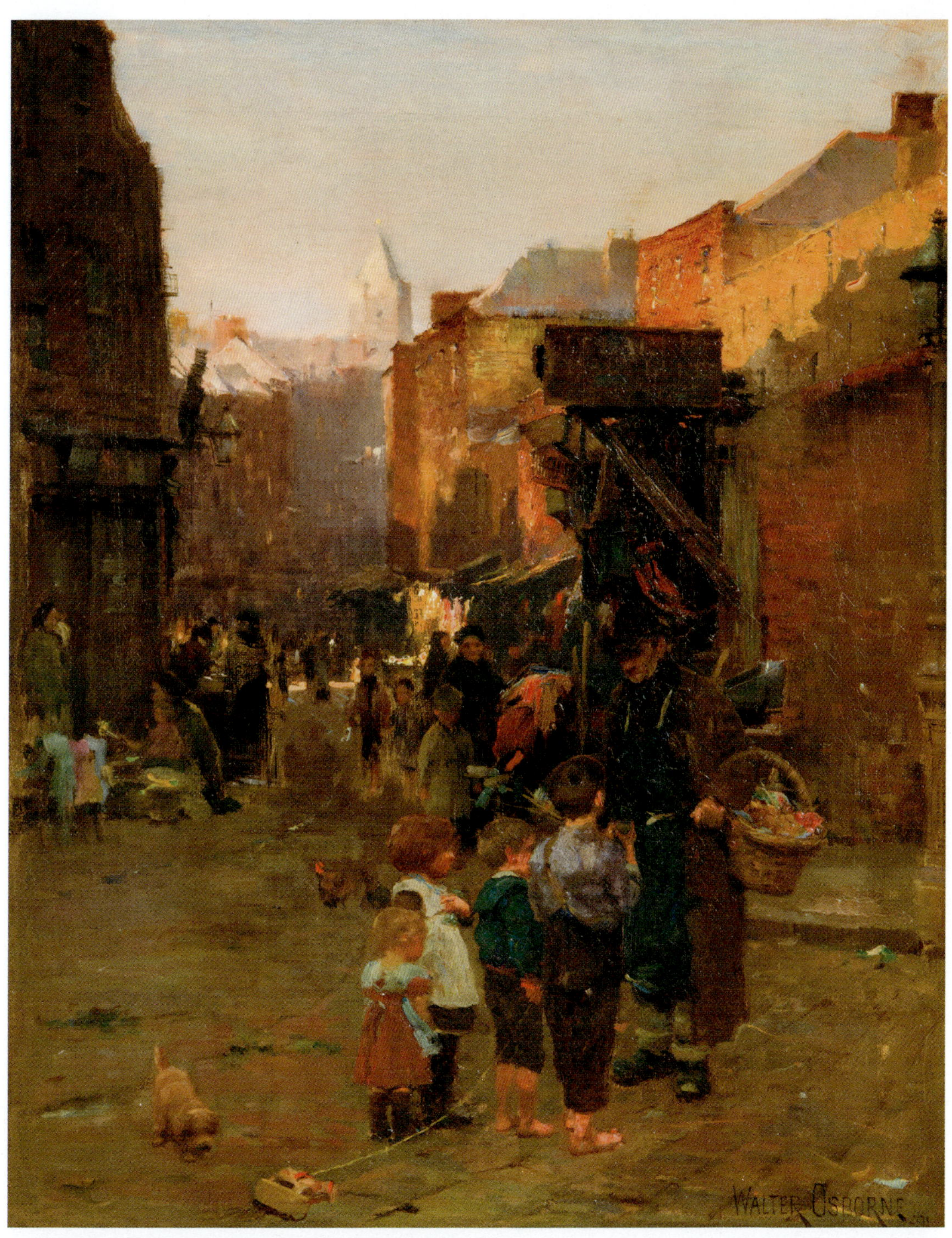

1.4   Walter Frederick Osborne, *Rags, Bones and Bottles*, 1891

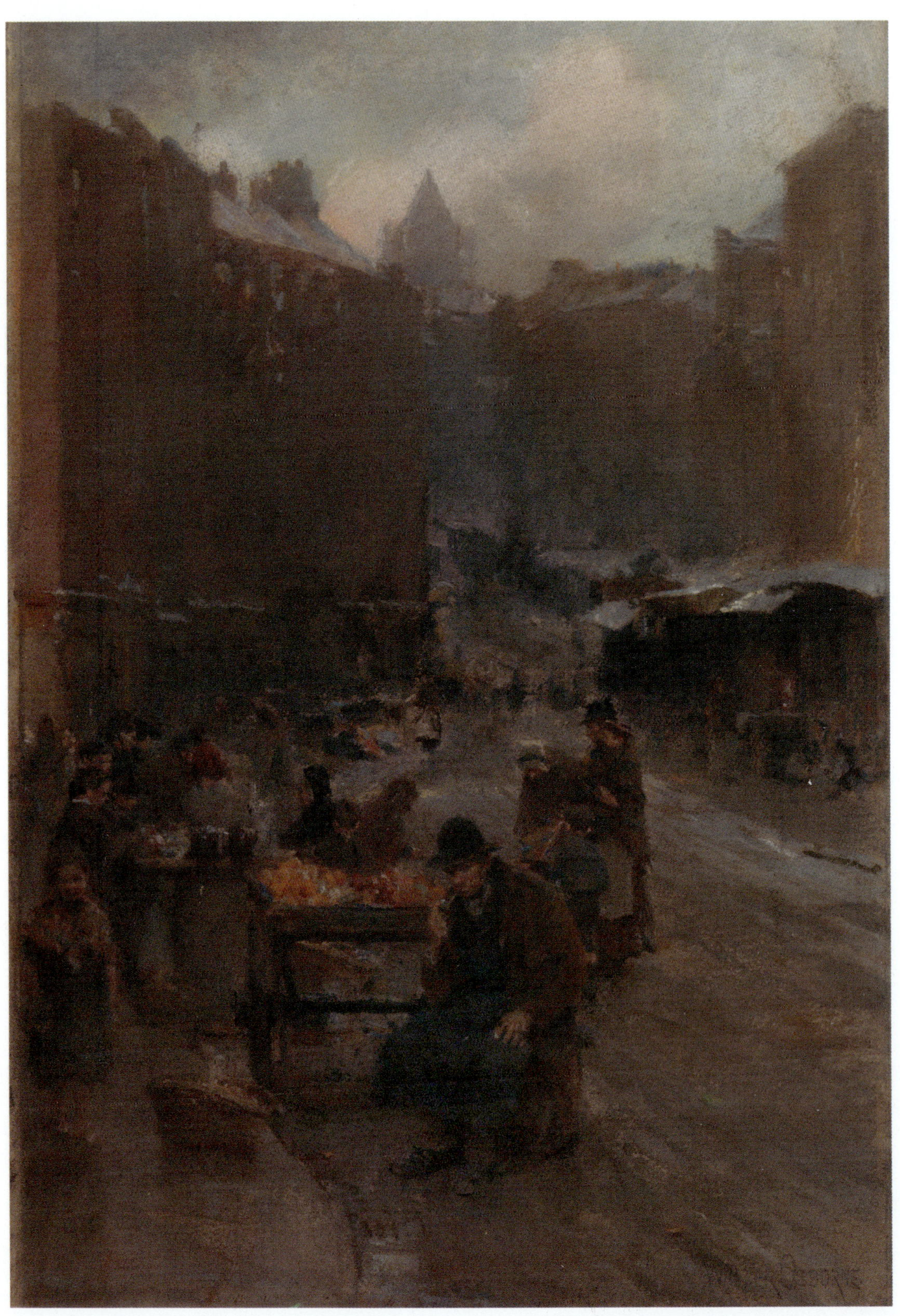

1.5   Walter Frederick Osborne, *Life in the Streets: Hard Times*, 1892

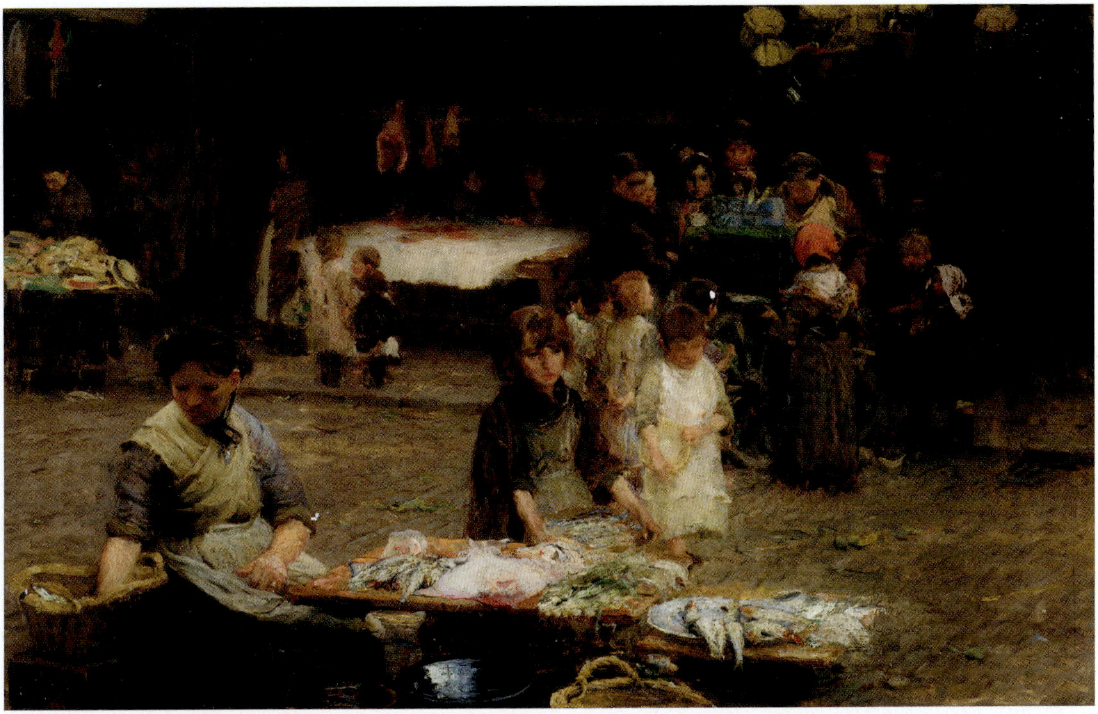

1.6   Walter Frederick Osborne, *The Fish Market*, 1893

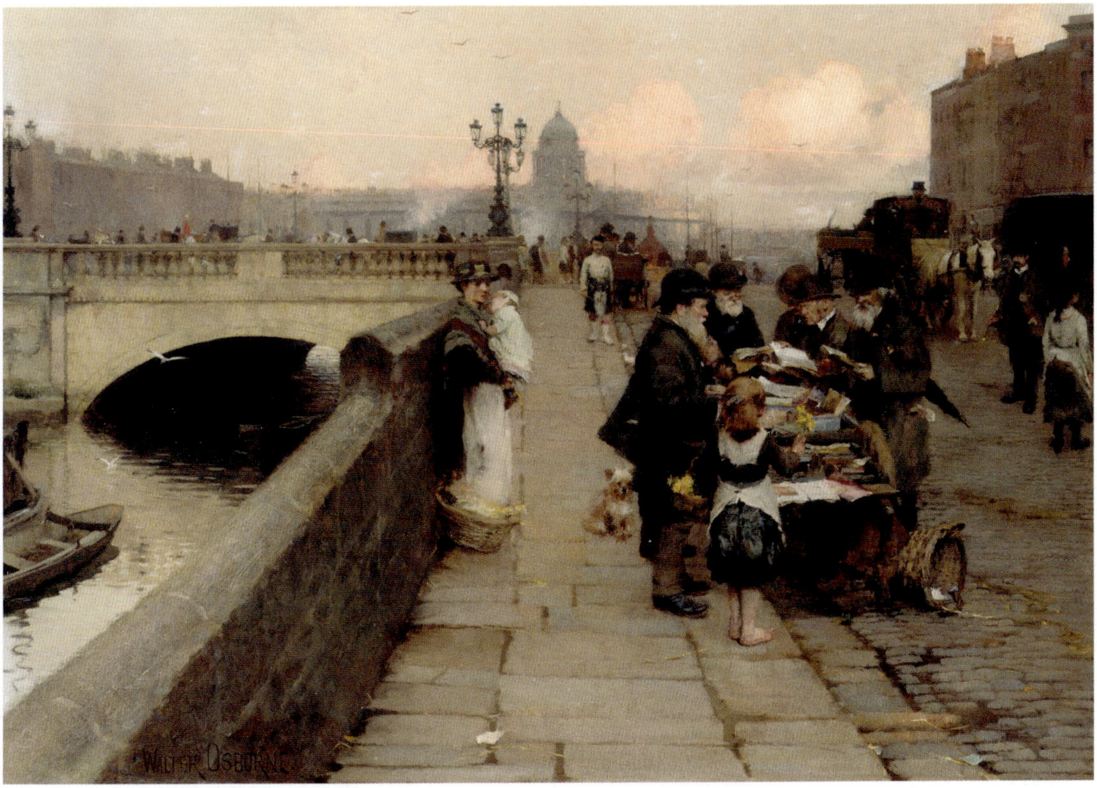

1.7   Walter Frederick Osborne, *Dublin Streets: A Vendor of Books*, 1889

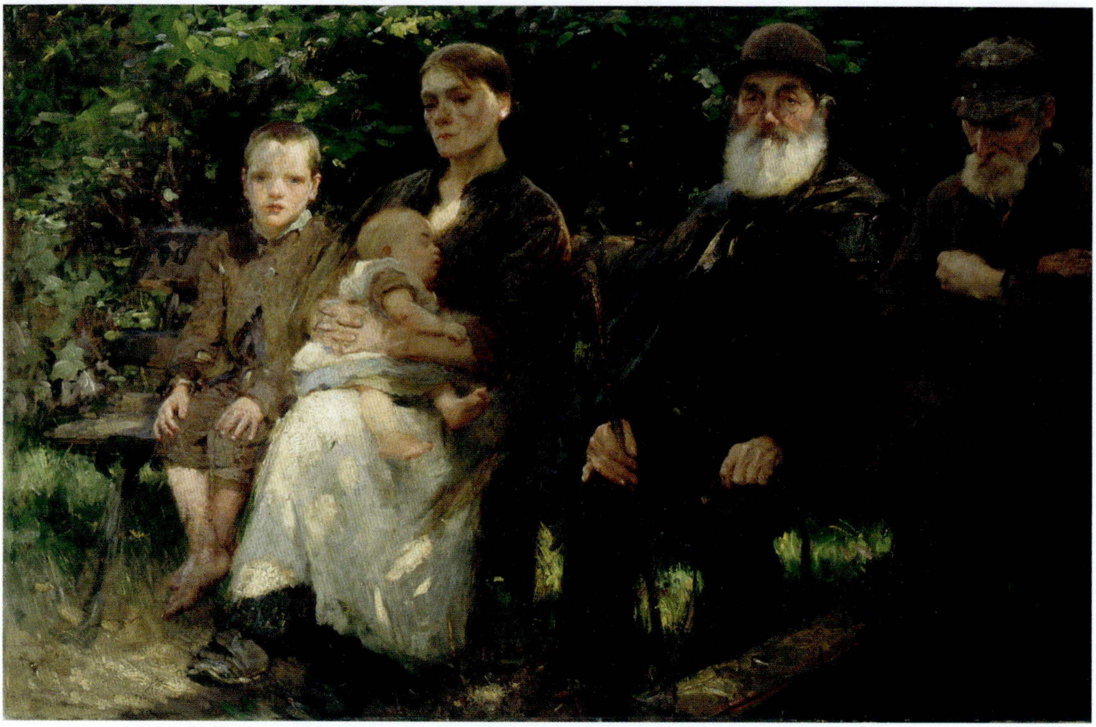

1.8   Walter Frederick Osborne, *In a Dublin Park, Light and Shade*, c.1895

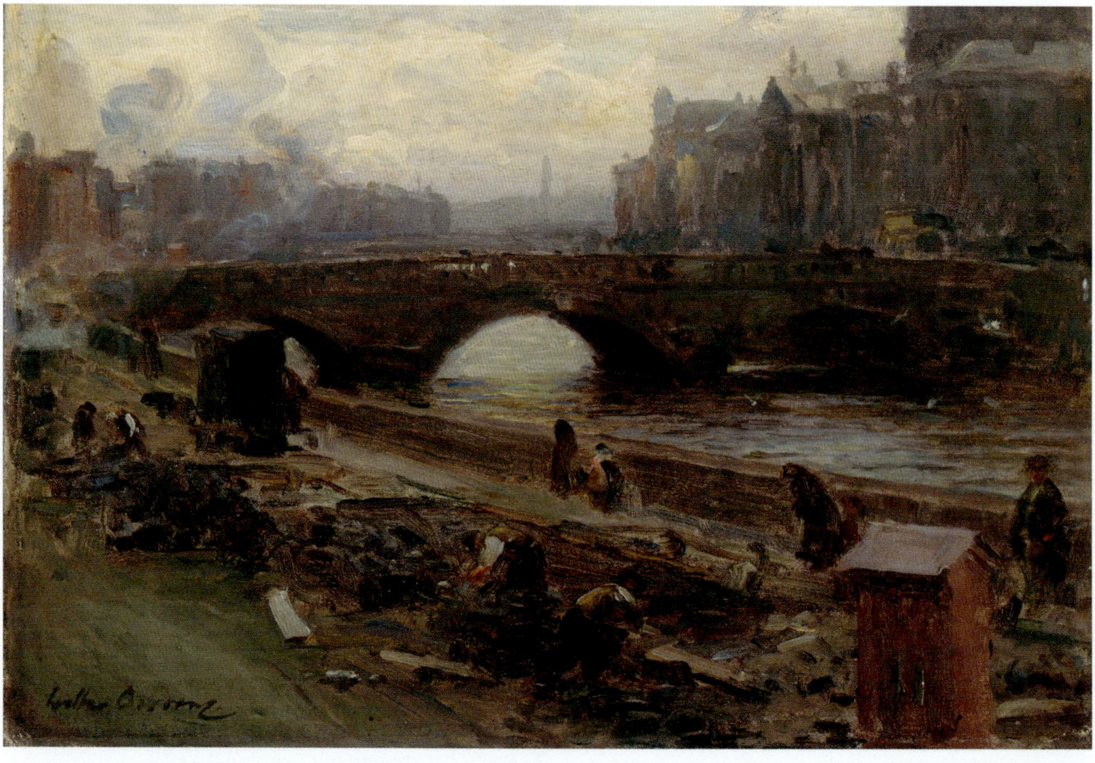

1.9   Walter Frederick Osborne, *The Four Courts, Dublin*

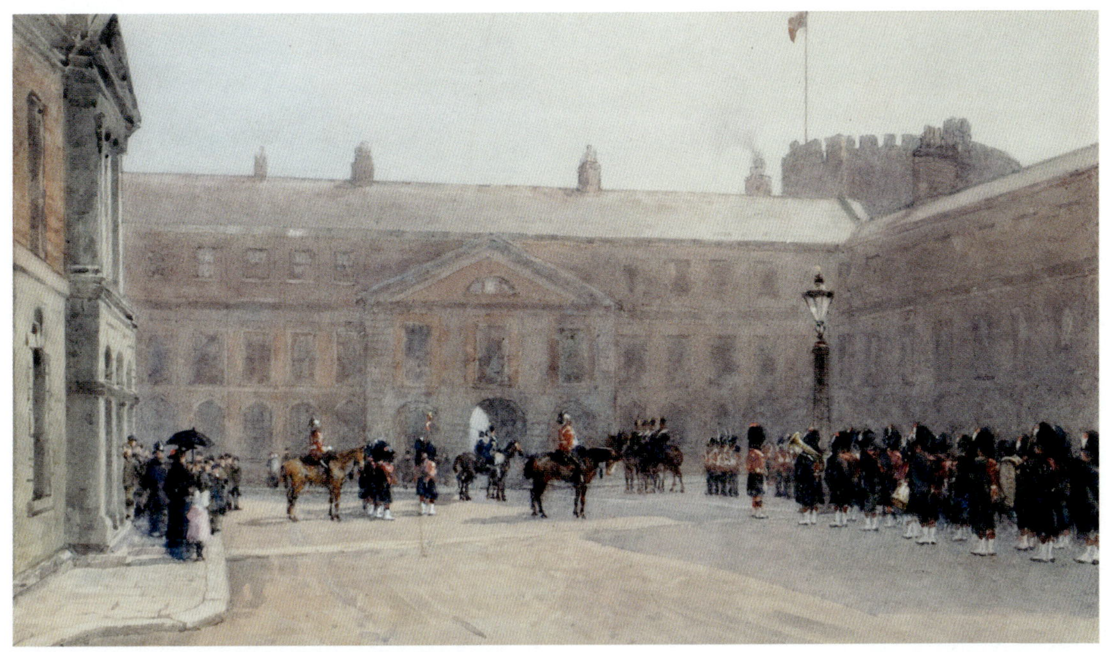

2.1   Rose Barton, *Relieving the Castle Guard*, 1891

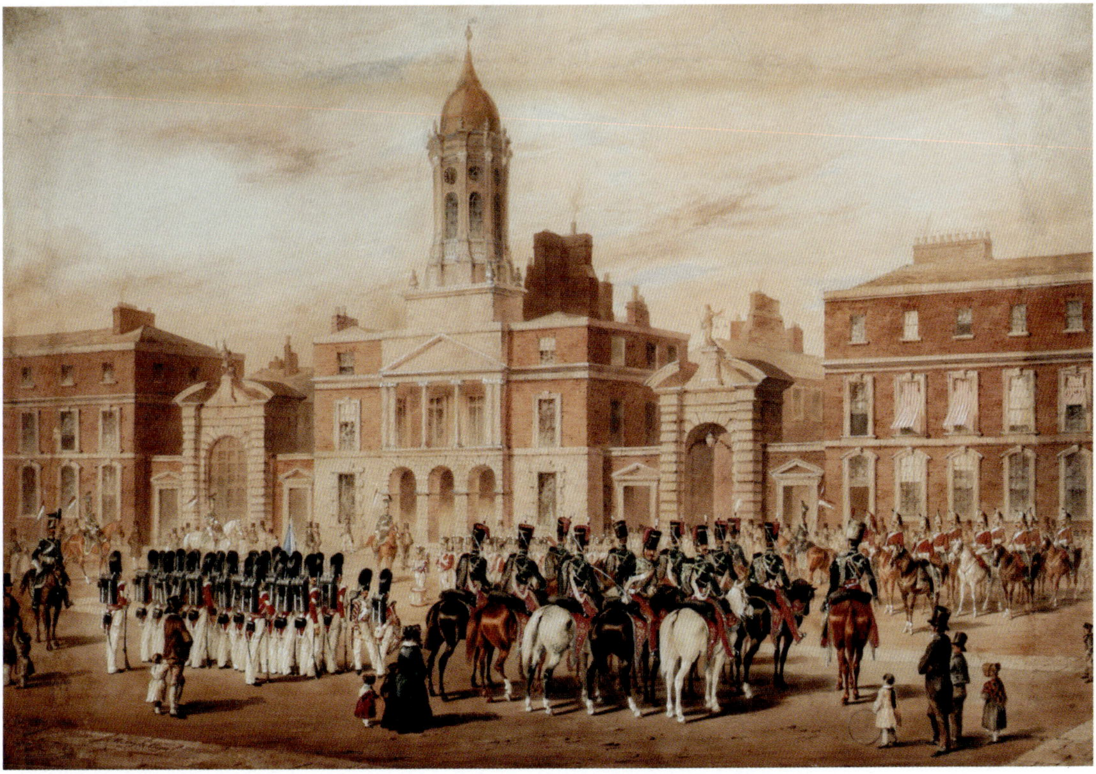

2.2   Michael Angelo Hayes, *St Patrick's Day, Military Parade at Dublin Castle*, 1844

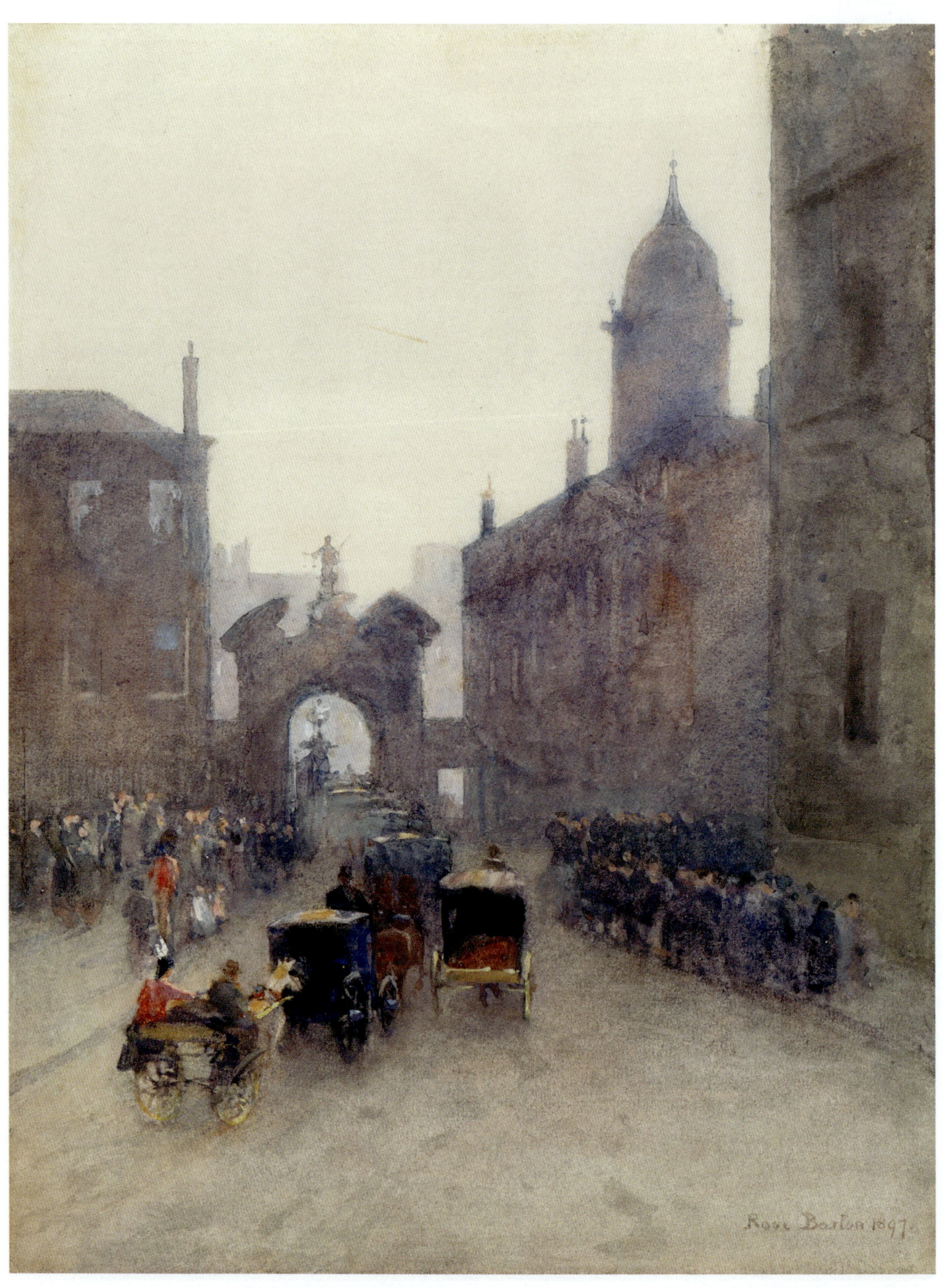

2.3   Rose Barton, *Going to the Levée at Dublin Castle*, 1897

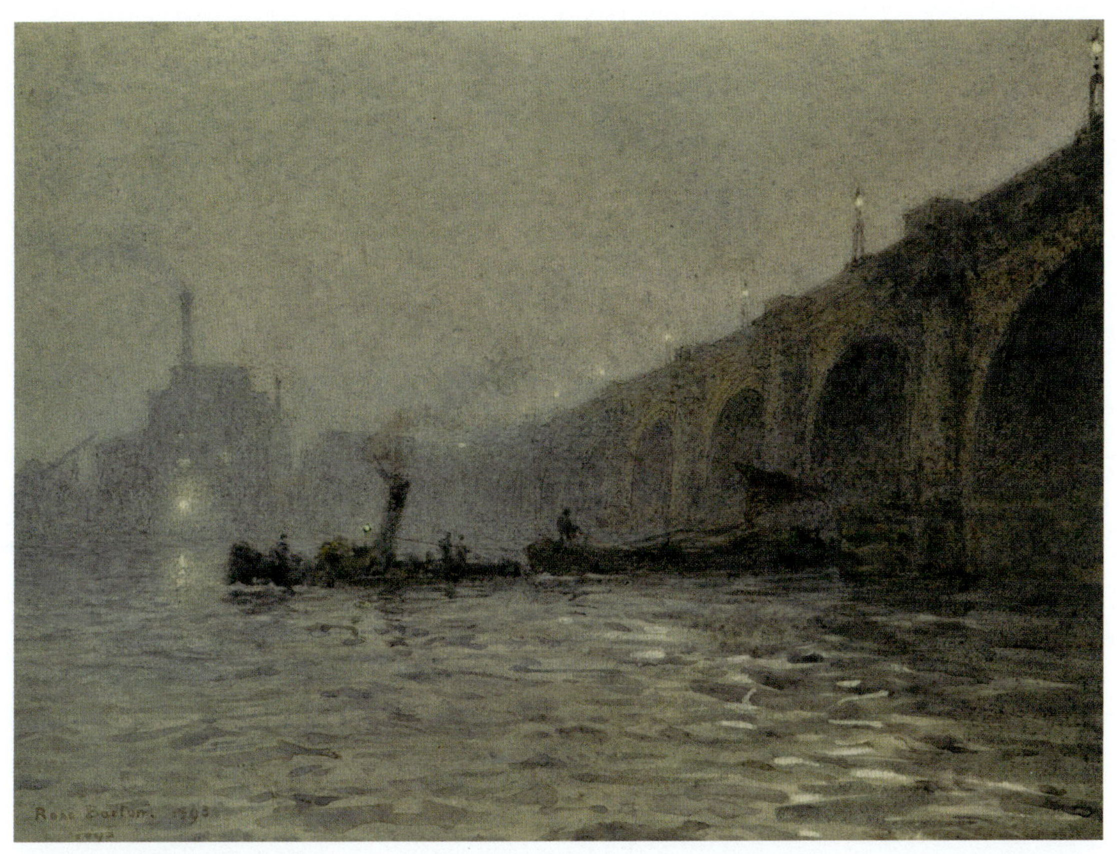

2.4   Rose Barton, *Waterloo Bridge, London,* 1893

2.5 Rose Barton, *South Kensington Station*, 1894

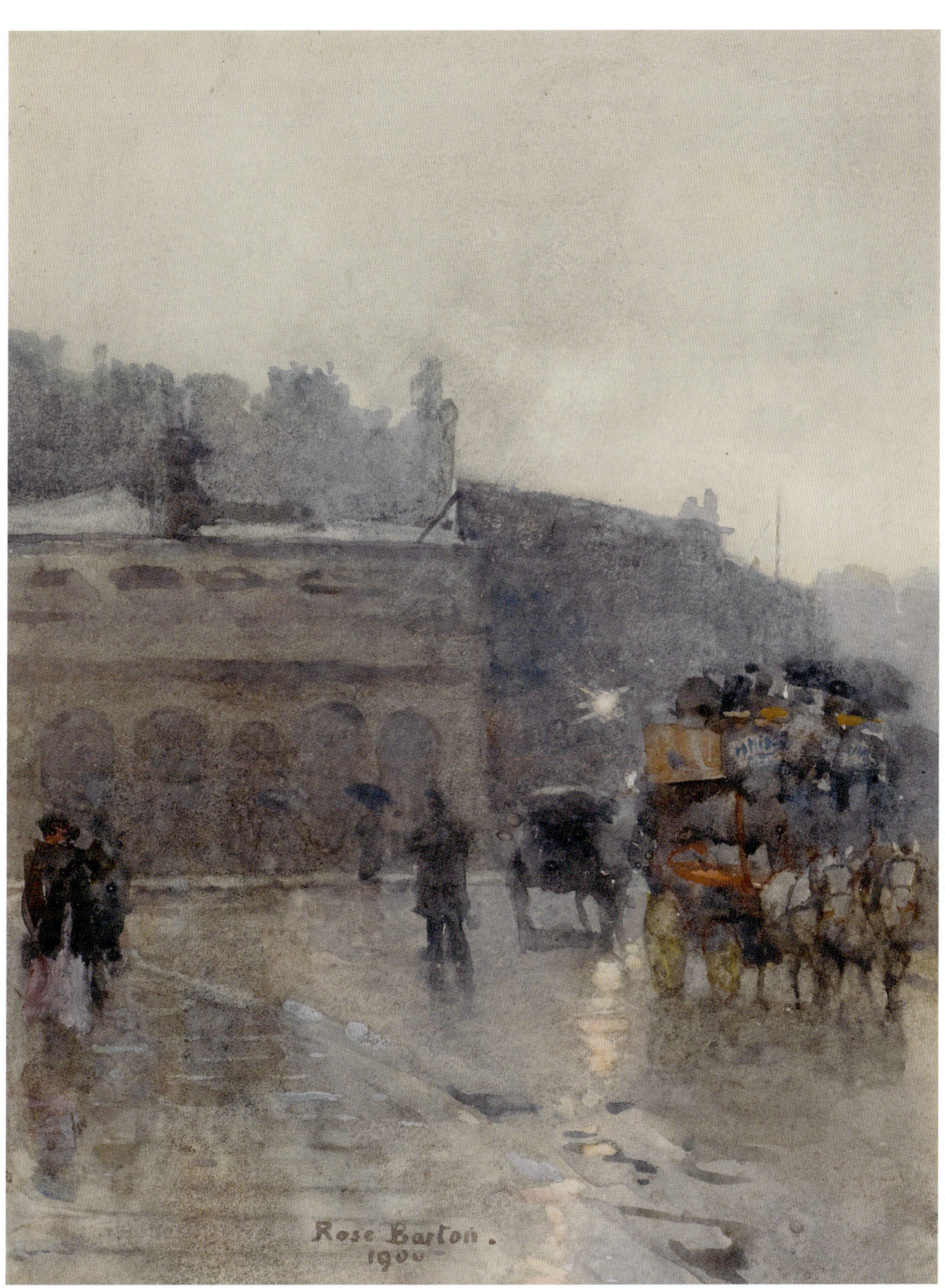

2.6   Rose Barton, *The Rotunda Rooms*, 1900

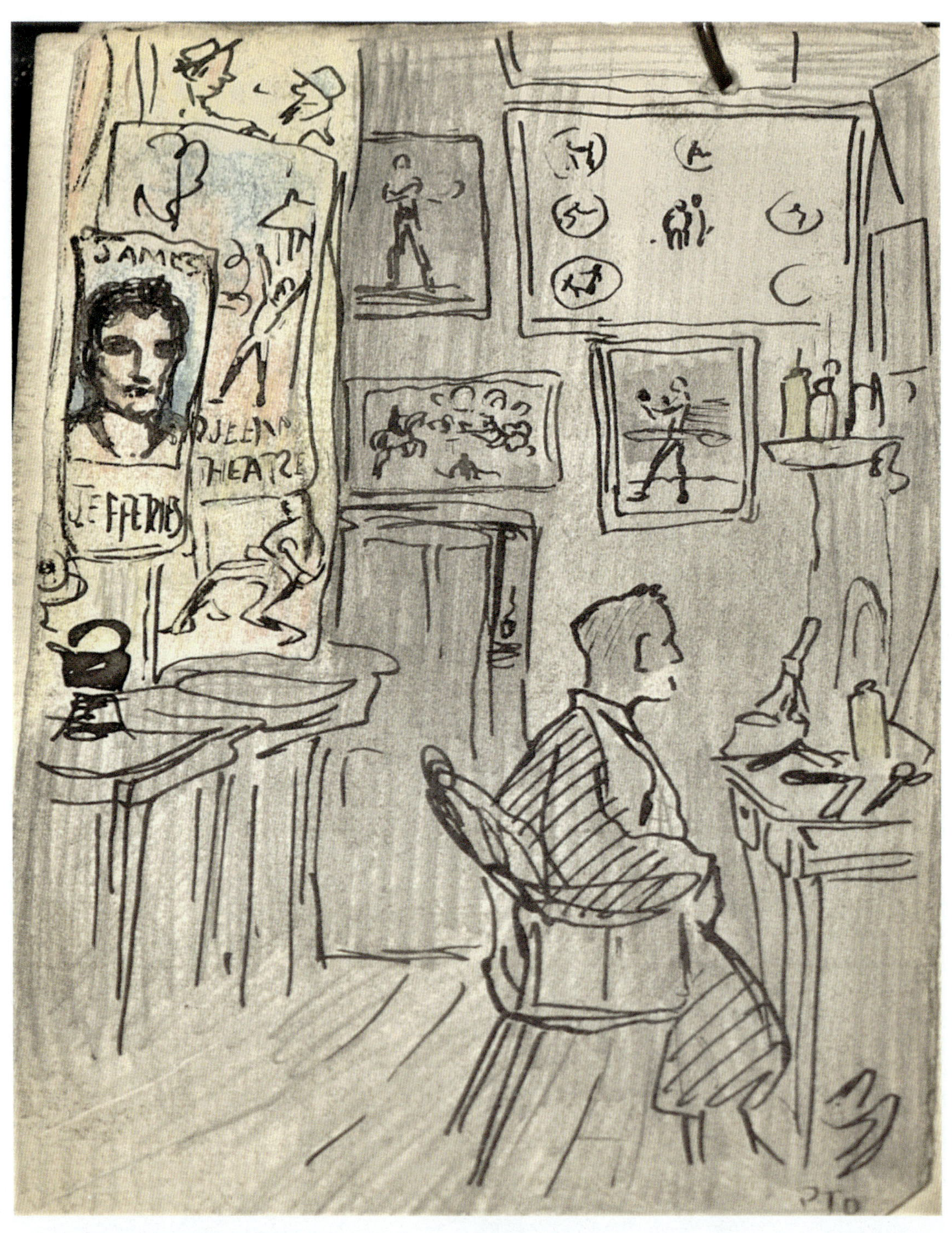

3.1   Jack Butler Yeats, *Rum Old Hairdressers near the Academy*, 1900

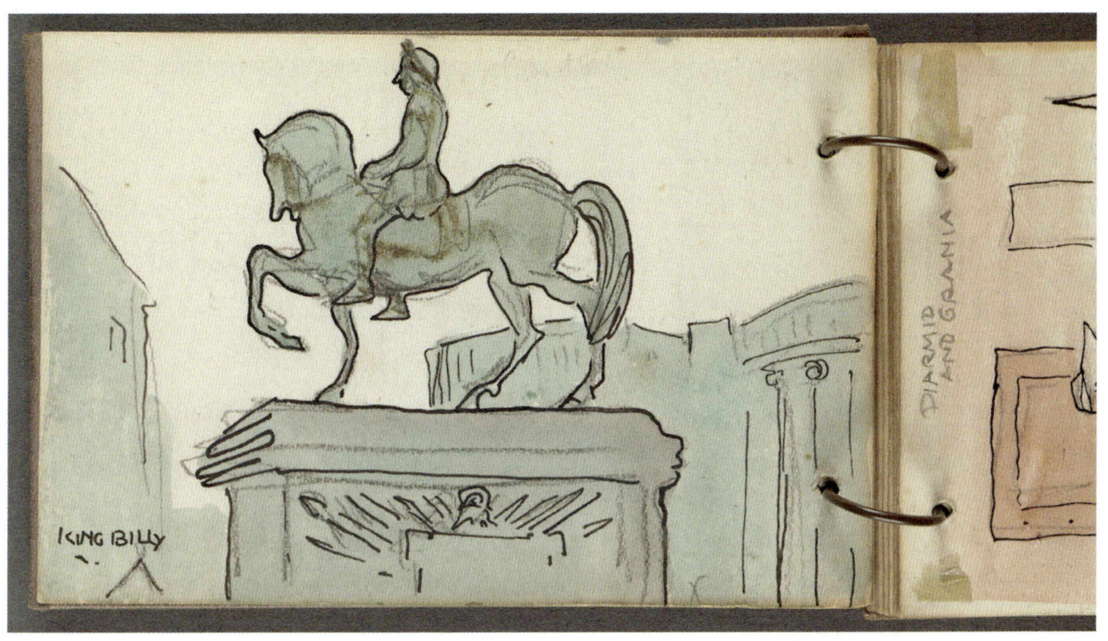

3.2   Jack Butler Yeats, *King Billy*, 1901

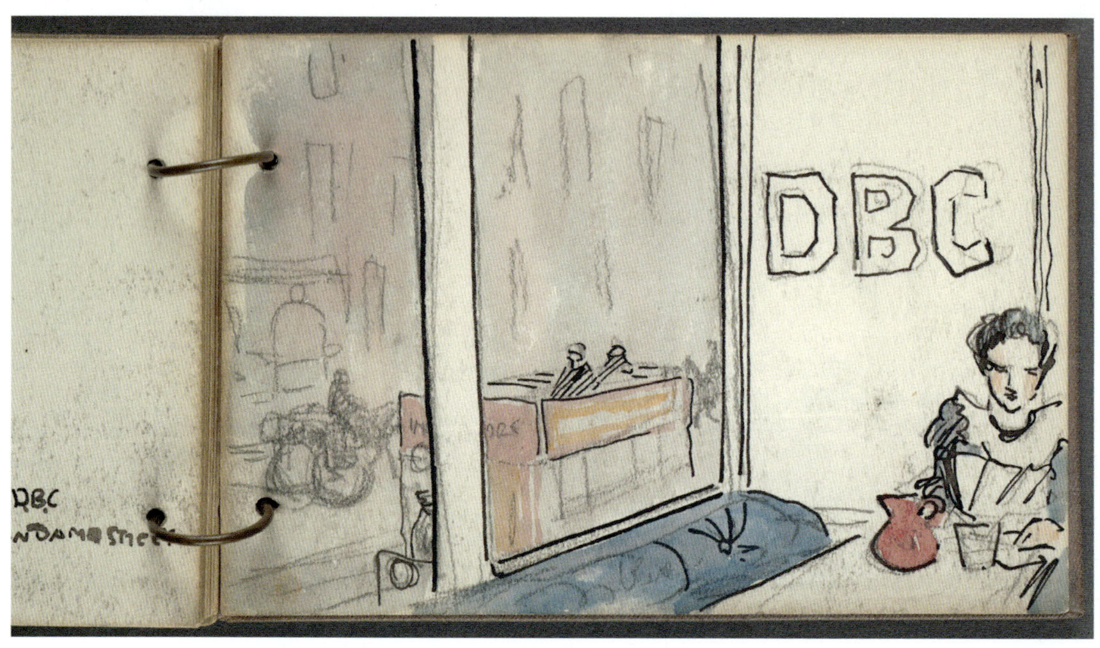

3.3   Jack Butler Yeats, *The DBC Cafe*, 1901

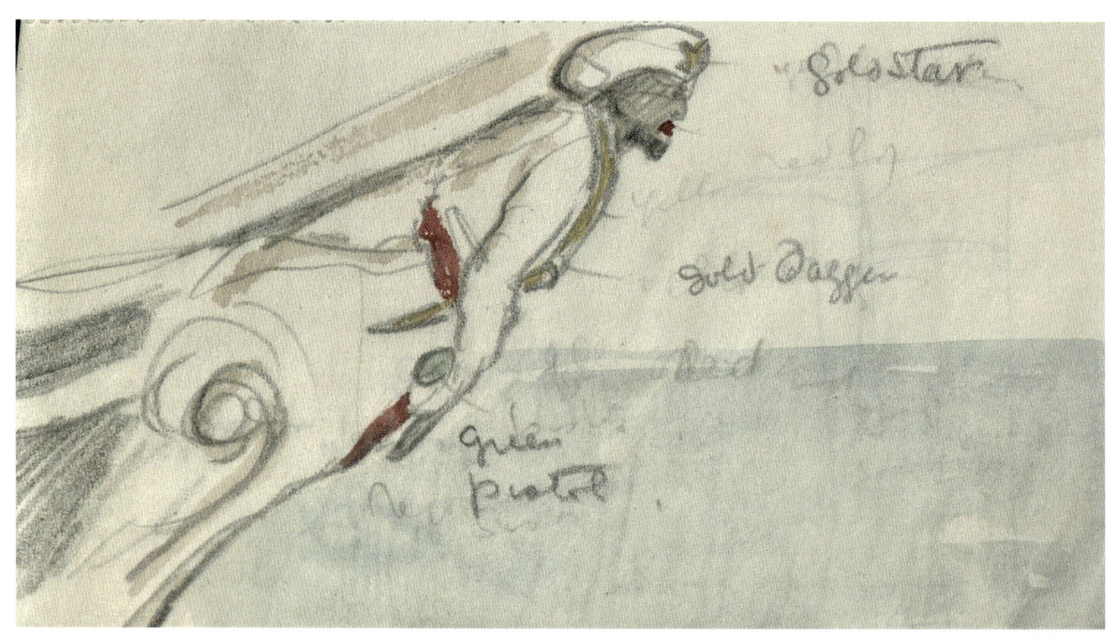

3.4   Jack Butler Yeats, *The Barcore*, 1908

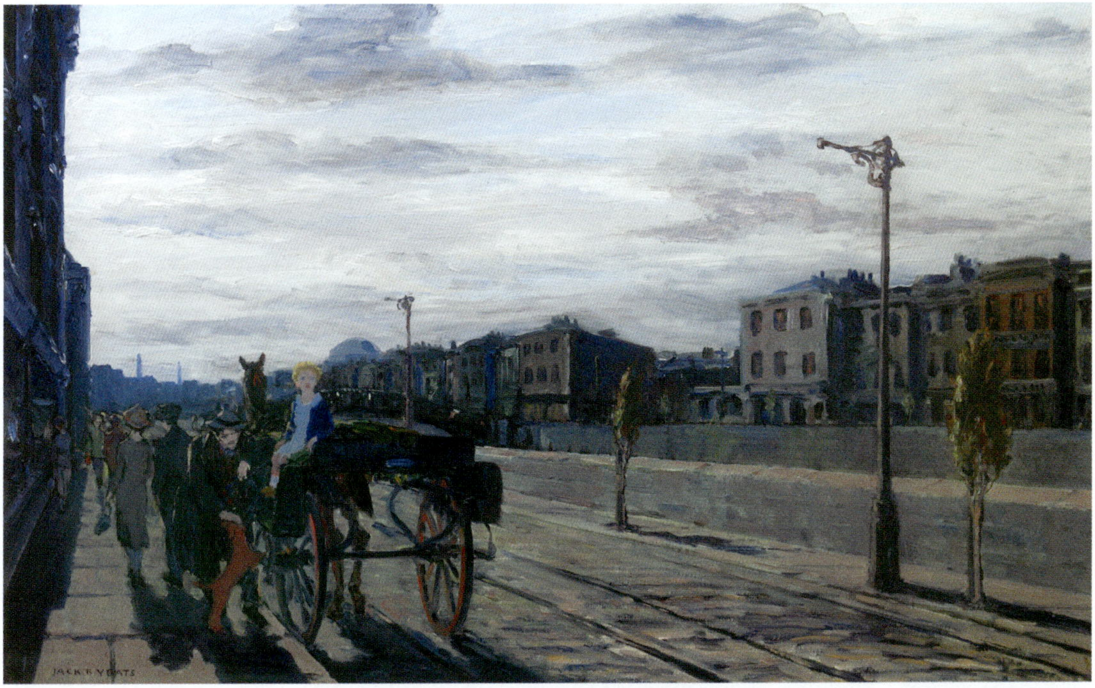

3.5   Jack Butler Yeats, *A Westerly Wind*, 1921

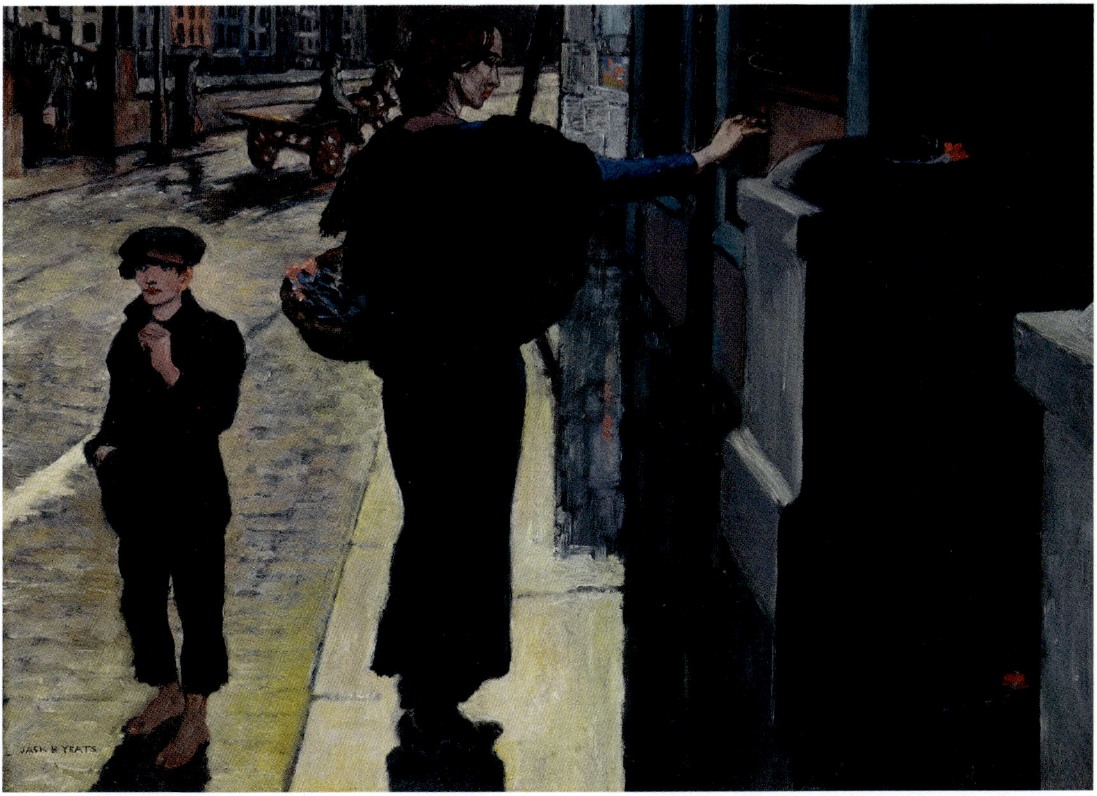

3.6   Jack Butler Yeats, *Bachelor's Walk, In Memory*

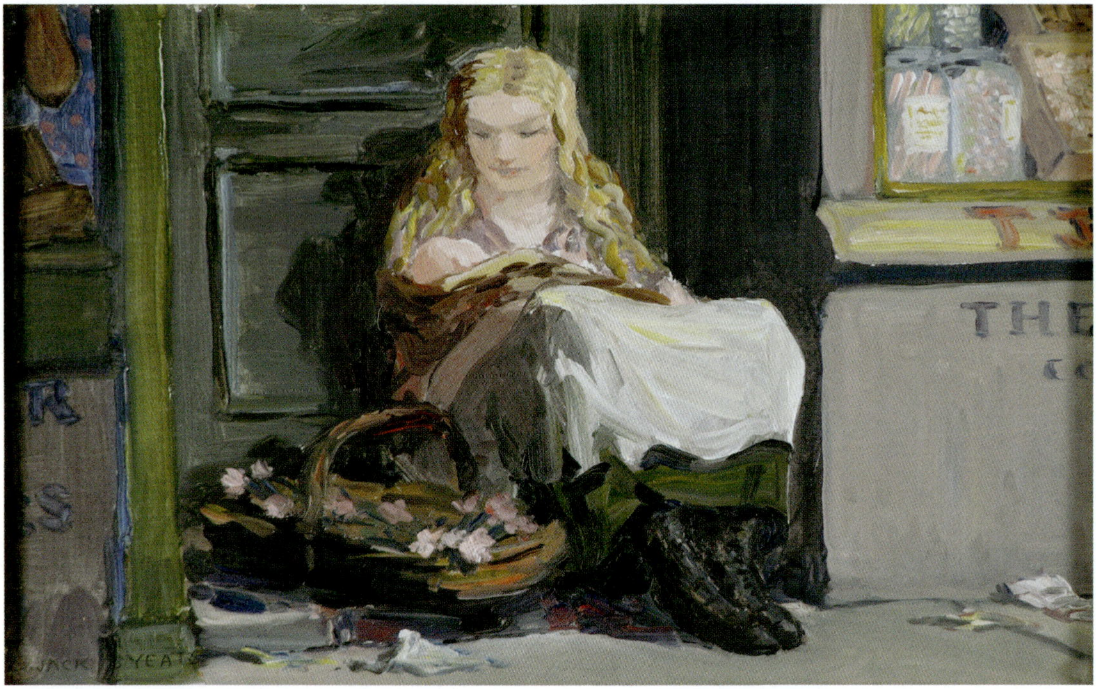

3.7   Jack B. Yeats, *In Capel Street, Dublin*, 1923

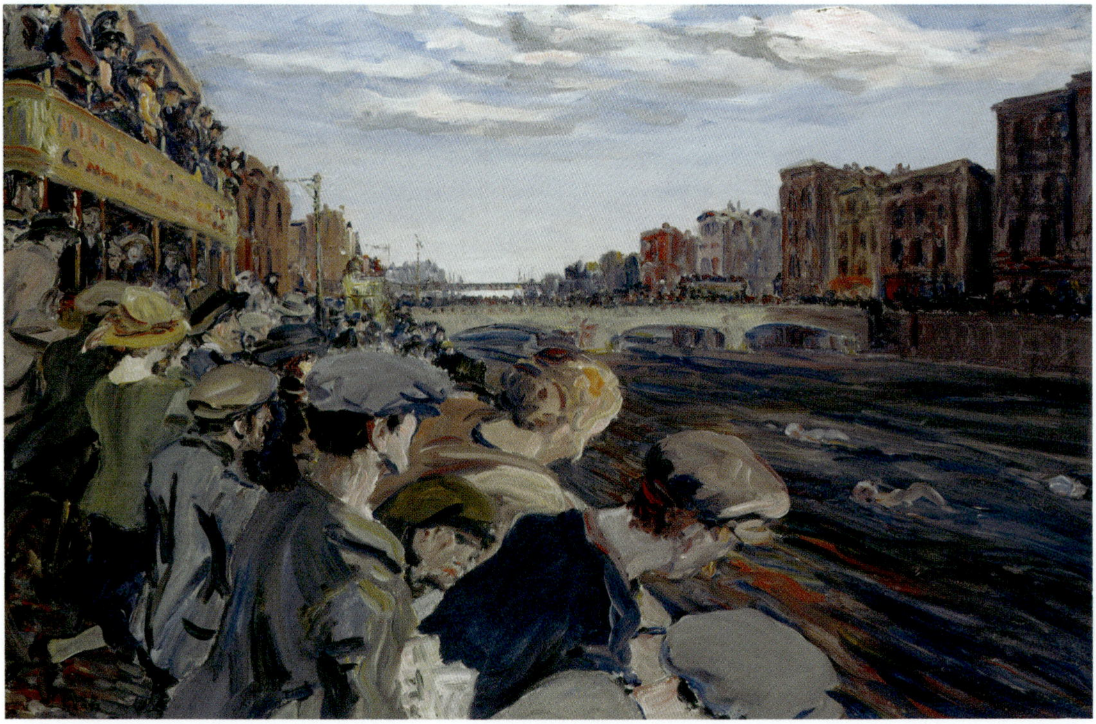

3.8   Jack Butler Yeats, *The Liffey Swim*, 1923

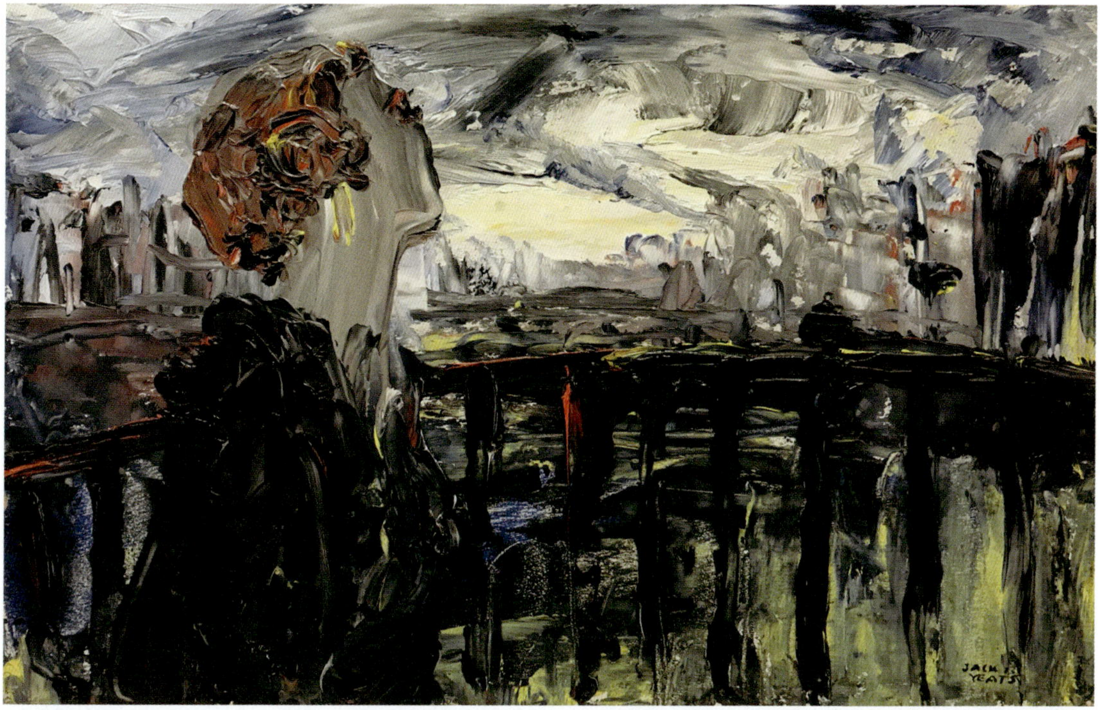

3.9   Jack Butler Yeats, *Crossing the Metal Bridge*, 1926

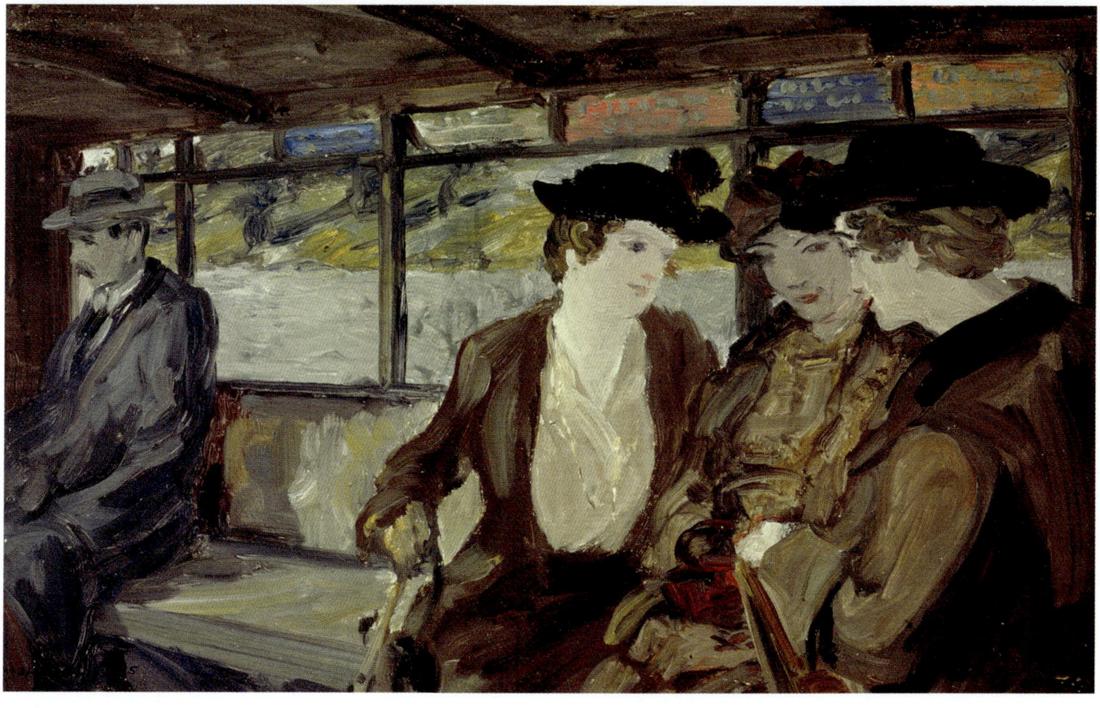

3.10   Jack Butler Yeats, *In the Tram*, 1923

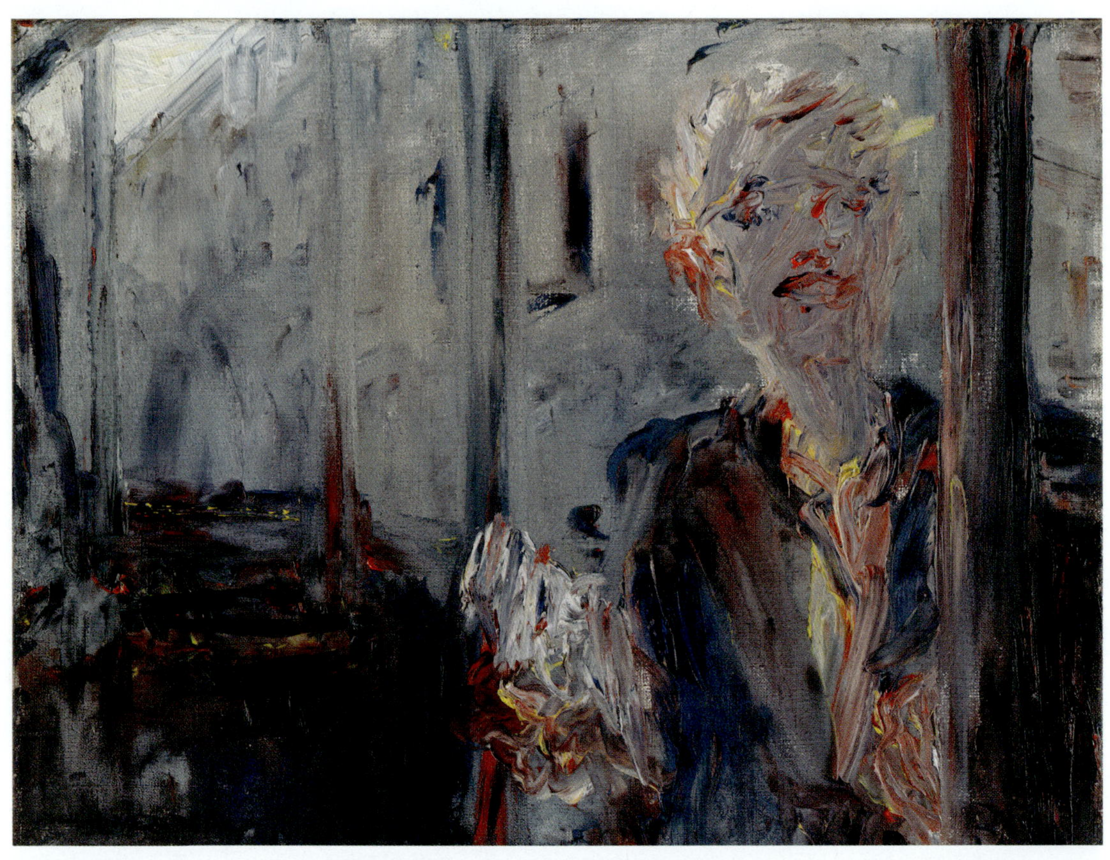

3.11   Jack Butler Yeats, *A Dublin Newsboy Boarding a Tram*, 1926

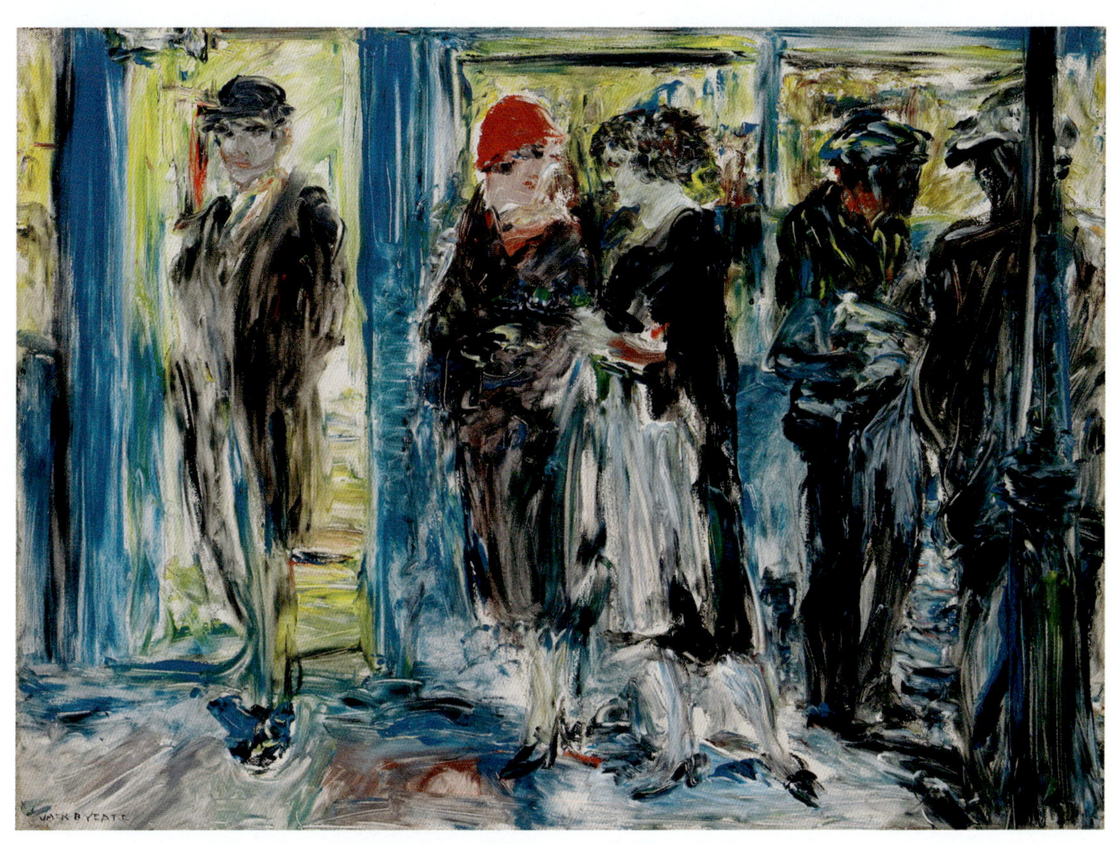

3.12   Jack Butler Yeats, *Flower Girl, Dublin*, 1926

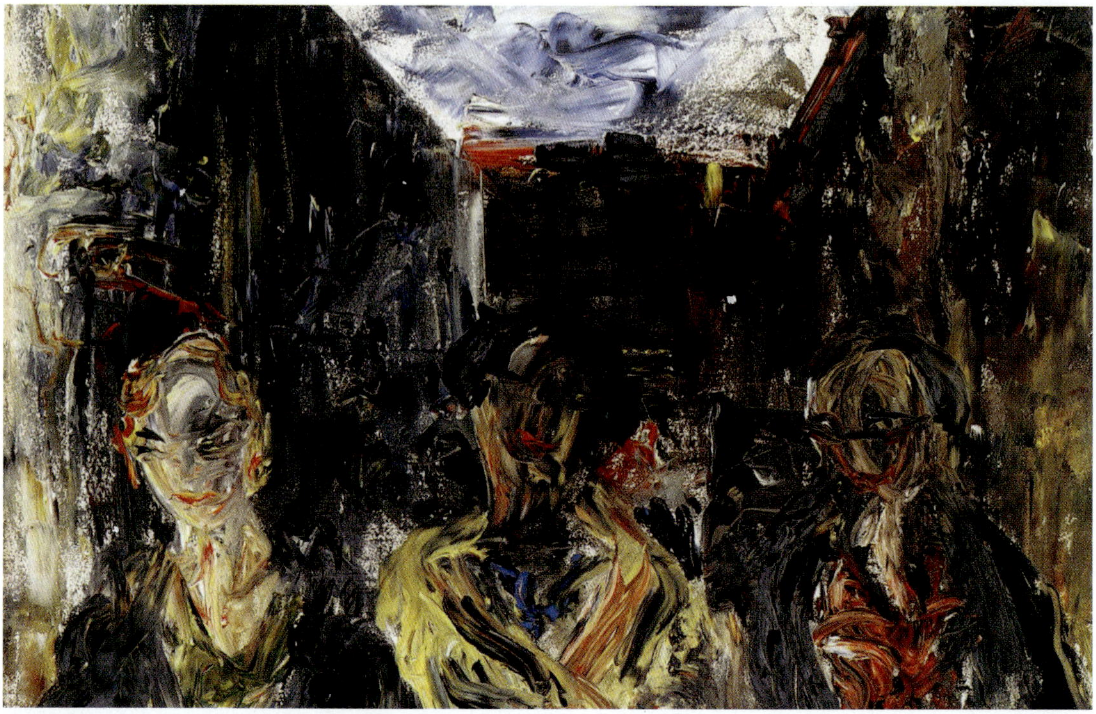

3.13   Jack B. Yeats, *Three Traders of Dublin*, 1927

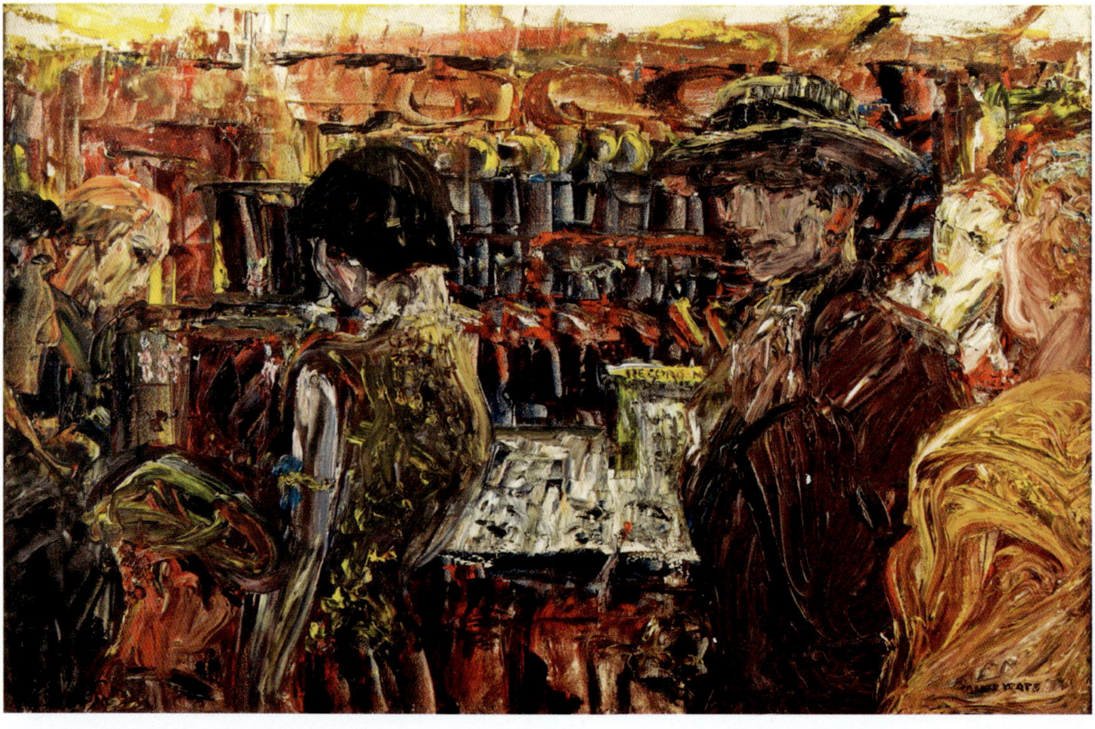

3.14   Jack Butler Yeats, *Jazz Babies*, 1927

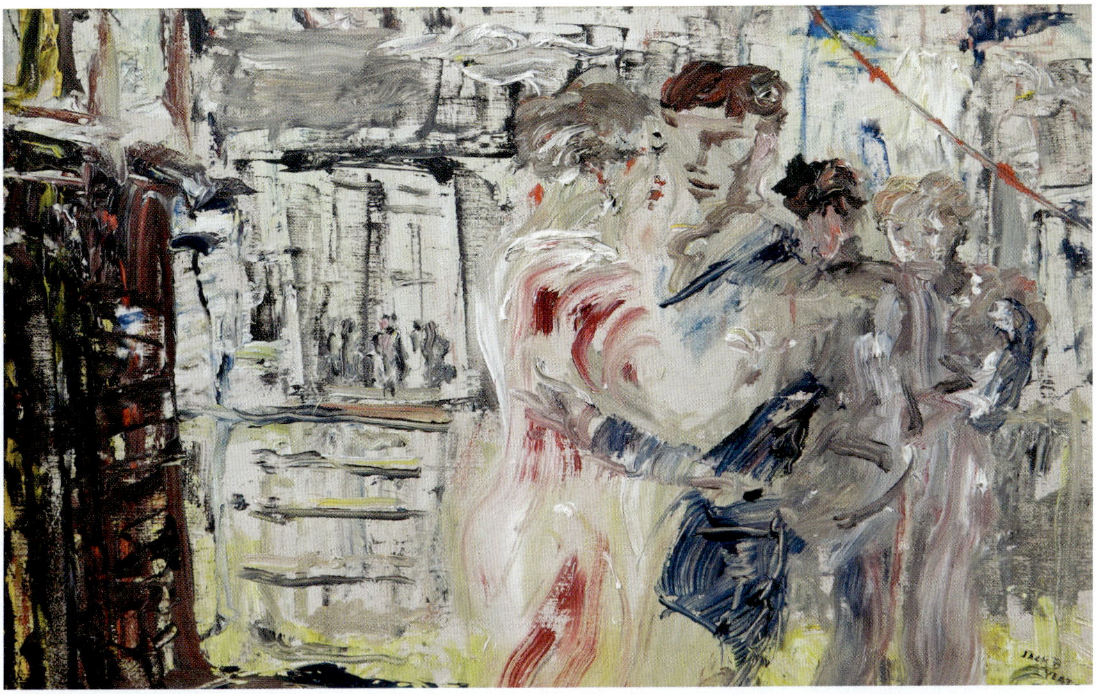

3.15 Jack Butler Yeats, *Dancing on the Deck of the Royal Iris*, 1932

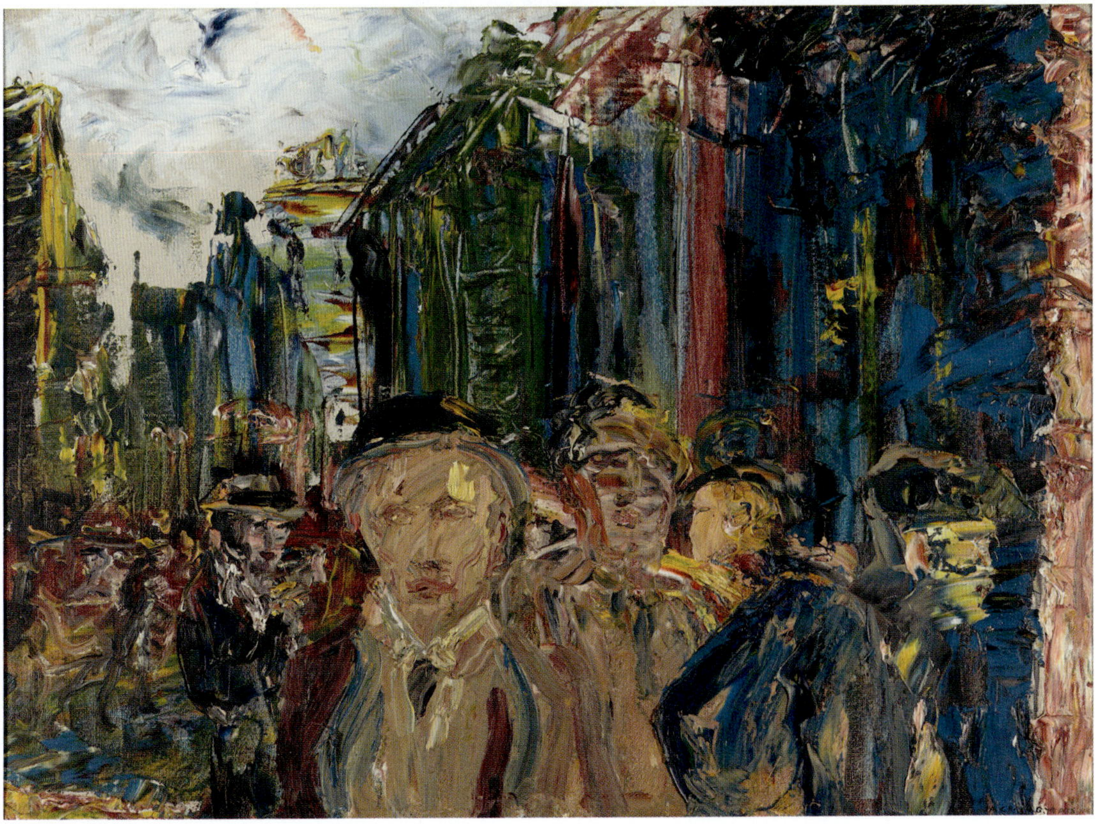

3.16 Jack Butler Yeats, *People in a Street*, 1936

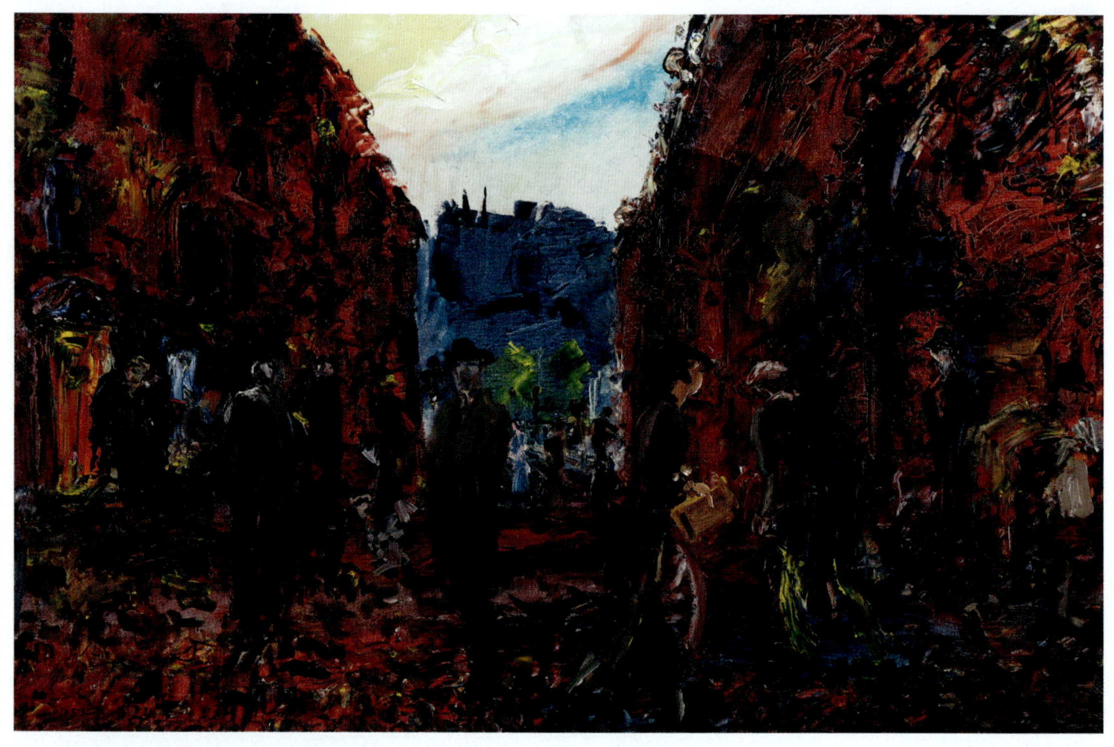

3.17 Jack Butler Yeats, *Morning in a City*, c. 1937

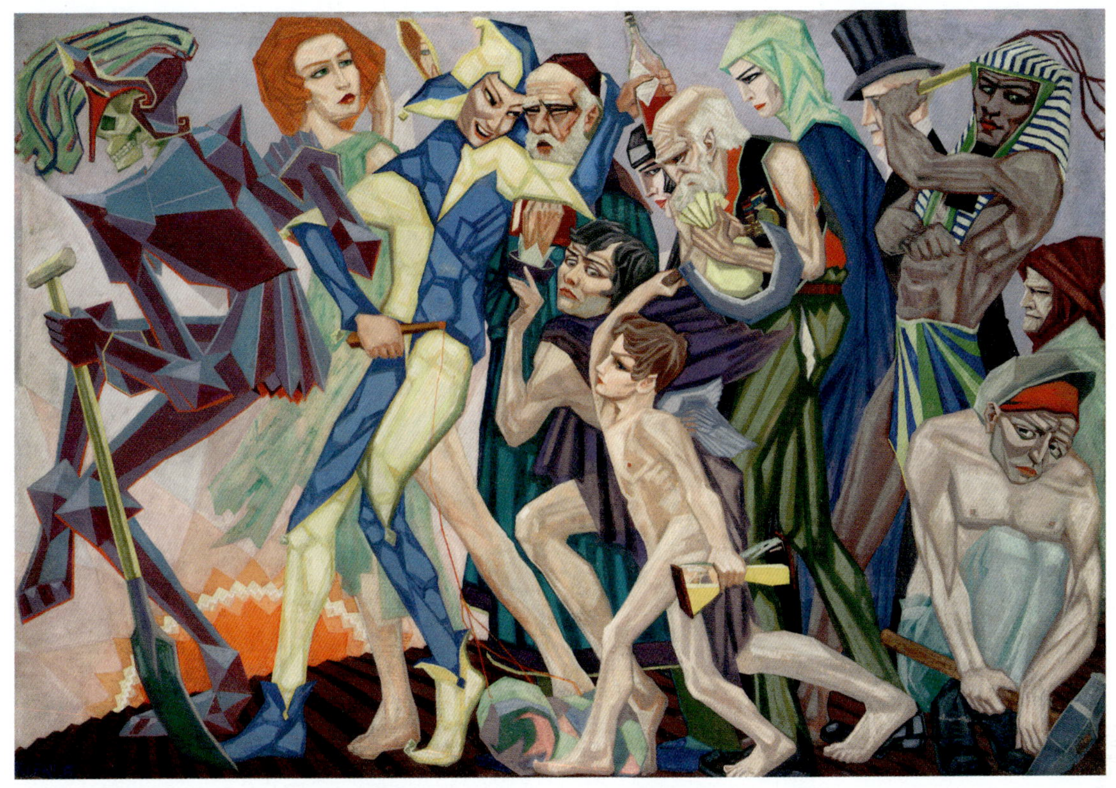

4.1   Harry Aaron Kernoff, *Death*, c.1934

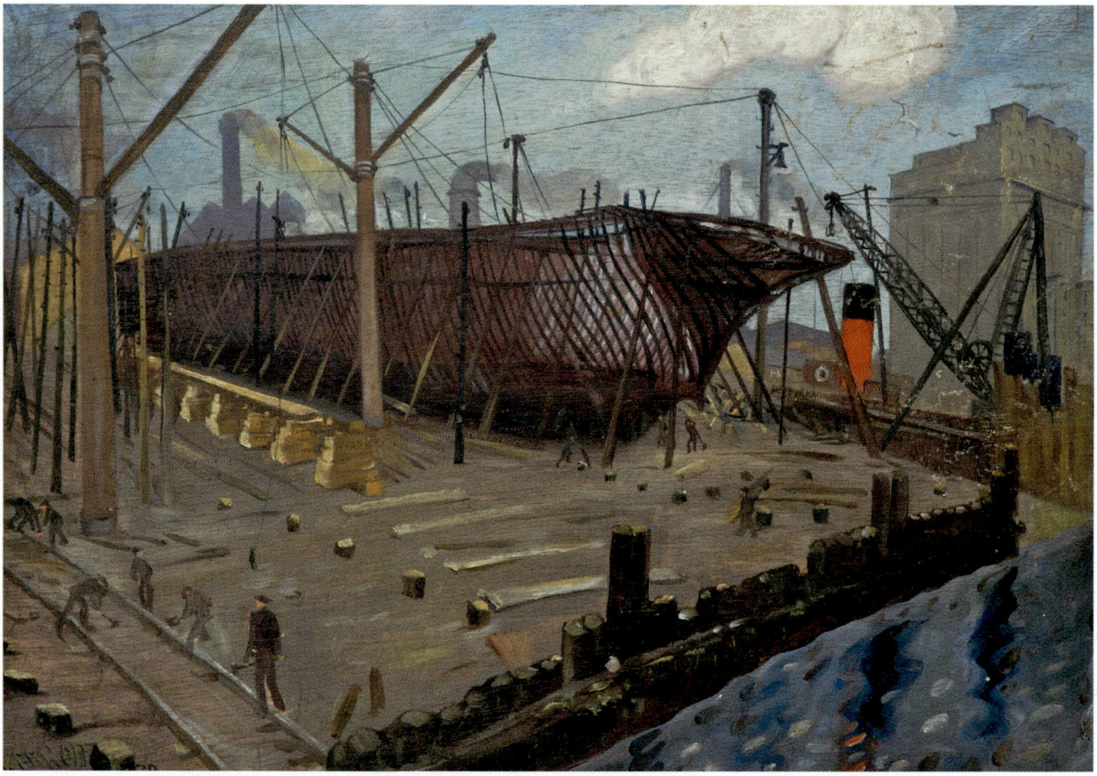

4.2   Harry Aaron Kernoff, *Dublin Dockyard*, undated

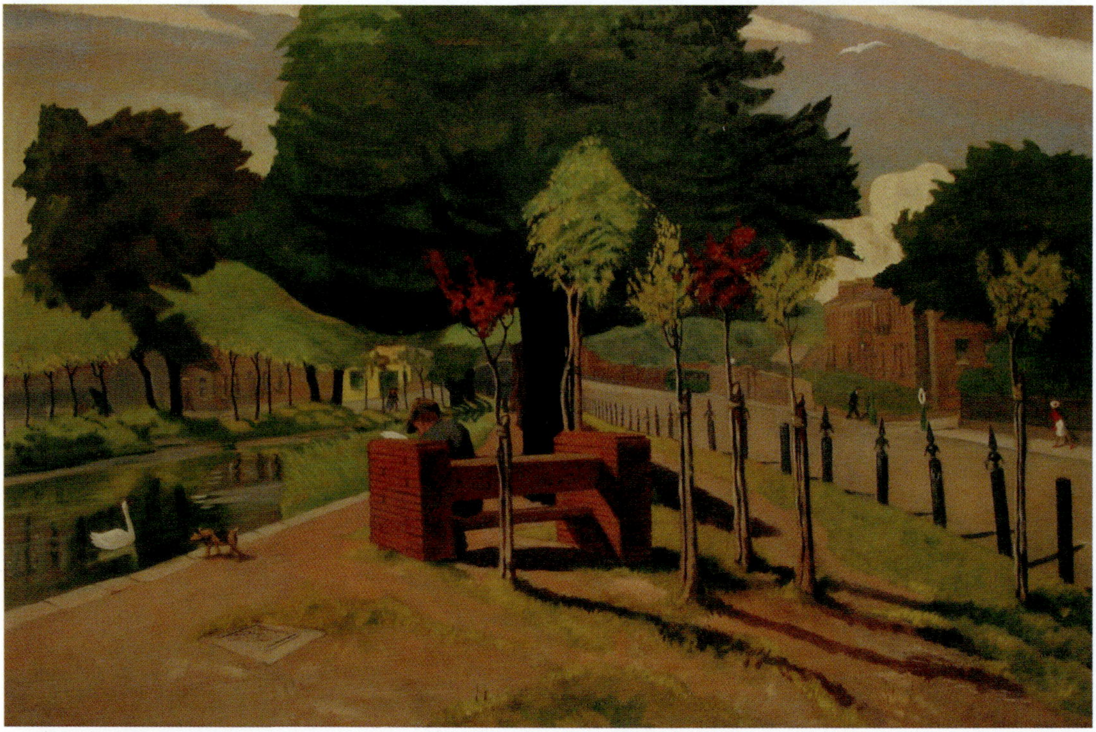

4.3   Harry Aaron Kernoff, *The Red Seat near Baggot Street Bridge*, c.1947

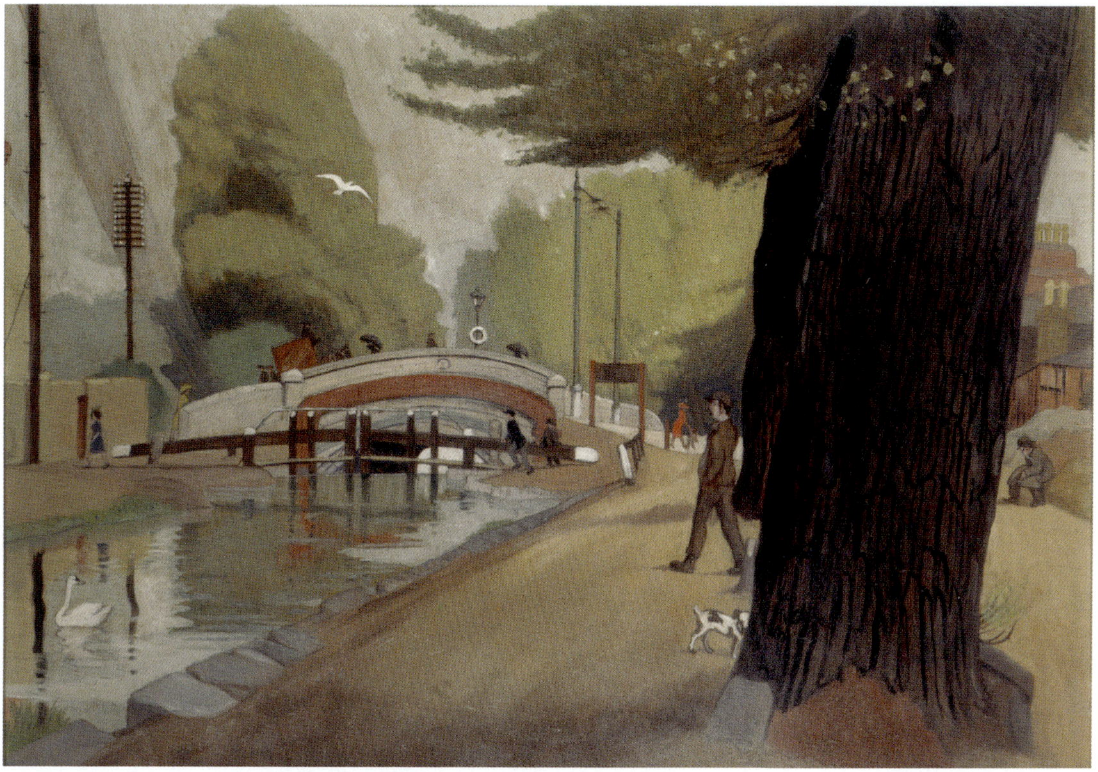

4.4   Harry Aaron Kernoff, *Summer's Day at Leeson Bridge*, 1936

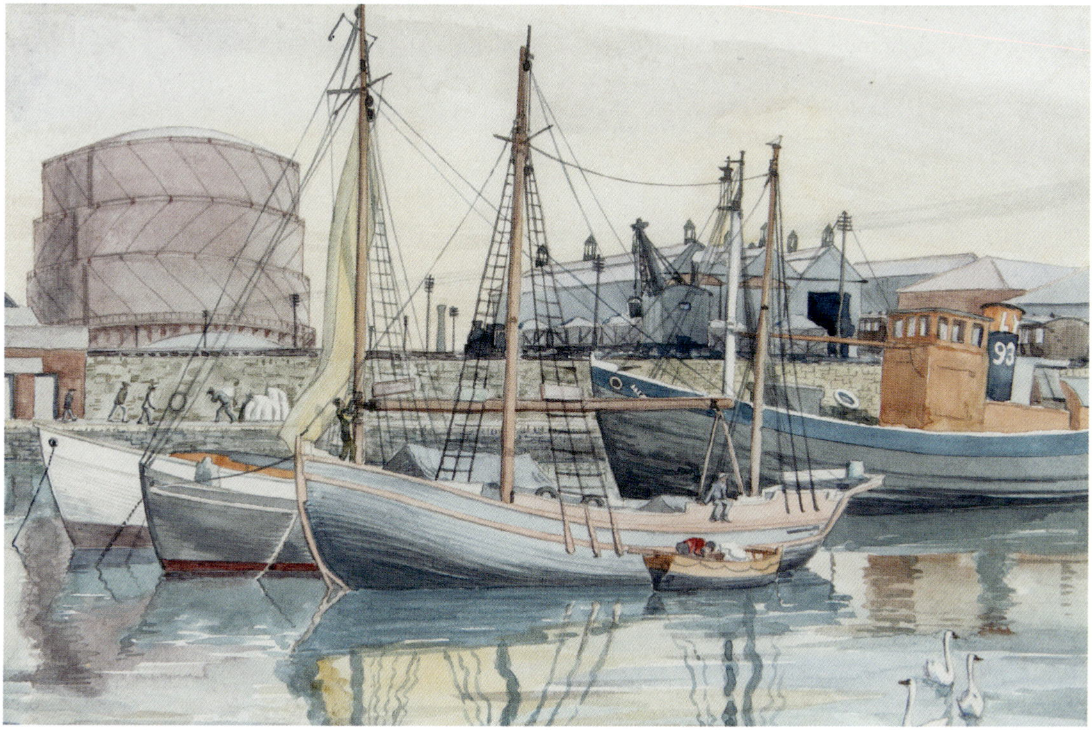

4.5   Harry Aaron Kernoff, *Boats at Anchor – Grand Canal Quay*, 1937

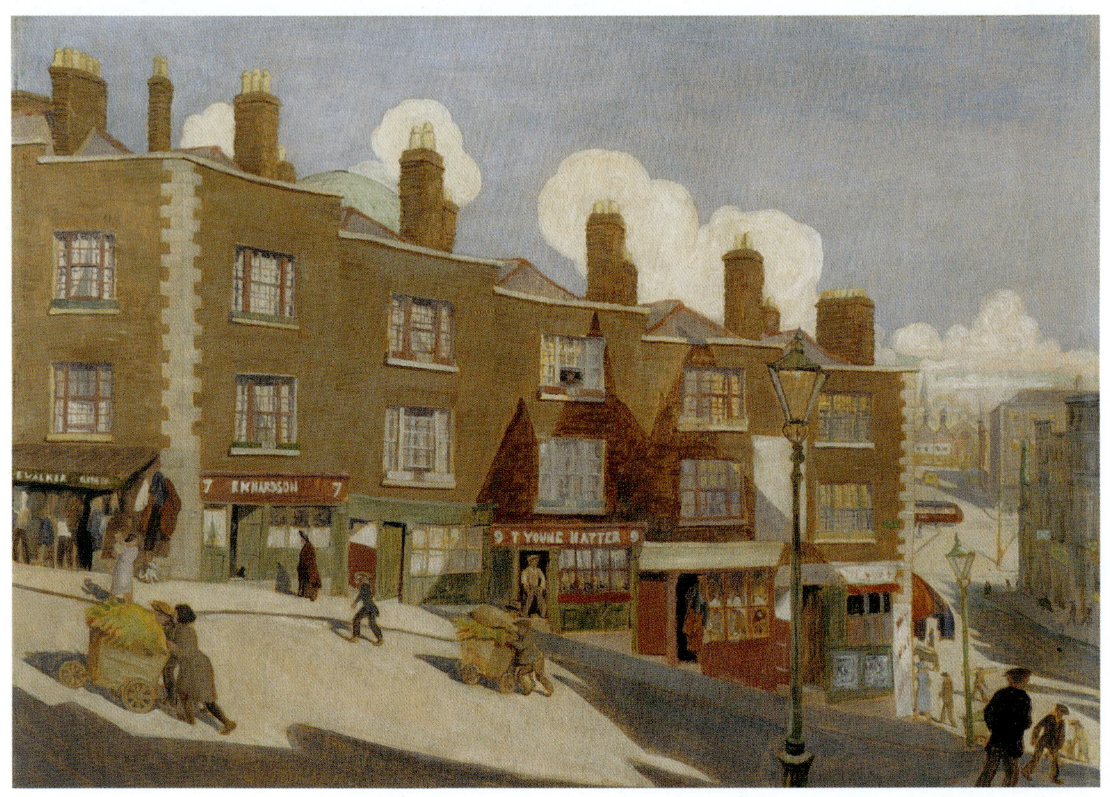

4.6   Harry Aaron Kernoff, *Winetavern Street*, 1934

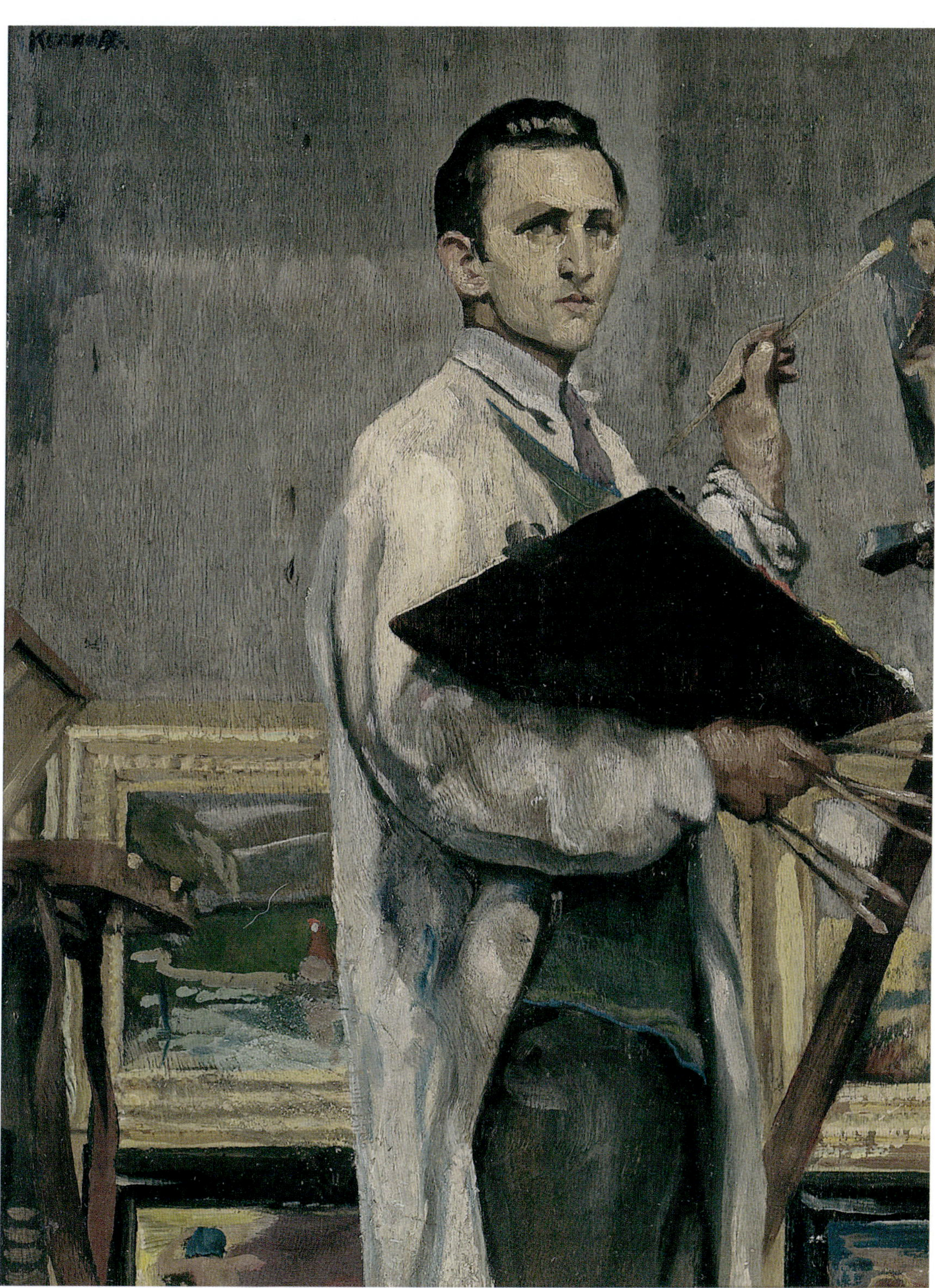

4.7 Harry Aaron Kernoff, *Self-Portrait*, 1929

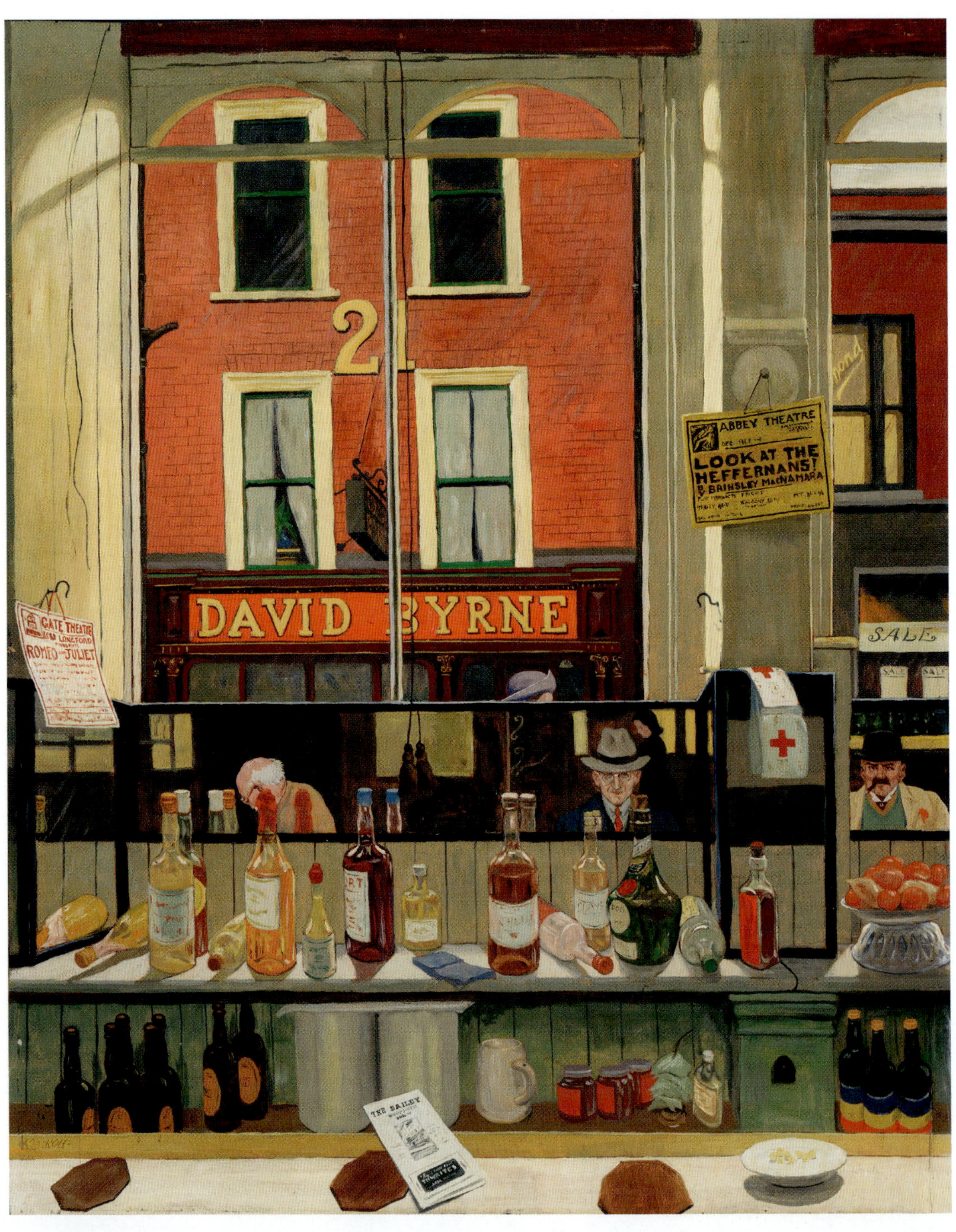

4.8   Harry Aaron Kernoff, *Davy Byrne's Pub, Dublin, from the Bailey*, 1941

'slough off their habitual identity', we can see not only the transformation of Yeats's own artistic outlook and style, but also his identification of the river as a place of crossing, transgression, and change, drawing on a rich visual tradition of the urban riverside as a site to be both celebrated and feared.

Circulation: the tram

In nineteenth-century urban paintings, the tram or railway carriage was frequently used to symbolise progressive urbanisation and the modernity of the city, as well as offering a convenient space to contrast differences in social class: as Laura Marcus has outlined, the 'railway and other modern forms of transport are not intrinsically modernist, but they have been an important inspiration for modernist cultural forms'.[55] Although the tram service had been in operation in Dublin since the late 1870s, Yeats was one of the first artists in Ireland to repeatedly depict the tram and its passengers as a subject, making it the central focus of five paintings completed over the course of the 1920s. Predating these, a small number of tram sketches appear in various sketchbooks, for example a 1901 pen and watercolour sketch depicts a trolley crossing the canal at Baggot Street bridge.[56] Trams were the main method of public transport in the city, and in the first half of the twentieth century, seventeen routes connected all sides of the city and suburbs: Yeats's own map of the city's tram routes is extant in his archive.[57] Given their importance as a method of circulation, it is unsurprising that the tram network featured heavily in literary descriptions of the city – perhaps most notably in *Dubliners*, where the horse-drawn trams are frequently mentioned, and in *Ulysses*, where the electrified successors are habitually taken by a range of characters. Early in the novel, Joyce described the central tram terminus at Nelson's Pillar where

> trams slowed, shunted, changed trolley ... The hoarse Dublin United Tramway Company's timekeeper bawled them off ... Right and left clanging ringing a double-decker and a singledeck moved from their railroads, swerved to the down line, glided parallel.[58]

Yeats was also likely aware of the other recent uses and history of the Dublin tram network. Even a cursory search for the term in the Bureau of Military History Witness Statements shows that trams were used for covert meetings, espionage, or for the transportation of arms; they were frequently searched by the Auxiliaries and other officials enforcing the city-wide curfew.

As outlined in the Introduction, the guerrilla war which played out across the city in the opening years of the 1920s, accompanied by curfews and search trucks, added to the tense mood in the city at this time. This close and confined atmosphere is further explored by Yeats in the opening pages of his 1936 novel, *The Amaranthers*, when a character – walking in a city at night – sees 'light hit the wall at the end of the street behind her, a strong shaft of light, it whisked about and then went out. She knew it was a search light from an armoured car.'[59] As

Samuel Beckett noted in his review of the book, Yeats did not overtly reference Dublin in his creation of the 'City', but passages such as these certainly resonate with its history.[60] Previous biographers of the artist have referred to a period of depression experienced by the artist in the mid-1910s as being connected to the trauma of the First World War, which went against the artist's pacifist principles, but the extent to which he absorbed the tensions of the revolutionary period into his painting as largely been confined to expressly nationalist readings of key paintings, such as *Bachelor's Walk*. Exploring the artist's series of tram paintings in relation to the wartime experience of the city, along with the more general experience of urban isolation, enables a more psychological reading of these works which further balances the artist's local and universal experiences of city life.

In 1923, the artist completed two contrasting depictions of tram interiors. Painted in the same naturalist style as works like *Bachelor's Walk* and worked on a small scale like *In Capel Street, In the Tram* (Plate 3.10) shows a group of well-dressed, middle-class women in conversation in a moving trolley. Grouped together on the right-hand side of the canvas, their closeness seems to emphasise the solitary isolation of the man seated in the opposite corner. The palette of the painting is relatively sombre, with the brown and grey tones lifted by the coloured window panes and the blurred green verdure of the landscape behind them.[61] In contrast to this rather sedate colouring and atmosphere, *A Full Tram* (1923, oil on canvas, private collection) gives quite a different portrayal of this mode of transportation and signals an important key change in Yeats's colouring and technique as he approached the mid-1920s. Significantly larger than its contemporary, the canvas is filled with strongly contrasting colours, from the golden yellow of the carriage roof, the brown tones of the passengers' clothing, to the dark shadows of the foreground. The viewer of the painting looks directly down the length of the carriage, peering over the shoulder of a woman as she enters the carriage. From this perspective, Yeats conveys a sense of the narrow, crowded space, and the long brush strokes that make up the carriage floor lend a strong sense of movement and dynamism to the composition.

As with *In the Tram*, here Yeats again includes the figure of a solitary man; however, in this instance the figure is more suggestive of the artist himself. Through the 1920s, the depiction of an isolated man became a recurrent motif in many of Yeats's urban paintings, often emulating the physical characteristics of the artist. Arnold described the appearance of the artist in the 1920s, noting that: 'his tall figure had become leaner as a result of his illness, and the bone structure of his face, which in later years was to become quite cadaverous, gave it a stern authority'.[62] The figure stands in the left-hand middle-ground of the composition, holding on to an overhead strap. His face is turned down, composed only of a series of short, suggestive brush strokes. None of the surrounding passengers engage with him (or with each other for that matter), although the gaze of the woman in the foreground does seem to be directed towards him. Standing just outside of the tram doors, and fashionably dressed in a cloche-style hat, she has attracted the attention of the two men in the left-hand foreground, who both turn their heads towards her. Through these figures the act of looking or observing is woven into the painting, echoing the wider discussion around the idea of the observer of modern life. In addition, Yeats conveys the sense of isolation of the people depicted: despite the full carriage, there is little sense of community or communal experience, and most of the figures shown seem engrossed in their own worlds and thoughts.

In the later part of the 1920s, Yeats embarked on three further tram scenes which once again demonstrate the dramatic change in his technique as he approached the 1930s. *A Dublin Newsboy Boarding a Tram* (Plate 3.11), painted in 1926 and now in the Harvard Art Museum, aligns Yeats's interest in the city's newspaper sellers with the transitory space of the tram carriage. Again, the painting shows the marked change in Yeats's painting technique: the application of paint across the breadth of the canvas is uneven, with only a thin wash of grey-blue applied in parts of the background, while the boy's face and clothing are worked in thick impasto. The face of the newspaper seller is only rendered in vague outlines, and the bundle of papers is loosely suggested through a thick area of white paint. The placement of the vertical line of the tram door, close to the edge of the canvas, suggests that the boy is peering, and perhaps shouting, quickly into the carriage to advertise his wares during a brief pause in the service. The city behind the figure is non-descript, indicated only by loose strokes of blue-grey. This contrasts strongly with *Crossing the Canal Bridge from the Tram Top* (1927, oil on canvas, private collection), completed by Yeats in the following year. In this composition, Yeats radically changes the viewpoint from the previous tram scenes: the viewer sits with the artist in the trolley and looks out at the blue canal and dark night sky. The brown-red frame of the tram window cuts across the window at an angle, enabling the viewer to experience the sensation of the rise and speed of the carriage as it crosses the humped bridge. The exact location is unidentified; however, the look and general outline of the buildings are suggestive of the stretch between Portobello and Baggot Street, where there were several crossing points. The colouring of the canvas is lifted by the green canal banks, along which commuters scurry through the evening light.

The final work of this series also dates from 1927 and presents a further perspective on the city. Removed from the confines of the carriage, the figure in *From the Tram Top* (1927, oil on panel, private collection) surveys the city around him, where thickly applied lines and dashes of paint suggest people on the pavement. Described by one critic as 'phantom-like', the man is also reminiscent of the figure shown in *A Full Tram*, and perhaps, then, of the artist himself.[63] Whereas *A Full Tram* showed the artist-figure as being observed by others, here the elevated position places him above those around him and firmly in the position of the onlooker. The sense of height in the painting is emphasised by the buildings that frame the canvas and that, like the tram, rise over the people below. Using brown, black, and ochre tones, along with the blank, dark windows, the buildings on the right-hand side have a menacing air, while also adding to the sense of confinement by blocking out the sky. Yeats's five tram paintings from the 1920s encapsulate the changes in his urban vision over the course of this decade, and mirror more broadly the transformation of his artistic style. From the illustrative focus on others seen in *In the Tram*, through to the more frenetic later canvases which seem to focus on both the alienation of the self – and of the urban environment itself. If the tram paintings reflect something of the tensions experienced by those living in Dublin in the early 1920s, a further strand of Yeats's urban painting was concerned with the aftermath of the revolutionary years, exploring the place of women and leisure in the new Irish Free State.

Painting modernity and morality in the Irish Free State

Yeats's early sketches of theatres and boxing clubs show the artist's interest in urban nightlife, taking in the serious and comedic, popular music halls, and more serious productions of the national theatre. This interest was not only reflected in the artist's sketches, but also through his collection of theatre programmes, playbills, and posters: including those for the Abbey and Gate theatres, as well as the Gaiety, Olympia, and the Theatre Royal. Alongside these, a collection of ballad sheets, with notations suggesting that the artist purchased them for a few pennies along the Dublin quays, give a rich insight into the city's musical culture in the early years of the twentieth century. These interests were combined by the artist in a series of paintings of theatre interiors through the 1920s, 1930s, and 1940s such as *Patriotic Airs* (1923, oil on canvas, NGI) and *Singing the Minstrel Boy* (1923, oil on canvas, The Model, Sligo) which present music hall interiors – a conflation of several Dublin theatres – and riff on nationalist themes. As the decade progressed, the context in which Yeats was living and working was shifting, as the Irish Free State settled and solidified after the turbulent years of the Civil War. Reflecting these changes, several paintings of the city at night, its nightlife, and entertainments from this period show a very different side of urban experience to the Sickert-like theatre scenes.

Pertinent among these shifts was the increasing conservatism of the state towards the moral aspects of modern life, particularly as related to sexual activity, dancing, and the influence of international cultural trends on traditional values. Much of this concern was directed towards women, and their private lives came under increasing scrutiny. As Maria Luddy has explored, prior to independence, the blame for sexual issues such as venereal disease or the rate of births outside of marriage was often laid at the British garrisons stationed in Ireland. However, when the incidence rates of such issues grew after 1922, it was more difficult to place the blame on this quarter. Rather, when the Inter-Departmental Committee of Inquiry regarding Venereal Disease (known as the Carrigan Committee) wrote their report, they identified a new target to blame for the spread of the disease: 'a young woman who engaged in sexual activity without looking for monetary gain'.[64] Their (unpublished) report labelled these women as prostitutes, thus allying 'the sexuality of young women with that of the stigmatized prostitute', rather than recognising the emergence of the more liberated 'new woman', in Irish society.[65] The new state's fear of prostitution in particular was exemplified by the Abbey Theatre board's worries over Seán O'Casey's inclusion of a prostitute in *The Plough and the Stars*, as well as the Legion of Mary's campaign to clear the infamous 'Monto' red light district. This area on the city's northside had appeared under the guise of 'Night-town' in *Portrait of the Artist* and *Ulysses*: in the former, Stephen visits a brothel, located in 'a maze of narrow and dirty streets. From foul laneways he heard bursts of hoarse riot and the drawling of drunken singers.'[66]

Despite the disruption of the revolutionary period, Dublin was not immune from the latest trends of modern popular culture. New fashions were not solely the preserve of women, as an article on 'Dublin's Beau Brummels' reported in December 1921. While women's fashions were seen to be limited to 'subdued shades … navy, brown, or terracotta', Dublin's modern young man 'delights in brilliant colours, and his resplendent garb is calculated to put shame to the colours of the rainbow'.[67] Women's interest columns gave advice on shorter skirt lengths, including a new Parisian style where 'the skirt finishes above the knee', the trend for larger handbags and small cloche hats, the height of heels, and, in 1923, a pattern for a flapper-style dress.[68] Throughout this period all of the large Dublin hotels and venues hosted jazz bands and cabaret acts; for example, in 1923 the 'Cocktail Syncopators' played at the Theatre Royal along with the 'Martinis', a group of dancers who were 'celebrated as what are called ballroom dancers, but their performance here is a whirlwind variety, such as no one could expect to see elsewhere'.[69] A report on a dance held at the Metropole Ballroom, O'Connell Street in 1927 featured 'Percival Mackay's band, and the cabaret "turns" by Miss Monti Ryan, Miss Dickie Dixon, and Mr Harry Robbins'.[70] Ryan was Irish, and during this performance she 'gave impressions of eccentric dancing, danced the "Apache," and gave exhibitions of the Charleston and the Blackbottom [*sic*]'.[71]

Admonitions directed towards women who followed these trends were frequently issued from the pulpit; for example, in his Lenten Pastoral in 1920, the Bishop of Limerick focused on 'the question of female dress and attendance at picture exhibitions' (meaning the cinema) as well as the dangers of modern dancing which 'were gradually creeping into their midst in the city'. The Bishop contrasted traditional Irish dancing, which was felt to be 'the maximum of gracefulness, exercise, and entertainment, with the minimum of danger'; while on the other hand, new dances 'from their very nature and from the bearing and attitude of those engaged in them, are not only dangerous, but immodest and sinful'.[72] In 1924, Cardinal Logue repeated these judgements in another Lenten Pastoral, which again targeted women's dress and dancing. The *Irish Times* reported that the Cardinal 'had often felt an impulse to pass over women presenting themselves for Holy Communion in such unbecoming dress' and that while 'he knew nothing of the character of the imported dances ... their names are bizarre enough, and from those that had seen them he formed the opinion that they are the outcrop of the corruption of the age, most objectionable on the score of morality'.[73]

The connection made between traditional Irish dancing and a purer form of entertainment by the Bishop of Limerick in 1920 was often used in criticism of modern dancing. In 1921, a reader of the *Freeman's Journal* wrote to the editor to add their voice to previous complaints that during the celebrations following the truce that closed the War of Independence, 'it was alleged that some of our bravest and best could find nothing better in the way of dancing than foreign importations, such as jazz and the like'. For this reader, however, it was the mix of traditional Irish and modern dancing that provoked the most ire, and they called for 'some authoritative body' to 'issue a warning against what is known as a "Ceilidh and Dance"'. The author called for a boycott of mixed dance events, stating that while 'those who desire jazzing and its kindred freaks are entitled to them ... a ceilidh should be exclusively a ceilidh and nothing else'.[74] Through the 1920s the Gaelic League objected to the proliferation of new dances, and at their annual conference in 1928 the general secretary, Frank Fahy, charged the league to take control of dancing so that 'Irish dances might be encouraged and placed above all other kinds of dances'.[75] Fahy's remarks were, according to the *Weekly Irish Times* report, supported by the League's President, Cormac Breathnach, who said that 'the young men of the country were blameable for the neglect of Irish dances, because they were satisfied with whirling around in "jazz" and other foreign dancing'.[76] That taking part in non-traditional dances was considered by some as unpatriotic is further illustrated in a letter to the *Irish Independent* dating to 1926, wherein the author felt that

> foreign dances and their dancers produce the type of mind which can write a play in which the Irish boy is represented as half a fool, laughed at by the Anglo-Irish for his accent, laughed at by a Dublin audience because he is 'only a country boy.' The Gaelic Leaguer is right – we want no jazzers.[77]

Returning to Yeats's paintings of urban scenes in the 1920s, a correlation can be found between the themes and issues outlined above and his representations of women in the city. When *Flower Girl, Dublin* (Plate 3.12) was exhibited in 1926, the criticism offered in the Irish press was once again limited to the painting's aesthetic qualities, with the *Irish Independent* noting that the painting was 'excellent – the contrasts not only in the colouring but in the figures and their expressions, being definitely brought out, and the whole making a characteristic Yeats and fascinating study'.[78] At the centre of the composition, a young woman proffers a tray of violets to another female figure. Rather than being shown in a long skirt and thick woollen shawl, this flower seller wears a shorter, more fashionable length skirt or dress, smart heels, and has her hair cut into a bob. In contrast, the other woman wears a fur evening coat and fashionable cloche hat, while the flower seller is bareheaded and is only covered by a black shawl.

Yeats makes clear the social distinctions between the two women through their attire. To the left, a group like that seen in *A Full Tram* stands together conspiratorially, observing, but not interacting, with the other figures in the painting. Opposite them, the possible companion of the woman in the red hat stands against the bright lights of a shop window and looks almost directly out to the viewer, drawing them into the narrative. With this painting, Yeats markedly deviates from the established modes of representing the urban flower seller, with the clothing and the setting of the painting signalling the modern urban environment, and the contemporary discussion around the appropriateness (or otherwise) of women's dress. While the depiction of the girl does not evoke the pastoral associations seen in earlier representations of this figure, including those in Yeats's own oeuvre, the underlying association between the flower seller and prostitution forms an important subtext for this painting, with both figures previously viewed in tandem as 'both sold delicate, transitory beauty for money on the streets in urban public spaces'.[79] The interaction between the flower seller and the more well-to-do woman recalls a scene in *Portrait of the Artist* where a flower seller implores Stephen to 'Buy that lovely bunch. Will you gentleman? The blue flowers which she lifted towards him and her young blue eyes seemed to him at that instant images of guilelessness, and he halted until the image had vanished and he saw only her ragged dress and damp coarse hair and hoydenish face.'[80]

The fluidity between the identities of the urban flower seller and street walker finds further articulation in a later painting by the artist. *Three Traders of Dublin* (Plate 3.13), first exhibited by the artist at the Goupil Gallery, London in 1927, depicts three women – strangely elongated and distorted – against a dark, narrow background in which the cityscape is reduced to its simplest forms: while the setting is undoubtedly urban it could be set in any part of the city to which the title alludes. The three traders, different to either of the flower-seller 'types' already discussed, fold their arms defiantly across their chests, and the usual signifiers for street traders, such as fruit or flowers, are not included. The frontal position of the figures is reminiscent of earlier urban scenes by German artist Ernst Ludwig Kirchner, such as *Street Scene (Friedrichstrasse, Berlin)* (1914, oil on canvas, Staatsgalerie, Stuttgart). Rosalyn Deutsch previously described these works as showing 'pictures of an unnatural, thoroughly dehumanised world', a view which certainly resonates with Yeats's depiction of these traders.[81] While it is unlikely that London viewers of the painting would have been aware of the minutia of local Dublin politics, it is also possible that Yeats was referencing a contemporary dispute between the Dublin traders and the city commissioners. When, in January 1927, the authorities began to implement a series of new regulations allowed by the Street Trading Act (1926), brought in 'to make Dublin a clean, hygienic and beautiful city', many traders resisted this reorganisation.[82] Newspaper reports from throughout the year show that women (who were prominent among the city's market and street traders), were prosecuted for protest and non-compliance: for example, in June, 'a number of women street traders were fined in sums ranging from 10s. to 40s. for breaches of the street trading regulations', and on the same occasion, 'a girl who threw her shoe at a Guard was fined 10s. while another was fined 10s. for striking the same Guard with a bread-board and using offensive language'.[83]

In this context, *Three Traders of Dublin* can be read as a depiction of three marginal figures within the Dublin landscape, threatened by the modernisation of the city around them. A way of life that had been connected with the urban space for centuries was being phased out, marking not only a move away from open markets and stalls, but also a desire to 'beautify' the city to make it a more attractive environment. However, this reading and understanding of the painting rests on a prior knowledge of the dispute and on the situation for traders in Dublin in the late 1920s. For an audience unfamiliar with this context, such as those who might have seen the work when it was shown at the Goupil Gallery, might the compositional connection to artists such as Kirchner (or other twentieth century urban painters) have been more apparent? Seen in a wider art historical context and within the established conventions of urban painting, it doesn't seem completely unlikely that these women may have been, or at least may have been interpreted as being, selling something other than fruit.[84]

As already alluded to, the flourishing of jazz and international music in Dublin and elsewhere in Ireland was also cause for concern in the 1920s. This new music and the societal freedoms it signified, however, were central to a painting exhibited by the artist in 1929. *Jazz Babies* (Plate 3.14) took its title from an eponymous term used to describe a 'vivacious young woman' in possession of the attributes now associated with the quintessential 1920s flapper.[85] The painting itself, mainly composed in variations of orange, red, and black tones, shows a group of people in an interior, including a fashionably dressed couple in the centre of the composition. Described elsewhere as a painting which shows 'Dubliners who might be taken for New Yorkers', the composition takes in a bar scene, with the repeated touches of a bright yellow suggesting strong electric lighting.[86] Rows of bottles fill the background, while a white-faced barman rests to the left-hand side, shown more in the manner of a painted clown in Yeats's circus paintings. Two figures, however, demand more of our attention. To the right, a tall man dressed in a brown coat and hat, who holds a hand to his lapel; and to the left, a woman dressed in a sleeveless top or dress, her arm adorned with a gold cuff and turquoise ribbon, and either a black cloche hat or shingled hair style. This stylish and contemporary evening wear suggests that she and her partner are the 'jazz babies' of the painting's title, enjoying an evening in the city, perhaps taking in one of the entertainments described earlier in this chapter.

Yeats returned to the theme of dancing in 1932 with *Dancing on the Deck of the Royal Iris* (Plate 3.15). The palette of this work is lighter, with white, pink, blue, and yellow used, perhaps, to reflect the lighter nature of the subject matter. The *Royal Iris* had arrived in Dublin in 1932, when it was purchased by Irish shipping company, Palmer and Wallace, from Liverpool where it had been used as a passenger ferry on the Mersey. The ferry had been involved in operations during the First World War and was subsequently granted its 'Royal' prefix.[87] In addition, the *Royal Iris* provided an excursion and pleasure-cruise service from Custom House quay around Dublin Bay through the summer months. An afternoon and evening service was available, and a 1934 advertisement stated that 'refreshments can be had on board, and the steamer's dance band gives a special programme of music'.[88] In 1932, the *Irish Independent* published an image of children trying out the band's instruments, and certainly several non-traditional instruments can be seen, such as a trumpet, clarinet, and snare drums. In the following year, the *Irish Press* published a photograph of people dancing on the boat, and although it was reproduced in black and white, the movement and enjoyment seen in Yeats's painting is also evident.[89] The artist collected such advertisements, as well as other ephemera, and gathered these together in two large scrapbooks, now in the Yeats Archive at the NGI. In the 'late' scrapbook, which contains material from the early 1930s onwards, the artist pasted advertisements for the 'S.S Royal Iris Dublin Bay Excursion Services', and the 'Cynthia Pleasure Cruises from Custom House Quay'.[90] In this painting, Yeats also records the subtle developments in women's fashion in the 1930s: the dancer's hair is longer and pinned up rather than bobbed, and her dress also has longer sleeves. Although the press pictures suggest that a trip on the *Royal Iris* was a family affair, Yeats's depiction of the entwined couple is imbued with sensuality: the long, loose strokes of paint and the tones of red and pink which run along the woman's arms (the colour also being used for her lips) give a feeling of slow, undulating movement. While the dancers are observed by two figures in the background, the feeling of unease noted in *Jazz Babies* (chiefly caused by the man's direct gaze) is not present here.

Both *Dancing on the Deck of the Royal Iris* and *Jazz Babies* represent social life and socialising in Dublin in the late 1920s and early 1930s; yet even as Yeats's painted and exhibited them, the criticism of jazz and dance halls increased, focusing on urban and rural areas alike. The strongest interventions from the government to place controls upon popular culture came with the Censorship of Publications Act (1929) and the Public Dance Halls Act (1935), which was 'designed to make it extremely difficult to hold a dance without the sanction of the police, the judiciary and the clergy'. As Paul Rouse has astutely noted, however, 'it was one thing to make the law but quite another to ensure that people changed their habits'.[91]

Conclusion: the veil of city life

If the themes of isolation and alienation ebb and flow through Yeats's urban paintings of the 1920s, they reached an apotheosis in *People in a Street* and *Morning in A City*, both painted in the late 1930s (Plates 3.16, 3.17). An intense and frenetic depiction of a crowd moving through the city, *People in a Street* is among Yeats's most consciously 'modern' depictions of Dublin. The crowd is framed by the tall buildings of Westmoreland Street, with the portico of the former House of Lords visible in the background, although producing a recognisable streetscape was likely not the main concern of the artist. The narrow street, with the sky reduced to a small section of the upper-left-hand side, gives a claustrophobic atmosphere while the touches of yellow evoke electric lighting and flickering shadows. With figures placed at the forefront of the canvas, the viewer is immediately immersed in the pressing crowd, with half-formed figures passing by on either side. In this painting, the energy of earlier works such as *The Liffey Swim* and *Dublin Night* meet the introspection of *A Full Tram* and *Crossing the Metal Bridge*, with the fragmented brush work of *Three Traders of Dublin*. As with these earlier works, Yeats takes elements that are specific to Dublin but also redolent of a universal urban experience. The claustrophobic atmosphere of this painting is repeated in *Morning in a City*: the deep carmine red turning the street into a type of inferno, filled with bustling figures. At the centre of the composition stands an isolated male figure, akin to that seen in previous paintings from the 1920s. Róisín Kennedy has suggested that in this painting the 'city is presented as being at the service of the artist'; yet, arguably, we might see this representation of the self (presuming that this is a type of self-portrait) or of an anonymous urban citizen, as simply being part of the multilayered and complex system of human life in a large city.[92] Observing the development of Yeats's urban painting from the early sketchbooks to these later canvases, there is little sense of the artist mastering the urban environment, but rather an acceptance that to live there is to experience (to some extent) feelings of isolation, of alienation, and of being a small constituent part of something larger and uncontrollable – a theme which visual artists had been exploring from the 1880s.

In 1922, Yeats published a small pamphlet titled *Aspects of Modern Irish Art*.[93] Among the artist's comments on painting and the nascent Irish state, he noted that:

> 'Life in Ireland is nearer to nature than is a country overspread with cities, not that cities do not hold plenty of things to appeal to the memory of the eye. But for the artist to live too long among houses and streets is liable to introduce too dense a veil between his eyes and nature.[94]

He later continued that it 'is most necessary that the phases of the life in our big towns and cities should be painted. But the artist will be bothered with many pitfalls, he is too often tempted to see things in the form that others have seen them and not with his own fresh eye.'[95] Through his sketches, illustrations, and paintings of Dublin, Yeats himself was one of the most prolific chroniclers of urban life in Ireland; however, as these comments suggest, he was also wary of the city as a subject. Was he affected by the 'veil' of city life, and led to paint 'a picture from another man's picture'?[96] Perhaps this is what accounts for the sense of isolation, alienation, and loneliness that pervades many of Yeats's urban paintings; yet, if so, he was certainly not alone in portraying it in visual or textual form. Indeed, these comments align in many ways with Duncan's concept of the imagined environment or archive of the city, suggesting that it is almost impossible to separate the real and imagined worlds of the modern city. Yeats's visions of the city can be considered alongside his contemporaries, such as the artists of the Ashcan School, in a transnational history of urban painting. These works must be considered in a matrixed context that considers not only the history of life in Dublin, but the shared experience of modern life in an urban space.

Although Yeats's portrayal of Dublin was markedly different to that of either Osborne or Barton, all three artists can be broadly grouped together as middle-class painters with Protestant backgrounds, even if this varied from landed gentry to sons of professional, suburban fathers. Class largely protected Barton from any overt gender discrimination, she had the means – both financial and social – to pursue her professional career as she pleased, suggesting that class was an influential factor for those pursing artistic careers. Obviously not every artist working in Ireland during this period was from as well-to-do backgrounds as the artists discussed so far: however, Harry Kernoff, the focus of the next chapter, provides an interesting counterpoint to Osborne, Barton, and Yeats.

Notes

1   R. Kennedy, 'Jack Yeats and Dublin', in D. J. Foley (ed.), *The Only Art of Jack B. Yeats* (Dublin: Lilliput Press, 2009), p. 158.

2   R. Zurier, *Picturing the City: Urban Vision and the Ashcan School* (Berkeley: University of California Press, 2006), p. 91.

3   Quidnunc, 'An Irishman's Diary: Mr J. B. Yeats', *Irish Times* (29 February 1928), p. 4.

4   'Mr Jack B. Yeats's Pictures', *Irish Times* (28 April 1919), p. 5.

5   B. Arnold, 'Jack Yeats: the need for reassessment', in Y. Scott (ed.), *Jack B. Yeats: Old and New Departures* (Dublin: Four Courts Press, 2008), pp. 47–8.

6   D. J. Murphy (ed.), *Lady Gregory's Journals*, vol. II, books thirty to forty-four, 21 February 1925–9 May 1932 (Gerrards Cross: Colin Smythe, 1987), p. 31.

7   R. Ellmann, *James Joyce* (New York: Oxford University Press, 1959), p. 715.

8   NGI Yeats Archive, Y1/JY/1/1/90/24, 'One of Guinness's cruises on the Liffey' [September] 1905.

9   Drouot Estimations, *Tableaux Modernes et Art Nouveau – Art Deco*, 21 November 2008, Lot 96.

10 Allen, *Modernism, Ireland and Civil War*, p. 143.

11 Letter from James Joyce to Grant Richards, 23 June 1906. In S. Gilbert (ed.), *Letters of James Joyce* (London: Faber and Faber, 1957), pp. 63–4.

12 NGI Yeats Archive, Y1/JY/1/1/27/39, 'Cumberland and Westmorland wrestling at Savigear's riding school Earls Court', [March–April] 1900.

13 NGI Yeats Archive, Y1/JY/1/1/38/9, 'The Lady Juggler' [September–October] 1901 and Y1/JY/1/1/38/15, [Saxophone Player], [September–October] 1901.

14 NGI Yeats Archive, Y1/JY/1/1/30/22, 'Limestone causeway where the Chinamen live' [January–February] 1901.

15 See Jack B. Yeats, *Untitled: Japanese Pirate (I); Untitled, Japanese Pirate (II)*, sold, Sotheby's *Yeats: The Family Collection*, 27 September 2017, Lot. 169.

16 See T. Cusack, 'Migrant travellers and tourist idylls: the paintings of Jack B. Yeats and post-colonial identities', *Art History* 2:21 (2003), 201–18. DOI 10.1111/1467-8365.00103.

17 For more on Yeats's London connections in the 1930s and 1940s, see N. O'Donnell, '"Irrigated neither by the Seine nor by the Thames": Jack B. Yeats's reception in London', *British Art Studies* 14 (2019). DOI https://doi.org/10.17658/issn.2058-5462/issue-14/nodonnell.

18 See É. O'Connor, 'America called: the Helen Hackett Gallery and the Irish Art Rooms, 1924–1934', *New Hibernia Review / Iris Éireannach Nua* 15:4 (2011), 16–33.

19 New York Public Library, The Henry W. and Albert A. Berg Collection of English and American Literature, sketchbook V3, 'Dublin 1901 Diarmid and Grania'.

20 J. Joyce, *Ulysses* (London: Penguin Books, 2000), p. 320.

21 NGI Yeats Archive, Y1/JY/1/1/39/2, 'Down at the quays, Dublin', November 1901 and Y1/JY/1/1/59/20, 'In the tattoo shop on the quays, Dublin', November 1901.

22 'About Tattooing', *Evening Herald (Dublin)* (23 February 1901), p. 1.

23 J. Joyce, 'An Encounter', in *Dubliners*, ed. M. Norris (New York and London: W.W Norton & Company, 2006), p. 15.

24 NGI Yeats Archive, Y1/JY/5/2/74, letter from Walter Sickert to Jack B. Yeats, c. January 1924.

25 Walter Sickert, quoted in R. Emmons, *The Life and Opinions of Walter Sickert* (London: Faber and Faber, 1942), p. 246.

26 NGI Yeats Archive, Y1/JY/1/1/157/23, 'Where the people were shot on Sunday' [30?] July 1914.

27 T. Allen, 'A Talk with Jack Yeats: Art and Drama Under Sinn Fein', *Westminster Gazette* (21 December 1921). Clipping included in NGI Yeats Archive, Y1/JY/4/2/1, scrapbook of clippings of reviews, articles, and comment on the work of Jack Butler Yeats for the period 1881–1925.

28 S. Bhreathnach-Lynch, 'Framing Ireland's history: art, politics and representation', in J. C. Steward (ed.), *When Time Began to Rant and Rage: Figurative Painting from Twentieth Century Ireland* (London: Merell Holberton, 1998), p. 41; see also B. Arnold, *Jack B. Yeats* (New Haven: Yale University Press, 1998), pp. 191–3.

29 R. Foster, '"The occupation of living": Jack B. Yeats and the Irish Revolution', in B. Rooney (ed.), *Creating History: Stories of Ireland in Art* (Dublin: Irish Academic Press, 2016), p. 257.

30 See M. Maguire, *Precarious Childhood in Post-independence Ireland* (Manchester: Manchester University Press, 2009).

31 The exhibition was titled *Drawings and Pictures of Life in the West of Ireland*, despite the fact that several Dublin paintings were included. This suggests Yeats's own awareness of the public preference for rural or coastal scenes.

32 See S. Rains, 'City streets and the city edition: newsboys and newspapers in early twentieth-century Ireland', *Irish Studies Review* 24:2 (2016), 142–58; and D. Fallon, S. McGrath, and C. Murray, 'Dublin's newsboys of old,' in *Come Here to Me! Dublin's Other History* (Dublin: New Island, 2012), pp. 1–5.

33 NGI Yeats Archive, Y1/JY/1/1/59/18, 'Barefoot news boy in the swell lounge' [? August] 1903.

34 For reviews in the *Irish Times* and *Freeman's Journal* see, 'Connemara and Dublin: Mr Jack B. Yeats' New Studies of Irish Life', *Irish Times* (28 April 1923), p. 7 and 'Mr J. B. Yeats' Pictures', *Freeman's Journal* (26 April 1923), p. 8.

35 'The Art of Mr J. B. Yeats', *Irish Independent* (26 April 1923), p. 4.

36 Ibid.

37 British Pathé, 'Funeral of Michael Collins', 1922, https://ifiplayer.ie/funeral-of-mich ael-collins/ (accessed 21 April 2020).

38 Zurier, *Picturing the City: Urban Vision and the Ashcan School*, p. 23.

39 Ibid., p. 31.

40 J. Marstine, 'Eight, the (ii).' *Oxford Art Online. Grove Art Online.* Oxford University Press. www.oxfordartonline.com/subscriber/article/grove/art/T025690 (accessed 21 April 2020).

41 See P. McEvansoneya, '"Dismal Art" or "Strong, realistic pictures"? Luke Fildes, Frank Holl and "social realism"' (PhD Diss., University of Leicester, 1992).

42 NGI Yeats Archive, Y1/JY/4/1/3, Jack Butler Yeats's address books [c.1910]–1931 and 1931–55. Yeats also owned a catalogue for an exhibition of Sloan's work held in New York in 1948 (NGI Yeats Archive, Y1/JY/18/11, Catalogue of John Sloan (1871–1951) retrospective exhibition, Kraushaar Galleries, New York, 2–28 February 1948).

43 M. S. Hutton, 'Walking in the city at the turn of the century: John Sloan's pedestrian aesthetics', in H. C. Coyle and J. K. Schiller (eds), *John Sloan's New York* (Delaware: Delaware Art Museum in association with Yale University Press, 2007), p. 83.

44 Ibid., p. 88.

45 'Royal Hibernian Academy,' *Irish Times* (6 April 1925), p. 6.

46 Kennedy, 'Jack Yeats and Dublin', p. 154.

47 T. Cusack, 'Introduction: exploring the water's edge', in T. Cusack (ed.), *Art and Identity at the Water's Edge* (Aldershot: Ashgate, 2012), p. 2.

48 See T. Cusack, 'Crossing the Shannon: Ireland's "Mighty Stream" and the making of the nation', *Visual Culture in Britain* 3:1 (2002), 77–97; and T. Cusack, *Riverscapes and National Identities* (Syracuse: Syracuse University Press, 2010), pp. 158–89.

49 Cusack, 'Introduction: exploring the water's edge', p. 3.

50 Egerton, *The Wheel of God*, p. 23.

51 'The Art of Mr J. B. Yeats', *Irish Independent* (26 April 1923), p. 4.

52 'London Letter', *Freeman's Journal* (8 January 1924), p. 4.

53 Marshall, *City of Gold and Mud*, p. 23.

54 Our Own Correspondent, 'Mr Jack Yeats' Pictures', *Irish Times* (17 March 1928), p. 6.

55 L. Marcus. *Dreams of Modernity: Psychoanalysis, Literature and Cinema* (Cambridge: Cambridge University Press, 2014), p. 2.

56 NGI Yeats Archive, Y1/JY/1/1/37/24, 'Baggot street bridge', 1901.

57 NGI Yeats Archive, Y1/JY/24/1/6/19, Irish maps collection by Jack Butler Yeats, Box 2, 1900–15.

58 Joyce, *Ulysses*, p. 147. Yeats was undoubtedly aware of Joyce's later novel. Copies of *The Little Review* in which parts of *Ulysses* were serialised are extant in the Yeats Archive: see Allen, *Modernism, Ireland, and Civil War*, p. 150 and NGI Yeats Archive, Y1/JY/23/1/17, eighteen issues of *The Little Review*, 1917–21.

59 J. B. Yeats, *The Amaranthers* (London: Heinemann, 1936), p. 30.

60 S. Beckett, 'An Imaginative Work!', *The Dublin Magazine* (July–September 1936), p. 81.

61 Both Pyle and Kennedy suggest that this is the Phoenix Park, and that the painting shows the interior of the Lucan tram. See Kennedy, 'Jack Yeats and Dublin', p. 155 and Hilary Pyle, *Jack B. Yeats: A Catalogue Raisonné of the Oil Paintings*, vol. I (London: Deutsch, 1992), p. 177.

62 Arnold, *Jack B. Yeats*, p. 202.

63 P. G. Konody, 'Art and Artists: Mr Jack B. Yeats' Pictures of Irish Life', *Observer* (6 July 1930), p. 14. Pyle also suggests that this figure could represent the artist himself. See Pyle, *Catalogue Raisonné*, vol. I, p. 299.

64 M. Luddy, 'Sex and the single girl in 1920s and 1930s Ireland', *The Irish Review* 35 (2007), 86.

65 Ibid.

66 J. Joyce, *A Portrait of the Artist as a Young Man*, ed. H. W. Gabler with W. Hettch (London: Vintage, 2012), p. 94.

67 'Dublin's Beau Brummels', *Irish Times* (28 December 1921), p. 6.

68 'Women's Work & Interests: Skirts Above the Knees New Paris Fashion', *Irish Times* (14 August 1920), p. 6. See also, 'Floral Fashions: Big Handbags and Small Hats', *Irish Times* (29 April 1922), p. 6; P. W. 'The Height of Heels', *Irish Times* (10 May 1923), p. 2, and 'Paper Patterns for Home Workers: Flapper's Dress', *Irish Times* (22 September 1923), p. 6.

69 'Theatre Royal', *Freemans Journal* (1 May 1923), p. 8.

70 'Last Night's Dance: London Band at Metropole Ballroom', *Irish Times* (11 October 1927), p. 8.

71 Ibid. The apache was 'a fast and racy dance routine … It features a violent male … displaying his machismo in brutal, erotic partnership with a scantily clad girlfriend.' See D. Craine, and J. Mackrell, 'Apache Dance' in *The Oxford Dictionary of Dance* (Oxford: Oxford University Press, www.oxfordreference.com/view/10.1093/acref/9780199563449.001.0001/acref-9780199563449-e-122 [accessed 21 April 2020]). The black bottom dance had become popular in 1926 and was similar to the Charleston.

72 'Women's Work & Interests: Bishop of Limerick and Female Dress and Dancing', *Irish Times* (28 February 1920), p. 6.

73 'Modern Dancing: Condemnation in Lenten Pastorals', *Weekly Irish Times* (8 March 1924), p. 5.

74 G., 'Irish Dance Programmes', *Freeman's Journal* (26 August 1921), p. 6.

75 'Jazz Condemned by the Gaelic League', *Weekly Irish Times* (15 September 1928), p. 6.

76 Ibid.

77 A. Nic Fhirdia, 'Gaelic League and Jazz', *Irish Independent* (29 September 1926), p. 9.

78 'Mr Jack B. Yeats', *Irish Independent* (2 October 1929), p. 6.

79 Marshall, *City of Gold and Mud*, p. 208.

80 Joyce, *Portrait of the Artist as a Young Man*, p. 208.

81 R. Deutsch, 'Alienation in Berlin: Kirchner's street scenes', *Art in America* 69 (1983), quoted in C. W. Haxthausen, 'Kirchner's images of Berlin', in C. W. Haxthausen (ed.), *Berlin: Culture and Metropolis* (Minneapolis: University of Minnesota Press, 1990), p. 86.

82 'Street Trading in Dublin: A Clean Sweep', *Irish Times* (8 January 1927), p. 5.

83 'Obdurate Street Traders: Refusal to Leave their Pitches', *Irish Times* (20 June 1927), p. 11.

84 See H. Clayson, 'Painting the traffic in women', in V. R. Schwartz and J. M. Przblyski (eds), *The Nineteenth Century Visual Culture Reader* (London: Routledge, 2004), pp. 299–312 and C. Schönfeld 'Streetwalking the metropolis: prostitutes in Expressionism', in C. Schönfeld (ed.), *Commodities of Desire: The Prostitute in Modern German Literature* (Woodbridge: Camden House, 2000), pp. 110–30.

85 L. V. Berrey and M. Van den Bark, *The American Thesaurus of Slang: A Complete Reference Book of Colloquial Slang* (London: Harrap, 1954), pp. 363–4.

86 Allen, *Modernism, Ireland and Civil War*, p. 161.

87 M. R. McRonald, 'The Irish connections', *Friends of the Ferries Across the Mersey* (blog), www.friendsoftheferries.co.uk/ferries-history/ (accessed 21 April 2020).

88 'Dublin Bay Cruises', *Irish Press* (23 June 1934), p. 10.

89 'Holiday Makers – Enjoying a dance on the pleasure steamers, Royal Iris, in Dublin Bay', *Irish Press* (30 May 1933), p. 9.

90 NGI Yeats Archive, Y1/JY/8/2, Jack Butler Yeats's late scrapbook, c.1930–45.

91 P. Rouse, 'Popular culture in Ireland, 1880–2016', in *Cambridge History of Ireland Vol. IV*, p. 588.

92 Kennedy, 'Jack Yeats and Dublin', p. 158.

93 See J. B. Yeats, *Aspects of Modern Irish Art* (Dublin: Brown and Nolan for Cumann Léigheacht an Phobail, 1922). He had presented a version of this as a lecture at the Paris Race Congress in 1922, as part of the Irish delegation. For more on this event, see P. Murray, 'The Irish Race Congress, 21–28 January 1922', *History Ireland* 9:4 (2001) www.historyireland.com/20th-century-contemporary-history/the-irish-race-congress-21–28-january-1922/ (accessed 21 April 2020); and M. Hayes, D. Hyde, and E. MacNeill, 'Report on the Irish Race Conference in Paris', January 1922, Documents on Irish Foreign Policy, NAI DFA ES Box 11 File 77, www.difp.ie/docs/1922/Irish-Race-Convention-Paris/239.htm (accessed 21 April 2020).

94 Yeats, *Aspects of Modern Irish Art*, p. 6.

95 Ibid., p. 7.

96 Ibid., p. 6.

4

Radicals, workers, and drinkers

Assessing the changes that took place in the painting of 'modern life' from the late nineteenth century, T. J. Clark recently posed the question 'why … was there in the twentieth century no "painting of modern life" – or none that Degas and Baudelaire would have recognised?'[1] A number of answers to this query were suggested by the author including, for example, the idea that 'modernity no longer presented itself as a distinctive territory, a recognisable new form of space', and that 'the ordinary life of the "modern" had become unglamorous, unspectacular, neither familiar nor unfamiliar'.[2] For Clark, however, a key factor in this change was the issue of social class, and this was markedly evident in relation to the representation of the industrial city. He wrote that this subject was

> not … for bourgeois bohemians. And why? Because, though the life of the streets never stopped throwing up incident and energy … middle-class artists, whatever their sympathies for the proletariat, were constantly faced by the fact of their own exteriority to the world a few miles away. Incident remained for them just that.[3]

Clark's essay, written in the context of the L. S. Lowry retrospective at the Tate in 2013, raises some interesting points for consideration in relation to the depiction of the city in early to mid-twentieth-century painting. His analysis points to a shift in how the city was viewed in contemporary culture, while also acknowledging how personal circumstances influenced how artists interpreted the urban world around them. This was certainly true for Harry Kernoff, who was, coincidently, compared to Lowry during his lifetime.[4] While Dublin was not as industrialised as the cities and towns depicted by Lowry, Kernoff embraced this side of Dublin's urban landscape in a way hitherto unseen, and was certainly influenced by his own background and beliefs. Despite the changes Clark perceived in relation to the representation of the urban sphere, one link to the previous century was artists continued use of walking, whether as a *flâneur* or other form of urban observer, and a fascination with the city's multifaceted and contrasting nature.

Although working in the same period as Jack B. Yeats, Harry Kernoff's artistic technique and choice of subject matter contrasts with his older peer, offering a different view of everyday life in Dublin and demonstrating the multiplicity of experience that characterises the modern city. Like Yeats, through his life Kernoff became a recognised figure in Dublin, conspicuous by his small stature and the large black fedora that he habitually wore. His travels around the city were made visibly evident through the drawings found among the artist's papers, and his fellow artist Maurice MacGonigal later noted that he 'walked the city with Kernoff, who wandered'.[5] Allied to Kernoff's movement through, and notation of, the cityscape is the close attention that the artist paid to the social conditions, arguably influenced by his own position as an outsider in the city and by his leftist politics. Kernoff can be identified alongside the different forms of urban observer present in the modern city, already discussed elsewhere in this volume. Despite the political climate during the early 1920s there was an increasingly vibrant social scene and artistic community in the city, and as a student and young artist Kernoff was at the heart of it; he later observed that 'You remember it was the jazz age … after the Irish Civil War. People were in a joyous mood and everywhere cabarets and dance halls were springing up.'[6] Tracing the development of the artist's career and changing representation of the city and its people, this chapter will examine Kernoff's depiction of Dublin from the 1920s through to the 1940s.

Artistic beginnings in Dublin's 'Little Jerusalem'

Born in London in January 1900, Kernoff was the eldest son of Isaac and Kate Kernoff, Russian-Jewish immigrants who had moved from Vitebsk (then part of Russia, and now in Belarus) during the 1890s. The 1901 Census records the young family as living at 5 Clarke Street, Mile End, Stepney, renting two rooms in a house mainly occupied by Russian immigrant families.[7] In April 1914, the Kernoff family moved to Dublin, with the Alien Register detailing that Isaac was employed by Louis Gurevich, also from Vitebsk.[8] Isaac soon established his own cabinet-making business in the city where Harry served as his apprentice. The Kernoff family lived initially at 12 Raymond Street before later moving to 13 Stamer Street where Harry lived and worked for the rest of his life, using the spacious attic as his studio. Stamer Street was part of the area then known as 'Little Jerusalem' due to the large number of Jewish families living in the area: this community had grown exponentially around the turn of the century due to mass emigration from Eastern Europe.[9] Based around the city's South Circular Road, the area that comprised 'Little Jerusalem' contained good housing stock, mostly built in the second half of the nineteenth century by speculative builders. The sound infrastructure of these houses (for example, there was proper sanitation and running water), along with the wide range of housing stock was important in enabling the newly settled community to thrive in Dublin.[10]

Serving as an apprentice cabinet-maker, the intention seems to have been for Kernoff to work with his father and eventually take over the family business. However, alongside his apprentice work he began to take introductory drawing courses at the Kevin Street Technical Schools before progressing on to evening classes at the DMSA in 1919. He continued to aid his father for some time, for example in 1924 the *Irish Times* described him thus: 'Mr Kernoff, who is a prolific painter, daily follows his trade as a Dublin cabinet-maker'.[11] His first success as an artist took place shortly before the Civil War ended, when he was the recipient of the Taylor Scholarship in 1923. This enabled the artist to attend the DMSA as a full-time day student, marking a significant progression along the road to becoming a professional artist. In 1927, Kernoff held his first one-man show in The Gallery, 7 Stephen's Green, another landmark occasion in his early career. This gallery belonged to the Society of Dublin Painters, and Kernoff had joined its ranks in 1927.[12]

The catalogue of the 1927 exhibition shows that even at this early point in his career, Kernoff was showing a wide range of urban scenes drawn from the city streets around him, as well as of the surrounding Dublin countryside and coast. The inclusion of urban scenes in the display drew the attention of the press, with the *Irish Times* noting that he 'sees colour and aspects of light without bias or conviction, and has been able to reveal their beauty through most commonplace scenes, as in "Georgian Houses", "Charlemont Bridge, Summer", the distinctive "Nocturnes" … and "Over the Bridge" – with their fine night skies and gas-light shadows'.[13] One of these 'Nocturnes' was *Harcourt Street Station* (Figure 4.1) and while the *Irish Independent* generally supported the *Times*'s positive review, the author did note that 'without the catalogue one would never know that the imposing edifice with the long central vista was Harcourt Street station'.[14] The palette of the painting is muted, and the artist has focused in on the central door of the building. Passengers and commuters rush past and through the station, and the glow of the streetlight casts long shadows along the pavement in the foreground, as well as a bright orange glow above the doorway to the building. The overall impression created by the artist in the painting is one of busy activity: the figures all move with purpose, rather than at a leisurely pace. Along with *Over the Bridge* (1924, oil on board, private collection; a similar composition was later reproduced as a woodcut, Figure 4.2) and other works, this series of nocturnes presents Dublin as a bustling and modern city: Kernoff reuses tropes, which, by 1927, were long established in urban scenography: for example, the swath of light which illuminates the bridge as the tram crosses, supplemented by the street lamps; the bustle of the commuters entering the station; or the ubiquitous advertising which covers the curved wall behind the waiting jarvies (Figure 4.3). The artist's focus on the area around Harcourt Street for many of these paintings is notable: no more than a ten-minute walk from his home on Stamer Street, it suggests his

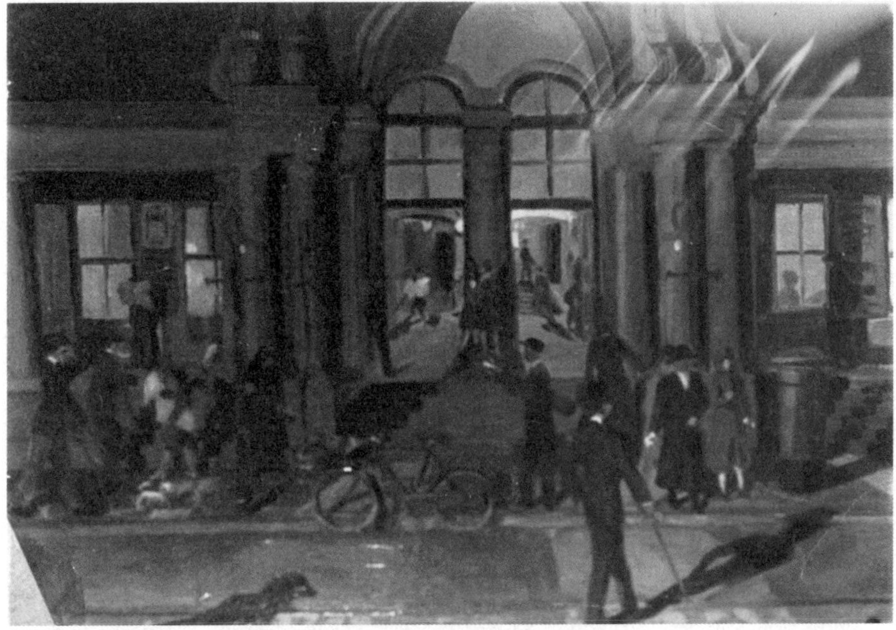

4.1   Photograph of Harry Kernoff, *Harcourt Street Station*, 1926.

growing connection to this part of the city, and his deep observation of daily life there.

Radical politics and Dublin's cabarets

Interviewed prior to the opening of his final exhibition in 1974, Kernoff recalled the late 1920s, saying that 'I remember, going back, there was Liam O'Flaherty and Brinsley MacNamara, the Radical Club, it went to pieces afterwards, but after that was the Studio Art Cabaret run by Mme. Cogley … I did portraits of MacLiammoir and Hilton Edwards and all that gang in 1928.'[15] The Radical Club emerged through the activities of Liam O'Flaherty in 1925, gathering together artists, writers, and poets for weekly meetings, conversations, and events. Reviewing the names of those involved with this venture, Nicholas Allen has argued that it 'suggests that "radical" in the 1920s encompassed any form of disaffection to the state, enlightened or reactionary', rather than engaging in radical or particularly innovative political activities.[16] While the core group of the Club was drawn from literary circles, there was also a focus on the visual and performing arts. In 1926, Kernoff exhibited with the 'Radical Painters Group' at the Daniel Egan Salon, 38 Stephen's Green, and was a close friend of the chair of the Club's cabaret committee, 'Toto' Bannard Cogley.[17] Kernoff designed settings and backdrops for Toto's other cabaret night, known as the Studio

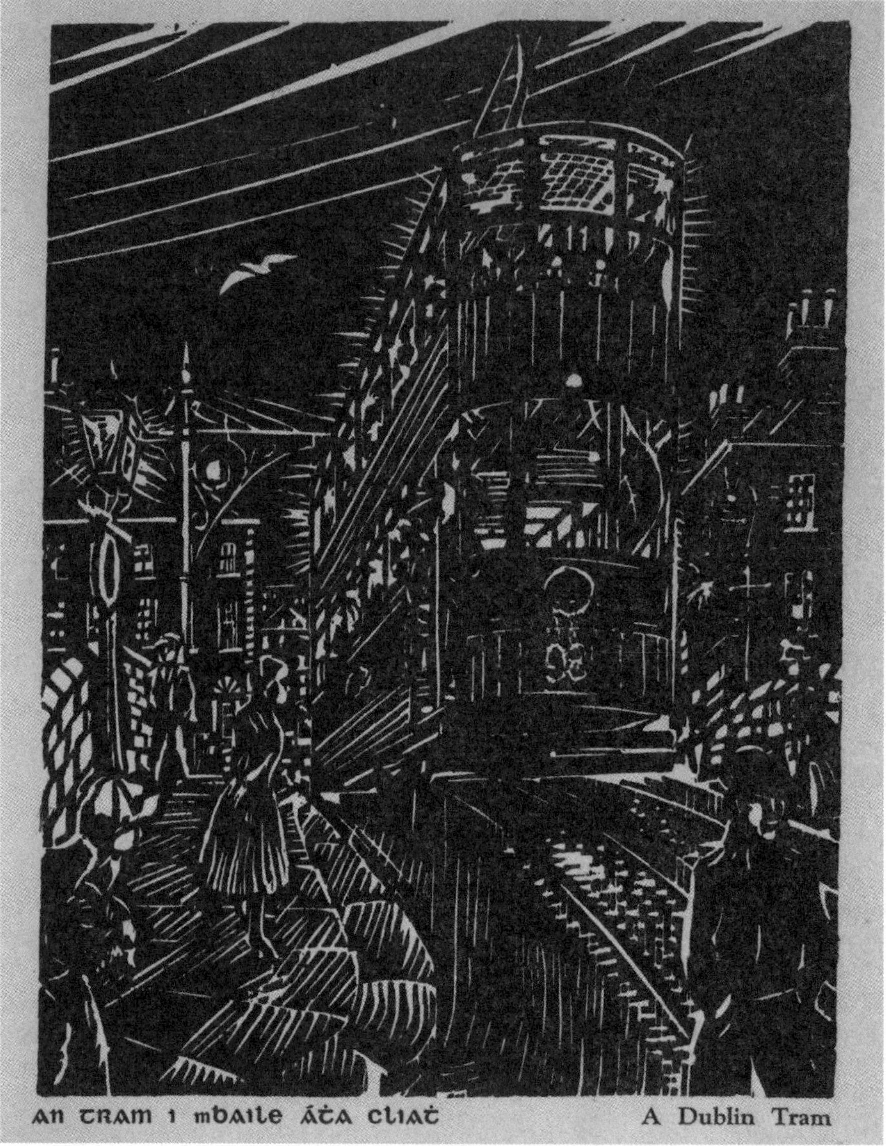

4.2 Harry Kernoff, *A Dublin Tram*, from Harry Kernoff, *Woodcuts* (The Talbot Press, 1942).

Arts Club, which initially operated from 41 Harcourt Street and later from 'The Little Theatre', 7 South William Street.

The cohort of people that Kernoff met through the Radical Club and the Studio Arts Club was important not only in the development of his work as

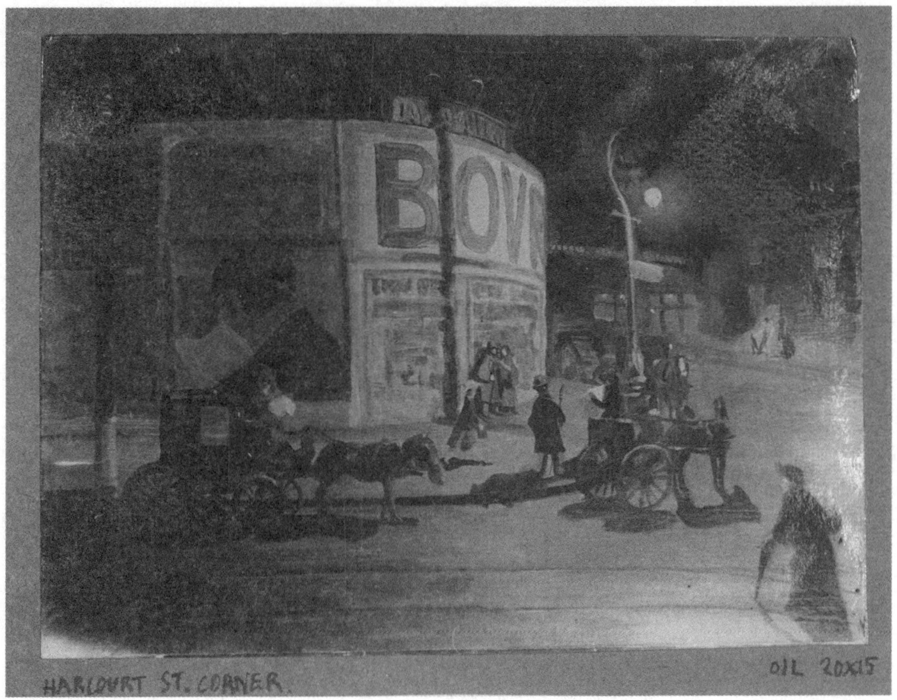

4.3   Photograph of Harry Kernoff, *Harcourt Street Corner*, undated.

a stage and costume designer, but also provided an opportunity for the artist to find patronage among those who attended the cabaret performances. For example, C. S. Andrews (a significant political figure in revolutionary and Free State Ireland), recalled that he met the artist at the Studio Cabaret during its time in Harcourt Street, and subsequently purchased *Harcourt Street Station*.[18] A sense of the personalities involved with this artistic circle was captured by Kernoff in a tableaux titled 'Noah's Ark' (Figure 4.4), which although patently made as a piece of theatrical ephemera, was photographed for posterity. Built along the end wall and tiered benches of the Harcourt Street venue, we see the faces of many of the Radical and Studio Arts Club members superimposed on the bodies of animals, while the ark floats serenely in the upper left-hand corner. These portraits match with extant works by Kernoff: those depicted include Cogley, the Bauhaus-trained artist Stella Steyn; as well as actors, critics, journalists, and playwrights such as Denis Johnson, Hilton Edwards, Michael MacLiammoir, P. S. O'Hegarty, Gerald Crofts, and Ria Mooney. In 1928, one newspaper described Kernoff's designs for a cabaret performance as being 'bizarre and attractive', and it is likely that they were similar in style to several large-scale paintings completed by the artist around this date.[19]

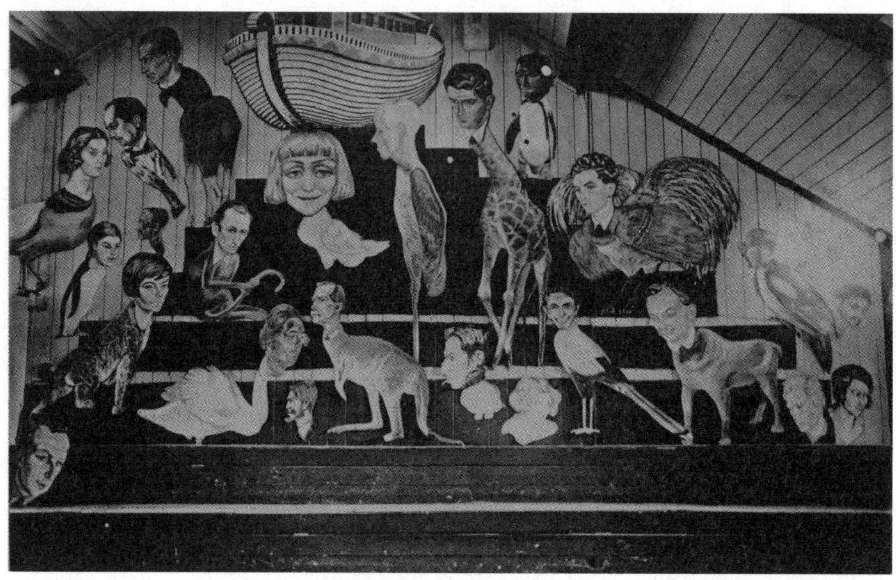

4.4   Photograph of Harry Kernoff, *Noah's Ark*, undated.

In addition to the decorations he produced for the Radical Club, Kernoff also became involved in theatre design during the 1920s. Elaine Sisson has discussed in some detail Kernoff's designs for two expressionist plays staged in Dublin in 1929 and 1930, drawing attention to the Cubist-inspired lines, the strong colouring, and suggestions of dramatic, cinematic lighting.[20] Made for productions at the Peacock and the Gate theatres, Kernoff was among a group of artists and dramatists exploring the theatrical and cinematic avant-garde in the 1920s, and throughout that and the following decade this collective of artists would have had opportunities to view modernist films across Dublin's many cinemas. A further collaboration between Kernoff and Cogley took place the following year, when he designed a number of backdrops for 'Erin Through the Ages', a historical pageant also held in Dún Laoghaire and which included a city panorama showing the Four Courts, the GPO, and the Custom House, along with three public sculptures from O'Connell Street (*Set designs for a pageant*, graphite on paper, NGI). The staging of historical pageants and tableaux in the 1920s and 1930s was used by the city and state authorities to 'not only affirm the legitimacy of the Dublin city commissioners as well as the Free State government and its army, but also to unite a public divided by civil war'.[21]

Returning to the artist's more experimental early paintings, this series of works stems from Kernoff's involvement in this iteration of 'jazz age' Dublin. It is identifiably different from that portrayed by Yeats (in paintings like *Jazz Babies*, for example), developing instead the hybrid form of European modernism which emerged around Dublin's theatre scene and which blended

elements of Cubism, Futurism, and Expressionism, usually with a strong incli-
nation for leftist politics. Kernoff's paintings from this time included *Jupiter
and the Muses*, *To the Inevitable*, *Dance of Death*, *Vortex* (Figure 4.5), and *Harmony
in Curves*. Now unlocated and known only through photographs, these were
exhibited by Kernoff in a range of venues between 1926 (when *Jupiter* was
shown at the Radical Club Painters' Group exhibition), at the Dublin Painters'
Gallery in 1928 and 1929, and later at the Gieves Gallery, London in 1931,
among others. A large canvas in the NGI titled *Death* (Plate 4.1), gives a vivid
sense of the scale and colouring of these now disappeared canvases. Indeed,
the composition of *The Triumph of Death* (Figure 4.6) is remarkably like the
NGI painting, save for its scale. On the reverse of the photograph, notes in
Kernoff's hand record that it was a 'mural dec[oration]', of 'Death leading
all back to the earth / except Revolution, who typifies progress. / Setting
Sun / Stormy colour scheme'. Through the different figures, Kernoff evokes
several 'sins', such as pride or vanity (through the modish woman looking
in a compact mirror), greed, wrath, envy, and gluttony. The inclusion of an
hourglass, held by a young herald, further underpins the artist's reference to
older art historical traditions, such as vanitas painting and the *danse macabre*.
In the larger, extant version, the figure of 'revolution' is clearly demarcated:
crouched in the lower right-hand corner, and attracting the wrath of the stylised Pharaoh figure, a red bandana suggests his political leanings, reinforced by
the hammer he holds. Political references pervade this series of paintings; for
example, through the 'censored' legal figure in *Vortex*, along with more general
evocations of conversations around evolution and religion. In Autumn 1930,
a profile of Kernoff was published in the Russian art journal, *Iskusstvo v Massi*
(*Art of the Masses*), outlining his career and successes up to that date, as well as
reproductions of five paintings. This included *Vortex*, described by the author
of the profile as 'an attempt at a satire directed against the capitalist system by
means of symbols (Art, labour, law, gender relations, philanthropy and others)
and shows that all of the soul of culture under capitalism is based on lies and
hypocrisy'.[22]

When *To the Inevitable*, a canvas like *Death*, was exhibited at the RHA in
1927, George Russell (writing under the pseudonym 'Y. O.') noted that:

> Mr Kernoff's big picture ... is clever, but I do not think it more than clever.
> The decorator has submerged the imaginative artist. The figure of Death which
> dances at the head of the procession is merely a decoration and there is nothing
> to awe us. I think this clever artist will react from his own fancies and become
> a realist. He has not enough of the poet in him to make his symbolic pictures
> purely poetical, but he has enough poetry, I think, to lift his realism out of the
> rut of dullness into which so many realists sink.[23]

While Russell's assessment of the trajectory of Kernoff's career now seems pres-
cient, the importance of this early involvement in Dublin's radical artistic circles
cannot be overlooked. It introduced Kernoff to a group of like-minded peers,

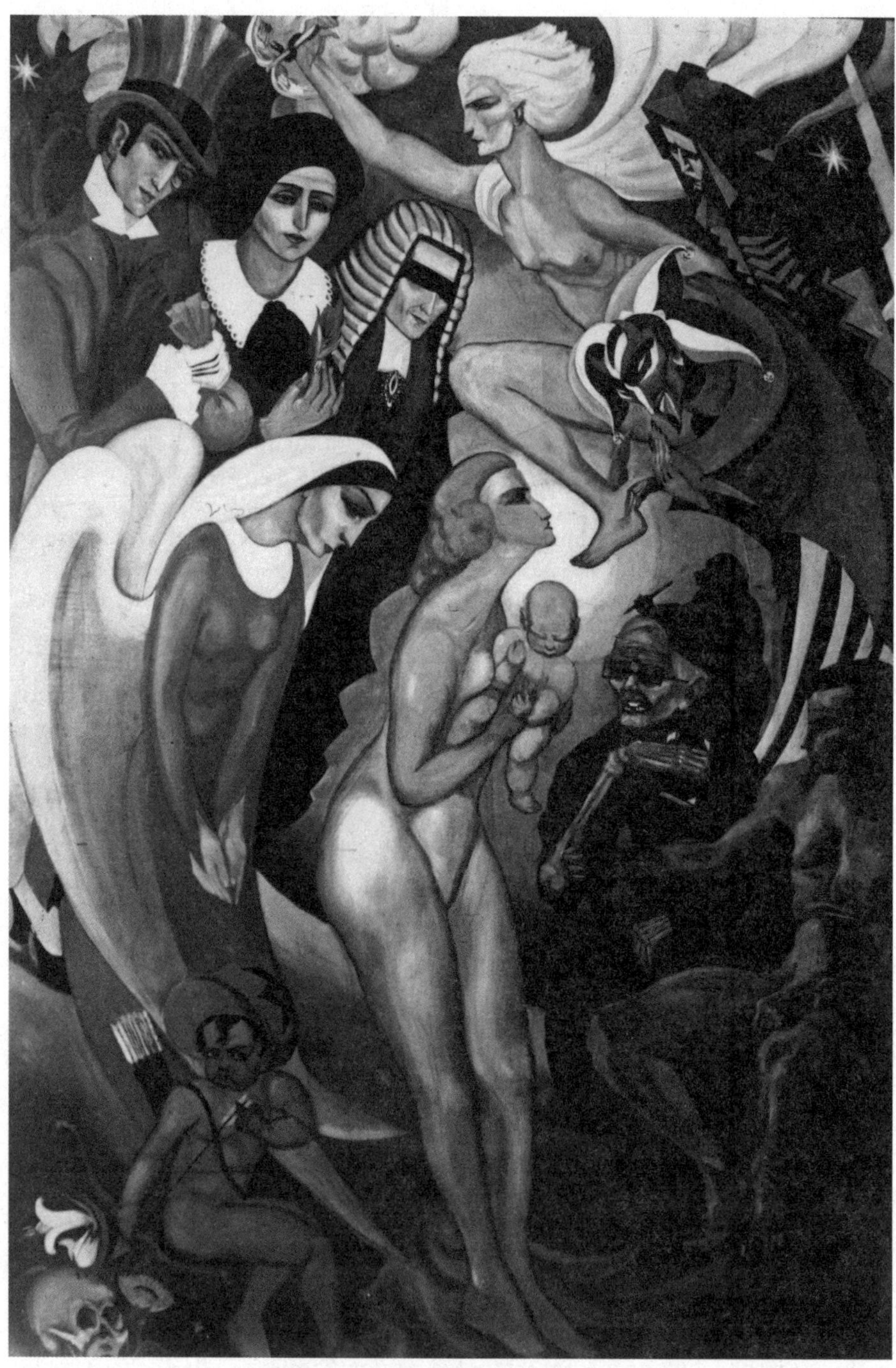

4.5   Photograph of Harry Kernoff, *Vortex*, undated.

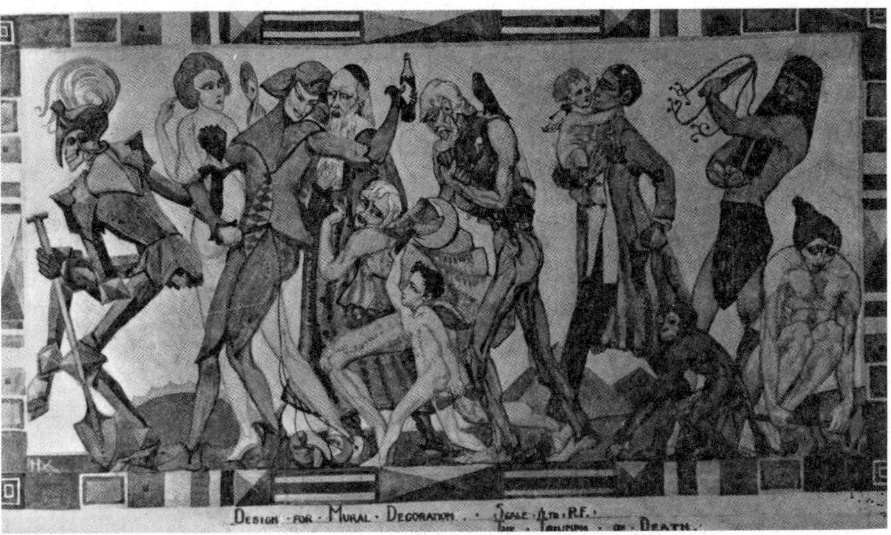

4.6   Photograph of Harry Aaron Kernoff, *The Triumph of Death*, undated.

particularly Cogley – with whom he remained friendly through the 1930s and 1940s and who he introduced to Ireland's socialist and communist circles.

This affiliation with the political left was strengthened in September 1930 when he visited the USSR with the Irish branch of the Friends of Soviet Russia (FSR). An article in the *Workers' Voice* records how the opportunity to travel to the USSR came about. In May 1930, the FSR International Committee in Berlin and the Foreign Relations Committee of the Soviet Trade Unions wrote to the Irish branch inviting them to send a delegation.[24] In addition to several drawings and sketches, Kernoff's recollections of this trip, along with those of his travel companions, were published in *The Watchword*, the newspaper of the Irish Trade Union and Irish Labour Party, as well as in a pamphlet by the FSR titled *The USSR through Irish Eyes*.[25] As the pamphlet outlines, the delegation travelled throughout the USSR over a six-week period, overseeing all aspects of life there including factories, communal farms, the Hermitage museum, cinema, theatre, and ballet. Kernoff naturally took a great interest in the place of the arts in the USSR, and his recollections demonstrate this close attention.[26] When considered in light of his own willingness to involve himself in different aspects of artistic life in Dublin, Kernoff's views of Russian art are noteworthy. He outlined that:

> artists in the Soviet Union are all in one union, the Art Worker's Union, this includes all craft workers and associative workers ... The artist has to produce four pictures or works of art a year, for which he gets his keep for the year. If he produces more, he can dispose of them as he pleases. Generally, a workers-club buys them or commissions him to do them.[27]

The apparent security of this system, including some financial stability, was evidently something Kernoff admired – perhaps unsurprising given the precarious nature of earning a living as an artist in Dublin. His writing reveals that he perceived that art was given a central role in the USSR, not only in terms of people purchasing it from exhibitions, but also in that it displayed a political and social function, especially as 'so much is being built, so many clubs, theatres, communal dwellings, rest-homes, schools, institutes etc., and these have to be decorated. Also their propaganda needs a great amount of pictorial and poster work of all description.'[28] Although he did not explicitly comment on the aesthetics of the art produced by the Soviet artists he encountered, he evidently admired it and noted that he collected 'about 130 samples of modern art in the Soviet Union … and have made an album with them'.[29]

In visiting the USSR in 1930, Kernoff was exposed to Soviet art and artistic support at an important juncture: the state was emerging from the cultural pluralism of the 1920s and engrossed in schemes of collectivisation and the implementation of the five-year plans. While art was certainly subordinate to the needs of the state, interference did not become dominant and explicitly policy-based until 1934, when Socialist Realism was 'proclaimed the approved method for Soviet artists in all media'.[30] Kernoff's enthusiasm for state support of artists and arts education continued throughout his life. In 1934, he wrote to the standing committee responsible for implementing reforms at the DMSA, stating that direct financial support for artists would 'ameliorate the artists [sic] position in Ireland, and to give certain artists of undoubted ability an income from the state, sufficient to allay their fears … so that they can work unhampered and produce their best works thereby'. Writing of this intervention, John Turpin argues that it shows Kernoff's awareness of the Works Project Administration in the United States, which supported artists in the years following the Wall Street Crash.[31] Kernoff was even more explicit in an article penned for *The Irish People* in April 1936, outlining the kinds of state support available to artists in America, France, and Britain, including the French policy of an artist's exemption from income tax (not introduced in Ireland until 1969), stressing that artists should be 'painting the life of the people'.[32]

Life on the left: unemployment, labour, and industry

As predicted by Russell, experimental paintings formed only a small part of Kernoff's oeuvre, and he increasingly gave more attention to the strand of his painting seen in the 1927 exhibition: urban realism. Many of these paintings fall under the umbrella of social realism, a general term used to 'refer to the work of painters, printmakers, photographers and film makers who draw attention to the everyday conditions of the working classes and the poor, and who are critical of the social structures that maintain these conditions'.[33] Manifestations of social realism can found in the work of artists across Europe and America through the inter-war period. In the American context, the work of the Ashcan

School earlier in the twentieth century was influential in motivating the next generation of artists to also look at the city for inspiration and to adhere to the principles of representational painting. In New York and Chicago, for example, artists were concerned with depicting everyday life in the city, recording everyday experience in an increasingly diverse urban environment.[34] In the 1930s, artists such as Ben Shahn and Raphael Soyer drew on their political allegiances and beliefs; Patricia Hills notes that many social realists 'were independent Marxists, some communists, some socialists, and some identified … with the humanist tradition'.[35] Certainly through the 1920s there were strong connections between artists in America and in the USSR, through both political assemblies and artistic groups such as the John Reed Club, which established branches in different cities.[36] While it is difficult to establish Kernoff's familiarity with artists like Shahn and Soyer, they all share similar artistic motivations and painting styles. A watercolour by Kernoff of *Yonah Shimmel's Knishe Bakery* (c.1939, watercolour on paper, private collection) suggests that he had some familiarity with New York, perhaps through photographs or books.[37] Looking to Britain, Kernoff was a frequent visitor to London – spending time with friends and family – and painted a small number of scenes from around the city and suburbs.[38] Although speculative, it is possible that through the 1930s and 1940s, the artist was aware of collectives such as the East London Group, or the involvement of visual artists, such as William Coldstream with the Mass Observation project (established in 1937) which led to some interesting representations of urban life, taking a regional city rather than the capital for its subject matter.[39]

Writing after the artist's death in 1974, John Nolan hailed Harry Kernoff as 'the artist of the workers', noting Kernoff's 'identification over many years with progressive, radical, working class ideas'. Nolan continued that 'in the 1920s and early '30s he [Kernoff] showed his sympathies with the struggles of the unemployed; his drawings of men without work, the poverty that was around him and of places of work showing both his understanding and sympathy for working people'.[40] One of Kernoff's most manifest displays of sympathy with the political left in Ireland came through his repeated depiction of Liberty Hall. Before the construction of the present Liberty Hall in 1965, a far less conspicuous building occupied the site on Eden Quay. Formerly a hotel, the building was purchased by the Irish Transport and General Workers Union as their headquarters in 1912. The building played a significant role in the political and social events of the period: it was used as a soup kitchen during the 1913 Lockout, served as the headquarters of the Irish Citizen Army, and housed the printing presses used to create the Proclamation of the Republic in 1916. The building suffered heavy shelling during the Easter Rising, but remained standing (with significant repairs) until 1958.[41] A pen-and-ink drawing of Liberty Hall by Kernoff is dated to 1928 (Figure 4.7), although records show that he first exhibited a version of the composition in 1927 at the RHA with the title *Liberty Hall, Night*. It may be that the pen-and-ink sketch now in the NGI is from 1927. The style of the signature and the addition of 'RHA' to the artist's name suggest

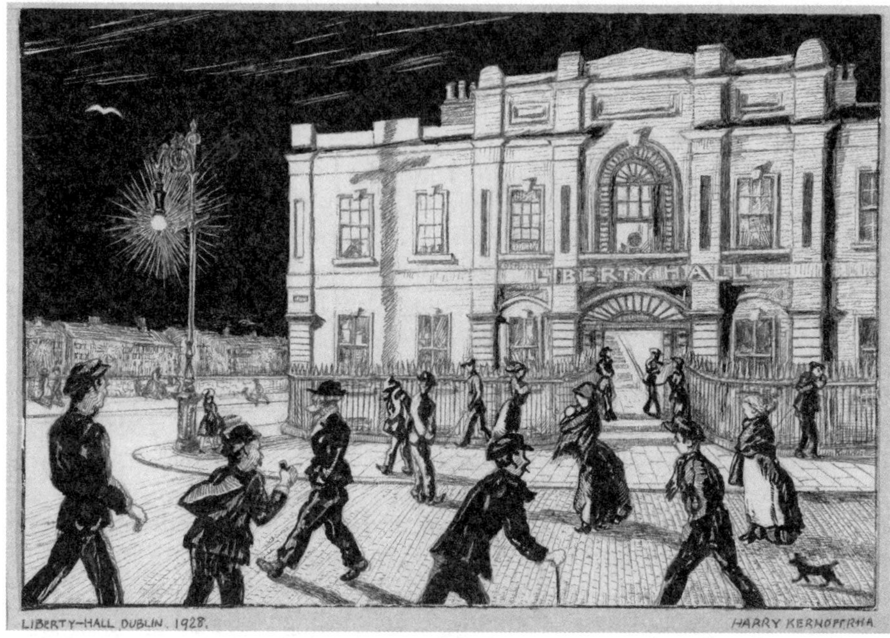

4.7   Harry Kernoff, *Liberty Hall,* 1928.

that these were later additions.[42] Certainly the scene depicted is set at night, with the building itself gleaming white against the ink-black sky, illuminated by a street light. In all the versions of this scene, the building is shown as having an open door and the shadows of people at work can be seen in the windows. A later version, titled *Liberty Hall, Summer's Evening* (watercolour on paper, private collection) from 1934 shows how Kernoff retained the core section of the composition but altered the figures in front of the building.[43] As with other works, Kernoff depicts a cross-section of Dublin's working population, from labourers and dockers to aproned women and busy mothers. To further emphasise the symbolism of the painting, Kernoff also included a young boy in a red jumper facing towards the illuminated building, underscoring its connection to the political left.

Beyond such landmarks, Kernoff did not have to look far to find subjects which reflected the varied composition of Dublin society. The docklands gave the artist the opportunity to make plain his empathy and understanding with Dublin's working class, and through such works he brought attention to everyday life and labour in Dublin through the 1930s, while also highlighting the presence of politics in the city environment; for example, through the inclusion of election posters or strike activity in his imagery. In 1931, Kernoff noted how, growing up in London, he had been fascinated by the dock district, and that in his view, 'no artist need go to Brittany or Holland to paint pictures; he will find plenty down by the London docks'.[44] This is certainly borne out in a number of drawings and paintings throughout the 1930s and 1940s, albeit showing the Dublin rather than the London docks. In recent decades the Dublin docklands have undergone significant redevelopment, encompassing areas on both the north and south sides of the Liffey: transformed by grand architectural projects such as Daniel Libeskind's Grand Canal Theatre, and an influx of leading technology firms, leading to the moniker 'silicone docks'. Newsreels and photographs from as late as the 1990s show, however, that in the intervening decades, little had changed from when Kernoff was sketching and painting the docklands in the 1930s. A good example of this can be found in the artist's numerous depictions of *Misery Hill* (c.1939, pastel on board, private collection), a narrow street that today branches off from Macken Street/Cardiff Lane and runs down towards the Grand Canal Theatre. From the mid-nineteenth century, this was one of the more industrialised areas of the city, with several gas companies operating in the area all of which were fuelled by imported coal. As the century progressed allied industries emerged, including a chemical works on Misery Hill which manufactured chemical manure, guano, and sulphuric acid.[45] A preparatory sketch (Figure 4.8) of this composition indicates that Kernoff first noted the scene on 27 August 1936; however, versions of the scene in both pastel and oil are undated.[46]

Regardless of small variations between these versions, *Misery Hill* shows three men walking down the centre of the street: in the right-hand corner a section of a gasometer can be seen in red, and the other buildings in the

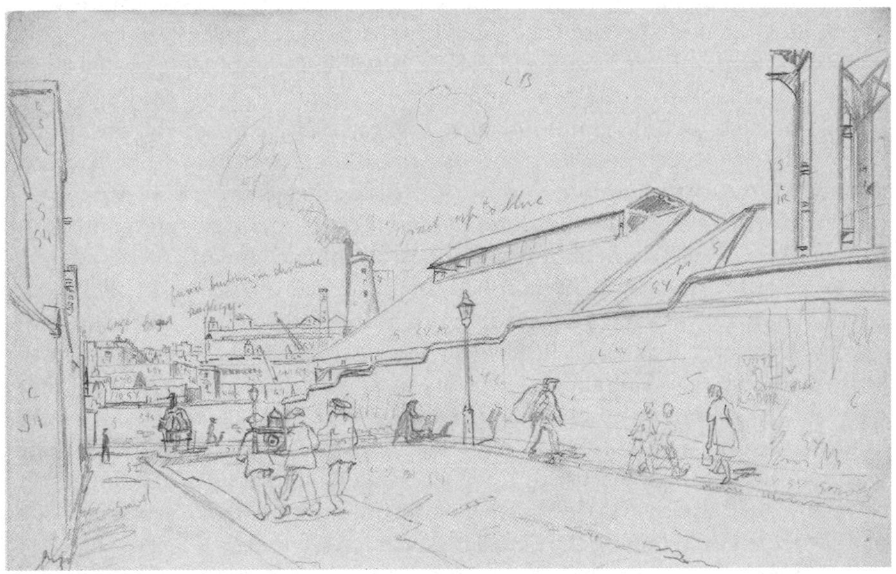

4.8   Harry Kernoff, *Misery Hill*, 1936.

painting reflect the then industrial landscape of the area. As with many of the artist's urban scenes, a political poster is included, seen on the wall beside the gasometer and reading 'Vote 1 Labour'. Along the sunnier side of the street, men and women go about their daily chores, contrasting strongly with a solitary figure standing alone in the shadows on the opposite side of the composition. Although the painting represents a rather down-at-heel part of the city, the sunlight and bright blue sky carry this painting away from the dark and grim atmosphere usually associated with the depiction of the industrial landscape, although the smoke belching from the distant chimney is a reminder of the environmental effects of industrialisation. The disparity between the subject and the colour palette is further reinforced when one considers the very real problems of unemployment and poverty across Dublin in the 1930s.

A watercolour dated to 1945, titled in recent years as *On the Dublin Quays – Johnny Forty Coats* (watercolour on paper, private collection) is a further example of how Kernoff introduced these themes into his painting.[47] The painting shows a rather dilapidated public house beside the river, with a boat and low warehouses visible in the background. In the fore- and middle-ground of the composition, various figures go about their day, with profession and social status indicated by clothing – such as a ship's captain in his blue uniform on the right-hand side, or the dock workers in flat caps. It may be assumed that the central figure, wrapped up in several layers of clothing and a large bag on his back is the man that the title alludes to: P. J. Marlow, or 'Johnny Forty Coats', was a homeless man known in Dublin through the 1930s and 1940s, and a contemporary photograph in the NLI shows some likeness to the figure in Kernoff's painting.[48] Kernoff did not shy away from depicting the more mundane (and perhaps, unsavoury) realities of city life: in a nook between the buildings, he depicts a makeshift *pissoir*, with a visible stream of urine running along the pavement and pooling on the street. Beside the side door of the 'wine and spirt merchant', a poster reading 'Vote 1 Jim Larkin' and a crude graffito of 'the IRA' can also be seen. The poster may refer to the 1943 elections, when both James Larkin (1878–1949), who had been a leader of the 1913 Lockout, and his son, also called James, won seats in the Dublin North East and Dublin South Central constituencies, representing the Labour Party. Despite the date 1945 appearing beside the artist's signature in the lower left-hand corner, Kernoff had first observed this scene on 18 October 1935 (Figure 4.9). As the preparatory sketch notes, the setting of the painting is Forbes Street, a side-street just off Sir John Rogerson's Quay, and when the artist made the sketch at about 11:00, it was a 'grey day': the figure of 'Johnny Forty Coats' is notably absent from the drawing. A comparison of the sketches in this collection with finished watercolour or oil paintings demonstrates that it was not unusual for the artist to leave a considerable amount of time between completing the sketch and the finished work, or for him to make several versions of a composition, retaining the detailed sketch for reference.

Although the work was irregular and often hard to come by, the docks were an important source of employment in Dublin through the first half of the

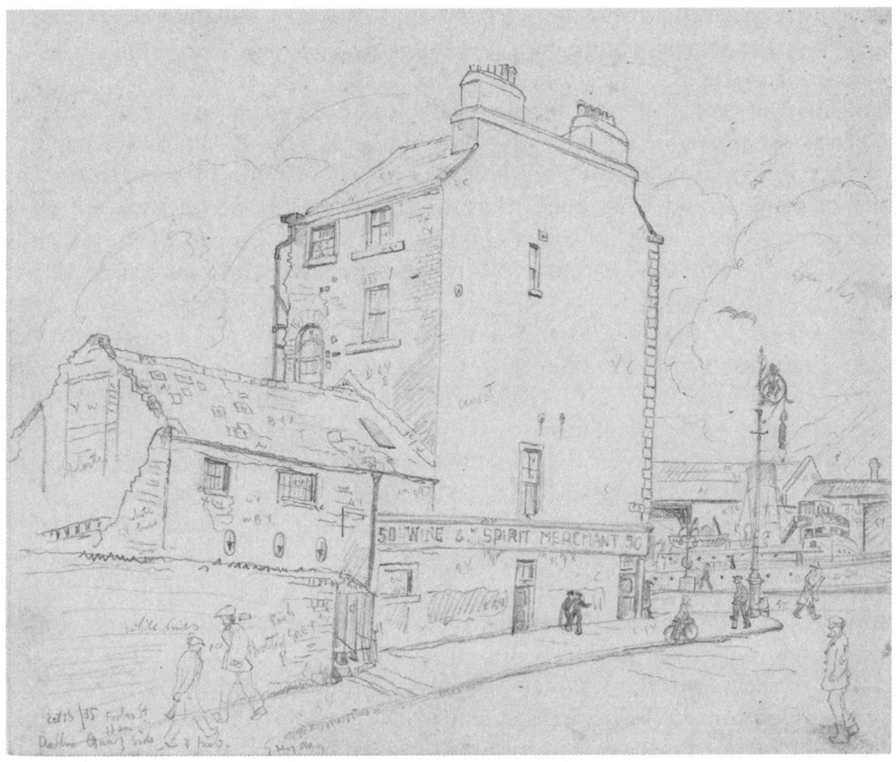

4.9   Harry Kernoff, *Dublin Quay Side, Forbes Street*, sketch for *On the Dublin Quays –
Johnny Forty Coats*, 1935.

twentieth century. As oral testimony records, employment on the docks and
the ships coming in and out of the port was often on a day-to-day basis, with
men gathering each morning in the hope of being selected for a day's labour.[49]
The plight of dock workers was captured in a monumental fashion by Maurice
MacGonigal in his painting *Dockers* (1934, oil on canvas, DCGHL). Although
ostensibly taking the same subject matter as Kernoff, MacGonigal's approach
and style were very different. Focusing on the figures themselves, rather than
the city or working environment, MacGonigal posed the three men in the
studio, after they were sent there by Larkin senior.[50] MacGonigal's emphasis on
the men themselves almost removes them from the urban setting of the docks,
and by arranging the figures so that they appear to look down on the viewer,
he further heroicises them. In contrast, Kernoff's depiction of workers and the
unemployed appears more ordinary, highlighting the different approaches of
the two artists. *Unemployed*, now only known through a contemporary newspaper photograph (present as a clipping amongst the artist's papers), shows a
man in similar clothing to Kernoff's other depictions of dockers or labourers,

facing the viewer with his empty hands upturned. Although they are barely visible in the reproduction, along the bottom of the canvas Kernoff included banners and figures: the *Irish Times* noted that 'the script of the banners explains the title'.[51] Where MacGonigal's dockers appear stoic, the figure in *Unemployed* appears vulnerable or almost pathetic. The sturdiness and solidity of MacGonigal's men is notably absent, perhaps justifying the criticism that the painting would have been more successful if 'the figure and face were more in conformity with the idea of labour'.[52] Despite this perceived fault, it is likely that Kernoff used a model for this painting. The same figure appears in a woodcut published in *Woodcuts* (Figure 4.10), also titled *Unemployed*, where the artist shows the man's head and shoulders, while a group of figures with the sign 'We Want Work' can be seen in the background. The original woodblock for this print (now in the NLI collection), is titled 'Unemployed (Jack O'Neill)'. Kernoff likely met O'Neill in 1930, as the latter was also part of the FSR delegation. As a representative of the 'Unemployed Movement', he was an eminently suitable model for *Unemployed.*

Over the course of his career, Kernoff published three books of woodcuts and sold numerous individual prints, many of which can now be seen on the walls of various Dublin pubs. In the 1920s and 1930s, however, book illustration constituted an important part of the artist's overall output: these commissions would not only have provided important income for Kernoff, but given the nature of the publications, placed him firmly within the band of artists charged with visualising both post-Independence Dublin and the nascent Irish Free State. In 1929, three drawings by Kernoff were included in *A Book of Dublin*, published by Dublin Corporation as part of its civic week celebrations (Figures 4.11, 4.12, 4.13). The aim of this publication was to 'bring together writers and artists … in a civic commemoration of the history, antiquities and commerce of the post-independence and post-civil war capital city'.[53] Alongside text on Dublin's industry and history, the book included reproductions by a wide range of contemporary Irish artists, including Paul Henry, Estella Solomons, Hilda Roberts, and Maurice MacGonigal, among others. Kernoff's drawings, dated 1928, showed the Guinness Brewery, Jacobs Biscuit Factory, and the grain silo of the Merchants Warehousing Company on the Alexandra Basin at Dublin Port. Reproduced in sepia, Kernoff's illustrations were most likely completed in pencil and charcoal, although the original drawings are now unknown. A later watercolour, *Watling Street* (1933, watercolour, private collection), offers a different perspective on the locale around the famous brewery, mimicking the composition of *Misery Hill* with the crumbling wall spanning the canvas. Given that the text of the *Book of Dublin* sought to emphasise what little industry Dublin had, as well as rebranding the city as the vibrant capital of the Irish Free State, it is notable that in each of his drawings Kernoff foregrounds the wires and posts of the electricity and telephone network. A tangible signifier of modernisation and progress, by including them Kernoff subtly alludes to Dublin as a site of modern industry.[54] In his representation of the Merchants' Warehousing

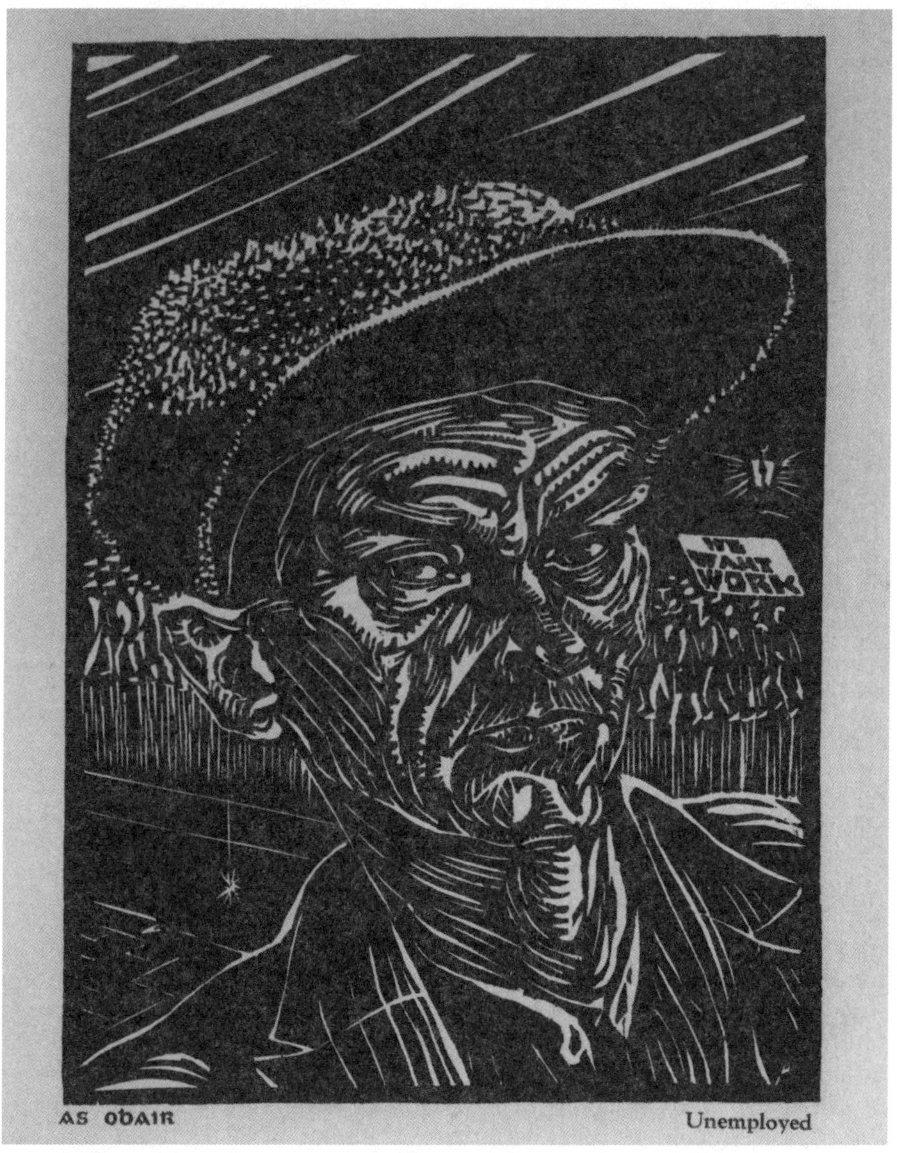

4.10   Harry Kernoff, *Unemployed*, from *Woodcuts* (The Talbot Press, 1942).

Company, Kernoff included men at work, a crane, and a pylon with thick black power wires. The drawing gives the impression that the building was still under construction, though this had been completed by 1926. Through the different types of wires in the three illustrations for the *Book of Dublin*, Kernoff suggests the progress in technology, communication, and electrification in the city. In

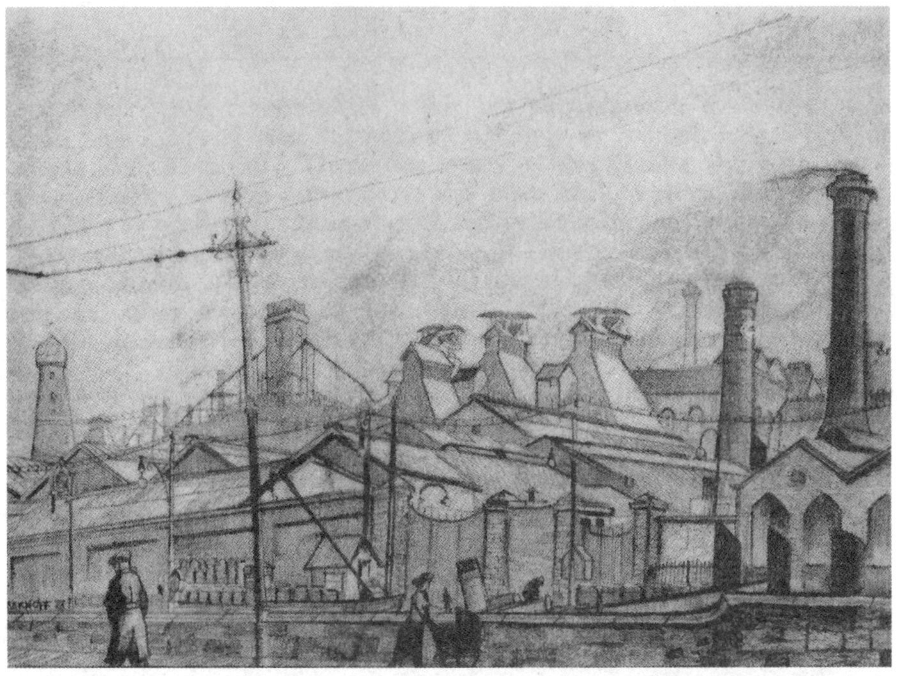

4.11   Harry Kernoff, *The Guinness Brewery*, from *A Book of Dublin* (Dublin Corporation, 1929).

The Guinness Brewery, we see telephone wires; tram wires in *Jacobs Biscuit Factory*; and in *The Grain Silo*, electrical wires can be seen.

The grain silo also appeared in the background of *Dublin Dockyard* (Plate 4.2), a painting that may have been exhibited under the title *Dublin Docks* in 1934, which was described as showing: 'a silent story of human potentiality in the big lattice frame hulk and the strewn apparatus of the dock'.[55] The painting shows the skeletal hull of a ship on the dry dock, with smoking chimneys protruding into the blue sky. As with the earlier *Book of Dublin* illustrations, Kernoff uses the wiring, crane stays in this instance, to accentuate the industrial nature of the scene, while in contrast to other depictions of similar subjects, the shipyard workers blend in with the grey ground of the dock. For example, Paul Henry's illustration of *The Grand Canal Dock, Ringsend* (charcoal on paper, 1928, NGI) demonstrates a different artistic approach to the subject. Described by Justin Carville as 'less of a depiction of the Dublin cityscape and more of an impression of its texture', this drawing shows the early influence of Whistler on Henry, and his interest in the contrasting aesthetics of soft mist and fog against the concrete industrial buildings.[56]

Kernoff's involvement with printed books continued through to 1931, when his work was included in *Saorstát Éireann: Irish Free State Handbook*. Among the

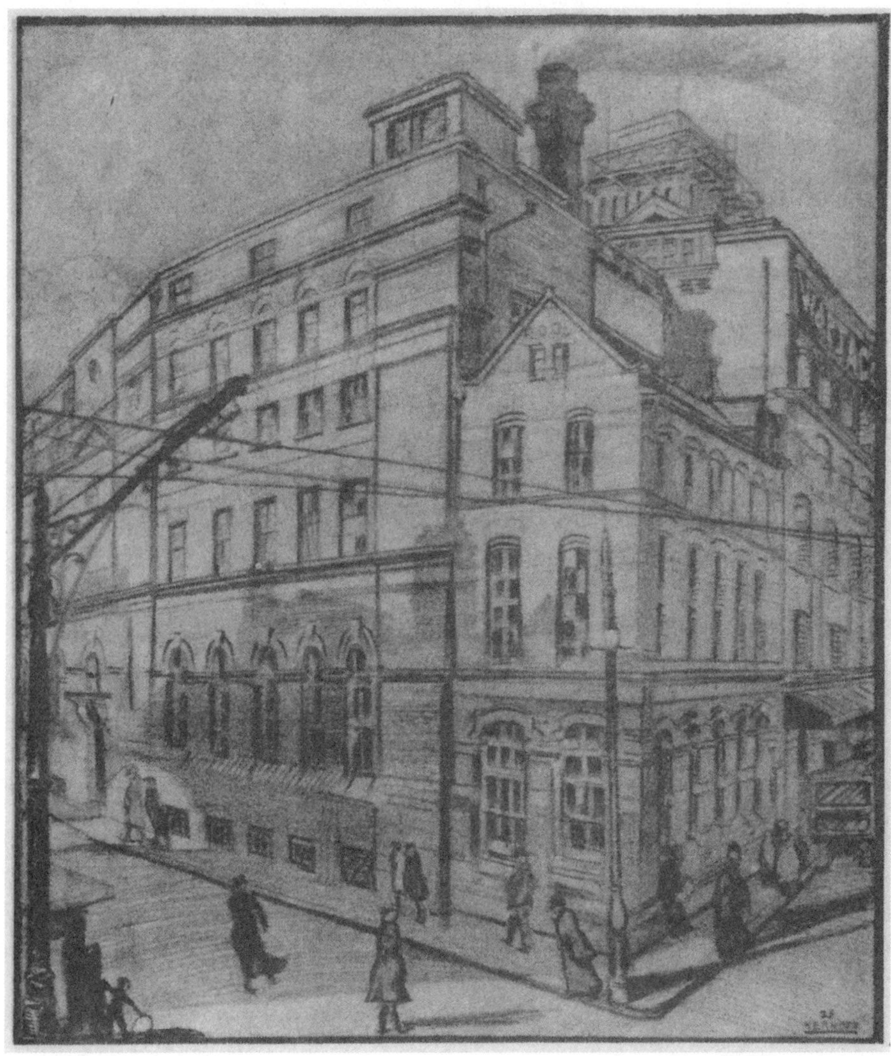

4.12   Harry Kernoff, *The Jacobs Biscuit Factory*, from *A Book of Dublin* (Dublin Corporation, 1929).

works reproduced were *Dublin Docks*, a drawing in charcoal and pencil (Figure 4.14). The dark tones of the media are well suited to the industrial subject matter, heightening the bleak atmosphere of the scene. Moving away from the buildings around the docks, this drawing brings the viewer down to the river itself, with the criss-cross of cranes, chimneys, and boats framing the water. The height and power of these features is emphasised by the small boat bringing a group of men back towards the quayside. From these depictions of scenes of

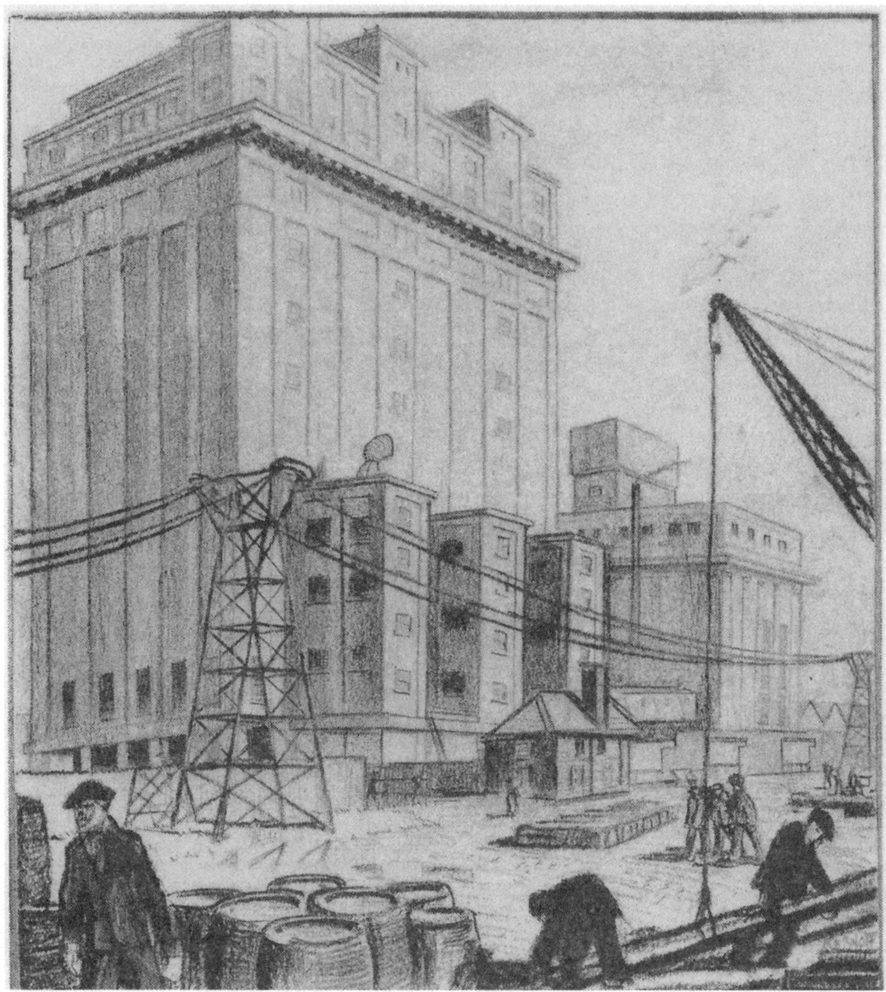

4.13 Harry Kernoff, *The Grain Silo of the Merchants Warehousing Company*, from *A Book of Dublin* (Dublin Corporation, 1929).

industrial sites around Dublin, it is perhaps unsurprising that a comparison was made between Kernoff and L. S. Lowry. While both artists have their own distinct pictorial styles, Lowry's interest and concentration on industrial towns do make for an interesting comparison with Kernoff. From the early 1920s, Lowry depicted scenes from around Salford and Manchester, detailing the realities of life in a highly industrialised urban centre. While Dublin was not anywhere near as industrialised as the cities and towns depicted by Lowry, the works discussed in this section demonstrate that he actively sought out what industrial areas of the city there were.

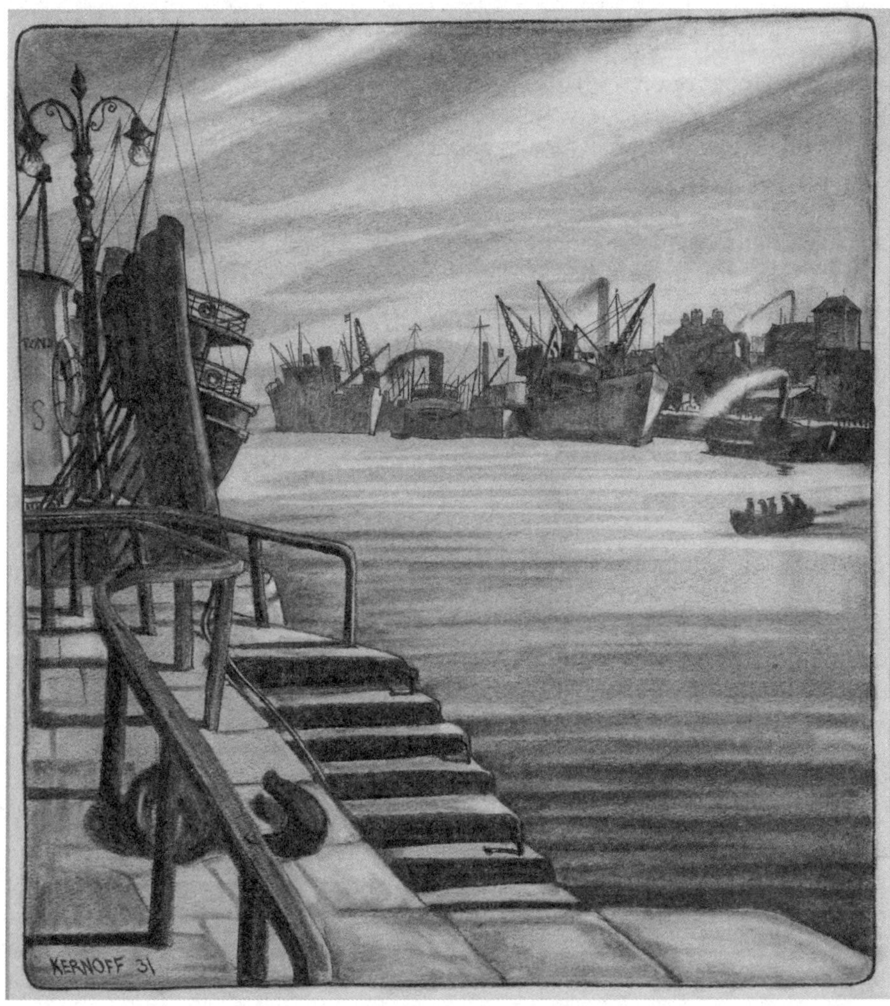

4.14 Harry Kernoff, *Dublin Docks*, 1931.

In and around the city

As the 1930s progressed, Kernoff's artistic style evolved into more mature, representational cityscapes, although he continued to be active in radical political circles. This decade saw the artist cement his professional reputation in Dublin (for example, in 1935 he was elected an associate of the RHA, and a full member in 1937) and beyond: two solo exhibitions were held in London in 1931 and 1938 respectively, and his work was included in several international exhibitions of Irish art. A visit to Paris in 1931 expanded the artist's range of city scenes, with works in oil and watercolour of the French capital exhibited at the Victor Waddington Galleries, Dublin in 1932. Alongside the more overtly political paintings already discussed, through the 1930s the artist also developed a separate strand of urban paintings, which focused on moments of solitude or leisure in and around the city. In keeping with many of the artist's depictions of labour and industry, these cityscapes and urban landscapes are usually brightly coloured, with blue skies and sunlit streets. The overall impression created by the artist is of a genial and friendly atmosphere, despite the social issues present in the city at the time, and which he did confront elsewhere. These paintings build and extend upon subjects already outlined in this chapter; for example, we see the artist return again to the quayside – however, in this seam of work it is the architectural and atmospheric details which interest him, rather than industry and labour. Representations of marketplaces and busy shopping streets are filled with vignettes of everyday life, and in depictions of Stephen's Green, the Phoenix Park, and the Grand Canal, leisure, solitude, and quietness come to the fore. In contrast to the 'jazz age' which Kernoff experienced after 1923, the 1930s were characterised by a far steadier pace of life in Dublin. Issues around housing and social provisions continued as the Irish Free State found its footing, and Dublin began to expand outwards with the development of new housing blocks on derelict industrial sites and larger garden suburbs.[57] While the effects of economic policy are more clearly seen in Kernoff's depictions of labour and unemployment, we can also understand the artist's more general city views in relation to the stultifying effects of censorship, stagnation, and protectionism. Kernoff's personal experience of the decade – with his involvement in radical political circles, his interest in developments abroad, and his commitment to life in Dublin – offer an interesting insight into the city.

Given its proximity to his studio on Stamer Street, it is perhaps unsurprising that Kernoff gravitated towards the banks of the nearby Grand Canal. The canal had traditionally marked the city boundary and was an important trade route linking Dublin to the canal and river network around the country. Later in the twentieth century it would also be memorialised by Patrick Kavanagh in his poem *Canal Bank Walk* and *Lines Written on the Seat on the Grand Canal*.[58] For Kavanagh, the canal bank was a green oasis, being a still and peaceful place on the edge of the city. This is redolent of the qualities found in Kernoff's paintings of the same location, often embellished with the addition of characterful swans and small dogs. Indeed, it is tempting to see Kernoff's *The Red Seat near Baggot Street Bridge* (Plate 4.3), showing a man sitting by the quiet water, as a visual counterpart to Kavanagh's words. This connection is strengthened by the fact that the poet and the painter were acquainted: having first met in the Palace Bar, in 1943 the pair embarked on a cycling holiday in Kerry together. In his 'City Commentary' column for the *Irish Press*, Kavanagh praised Kernoff's painting for being 'a vital painter who takes everyday things like Dublin houses and parks for his subjects'.[59] For Kernoff, the route along the waterway would ultimately bring him to Grand Canal Dock and onwards to the docklands. This stretch at the edge of the city also formed part of the artist's social life, as from the 1940s onwards Kernoff was associated with the artistic community that sprang up around Parsons Bookshop at Baggot Street Bridge, marking a new generation of writers and artists in Dublin's cultural life.[60] The attraction of the canal for artists of all shades in Dublin is further exemplified by Elinor Wiltshire's photographs around Portobello, made around 1959, which form an interesting visual counterpart to Kernoff's paintings.

Several depictions of the Grand Canal were included in Kernoff's 1936 exhibition at the Waddington Galleries. From Portobello Harbour to Grand Canal Dock, the paintings in both oil and watercolours all exude a quiet charm, filled with small and well-observed details, such as a pair of curtains adorning a window, a shop sign, or a loitering figure. Despite its title, the colouring of *Summer's Day at Leeson Bridge* (Plate 4.4) is more suggestive of early autumn, with the foliage of the trees clearly about to turn from green to orange and red.[61] Moreover, the composition is identical to a preparatory sketch that bears the inscription 'wet grey day, 12pm, Leeson St Bridge, Dublin 2, 2–8-35 Aug'.[62] Given this inscription, it is possible that *Summer's Day at Leeson Bridge* may actually be 'Soft Day at Leeson Bridge'. A particularly Irish colloquialism, a 'soft day' is used to refer to a grey, often misty day, with frequent but light showers of rain. Looking closely at *Summer's Day at Leeson Bridge*, the artist included a predominantly grey sky, with light sweeping strokes of darker grey and brown suggesting a light drizzle of rain. On the bridge itself, some figures are shown with umbrellas, while others wear brightly coloured summer dresses, perhaps indicating the changeable nature of a 'soft day'. There is no such ambiguity in *The Peppercanister from Percy Place* (watercolour on paper, private collection). The initial sketch titles the scene 'Huband Bridge & St Stephen's Church, Mount Street Dublin' and is dated 8 June 1939. In addition, Kernoff noted the time (3–4pm), and the sketch was drawn from '1st floor, V Murphy's flat' (Figure 4.15). Moving figures bring life to this scene, and it is further enhanced by details such as the small dog and the bright green post box on the far side of the bridge.

The artist's journey down the canal way continued to Grand Canal Dock, past *Boland's Mills* (1931, watercolour on paper, private collection), which had been occupied during the 1916 Rising, and into the dock area of *Boats at Anchor – Grand Canal Quay* (Plate 4.5) where a serene view of the docked boats eclipses the industrial background. The sense of stillness from this watercolour is repeated in *On the Liffey*, a view of City Quay (undated, oil on board, private collection). While the painting itself is undated, Kernoff sketched the view of the crane and surrounding buildings on 8 August 1935 (Figure 4.16). Though some small figures are visible around the base, the overall impression is one of quietness: the artist has focused on the imposing structure of the crane itself, which stands proudly over the surrounding buildings. One of several four-ton cranes installed in the docklands in 1931, in this painting Kernoff captures the continuing importance of the dock area to industry in Dublin, despite the ongoing economic difficulties. In both the sketch and the finished painting, the

4.15   Harry Kernoff, *Huband Bridge, Saint Stephen's Church (Peppercanister), Mount Street, Dublin from 1st Floor V. Murphy's Flat*, sketch for *The Peppercanister from Percy Place*, 1939.

viewpoint suggests that the artist observed the scene from the water, rather than from the opposite quay, which invites the intriguing prospect that the artist was as familiar with the city by water as he was by foot. It is possible that like Yeats, Kernoff made use of the Liffey ferries to gain a different perspective on the Dublin docklands. A further moment of repose is captured in *From the Custom House Steps, Dublin* (watercolour on paper, private collection) sketched and painted in 1933, with the artist placing himself among the dock workers who take in the view across the water towards the far dockside and Tara Street railway station (Figure 4.17).

Moving further into the city centre, *St Stephen's Green* (1935, watercolour on paper, private collection) offers one of Kernoff's most encompassing views of the city centre. The preparatory sketch for this painting notes that it was made during a tram strike and suggests that the artist's focus was on Fusilier's Arch, a memorial to members of the Royal Dublin Fusiliers who fought in the Second Boer War (Figure 4.18).[63] Once more it is the small details which bring life and movement to this painting, showing Kernoff's forensic notation of the scene. For example, the row of shops and buildings that make up the background of the painting are all identifiable from their signage and awnings, including The Green Cinema which was screening Charlie Chaplin's *Modern Times*. The

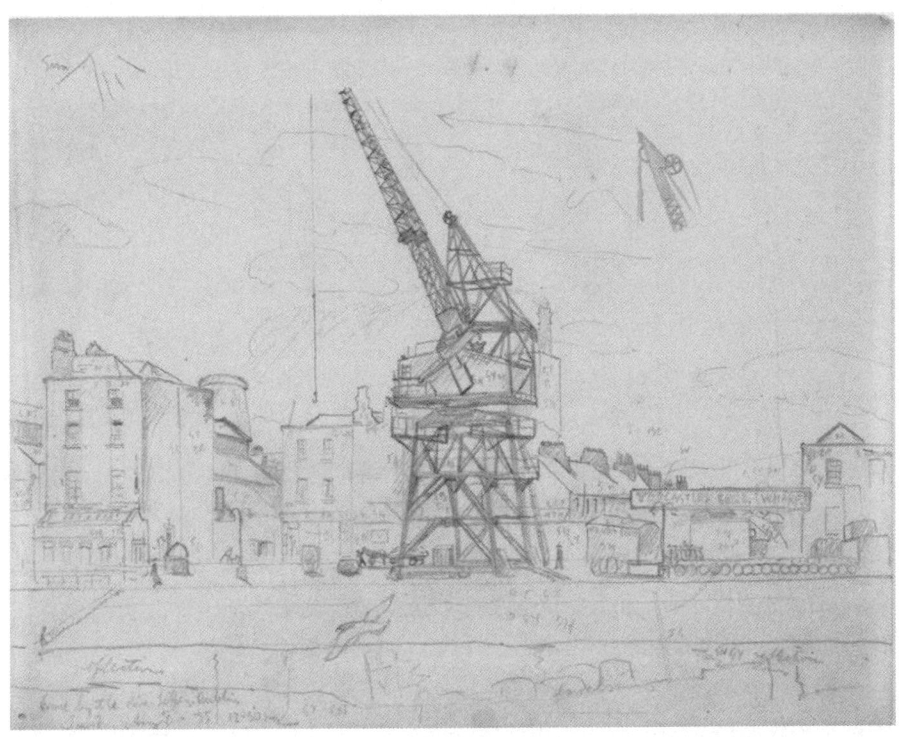

4.16   Harry Kernoff, *Crane by the River Liffey, Dublin*, sketch for *On the Liffey*, 1935.

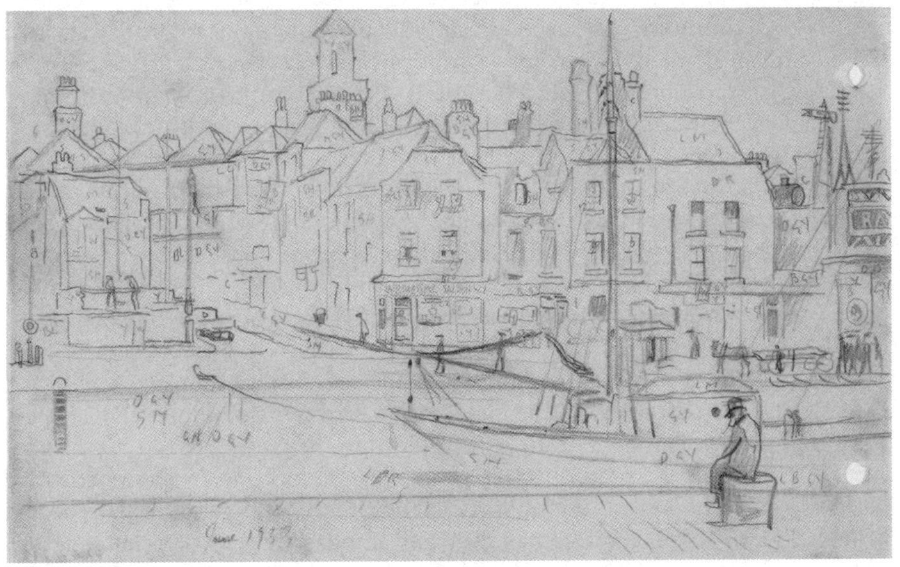

4.17   Harry Kernoff, *Quay and Street*, sketch for *From the Custom House Steps*, 1933.

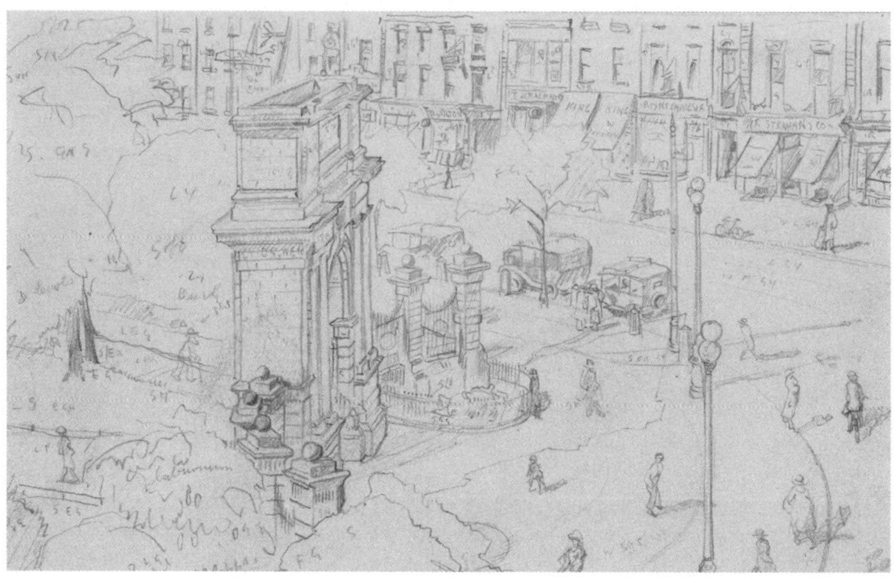

4.18   Harry Kernoff, *The Boer War Memorial, Saint Stephen's Green, Dublin*, sketch for *St Stephen's Green*, 1935.

streetscape is populated with small figures, painted in Kernoff's characteristic style. Interior views of the Green complement Osborne's earlier views of the same space: while to a large extent the later artist focuses on capturing a sense of pleasure in a sunny day, rather than using the park space to explore social class, there is still an element of this. For example, in *Pink Hawthorn, St Stephen's Green* (undated, watercolour, private collection) Kernoff reintroduces the 'Johnny Forty Coats' figure seen in *On the Dublin Quays*, and as with the dockside painting, this figure does not appear in the preparatory sketch.[64] The heavily coated figure contrasts strongly with the bright colours of his surroundings, and with the neatly dressed figures who are also enjoying the amenity. Why did the artist choose to place this figure in these compositions? Given the extent to which Kernoff himself walked around Dublin, perhaps he was drawn to other 'wanderers', or was particularly aware of those who were outside of the mainstream of Dublin society.

When viewing many of Kernoff's paintings of the city centre, it is difficult to avoid the fact that many of the locations he recorded are now no longer part of Dublin's urban fabric. Repeating the interest in the signage of the city's shops seen elsewhere, in *Winetavern Street* (Plate 4.6) Kernoff again shows the city bathed in sunlight while the shop owners and others go about their daily work. Using more of these small figures, Kernoff emphasises the steep pitch of the hill through the men and women pushing seemingly heavy carts up its height. The crest of the hill also offers a view over the north side of the city. *Winetavern*

Street offers another instance of how the artist reused and repurposed a composition in various media. The 1934 oil version was bought by the Friends of the National Collections and presented to the Municipal Gallery, and in 1937 a further watercolour version was exhibited. In a review of this exhibition, a commentator in the *Irish Independent* noted that while 'water-colours are apt to be subdued and insipid compared with oils ... Mr Kernoff's water-colour work is vivid, airy and arresting. To take one example, his No. 54 is a study of Winetavern Street ... Personally, I prefer the water-colour in this exhibition to the oil painting.'[65] In 1940, the artist also produced a pen and ink drawing based on his original sketch, along with a hand-coloured woodcut version of the same drawing. Finally, he also produced additional versions in both oil and watercolour, also in 1940 (private collection). Given that the original painting had been purchased by a prestigious group, it is possible that Kernoff sought to build on this success and on the public's knowledge of the painting by making additional versions available for purchase. In December 1937, the *Irish Independent* noted some of the remarks at the opening of a Kernoff exhibition: 'Lord Longford said that Mr Kernoff is perhaps the most original of our Dublin artists and that many of his most beautiful paintings will in future have historic as well as artistic value, as they depict a Dublin that is passing.'[66] The houses depicted on Winetavern Street were largely demolished in 1964, while nooks such as *Queen's Mews Court* (c.1939, oil on panel, private collection) – captured in a characteristically sunny painting, complete with graphic advertising and washing wafting in the breeze – have since been subsumed into new building complexes.

Moving from the eastern docklands to the western boundary of the city, in the Phoenix Park Kernoff found a further subject for showing a pastoral idyll within the Dublin landscape. Following the creation of the Irish Free State, the Park was no longer the administrative and military site that it had been in the nineteenth and early twentieth century but remained an important centre of recreation for Dubliners.[67] In 1932, around one million people gathered in the area of the park known as the '15 acres' to celebrate the Pontifical High Mass at the closing of the Eucharistic Congress; however, the photographs of this lavish ceremony are in stark contrast to Kernoff's vision of the space. From around 1932–37, he sketched and painted multiple views ranging from a bustling view of the bandstand on a sunny afternoon, to views of the Liffey and Inchicore, and repeated views of an area populated with native silver birch trees. As a collection of works, these views are more allied with the artist's depictions of Dublin's coastal towns, villages, and beaches, forming an important visual record of Dublin at leisure in the middle decades of the twentieth century. While a full exploration of these paintings lies outside of the present study, it demonstrates Kernoff's participation in a long tradition of urban landscape painting which encompasses scenes of work and leisure in both an urban centre and its immediate suburbs.

Drinkers and the Dublin pub

In her memoir of Dublin in the 1950s, the British writer Honor Tracy recorded her visit to a Dublin pub on her first morning in the city. After purchasing a newspaper, the author

> made [her] way into a snug that had long been a favourite … In the greenish twilight, with an air of having never moved since the beginning of time, sat still three old gentlemen with the bottle noses and the split boots, and the seedy bowler hats which they would gravely remove at the entrance of a woman. At no matter what time of the day, except in the Holy Hour, they were to be found in session.[68]

In twentieth-century Dublin stories, whether fiction or non-fiction, the location of the public house is hard to avoid, whether used as a space for quiet contemplation (as it was for Tracy), or a site for revealing attitudes towards politics, nationalism, and difference (think, for example, of the altercation between Leopold Bloom and The Citizen in *Ulysses*, or Act Two of Seán O'Casey's *The Plough and the Stars*). From the 1930s onwards, several of the city's watering holes became particularly associated with writers and artists. Dublin's literary pubs attracted 'not only writers but artists, professors and amateur philosophers'.[69] For (male) writers such as O'Flaherty, Kavanagh, Brendan Behan, and Austin Clarke, the pub was one of their main places for socialising in Dublin, although Samuel Beckett found their presence in these haunts overwhelming.[70] The atmosphere of one of the coteries was captured by Alan Reeve in his caricature, *Dublin Culture*, first published in 1940, which shows the back room of the Palace Bar, Fleet Street. At the front table, nestled between Patrick O'Connor and Sean O'Sullivan is the diminutive figure of Kernoff, hidden under his large fedora and behind large spectacles. He is shown as being significantly smaller than his peers, and his nervous glance suggests a slight unease with the situation. This work was included in an exhibition of Reeve's work at Brown Thomas, Grafton Street, and on seeing the show the author of the 'Irishman's Diary' column commented that it was 'the most interesting of its kind that has been held in Dublin for many a day'. The author added, 'it might represent a group of Dublin's *intelligentsia* sipping afternoon tea in the Y.M.C.A., but it doesn't', suggesting, with little subtlety, the real location to the column's readers.[71] What *Dublin Culture* shows is how central the life of the pub was to Dublin's social scene at this time, particularly in literary and artistic circles, and how it had evolved from Kernoff's own 'Noah's Ark' in the 1920s.

By placing himself within this sphere, Kernoff further sought to ground himself within the social and cultural fabric of Dublin. This was made further manifest by a collection of paintings which recorded the names, characters, and interiors of some of the city's pubs. The artist's position within the city's pub culture can still be seen in a more tangible way with several of his paintings and prints still hanging on the walls and behind the bars of establishments such as Neary's, Davy Byrne's, and The Palace. The names of these and many other Dublin pubs appear in the background of *A Bird Never Flew on One Wing* (1947, oil on board, private collection), creating a more unusual portrait of the city. Different versions of the composition are extant, including versions in oil, woodcut, and coloured engraving, with each noting a slightly different range of names. The composition centres around two men clearly enjoying the refreshments offered in the hostelries listed behind them: in his representation of the two men, Kernoff draws on previous figures of jarvies and workers. Exhibited at the RHA in 1947, the *Irish Times* noted that it was 'a humorous work by Harry Kernoff, whose incisive style adds a bite to his witty remarks'.[72] The names in the background show just how many pubs there were in Dublin and their centrality to the city's social scene. The two figures both have elements of caricature, especially in their facial features, perhaps reflecting the artist's interest in the city's 'characters'.

Davy Byrne's on Duke Street was (and remains) one of the most famous of Dublin's literary pubs, celebrated for the reference to it in Joyce's *Ulysses*. In the text, Leopold Bloom pauses at the pub for refreshment, having a gorgonzola sandwich and a glass of red wine – describing how the eponymous owner 'doesn't chat. Stands a drink now and then.'[73] Kernoff used Davy's as a setting for three different works, two showing the interior and the other the exterior from another well-known bar, the Bailey. Taking these in chronological order, in 1936 Kernoff completed his first interior scene of the bar, *In Davy's Back Snug* (1936, oil on board, private collection). The painting shows Martin Murphy, a stage builder at the Gate Theatre, and Davy Byrne himself in the foreground, while two others can be seen in the background. While the artist does not appear in corporeal form, his presence is signified by three inclusions in the middle-ground: a fedora hat hangs on the wall, an exhibition of his pictures is advertised on a poster, and below this on the mantelpiece, a small wine glass filled with an orange liquid can be seen. A second interior scene from Davy Byrne's is *In Davy's Parlour Snug: Portrait with Davy Byrne and Martin Murphy* (c.1938, oil on board, private collection). In this, Kernoff depicts himself sitting with Byrne and Murphy. The small glass of orange is in front of him, and his fedora is shown placed firmly on his head. While the finished oil is quite stylised, with broad brush strokes used to emphasise the sitter's facial features, a preparatory watercolour is painted more naturalistically. There is a strong contrast between Kernoff's self-portrait here and Reeve's 1940 caricature. While there are some fundamental artistic differences between a self-portrait and a caricature, Kernoff's self-portrait shows the artist as being confident, and very much on a par with Byrne and Murphy.

By the time Kernoff completed this triple portrait in the mid-late 1930s, he had already completed several other accomplished self-portraits in various media. A self-portrait drawing from 1923, when he won the Taylor Prize and entered the DMSA as a full-time student, shows the youthful artist. Drawn using light, quick graphite lines, the sketch is similar in quality to the artist's life drawings from the same date.[74] Life drawing was the bedrock of the system at the DMSA, and Kernoff's sketches show how students were expected to master different poses and attitudes. In addition to learning key drawing skills at the DMSA classes, Kernoff and his contemporaries may also have been encouraged to practise self-portraiture by his teacher, Seán Keating. As a student himself, Keating had been encouraged by William Orpen to use self-portraiture as a way of maintaining a daily routine of practising art.[75] This development and lineage is most evident in a 1929 full length self-portrait (Plate 4.7). Borrowing from Orpen's academic style, Kernoff placed himself before the easel, holding his palette and several brushes. Behind him, finished pictures in large gold frames can be seen, and to the left-hand side an open paint box rests on a stool or high table. With an open smock covering his clothes, Kernoff presents himself as the consummate artist, ready to move on from the opening years of his career.

Surveying the history of self-portraiture in Western art, Omar Calabrese has noted that there are 'at least four motives for the self-portrait: (a) exhibition of virtuosity and economy of means; (b) affirmation of success; (c) staking a claim to artistic merit; (d) the exploration of the private realm'.[76] In relation to Kernoff's 1929 self-portrait, we can certainly read it as staking a claim to artistic merit and as an affirmation of his achievements to date. Writing on migrant artists in Chicago in the period 1910–50, Sarah Kelly Oehler further commented that 'portraiture was one means by which migrant artists could position themselves within their new community. They could use the genre to define themselves as they wished to be seen, calling attention to certain traits while downplaying others.'[77] The artists discussed by Oehler refer to a wide range of migrants who found their way to Chicago through this period, echoing Kernoff's own journey to Dublin in 1914. In Oehler's study, a common trend was for artists to represent themselves at work; for example, Emil Armin's *Self-Portrait* woodcut. By showing themselves in this way, these self-portraits allowed artists to present themselves as something other than 'migrant'. Rather than being defined by their language, accent, name, or appearance – as might be perceived when face to face with the artist – the artwork allowed such signifiers to be circumvented, and for the focus to rest on the person and profession depicted. In the case of Raphael Soyer, the use of self-portraiture also allowed the artist to claim his place within a fine art tradition, as seen in his *Self-Portrait with Self-Portraits of Rembrandt, Corot and Degas* (1959, oil on canvas, collection unknown).[78] For Kernoff, the practice of self-portraiture was not only a method of mapping his artistic progress but, as seen in many of the pub paintings, a deliberate tool of self-fashioning, literally locating the artist in this important part of Dublin's social scene.

Davy Byrne's Pub, Dublin, from the Bailey (Plate 4.8, Figure 4.19) is not only one of Kernoff's most accomplished paintings, but it also includes a fascinating self-portrait. Amid the detritus of the bar and counter, the artist's image is reflected in the mirror that runs along the shelving at the window. This is one of the few self-portraits where the artist makes direct eye contact with

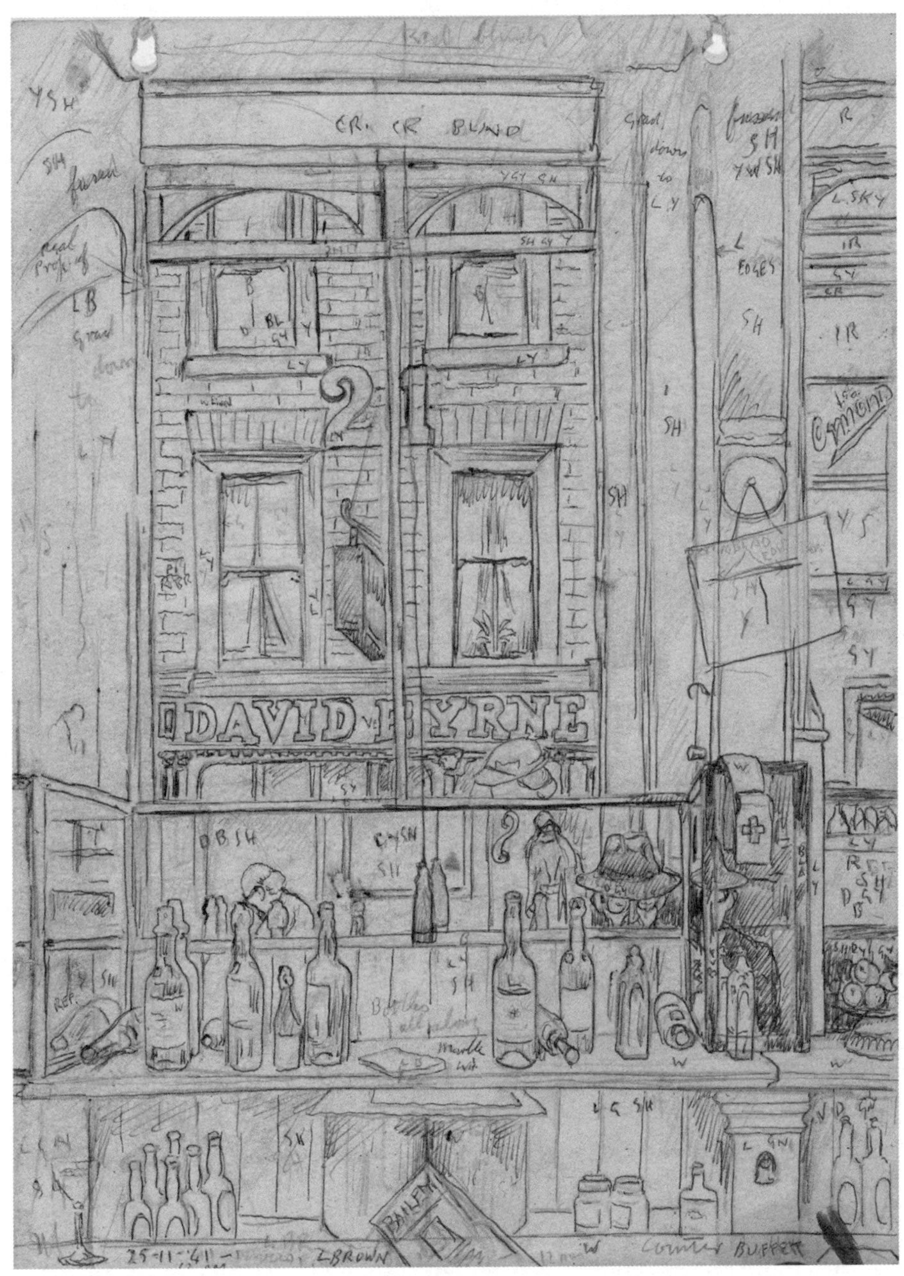

4.19   Harry Kernoff, *Davy Byrne's Pub, Dublin, from the Bailey*, 1941.

the viewer, and his undeviating gaze draws the viewer into the painting. In addition to his initial and extremely detailed sketch, Kernoff also completed at least three preparatory watercolours and one oil sketch (1941, oil on board, private collection) of this composition.[79] These preliminary versions show that he thought very carefully about each aspect of the final work, together with the inclusion of a self-portrait. The initial drawing is dated to 25 November 1941, and broadly reflects the structure of the finished painting. In this drawing, and the oil sketch, the figure reflected in the mirror does not resemble the artist – although Kernoff does include the small glass of orange seen in his other *Davy Byrne's* paintings. The two watercolour sketches have small differences: while one shows the glass of orange, in the other this has been replaced by an elegant cocktail glass. Another detail that shows the artist's concentration on this composition is his reworking of the theatre posters that ultimately hang on either side of the windowpane. The finished oil painting uses these posters to feature Dublin's two most prominent theatres – the Abbey and the Gate. In the first instance, Kernoff showed a blank notice and gave no indication or even a clear colour reference for what it was to show. In one watercolour version and the oil sketch, he added the details of the Abbey Theatre and the name of Brinsley MacNamara's play *Look at the Heffernans!* Kernoff contemplated including two different posters – for the RHA Annual Exhibition and for *The Plough and the Stars* at the Abbey. Ultimately the final version of the painting stays with *Look at the Heffernans!* and to include both the Gate Theatre and to contrast comedy and tragedy, the right-hand poster advertises a Lord Longford production of *Romeo and Juliet*. Newspaper records show that while the Gate production tallies with the date given on the initial sketch, the MacNamara production had played at the Abbey in 1940. The artist's deliberations over the exact composition of *Davy Byrne's Pub* suggest a strong concern for getting the final arrangement just right; however, even after the painting was exhibited abroad, the artist made a further change. In 1950, the painting was included in an exhibition organised by the Cultural Relations Committee (part of the Department of External Relations, now the Department of Foreign Affairs and Trade). Overseen by Elizabeth Curran and titled *Contemporary Irish Painting*, the exhibition toured to three venues in North America: Providence, Rhode Island; Boston, Massachusetts; and Ottawa, Canada. An illustration of *Davy Byrne's from the Bailey* in the catalogue shows an additional figure beside the artist's self-portrait, a man eating from a bowl. However, this has since been removed from the canvas, although the outline can still be seen on close examination.

In this painting, Kernoff placed himself in the heartland of Dublin's literary pubs and more specifically between two establishments famed for their inclusion in a much talked-about literary representation of the city. Unlike other self-portraits, in this work the artist confronts the viewer directly (albeit through his reflection) using a frontal pose. Describing this pose, Calabrese notes 'there is a figure that looks out at us; we can identify the fact that he looks at us only while we are looking at him, so thereby we are reproducing an exchange of words'.[80] In the case of this painting, Kernoff can be seen to be acknowledging his presence within Dublin's urban environment, rather than offering the viewer a reflection of what he sees around him, as in his more general city views. With the choice of location, and the carefully mediated composition, this painting can be read as both a comment on Dublin's cultural life at that time, as well as a statement on Kernoff's place within that environment. Using self-portraiture in this and other examples of his Dublin pub paintings, Kernoff made a clear attempt to position himself within a community, and perhaps to downplay his migrant roots. Over the course of his career, Kernoff became a familiar and important figure in Dublin's political, social, and artistic circles. There is, however, often a sense of loneliness or solitude in his paintings – and – in some of the pub paintings, of overstretching, of being overeager to represent his experience of Dublin life. Scattered throughout the Kernoff archives are reminders that, regardless of how well the artist seemed to integrate into the Dublin art world, he was often seen as an outsider or, simply because of his religion, different to his peers. For example, in 1939, Seán Moylan (TD for Cork North) wrote to Taoiseach Éamon De Valera to recommend Kernoff for a teaching assistant position in the National College of Art (formerly the DMSA). Outlining his case, Moylan stated that Kernoff was 'not an Irishman but he is so long here that he has in great measure adopted our Irish outlook'.[81] An undated portrait sketch of the artist was sent to him by Maurice MacGonigal as a holiday card, with the greeting, 'Best wishes for whatever you do be having': Kernoff's isolation from his peers due to religion was further emphasised by his diary notes from 26 December 1964, when he wrote: 'St Stephen's Day or Boxing Day / Very dark walk / Various family pubs, arts clubs, no one there.'[82]

Conclusion: a Londoner who loved Dublin

Kernoff continued to paint the city throughout the 1950s and 1960s, producing and exhibiting his work until his death on 25 December 1974, with the majority of urban works from this period being worked from sketches made during the early decades of the century. His representational views of the city were largely eclipsed by contemporary developments in the Dublin art scene and the arrival of a new generation of artists who forged a new radicalism, much as Kernoff and his peers had done in the 1920s. The importance of Kernoff's city paintings from the 1920s until the late 1940s is profound, as they capture so many facets of Dublin life in this period. The 'jazz age' paintings capture the energy of the post-revolution city and segue into Kernoff's involvement in the city's theatrical and radical circles. His depictions of the city at this time, together with designs for costumes, tableaux, and stage designs, contribute to the 'fragmentary but suggestive' evidence which reveals a 'city where artists, actors, musicians and politicians mingled in the margins of a miniature Berlin, experimenting in radical forms, burlesque and low comedy, pamphlets and periodicals, the erotic and irreverent'.[83] As the artist matured, so did his visions of the city he lived in: his concentration on the docklands, particularly the area around the Grand Canal basin, marks a significant departure in the representation of Dublin generally and is made even more meaningful by the artist's continued commitment to leftist and anti-fascist politics in the 1930s. Contrary to the painters alluded to by Clark in his writings on Lowry, Kernoff was not 'exterior' to the difficulties faced by Dublin's labourers and dockers, and was one of very few artists working in Ireland at this time who showed an ongoing commitment to the representation of labour and unemployment.

Shortly before the artist's death on 24 December 1974, he was interviewed by Cathal O'Shannon for an RTÉ programme titled 'Going on 75', which profiled people who had been born in 1900, and asked what changes they had noticed over the intervening three-quarters of a century. Filmed in Kernoff's attic studio, with a large sketch pinned to the easel beside him and a row of portraits hanging behind, the artist recounted (in a marked London accent) his arrival in Dublin in 1914 and his subsequent career. An obituary published in early 1975 bore the headline 'A Londoner Who Loved Dublin': a simple yet effective way of summing up Kernoff's relationship with his adopted city.[84] Through his art, Kernoff assessed and signified his own sense of place: establishing himself within the cityscape through the performative act of painting it and self-locating within his images. The artworks he produced were truly 'realist', depicting his reality, complete with natural, man-made, and social realities. Kernoff's long career in Dublin meant that he not only overlapped with Yeats, but also with the two artists discussed in the last chapter of this book: Estella Solomons and Flora Mitchell. If Lord Longford felt that Kernoff depicted a 'Dublin that is passing', this theme manifested itself even more strongly in the works of these two artists and, more particularly, the publications they contributed to.

Notes

1 T. J. Clark, 'Lowry's Other England', in T. J. Clark and A. M. Wagner (eds), *Lowry and the Painting of Modern Life* (London: Tate Publishing, 2013), p. 39.
2 Ibid.
3 Ibid., p. 46.
4 In 1974, John Ryan commented that 'W.S. Lowry [*sic*] is the only other painter I can think of who matches the feeling of radical humanism he shows in his portrayal of the (not always breath- taking) urban environment in which so many of us spend our lives'. J. Ryan, 'Harry Kernoff RHA', in *Harry Kernoff: A Selection of Dublin Paintings* (Dublin: Godolphin Gallery, 1974), n.p.
5 Snoddy, *Dictionary of Irish Artists: 20ᵗʰ Century*, p. 311.
6 NLI, Harry Kernoff Papers, Ms 20, 918, *Daily Express* (23 February 1931), p. 7.
7 1901 Census Return Form.
8 S. Rosenblatt, *Alien registration file 1914–1922 (a police record, Chancery Lane, Dublin, Ireland): Ada Shillman (midwife) birth records, Dublin 1893–1908* (Dublin: The Jewish Genealogical Society, 2005), p. 79.

9 For a full account of the history of Ireland's Jewish community, see D. Keogh, *Jews in Twentieth-century Ireland: Refugees, Anti-Semitism and the Holocaust* (Cork: Cork University Press, 1998).

10 C. Ó Gráda, *Jewish Ireland in the age of Joyce: A Socioeconomic History* (Princeton: Princeton University Press, 2006), p. 105.

11 'Irish Artists: The Exhibition at Balls-Bridge', *Weekly Irish Times* (9 August 1924), p. 17.

12 S. B. Kennedy, *Irish Art and Modernism: 1880–1950* (Belfast: Institute of Irish Studies, 1991), p. 20.

13 'Impressions and Landscapes: Mr Harry A Kernoff's Work', *Irish Times* (21 April 1927), p. 7.

14 'Interesting Picture Show', *Irish Independent* (21 April 1927), p. 6.

15 'Arts and Studies: Harriet Cooke talks to Harry Kernoff', *Irish Times* (17 May 1974), p. 10.

16 Allen, *Modernism, Ireland and Civil War*, p. 54.

17 'Toto' was the affectionate name given to Desirée or Marguerite Bannard Cogley, also known as Daisy Bannard or Helen Cogley Carter. See E. Sisson, 'Experiment and the Free State: Mrs Cogley's cabaret and the founding of the Gate Theatre, 1924–1920', in D. Clare, D. Lally, and P. Lonergan (eds), *The Gate Theatre, Dublin: Inspiration and Craft* (Dublin: Carysfort Press, 2018), p. 1.

18 See J. Eckett, *Art on the Move: Hidden Treasures from the CIÉ Art Collection* (Dublin: Córas Iompair Éireann, 2006), p. 24.

19 'Studio Cabaret: Enjoyable Entertainment', *Irish Times* (5 March 1928), p. 4.

20 See E. Sisson, 'Experimentalism and the Irish stage: theatre and German Expressionism in the 1920s', in E. Sisson and L. King (eds), *Ireland, Design and Visual Culture: Negotiating Modernity, 1922–1992* (Cork: Cork University Press, 2011), pp. 39–55.

21 J. FitzPatrick Dean, 'Rewriting the past: historical pageantry in the Dublin civic weeks of 1927 and 1929', *New Hibernia Review* 13:1 (2009), 22–3.

22 D. Lyakovitz, 'Revolutionary artists of the west: Harry Kernoff', *Iskusstvo v Massi*, no. 10–11 (October/November 1930). Trans. Maurice Casey: https://goodbyetwilight.wordpress.com/2018/01/02/too-revolutionary-for-capitalist-society-a-1930-soviet-profile-of-an-irish-artist/ (accessed 21 April 2020).

23 Y. O., 'The Hibernian Academy', *The Irish Statesman* (16 April 1927).

24 'FOSR meeting in Dublin', *Workers' Voice* (24 May 1930), p. 2.

25 See H. Kernoff, 'A Dubliner abroad: art in the new Russia', *The Watchword* (6 December 1930), pp. 7–8. *The Workers' Voice* noted that the delegation comprised of Hannah Sheehy-Skeffington, Sighle Dowling (President of the Irish Women Worker's Union), David Fitzgerald, Harry Kernoff ('the Dublin painter'), Jack O'Neill (representing the Unemployed Movement), and Charlotte Despard. The delegates spoke at a public meeting in the Mansion House, Dublin on their return. See 'Mansion House Meeting: Irish delegates returned from Russia', *Workers' Voice* (27 September 1930), n.p.

26 See E. Sisson, 'Designing Modernism: Harry Kernoff, Russia, and postindependence Ireland', *Éire-Ireland*, 52:3&4 (2017), 31–56.

27 NLI, Ms 24, 942, Harry Kernoff Papers, 'Observations re art and theatre in the USSR'.

28 Ibid.

29 Ibid.

30 D. Elliott and P. Juszkiewicz, 'Socialist realism', *Grove Art Online. Oxford Art Online.* Oxford University Press. www.oxfordartonline.com/subscriber/article/grove/art/ T079464 (accessed 21 April 2020).

31 Turpin, *A School of Art in Dublin since the Eighteenth Century*, p. 290.

32 H. Kernoff, 'Root causes of the lack of artistic appreciation in Ireland', *The Irish People* (14 March 1936).

33 J. G. Todd Jr, 'Social realism', *Grove Art Online. Oxford Art Online.* Oxford University Press. www.oxfordartonline.com/subscriber/article/grove/art/T079466 (accessed 21 April 2020).

34 See S. K. Oehler, *They Seek a City: Chicago and the Art of Migration, 1910–1950* (Chicago: The Art Institute of Chicago, 2013).

35 P. Hills, 'The socially concerned painters of the 1930s: an introduction', in *Social Concern and Urban Realism: American Painting of the 1930s* (Boston University Art Gallery: Boston, 1984), p. 9.

36 A. Hemingway, *Artists on the Left: American Artists and the Communist Movement, 1926–1956* (New Haven: Yale University Press, 2002), p. 20.

37 Kernoff was an assistant to Maurice MacGonigal on a mural for the Irish pavilion at the World's Fair held in New York in 1939; however, there is no evidence to suggest that he travelled to the city on that, or any other, occasion. Still operating today, Schimmel's knish bakery opened in 1910, although it is thought that Schimmel began selling knishes in Coney Island in the 1890s. See S. Roberts, 'Celebrating the freshest 100-year-old knish', *City Room, Blogging from the Five Boroughs* (blog), *The New York Times* (13 January 2010), http://cityroom.blogs.nytimes.com/2010/01/13/ knish/?_php=true&_type=blogs&_r=0 (accessed 21 April 2020).

38 A good example of Kernoff's paintings in England is *Bend in the Road, Richmond, Surrey* (1947, oil on board, National Museums of Northern Ireland).

39 See B. Laughton, *William Coldstream* (New Haven and London: Published for the Paul Mellon Centre for Studies in British Art by Yale University Press, 2004), pp. 53–7 and D. Buckely, *From Bow to Biennale: Artists of the East London Group* (London: Francis Boutle Publishers, 2012).

40 J. Nolan, 'The Artist of the Workers', *Irish Times* (30 December 1974), p. 10.

41 C. Casey, *Dublin: The City within the Grand and Royal Canals and the Circular Road with the Phoenix Park* (New Haven: Yale University Press, 2005), p. 152.

42 Kernoff was not elected to the RHA until 1936, suggesting that the drawing was mounted and dated after this date. It may also be that this is a retrospective image, showing Liberty Hall as it was in 1928.

43 See Whytes Irish and British Art, 1 October 2012, Lot 64.

44 NLI, Ms 20, 918, Harry Kernoff Papers, clipping of R. M. Fox, 'A Worker Artist', *Amalgamated Engineering Union Monthly Journal* (October 1931).

45 T. Bunbury, *Dublin Docklands: An Urban Voyage* (Dublin: Montague Publications Group on behalf of the Dublin Docklands Development Authority, 2009), p. 200.

46 H. Kernoff, *Misery Hill*, oil on board private collection, reproduced in *Selection of Results 2004*, DeVeres Art Auctions, p. 15.

47 Title given in catalogue for *Important Irish Art*, James Adam in association with

Bonhams, when the painting was sold from a private collection, Lot 39, 46, December 2002.

48 'Dublin Character P. J. Marlow also known as Johnny Forty Coats', *Independent Newspaper Collection*, NLI, IND6.774.

49 For example, see 'Testimony of Nellie Cassidy' from K. C. Kearns (ed.), *Dublin Tenement Life: An Oral History* (Dublin: Gill and Macmillan, 2006), p. 88.

50 See M. Cappock, 'Dublin divided: September 1913', in L. Sisley and M. Cappock (eds), *Dublin Divided: September 1913* (Dublin: Dublin City Gallery The Hugh Lane, 2013), p. 52.

51 'Kernoff Pictures: Exhibition at College Street', *Irish Times* (29 March 1934), p. 4.

52 Ibid.

53 J. Carville, 'Introduction: visual culture and the making of modern Dublin', in J. Carville (ed.), *Visualizing Dublin: Visual Culture, Modernity and the Representation of Urban Space* (Bern and Oxford: Peter Lang, 2014), p. 1.

54 See S. Mannion, 'Celtic arc light: the electric light in early twentieth century Dublin', in Carville (ed.), *Visualizing Dublin*, pp. 111–31.

55 'Kernoff Pictures: Exhibition at College Street', *Irish Times* (29 March 1934), p. 4.

56 Carville, 'Introduction: visual culture and the making of modern Dublin', p. 3.

57 See E. Rowley, *Housing, Architecture and the Edge Condition: Dublin is Building, 1935–1975* (London: Routledge, 2018), pp. 60–91.

58 See P. Kavanagh, *Collected Poems*, ed. Antoinette Quinn (London: Penguin, 2005), p. 224, p. 227.

59 Piers Plowman [Patrick Kavanagh], 'City Commentary', *Irish Press* (8 October 1942), p. 3.

60 See B. Lynch, *Parsons Bookshop: At the Heart of Bohemian Dublin 1949–1989* (Dublin: The Liffey Press, 2006).

61 This title was given when the painting appeared at auction in 1998. See Sotheby's, *The Irish Sale*, 21 May 1998, London, Lot 400.

62 See H. Kernoff, 'Leeson Bridge, Grey Day', graphite on paper, NGI 7766.363.

63 Another version of this composition was sold through Adams in 2014, with autumnal rather than green, summer leaves. See Adam's Important Irish Art Sale, 1 October 2014, Lot 127.

64 H. Kernoff, 'Stephen's Green', 20 May 1940, graphite on paper, NGI. 7766.420.

65 D. S. 'A Painter of Old Dublin: Mr Kernoff's Art', *Irish Independent* (2 December 1937), p. 11.

66 Ibid.

67 The building formerly known as the Viceregal Lodge, residence of the lord lieutenant and his family, was used temporarily by the governor general of Ireland, but lay empty for many years until it was renamed Áras an Uachtaráin (house or residence of the President) in 1938.

68 H. Tracy, *Mind You, I've Said Nothing! Forays in the Irish Republic* (London: White Lion Publishers, 1973), pp. 29–30.

69 K. C. Kearns, *Dublin Pub Life and Lore: An Oral History* (Dublin: Gill and Macmillan, 1996), p. 64.

70 N. Allen, 'Beckett's Dublin', in F. Croke (ed.) *Samuel Beckett: A Passion for Painting* (Dublin: National Gallery of Ireland, 2006), p. 45.

71 'Irishman's Diary', *Irish Times* (5 June 1940), p. 3.

72 'High Standard at R.H.A. Exhibition', *Irish Times* (21 April 1947), p. 4.

73 Joyce, *Ulysses*, pp. 217–18. A portrait of James Joyce by Kernoff now hangs in Davy Byrne's, where Kernoff also painted the original murals. Although later repainted by Cecil ffrench Salkeld, parts of the extant murals contain recognisable elements by Kernoff.

74 See H. Kernoff, 'Self-Portrait', 1923, 1923, NGI.3143.

75 See É. O'Connor, *Seán Keating: Art, Politics and Building the Irish Nation* (Dublin: Irish Academic Press, 2013), pp. 51–2.

76 O. Calabrese, *Artists' Self-portraits*, trans. Margurite Shore (London: Abbeville Press, 2006), p. 320.

77 Oehler, *They Seek A City: Chicago and the Art of Migration, 1910–1950*, p. 42.

78 This portrait is reproduced in S. Baskind, *Raphael Soyer and the Search for Modern Jewish Art* (Chapel Hill: University of North Carolina Press, 2004), p. 43.

79 Details of the preparatory works can be found in the following auction records: Whyte's Irish Art Sale, 21 February 2006, Lot 106; Whyte's Irish and British Art Sale, 1 October 2012, Lot 61.

80 Calabrese, *Artists' Self-Portraits*, p. 142.

81 NLI, Harry Kernoff Papers, 1939, Ms 20, 917, letter from Seán Moylan to Éamon De Valera.

82 NLI, Harry Kernoff Papers, 26 December 1964, Ms 19, 405–19, 414, Diaries of Harry Kernoff.

83 N. Allen, 'Cabaret, sex and independence: publishing in the early Free State', in M. Fanning and R. Gillespie (eds), *Print Culture and Intellectual Life in Ireland 1660–1941* (Dublin: The Woodfield Press, 2006), p. 186.

84 NLI, January 1975, Harry Kernoff Papers, clipping of B. Lynch, 'A Londoner who loved Dublin', unidentified newspaper clipping.

∞ 5 ∞

Glamorous, old, and vanishing Dublin

In 1931, the Royal Institute of British Architects held their annual conference in Dublin, hosted and welcomed by colleagues in their sister organisation, the Royal Institute of the Architects of Ireland. The first day of the conference was dedicated to an introductory talk on architecture in Ireland (ancient, medieval, and Georgian), after which delegates could select one of four tours around the city centre, all of which would be followed by tea. Reading through the routes selected for the delegates, it is striking that despite the intervening years, they would not have been out of place in a mid-nineteenth-century guidebook, with the Government Buildings on Merrion Street the only nod to twentieth-century construction in the city. To further introduce Dublin to the conference delegates, the organisers reprinted the 1929 *Book of Dublin* (discussed in Chapter 4) as part of the official handbook. In his introduction, the conference secretary Harry Allberry noted that despite improvements in transport, paving, lighting and cleansing, and some large-scale rebuilding, 'the soul of Dublin, that peculiar fascination which renders it so different from practically every other capital, still remains as of old'.[1] Undoubtedly what Allberry was referring to was the historic core of 'old Dublin' as imagined and codified in the late nineteenth and early twentieth centuries, and which continued to be seen as a key characteristic of the city.

Indeed, interest in and the study of 'old Dublin' was soon formalised through the foundation of the Old Dublin Society (1934), which sought to promote the history of the city through a series of talks, lectures, and site visits. In 1938, the Society began to produce a journal – the *Dublin Historical Record* – publishing papers that were delivered to the members, and thus forming one of the earliest records of local research on the city's history. Within the longer narrative of 'old Dublin', as outlined in Chapter 2, it is at this point in the early-mid twentieth century that a subtle shift occurs in the tone of the 'old Dublin' story. While the eighteenth-century and the city's Georgian-built heritage was still at its core, the overly nostalgic tone diminished, and the sovereignty of the pre-Union

165

Parliament was reclaimed in light of Irish independence and contemporary nationalism. This is reflected in subtle ways through the activities of the Old Dublin Society; for example, in December 1934 a paper titled 'Hidden and Vanishing Dublin' recounted the history of Fenian activity in the city during the 1860s, a topic later published in an early issue of the Society's journal. The conservation agenda set forth by the Irish Georgian Society in the early part of the century was not forgotten, and voices from within the architectural profession, and from amateur historians, called for the protection of the city's built heritage and stricter planning regulations to avoid making 'Dublin a dreary wilderness of hugger-mugger'.[2] Following on from the exploration of *Picturesque Dublin: Old and New*, and the relationship between Gerard's text and Barton's images, this chapter will look at two later representations of Dublin in guide-type books: etchings by Estella Solomons reproduced in *The Glamour of Dublin* (1928) and Flora Mitchell's *Vanishing Dublin*, written by the artist in 1966 and illustrated with pen and watercolour drawings produced in the 1950s and 1960s. The city views created by these two artists, and their critical reception, show how ingrained the idea of 'old Dublin' is in conversations around Dublin, its history, and representation.

Estella Solomons and *The Glamour of Dublin*

In a brief note on the fly pages of *The Glamour of Dublin*, D. L. Kelleher noted that 'Dublin, despite its housing, is one of the most profoundly optimistic cities in Europe. It is a heroic optimism that outlives every war and lays the most sardonic ghosts of the after-war period.'[3] First published in 1918, *The Glamour of Dublin* sought to outline Dublin's historic past along with more recent events such as the labour movement and the 1916 Rising; a subsequent edition was published in 1920, but like its predecessor, was issued without illustrations. This was the most significant change when the third edition was published in 1928: eight etchings by Estella Solomons were included, selected from her considerable corpus of Dublin scenes. In its declaration of optimism, along with some acknowledgement of Dublin's problems, this text is expressive of a renewed energy found in the description of Dublin following the upheaval of the revolutionary period. The guidebook's author, Daniel Laurence Kelleher, had penned several travel and guidebooks by this date, including *Paris, Its Glamour and Life* (1914) and *Lake Geneva* (1914). Through the 1920s he added *The Glamour of Cork* (1919), *Round Italy* (1923), and *Ireland of the Welcomes* (1929) to this impressive record. Prior to authoring guidebooks, Kelleher had been associated with the Cork Realists drama group and published three volumes of poetry. It seems likely that Kelleher, Solomons, and her partner (later husband) writer and editor Seamus O'Sullivan were acquainted through Dublin's literary and nationalist circles.

By 1928, Solomons's etchings would have been familiar to many in Dublin, having been both published and exhibited widely by this date. For example, in

1917, O'Sullivan included a reproduction of an original drawing by Solomons as a frontispiece to *Mud and Purple: Pages from the Diary of a Dublin Man* – a semi-autobiographical, literary, *belle-lettres*-style text, as well as reproducing her oil portrait of Jack B. Yeats and etchings of *Marsh's Library* and *Hoey's Court* (Figure 5.1) in the first volume of *The Dublin Magazine*, a literary journal which he founded and edited in 1923. In 1920, her *A Georgian Doorway* was included in *The Book of Saint Ultan*, published to raise funds for a children's hospital named after the saint, and in 1926, two further Dublin scenes were included in Padraic Colum's *The Road Round Ireland*. These publications further reveal how Solomons was embedded in Revivalist literary circles, as well as within the nationalist cause championed by the founders of St Ultan's, Kathleen Lynn and Madeline ffrench-Mullen, both of whom had been active in the 1916 Rising.[4] Materials in the artist's papers suggest that she intended at some point to produce her own publication using her etchings: a collection of twenty-five works were gathered by Solomons under the title 'for book', and included scenes from around Dublin city and county.[5]

A sketchbook dating to 1906 is evocative of Solomons's genteel, middle-class upbringing in Edwardian Dublin. Fluid sketches of a young woman (most likely her sister, Sophie), sewing, reading by the fire, or standing at a window, show her dressed in simple yet elegant clothing, with her hair pulled up in a coiffure typical of the period.[6] The well-to-do Solomons family lived on Waterloo Road, situated just outside of the city centre; her parents, Maurice E. Solomons and Rosa Jane Solomons (neé Jacobs), were known for their generous philanthropy and their involvement with the Jewish community in Dublin. Following her education in Dublin and Hanover, the young artist enrolled in the DMSA (1898–1901), before attending the Chelsea Art School (a private school founded by William Orpen and Augustus John) London, for three years from 1903. An early cityscape, *Cheyne Row, Chelsea* (c.1903, oil on canvas, private collection) visually places Solomons in London and uses a muted, naturalist palette. Despite the relatively long duration of her stay in London, little is known about the artist's activities there, and her name does not appear in catalogues of various group exhibitions then taking place.[7] The circles of Orpen and John would have introduced Solomons to the more bohemian side of London society, and this may have been important in the development of her political beliefs. Before returning to Ireland, she also spent some time at the Académie Colarossi, Paris, further expanding her artistic and visual education.

In Dublin, Solomons was involved in Revivalist circles, and like many of her colleagues from the DMSA was committed to the idea of Irish independence from Britain. Although this might seem to contradict much of her middle-class upbringing, she was part of a large circle of cultural figures in Dublin who contributed in different ways to the nationalist cause, often in contrast to the politics of their families. Indeed, she may have been influenced by other family activism at this time: her mother, Rosa Solomons, was involved with the Irish Women's Suffrage and Local Government Association, and a cousin, Louise Jacobs, was a

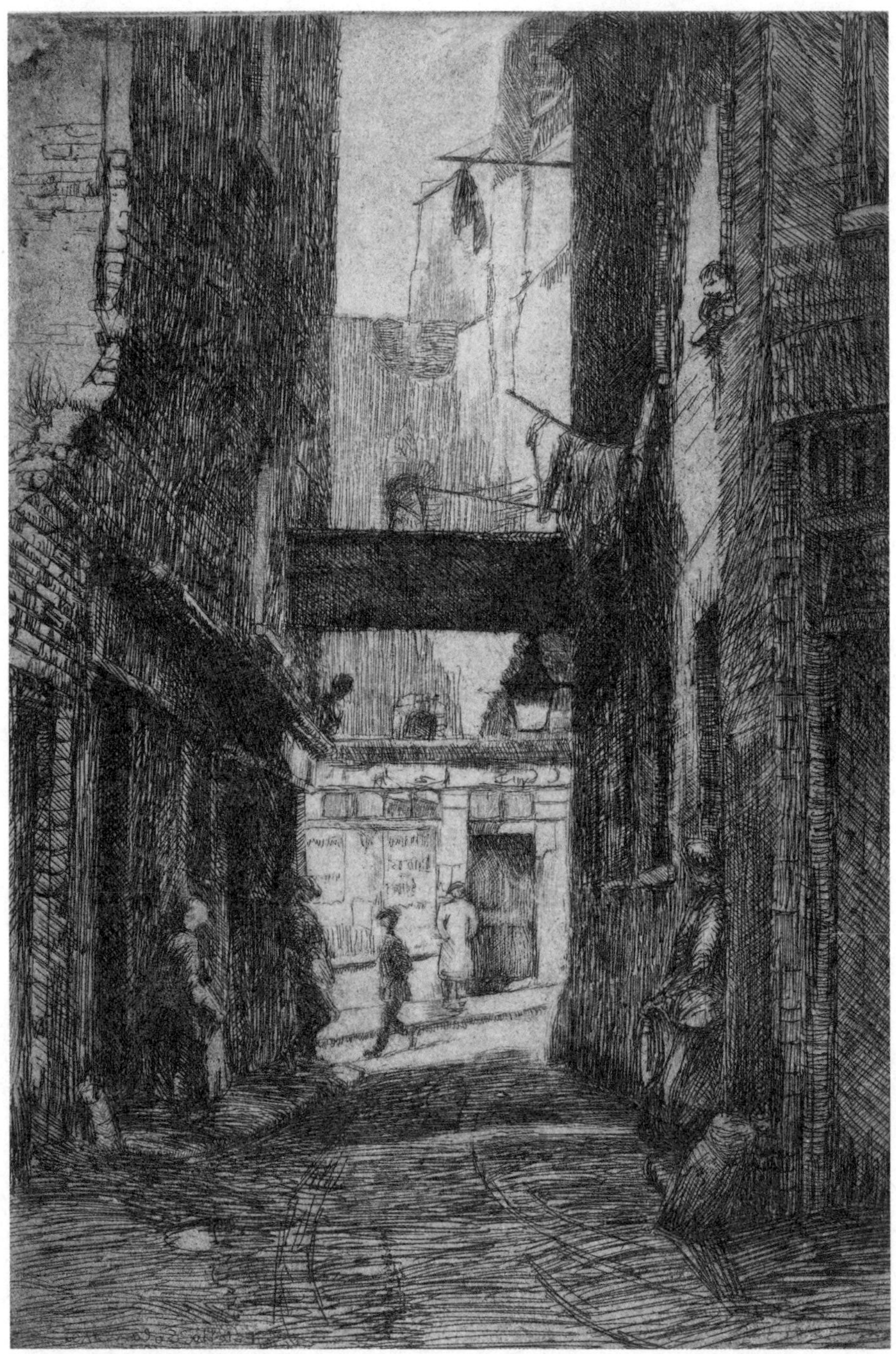

5.1   Estella Frances Solomons, *Hoey's Court*, undated.

suffragist artist and activist in Britain. From 1911, Solomons was listed among the artist-members of the Five Provinces Branch of the Gaelic League: established in 1905, this branch was generally associated with a large Protestant membership (it was colloquially referred to as the 'Branch of the Five Protestants', and it is likely that Solomons was among only a handful of Jewish Gaelic League members) but it was also notable for the large number of artists and academics associated with it; for example, Sadhbh Trinseach, Lily Williams, Stephen Gwynn, and T. W. Rolleston were members.[8] From 1910–15, the Branch held an annual exhibition at 7 Stephen's Green at which Solomons frequently exhibited her Dublin etchings and other paintings. In 1916, she was active in the Irish National Aid and Volunteer Dependents' Fund, helping to raise donations for a Gift Sale in December 1916, to which she, her family, and on her request, artists Augustus John and John Lavery, donated silverware, prints, books, sketches, and in the case of the latter, a blank canvas on which he would paint the portrait of the highest bidder.[9] The following year, Solomons furthered her commitment to the nationalist cause by joining the ranks of the Ranelagh Branch of Cumann na mBan with her friend Kathleen Goodfellow, where they were trained in surveillance and in the use of arms.[10] Goodfellow, who wrote under the pseudonym of 'Michael Scot', was a lifelong friend of Solomons who painted several portraits of her, as well as an author of short stories which reflected on conditions in Ireland during the War of Independence. Among these, *Three Tales of the Times* dealt explicitly with the outrages of the Black and Tans in Ireland, and Solomons and Scot later gifted a copy of this to Jack B. Yeats.[11]

Solomons had first taken a studio on Pearse Street (then known as Great Brunswick Street) in 1910 and retained a presence on the street into the 1920s, occasionally moving between different houses. This address brought her into the heart of the city, and throughout the revolutionary period the studio was both a cultural salon and a safe-house for those whose, as O'Sullivan described it, 'political and national activities had brought them a very undesirable amount of notice'.[12] While the studio was located at number 17, the author James Stephens lived in another flat at the same address, further demonstrating how the artist was embedded in Dublin's literary circles. During these years, Solomons painted several of the leading revolutionary figures in this studio, creating an important visual record of those involved in active service.[13] However, more pertinently, in the early years of her tenancy, it was also where she completed a number of paintings which further connect Solomons with the tradition of urban painting in Ireland – most notably with the legacy of Walter Osborne. The older artist had briefly taught Solomons at the DMSA, perhaps fostering her interest in 'views in the city, shadowy archways, old-fashioned lanes, famous buildings or rows of houses from an unusual angle'.[14]

This is most evident in two undated paintings which appear to have been painted on the rooftop of a city centre building: *Street Urchins with Bird Cage* (oil on canvas, private collection) and *Boy on a Roof Garden* (oil on canvas, private collection). These works develop the muted greys and greens seen in *Cheyne*

Row: in the former work strong sunlight highlights the features of an older girl, while a younger boy stands in shadow. While not as 'ragged' as the children seen in Osborne's works, the boy stands barefoot, and the girl's clothing is depicted as being constructed from plain and durable fabrics. The boy's stance is almost exactly replicated in the latter painting, with further visual detail and colour added through the young green leaves on the saplings, and a spray of yellow daffodils in a green-painted planter. The interior space of the studio also provided Solomons with a ready-made setting for more contemplative works, as seen in *A Woman Reading at a Desk by a Window* (c.1918, oil on canvas, private collection) and *Afternoon Tea* (c.1918, oil on canvas, private collection). In both works, a small sash window frames the composition, its size suggesting the upper storey of a tall Georgian house: turning again to O'Sullivan's description of the studio, we learn that 'the studio was, at that time, on the top floor of the tall house, and the ascent to it toilsome enough'.[15] Added to this, large curtains of green and either white or brown-orange fabric in the background of both paintings is suggestive of both a neutral backdrop for portrait painting, as well as subtly referencing two elements of the Irish tricolour flag. The composition and stillness of these works also seems to suggest an interest in Dutch painting, reinforced in *Afternoon Tea* by the large white cap worn by the maid figure, whose pose and brown costume echoes the genre paintings of Vermeer and his contemporaries. This is contrasted, however, with the short and severe bob of the woman in blue, which firmly places the painting in the early twentieth century.

Previous biographers have tied Solomons's interest in etching to her experience at a Rembrandt exhibition seen in Amsterdam in 1906; however, it is likely that she had been aware of, and perhaps practising, the medium before this date. Although she was exhibiting etchings from around 1911, further formal education was later available to the artist: Angela Griffith suggests that Solomons, along with other contemporaries, would have received private tuition in etching from George Atkinson, a teacher at the DMSA from 1914 onwards.[16] In the same year, and along with Mary Duncan and Albert Power, Solomons showed 'etchings which will have an interest for lovers of old Dublin' at an exhibition in the Pearse Street studio.[17] This was the first time that Solomons' etchings were given more than a passing mention by the press; in addition to the comment just mentioned, the *Irish Times* also reported that the works 'of Miss Solomons are practically all scenes in Dublin, and gain their effect by the broad treatment, suggesting, rather than fully defining the detail. The "Old Shop, Dublin" (No. 78) is, perhaps, the best example.'[18]

In March 1916, just a short time prior to the Rising, Solomons ordered and likely received an etching press from Herbert Weil, a London-based supplier of lithographic, letterpress, and engraving materials and equipment. Writing to the artist on 29 March 1916, Weil noted that although the press was ready for dispatch, the London and North Western Railway Company had paused the carriage of goods to Dublin. However, he was able to write to the artist two days later to say that the press was on its way to Solomons's studio.[19] The disruption to the railway service was likely caused by wartime restrictions, which were also to have a more material effect on Solomons (and other artists) then interested in depicting Dublin. In 1914, the Defence Against the Realm Act (DORA) placed sanctions on those wishing to sketch Dublin's streets and coastline unless they obtained a permit from the Dublin Metropolitan Police (DMP). In June 1915, Joseph Malachy Kavanagh (Secretary of the RHA) recommended that Solomons be granted a permit, but no further documentation relating to this application is extant.[20] However, in 1917, the Provost Marshall of the DMP wrote to Solomons outlining that they had received a report that she had been 'sketching on Wellington Quay without a permit. Will you please explain in view of the fact that the permit issued to you on 6 November, 1915, only authorised you to take sketches in the Phoenix Park and Botanic Gardens.'[21] On receiving Solomons's reply, the Provost Marshall stated that 'no further permit can be issued at present for the purpose of sketching in the Dublin area. Any further infraction of this Regulation will result in the permit you now hold being withdrawn.'[22] The extent to which artists applied for and were granted sketching or painting permits during this period is unknown, as any research relies solely on finding records within an artist's personal archive. Although some records from the DMP were transferred to An Garda Síochána (established in 1923), no archives relating to the granting of permits are extant.

Solomons and Duncan held a further shared exhibition in 1919, this time at their Pearse Street studio. They both continued to explore urban subject matter: one review noted that the artists (despite, perhaps, the restrictions) had 'drawn much of their inspiration from the quaint corners of old Dublin, and they have sketched the slum-dwellers with a feeling of genuine sympathy. They reveal not so much their shabbiness, as their tragic dignity.'[23] Solomons's etchings were described in similar terms in the *Freeman's Journal*, where the critic praised her etching, noting that in '"The Merchant Tailors" Arch (Figure 5.2) and "Georgian Doorway, Bolton Street" she sums up not a little charm of old Dublin'.[24] Reviews from exhibitions throughout the 1920s continue in this vein. In 1920, it was said that her representation of *Hoey's Court* 'breathes the very air of bygone Dublins'[25] and in 1921 as 'depicting picturesque old nooks in the quaint old byways of Dublin'.[26] Her representation of 'the older and more tumble-down parts of Dublin' was noted in 1923, and in 1926 the *Irish Times* review noted that 'these etchings of old Dublin will be treasured by connoisseurs, not only for the fine work that is in them, but also because they give us, as no camera-study can give us, the atmosphere and charm of places which are fast disappearing before the onroad [sic] of civic improvement'.[27]

This language continues the tone already established in considerations of artists' depictions of 'old Dublin', emphasising the 'quaint' and 'picturesque' elements of the streetscape. These reviews of Solomons's work strongly echo the language used in the late nineteenth century – for example, in Gerard's *Picturesque Dublin* – and show how this aestheticised view of the city continued to hold a firm place in conversations around Dublin's architecture and

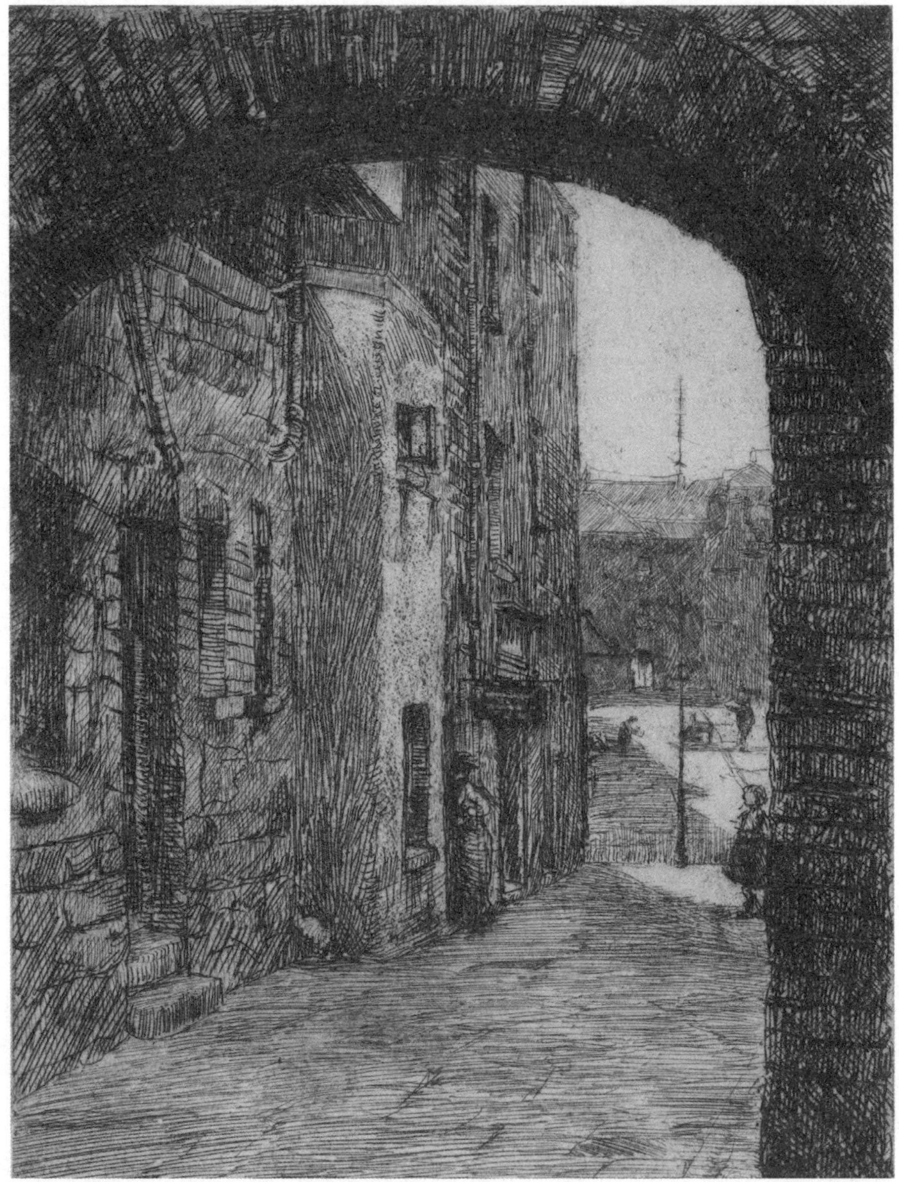

5.2   Estella Frances Solomons, *Dublin Alleyway (Merchant Tailors' Arch)*, undated.

infrastructure. As with earlier discussions, the hardships felt by those living in the city's tenements are reduced to an aesthetic that evokes the past, further evading the difficult reality of the city's social conditions.

Although Solomons drew her inspiration from the city centre from around

1910, her imaging of the city was mediated through ideas and discussions of 'old Dublin' and the picturesque qualities imagined therein. The critical responses to Solomons's etchings of Dublin framed the reception of the artworks in these terms, and the nature of the medium and its atmospheric effect reinforces this. It is notable that against this view of the 'picturesque slum' or the 'quaint nooks' of the city there was a concurrent discussion ongoing over the continuing crises around housing and poverty in the city. The *Darkest Dublin* series of photographs produced to accompany the Dublin Housing Inquiry in 1913 had given visual form to the slums, depicting, as Justin Carville describes, 'the narrow lanes of slum districts, the decay of tenement housing, collapsed dwellings, and the congested courts that became a central feature of much moral outrage at the unsanitary living conditions of Dublin's working classes'.[28] Many of these photographs were taken in 'old Dublin' – the Liberties, the Coombe, Patrick Street, and around Christ Church Cathedral – and while they are often atmospheric and artistic, the photographic medium was considered to be a scientific tool, and as these images were accompanied by first-hand observations of the tenements, they were invested with 'the purchase of the real'.[29]

Against the belief that such photographs held legal purchase, Carville notes a different way they were viewed that may further inform our understanding of artist's depictions, and audience responses to views, of 'old Dublin'. Many of the *Darkest Dublin* images were presented as lantern slides, and around the turn of the century public lectures using this type of medium had become a popular entertainment. Alongside these, the recording of slum districts had grown increasingly popular across Europe and America, borrowing from 'ideas of the colonial voyage to dramatize the narrator's position as an explorer of the urban landscape'.[30] Aimed at a middle-class audience, such events transfigured the image of the slums into a form of spectacle, allowing the audience to access them at a remove rather than walk for themselves among the run-down and overcrowded streets. These ways of presenting slum areas to a middle-class audience can be considered as further contributing to the aestheticising of such districts and the idea of the 'urban picturesque', as discussed in Chapter 2.

The eight etchings selected for reproduction in *The Glamour of Dublin* reflect the span of Solomons's city views, encompassing notable buildings, narrow courts and by-ways, the docklands, and the surrounding countryside. In order of appearance, these were: *The Leinster Market, 1915*; *The King's Inns, Henrietta Street* (Figure 5.3); *Carlisle Court*; *Winetavern Street*; *Hoey's Court, the Birthplace of Dean Swift*; *The Merchant Tailors' Arch*; *The Quay, South Wall*; and *The Hell Fire Club*. Of this collection, only *Carlisle Court* and *The Hell Fire Club* had not previously been exhibited by Solomons, although a preparatory sketch for the former of these is dated 1923.[31] Solomons rarely dated her work, so the first exhibition date may be the closest indicator to when the composition was first conceived, although this is not definitive. What is clear in the case of those included in *The Glamour of Dublin*, however, is that in some instances the etchings were over ten years old, and as such were not contemporaneous with the text or created specifically for the publication.

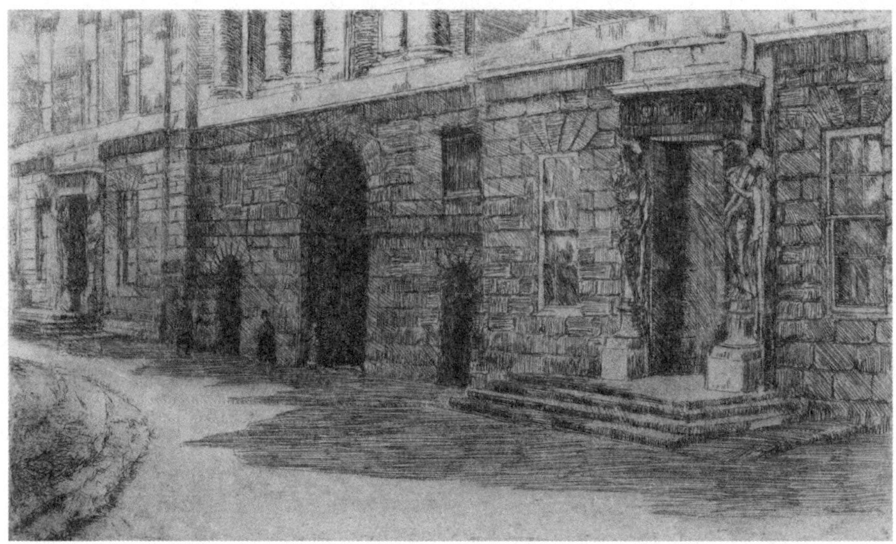

5.3   Estella Frances Solomons, *The King's Inns*, undated.

The opening pages of the 1928 guide reveal the momentous changes that had taken place since the publication of *Picturesque Dublin* in 1898. The journey through the city beings with the Parnell Monument on O'Connell Street, allying his words ('No man has a right to fix a boundary to the march of a Nation') to the actions of the 'nest of poets and impassioned young fellows', who fought on the street in 1916.[32] While the 1918 and 1920 editions had included an entry on Dublin Castle (a key site in Gerard's text), this was removed from the 1928 publication. In the first two editions, Kelleher had given it short shrift, referring to the statue of Justice as 'literally turning her back these long years upon the people, her balance only for the eyes of the supreme Ambassadors and Lord Governors imported into the Throne-room from that queen city of shopkeeping on Thames'.[33] For many of the entries in the guide, Kelleher links a street or site with a notable person who had been born, lived, or visited there. For the entry on the Coombe, which had featured so heavily in nineteenth-century accounts of the city, Kelleher mentions, but does not focus on, the poverty of the area, writing instead about the life and death of Anne Devlin, a republican who had aided Robert Emmet during the 1803 Rebellion and who, despite her involvement, died in poverty and obscurity in the Liberties.[34]

Solomons's depiction of the *Leinster Market* (Figure 5.4) makes a direct link with Walter Osborne, who had collected photographs of the narrow thorough-fare and written to a friend 'Come someday and I will show you the good things in that street. There are about fifty pictures in it. Do you know the Leinster Market?'[35] This suggests that Osborne had considered the Leinster Market as a

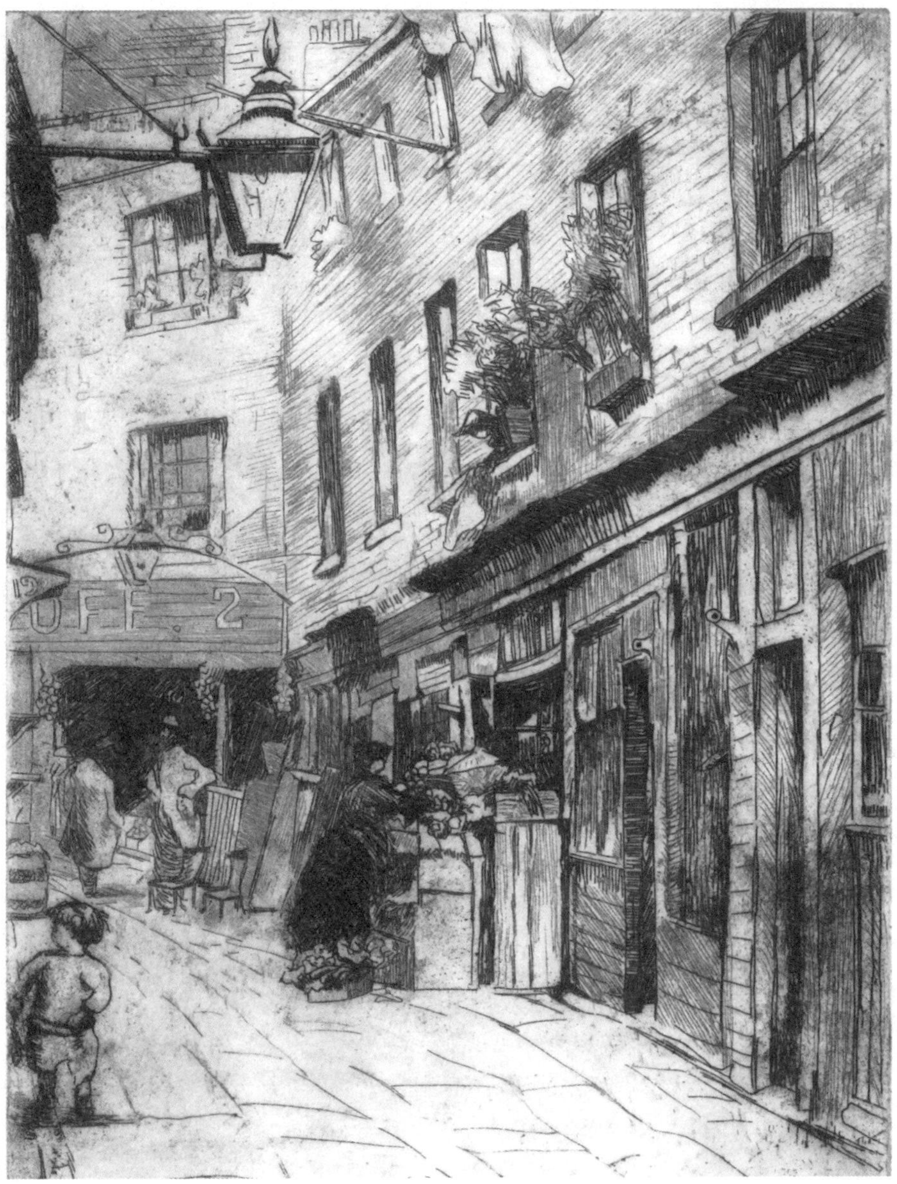

5.4   Estella Frances Solomons, *The Leinster Market*, c.1915.

subject, although he does not seem to have completed a painting of it. Solomons may also have seen Myra K. Hughes's depiction of the covered market at an exhibition in 1910 (Figure 5.5).[36] Using the natural perspective of the crooked lane, Solomons shows the tall Georgian buildings that encase the street market:

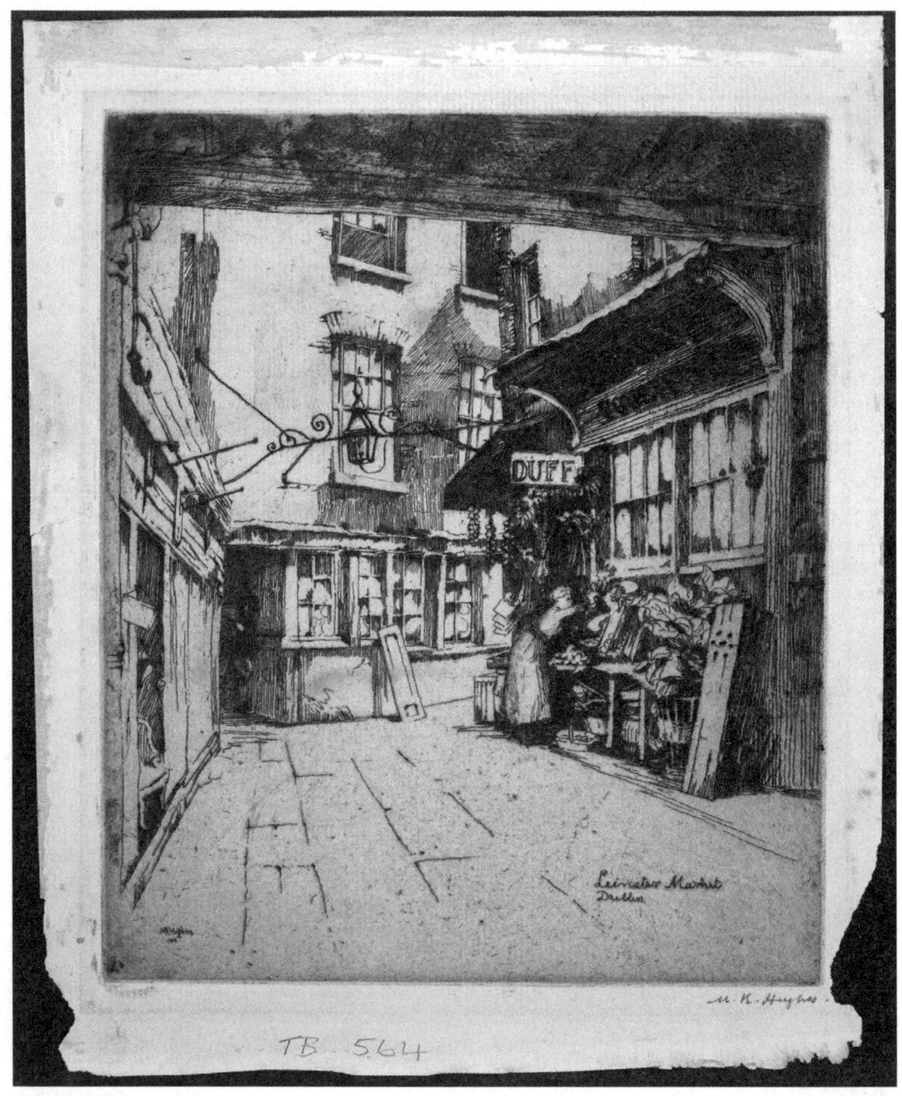

5.5   Myra K. Hughes, *The Leinster Market*, 1909.

many of the wooden shutters on the ground level are closed, and some small stalls and items of furniture are outlined, tended to by vaguely outlined figures. A small child on the left-hand side further peoples the composition, referring to the trope of the urban urchin. The verticality of this composition is repeated in *Carlisle Court* (Figure 5.6); *Hoey's Court, the Birthplace of Dean Swift*; and *The Merchant Tailors' Arch*; bringing the viewer into the enclosed spaces of the different locations. Framed by the surrounding architecture, glimpses of everyday life

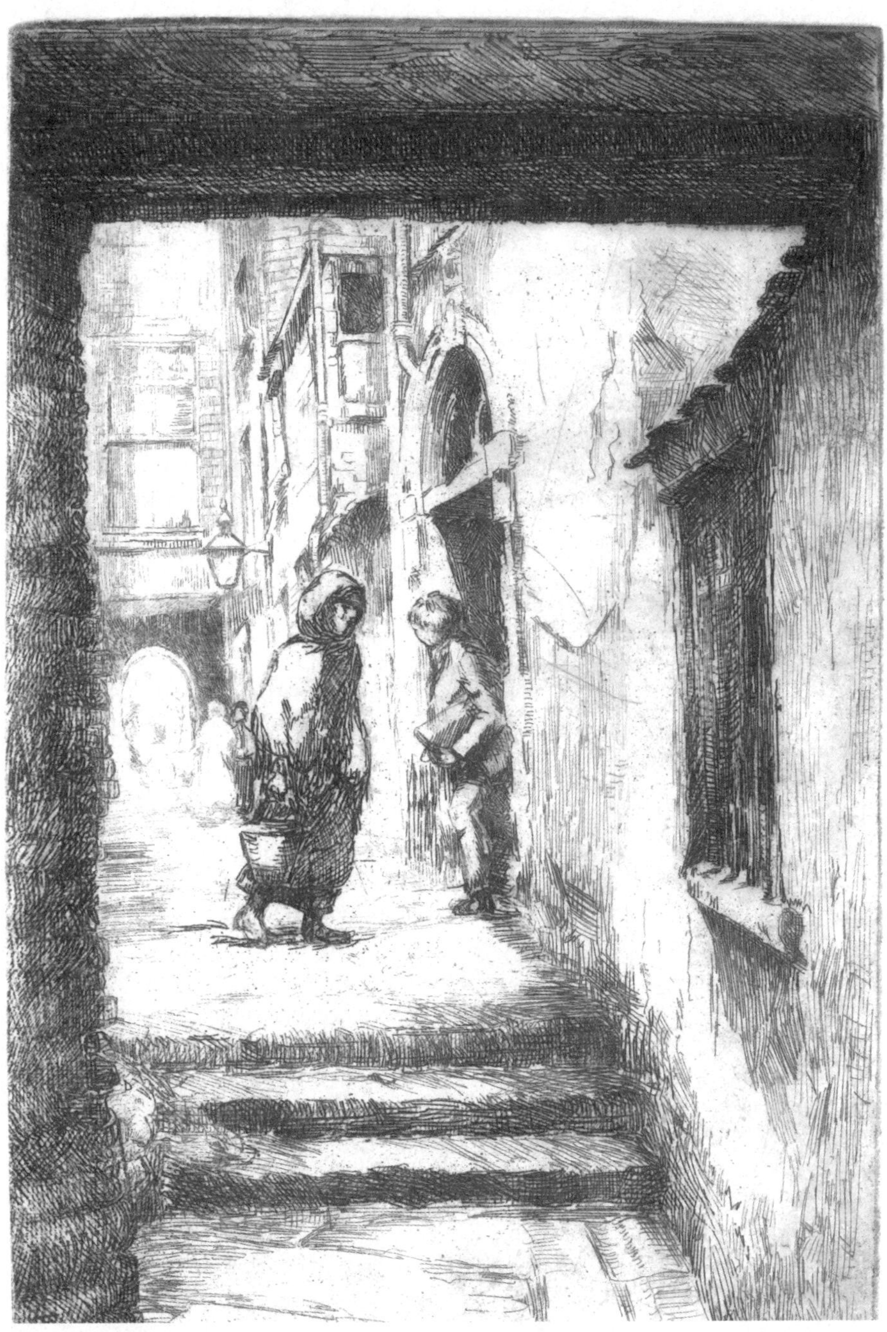

5.6   Estella Frances Solomons, *Carlisle Court*, undated.

and activities such as grocery shopping and calling on neighbours are included, giving some movement and life to the artworks.

If Barton's gentle wash drawings evoked a kind of misty or ethereal atmosphere, the close dark lines of these etchings suggest something darker and anachronistic. The clothing of some of the figures (for example the woman in a wide, bustle-like skirt in *The Leinster Market* or the heavy shawl of the older figure in *Carlisle Court*) are more redolent of the nineteenth century than the early twentieth century. When compared to other twentieth-century representations of Dublin – by Jack B. Yeats or Harry Kernoff, for example – Solomons's etchings offer a more antiquated vision of Dublin. This is starkly evident in her view of *Winetavern Street*, which shows the same row of shops that Kernoff depicted in the 1930s and 1940s (Figure 5.7). While both views share a sense of busy activity created by the figures working and moving in the street, Solomons's framing of the scene through the arch of Christ Church Cathedral introduces a more Gothic tone to the composition. The absence of the blue sky and other bright colours of Kernoff's view emphasises the despondent air of the dilapidated row and the second-hand shops housed there.

Although her infraction of the DORA regulations on Wellington Quay places Solomons at the riverside, she does not seem to have been as strongly drawn to the river or port as a subject. A notable exception is an etching titled *The Quay, South Wall*, reproduced in the *Glamour of Dublin* (Figure 5.8). Showing City Quay from Custom House Quay on the opposite side of the river, Solomons locates the viewer further downstream than Kernoff in *From the Custom House Steps*. The steeple of the Immaculate Heart of Mary Church adds height to the composition, and towers over the disjointed houses beside it. The industrial activity of the docks is hinted at by the edge of a crane winch which intrudes on the left-hand side of the composition, and a series of close lines which suggest activity on the dock wall. The schooner and rowboat docked at the quay also pre-empt Kernoff's later watercolour, suggesting that he may have been familiar with Solomons' earlier depiction of City Quay, as well as the idea that this type of boat was a common sight on the River Liffey. Solomons's interest in the riverside, and her depiction of *City Quay*, may hint to her interest in and knowledge of the Etching Revival more broadly, and Whistler's dockside views. For example, the composition of this work bears a striking resemblance to the American artist's *Black Lion Wharf* from 1859 or *Free Trade Wharf*, 1877 (Figures 5.9, 5.10).

Returning to Kelleher's preface to the *Glamour of Dublin*, there is little 'heroic optimism' to be found in Solomons's etchings. There is, however, another strand to Solomons's Dublin etchings that chimes further with the literary circles of which she was part of throughout her lifetime. In 1926, Solomons and O'Sullivan married after a long courtship: they had waited for both of her parents to die rather than have tensions frayed by a mixed religious marriage, although the letters of congratulation suggest that Rosa Solomons at least had been aware of the relationship.[37] As noted earlier, O'Sullivan had used a number of Solomons's

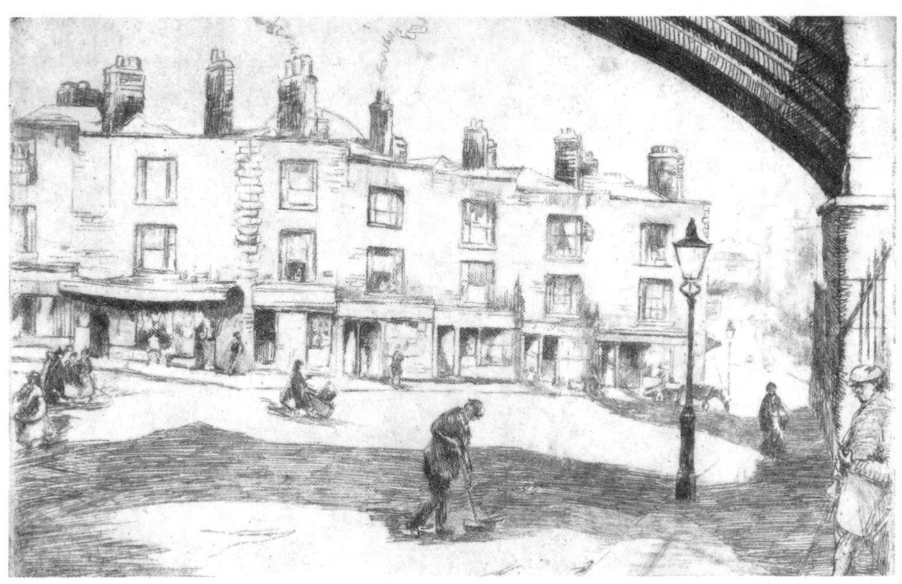

5.7   Estella Frances Solomons, *Winetavern Street*, undated.

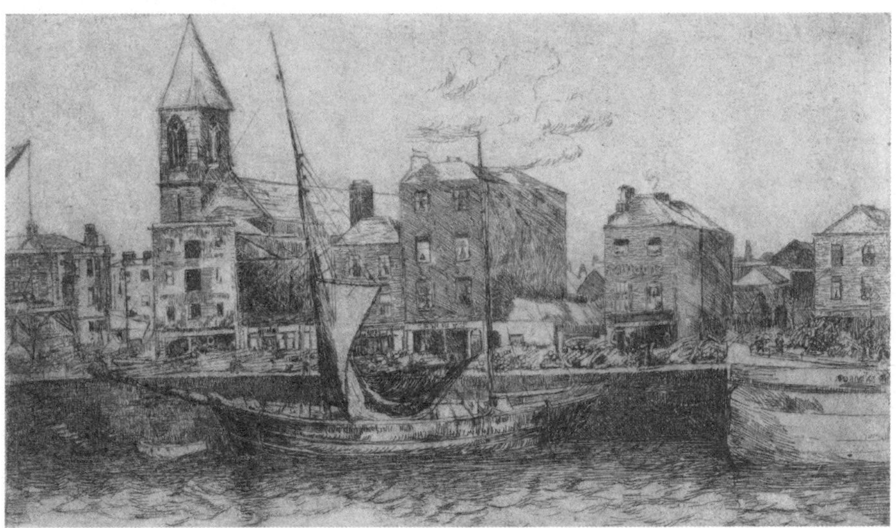

5.8   Estella Frances Solomons, *City Quay, Dublin (The Quay, South Wall)*, undated.

Dublin etchings to illustrate his publication projects. He was unusual among the writers associated with the Revival because of his focus on urban themes, and the streets, houses, and characters of 'old Dublin' echo throughout his writings. In a dedication to Oliver Gogarty, printed in the opening pages, O'Sullivan wrote

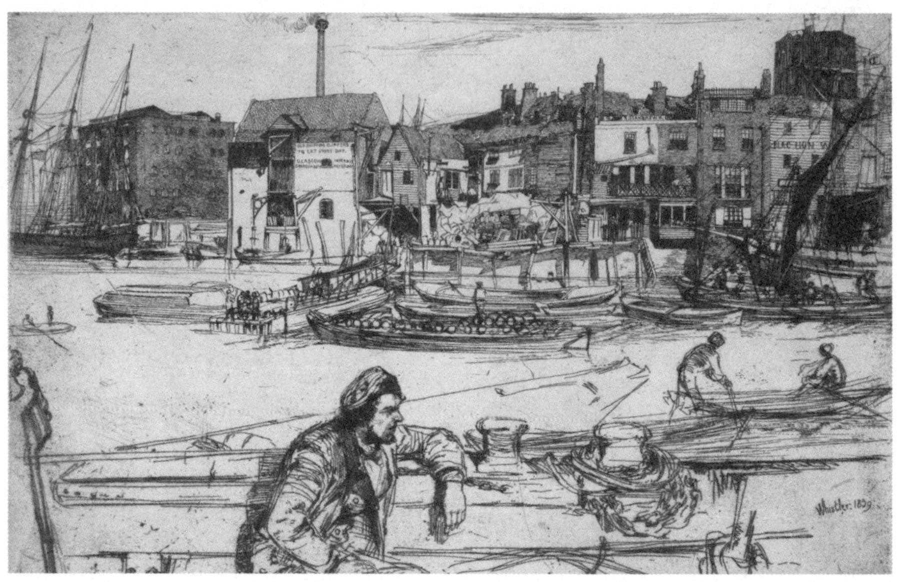

5.9   James Abbott McNeill Whistler, *Black Lion Wharf*, 1859.

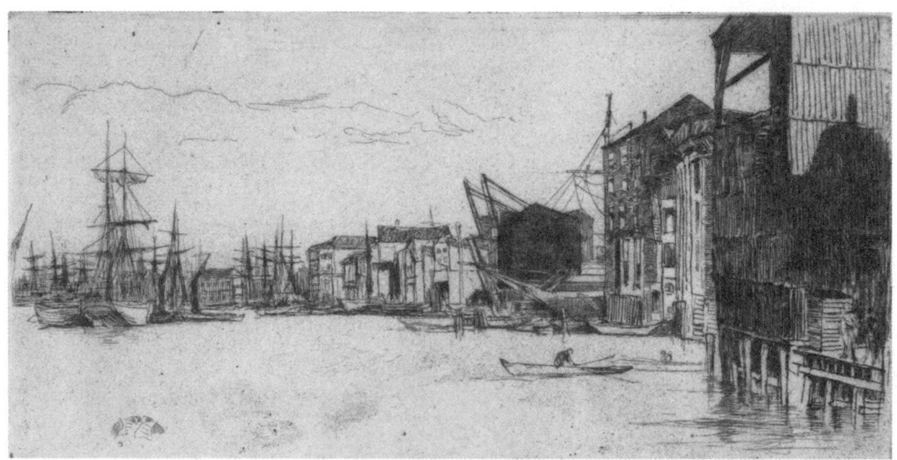

5.10   James Abbott McNeill Whistler, *Free Trade Wharf*, 1877.

of 'Where those old lovely streets still hold / About them proudly, fold on fold / Their ancient purple, through the stress / Of a late age's littleness / Prevail around, and only they / Are mindful of a kinglier day.'[38] O'Sullivan's interest in 'that old courteous century' is reflected in further stories in the collection, such as the city's Georgian details, the antiquated writings of Charles James Lever, and the strange atmosphere evoked by the city at night.[39] The atmosphere evoked by O'Sullivan in his writings is distinctive but clearly draws on the nostalgic tone evident in nineteenth-century texts: for example, in 'Fanlights' he notes the 'strange and half-deserted squares, once the centre of that long-departed society which has at one time come near to placing Dublin in the first rank of European cities'; the houses which fill these squares are fronted by 'dusty hall doors not infrequently adorned with quaint and beautiful knockers', 'great square windows', and a fanlight adorned by a stuffed bird.[40] With their deep contrasts of light and dark, the concentration of line and shadow, and a focus on 'old Dublin', Solomons's etchings echo the atmosphere and themes of O'Sullivan's writing. Considered in tandem, we can see in their work a clear development of the 'old Dublin' theme in the post-independence period: one that revels in, rather than mourns, the city's past and which offers aesthetic and emotional pleasure to those who can appreciate this aspect of its history.

Vanishing Dublin: Flora Mitchell's changing city

In May 1966, the regular column in the *Irish Times*, 'An Irishwoman's Diary', included a small feature on Flora Mitchell to mark the publication of *Vanishing Dublin*. Here, the artist, then in her mid-70s, commented that 'I'm driven about now and when we get to Winetavern Street, it's gone. So too has the Irish House. Where's everything? I can hardly find my way about the city now.'[41] The 1960s marked a period of sustained redevelopment in Dublin, with several older streets and blocks of houses restructured, redeveloped, or demolished. If Gerard and Barton were concerned with the disappearance of 'old Dublin' through social and political change, Mitchell was witness to the literal disappearance of many of the streets and buildings represented in the 1898 publication. The idea of a 'vanishing' city had emerged contemporaneously with 'old Dublin' and was driven by a similar sense of nostalgia: for example, in 1894, Roland W. Paul wrote and published *Vanishing London*, and in 1903, L. Ingleby Wood produced *Vanishing Edinburgh and Leith*, both of which contained original artworks produced by the author.[42] At least one Irish artist in the nineteenth century considered publishing a similar volume on Dublin: extant in the NGI Prints and Drawings collection is a manuscript for 'Vanishing Dublin: 30 Sketches in and Near Dublin' by Joshua Allen dating to 1888.[43]

Born in Omaha, Nebraska, Mitchell had moved to Ireland with her family at the turn of the twentieth century, when her father joined the Jameson distillery firm.[44] The 1901 Census records that Mitchell was living with relatives in Drogheda, but by 1911, when she was 20 years old, she was living with her mother in Ranelagh, a prosperous suburb to the south of Dublin city. In the early years of the twentieth century, Mitchell enrolled at the DMSA for three sessions, 1905–6, 1908–9, and 1910–11: from 1906–8, she attended Princess Helena College, in Ealing, London.[45] Snoddy notes that as a student, Mitchell was 'particularly attracted by the lesser-known courts, alleyways, bridges, byways and narrow streets of Dublin': from 1912–14 she exhibited a number of urban scenes at the Dublin Sketching Club, which included, for example, views of Sackville Street, the O'Connell Monument, College Green, Grafton Street, and the Shelbourne Hotel, all constituting larger and more recognisable public sites than those suggested by Snoddy.[46] The Mitchell family were resident in Dublin during the 1916 Rising. A letter written by her mother describes the family's shock at the events of Easter week. Written over the course of the Rising, the letter recounts both rumours and facts that reached the suburb of Ballsbridge, conditions at the shops on nearby Baggot Street, and the efforts of the Mitchell family and neighbours to provide provisions for British troops in nearby Herbert Park.[47]

In the mid-1910s and into the 1920s, Mitchell was concerned with depicting the urban landscape in a series of pen-and-ink drawings and, it seems, a small number of etchings. While the drawing technique prefigured her later watercolours of Dublin and London, these earlier works confined themselves to black ink on white or grey backgrounds. Of those works that are extant, two show depictions of Dublin following the 1916 Rising and have been identified by Brendan Rooney as copies of photographs reproduced in T. W. Murphy's *Dublin After the Six Days Insurrection* souvenir publication.[48] These are notable for the fact that while Mitchell studiously translated the buildings, she removed the people from the cityscape, a technique the artist later repeated for two views of the Four Courts made after its partial destruction during the Civil War in July 1922. An exterior view shows the decapitated dome, and the damage caused to the buildings on either side (similar to Kathleen Fox's view, referred to in the Introduction), and a second of the ruined central hall.[49] The close hatched lines were used to great effect by the artist in a *Dublin Dock Scene* (1929, ink on paper, private collection): an imposing view of a crane and ship masts around Dublin port, prefiguring Kernoff's later focus on similar industrial infrastructure on the quays.

In 1927, two illustrations in the *Dublin Civic Week Handbook* reproduced etchings by Mitchell. These depicted the Royal College of Surgeons as viewed from inside Stephen's Green and the Government Buildings on Merrion Street. Here, Mitchell repeats the closely hatched lines seen in her pen-and-ink drawings and a similar emphasis on the architectural structures rather than on any human element of the scenes. Although the location of the original etchings (or indeed any other examples of Mitchell's work in this medium) are unknown, it is likely that Mitchell was aware of printmakers such as Solomons, Duncan, and other artists involved in Ireland's etching revival at this time. Along with Hilda Roberts and Kernoff, these artists were also represented in the *Handbook*: Solomons contributed her views of *Marsh's Library* and *The Leinster Market*, with the latter described as 'an interesting remnant of the old Dublin which is now passing'.[50] Two further works by Mitchell were reproduced in *A Book of Dublin* (1929): a view of Dun Laoghaire and of the Governor General's House in the Phoenix Park (formerly the Viceregal Lodge, and now Áras an Uachtaráin – home of the Irish President). Mitchell did not confine herself to Dublin, and contemporaneous views of Belfast, Drogheda, and Limerick are also extant.

Despite the inclusion of Mitchell's works in these publications, which were important markers of the city's sense of civic identity and progress in the early years of the Irish Free State, her works did not appear again in public exhibitions until 1935 when similar Dublin scenes were included in the Watercolour Society of Ireland's annual exhibition. In 1930, she married William George Jameson and the couple spent much of their time in Cowes on the Isle of Wight. William was a sailing master on the royal yacht *Britannia*, and they often socialised with the royal family. An autobiographical record by Mitchell recalls this period of her life, recording numerous sailing trips and details of their social life in Cowes. While the account does not mention her art, it does reveal something of Mitchell's relationship to Ireland, or more explicitly, how she viewed the relationship between Ireland and Britain. For example, recalling a conversation with George V and Queen Mary, Mitchell noted that she was asked 'many searching questions as to our life in Ireland, the general situation there of which I am absolutely ignorant I fear!'[51] While the royal family seem to have regarded the Jamesons as Irish, it is clear that Mitchell, at least, saw herself as British, demonstrated, for instance, by her identification with the monarchy: she commented at one point that 'they [the Duke and Duchess of York] both look so young and full of life ... it makes one think how fortunate we are to have a really glamorous Royal family'.[52] Mitchell, of course, had close family ties to England: both of her parents had been born there and by the time of the artist's marriage in 1930, her parents had moved from Dublin to Ferndown, Dorset.

Mitchell's marriage to Jameson was to be short lived. William died in November 1939, and nothing is known of the artist's activities in the 1940s and early 1950s. Her artistic project of recording Dublin's streets and buildings seems to have firmly re-established itself around 1955 when she held a solo exhibition at the Dublin Painters' Gallery on Stephen's Green. Writing in the *Irish Times*, 'G. H. G.' noted that her Dublin scenes were not only 'accurate, so far as the superficial details of the scenes are concerned', but also 'convey[ed] a good deal of the atmosphere of the city. As works of art, Flora Mitchell's drawings are good enough to hang in any company, and, as souvenirs, they are cheap enough to have a considerable sale.'[53] Perhaps the growing concern over the changing landscape of Dublin spurred the artist on: after her hiatus of the 1930s and 1940s, Mitchell followed this exhibition with similar shows in 1957 and 1959. Around the opening of the 1959 exhibition, 'An Irishwoman's Diary' carried a profile of the artist's work, stating that over the past five years, Mitchell had produced over 200 views of 'odd corners in old Dublin'. 'Candida' continued that after two exhibitions of these scenes, the artist felt that there was little more to record in Dublin, and as a result travelled to London for a season to work there, with the hope of holding a private exhibition.[54] Despite this shift in focus, the artist implored that builders in Dublin '"stick to brick ... The old magic of Dublin lies primarily in its colour," she maintained, "and it rests with us to do all we can to build for the delight of Dubliners to come."'[55] Mitchell's artistic return could not have been better timed. The 1950s and 1960s was one of the most intense phases of Dublin's redevelopment to date, with the medieval and Georgian core facing imminent threat. In 1952, architectural historian Maurice Craig had published a crucial volume on the city's buildings – *Dublin, 1660–1860* – and in 1958, the Irish Georgian Society (largely dormant since the early part of the century) was reconstituted and enthusiastically campaigned for the preservation of Dublin's eighteenth-century architecture. The effects of urban change were noted not only by Mitchell, but across various art forms into the 1970s: for example, in the well-known song 'The Rare Ould Times', the narrator Sean Dempsey laments how 'Dublin keeps on changing, and nothing seems the same … the grey unyielding concrete, makes a city of my town.'[56]

Published by Allen Figgis, *Vanishing Dublin* gathered fifty of Mitchell's watercolours of streets, buildings, and other landmarks from the city centre. Reproduced in full colour, a short text giving some historical or local details accompanies each illustration, giving some of the artist's own observations. The original watercolours for *Vanishing Dublin* were regarded as sufficiently important to be purchased by the NGI in 1969 for £1000, a substantial sum at that time, and additional material was later bequeathed to the institution.[57] This includes several sketchbooks filled with Mitchell's preparatory drawings for many Dublin scenes, ranging from single drawings to sketchbooks. If Osborne, Barton, Yeats, Kernoff, and Solomons drew their inspiration from their journeys through the city on foot, Mitchell's method was more befitting of the 1960s: she was driven through the city and working from the car. The 1950s and 1960s saw a rapid increase in car ownership in Dublin city and county, and throughout these decades issues of congestion and parking were in constant public debate.[58] If the *flâneur* immersed themselves in the crowd, Mitchell was more likely to be caught in a traffic jam.

In her introduction, Mitchell invites the reader to travel with her through the city from the comfort of their own homes, rather than moving through the streets themselves, stating that there was 'no need to leave our chair by the fire. We can weave ourselves a tapestry from the threads of yesterday and today, threads of what we have seen, have heard, have read, or even dreamed.'[59] The warmth and colour of the 'old' city that Mitchell's watercolours suggest is contrasted with the city's newer buildings and 'the realization that soon it [Dublin] must become just another city of concrete and glass, colourless and stereotyped'.[60] In a similar manner to Frances Gerard's opening to *Picturesque Dublin*, Mitchell places herself and the reader at a distance from the contemporary city: through tone, historical references, and scant attention to those living in Dublin's remaining tenements, Mitchell claims the aesthetic of 'old Dublin' from her nineteenth-century predecessors.

In a further echo of *Picturesque Dublin*, Mitchell begins the armchair journey through Dublin at the fringes of Dublin Castle, the Coombe, and the Liberties, where the accompanying text draws attention to 'Dutch-type houses', the birthplaces of Thomas Moore and Jonathan Swift, and the old 'cries' of fish sellers, now replaced with those for oranges and apples.[61] One of Mitchell's most striking images appears early in the book: a view of Weaver's Hall – the niche above the door now vacant, the running board for the Weaver Furnishing Company broken, and a scattering of posters pasted across the blind windows and doorway.[62] In her notes, Mitchell commented that 'the building is now roofless and has been listed for total demolition for several years past'; although her depiction of the building is undated, by the time *Vanishing Dublin* was published in 1966 it was no longer standing. It is possible that Mitchell made use of contemporary photographic sources for some of the works in *Vanishing Dublin*, perhaps in tandem with her own sketches. A comparison between her view of Weavers' Hall with a photograph taken by Hugh Doran in 1961 (now housed in the Irish Architectural Archive) is certainly suggestive, with the detail given to the broken shop sign and posters covering the doors and window being quite exact. Moving on to Patrick Street, Mitchell returns to the vantage point previously seen in the photographs used by Walter Osborne as source material for *Near St Patrick's Close*, viewing the cathedral spire from the natural rise of the street at Nicholas Street.[63] The view, evidently, has changed dramatically: Mitchell's scene reveals the unifying and straightening effect of Lord Iveagh's redevelopment: the purpose-built tenement buildings along the left-hand side of the composition making up part of the Iveagh Buildings, green foliage emerging from the railings of St Patrick's Park, formerly the site of the rookeries described by Gerard.

Vanishing Dublin opens with an illustration and description of *York Street*, a narrow street which links Stephen's Green to Mercer Street, along the side of the Royal College of Surgeons.[64] The illustration shows a solid block of brick Georgian houses, with a mismatch of door and window frames. Assorted arrays of net curtains are on show, and a group of children play on the corner of the pavement. Mitchell's written description references the change the houses underwent from single-family homes to tenements, noting the

> families whose battle against poverty is bravely hidden behind lace curtains, and the happy games of the numberless children, well dressed and cared for, who play in the old street. If we could look behind the often-glassless fanlights … our sympathy would indeed be aroused for those who have suffered much hardship and overcrowding here during the past century. And every day the crash of demolitions comes closer, closer.[65]

This depiction of *York Street* is dated to 1964, suggesting that Mitchell's interest in the location came at a crucial time in the street's history. The period 1963–64 marked a crisis point for Dublin's tenement housing generally, with the collapse of two tenement buildings on Bolton Street and Fenian Street within a two-week period in June 1963.[66] Many other buildings were condemned and tenants evacuated, with many taking part in protests over housing conditions. The urgency of the crisis placed huge pressure on Dublin Corporation, as there was no housing available for most of the displaced families. The houses on York Street had been cleared prior to this emergency in October 1962. However, several families were then found to be squatting in the condemned buildings and were forcibly removed by the Gardaí in July 1964. The families refused to leave the street and instead scattered their possessions along the pavement in protest.[67] Other tenement buildings were also depicted by Mitchell, including *Dominick Street, Dorset Street, Paradise Court, Henrietta Street,* and *Hamilton Lane.*[68] In her notes for the first of these, the artist noted that the tall houses had already been emptied ahead of demolition, describing them as 'blind-eyed, waiting for their end'.[69] The street, Mitchell wrote, was still redolent of the past and one can imagine 'the street filled with swinging hoops, periwigs, swords, flashing buckles, satins, cascades of lace and great erections of feathers ... all the paraphernalia of social Dublin in the seventeen hundreds'.[70] This grandeur was in contrast to the street from the early nineteenth century, when 'the ensuing hundred years brought the street down to tenement occupation, the noble mantelpieces torn out and sold; the oak staircases burned for firewood; the gilt and plaster ceilings begrimed and rotten; till ... only the dark shell remained to be brought to the ground'.[71] The houses shown in the *Dorset Street* illustration had already been demolished by the time the book was published, and the artist focused again on the history of the lost buildings. Describing *Henrietta Street,* Mitchell commented that 'these sixteen houses can be said to be our last existing link with the social importance of Dublin prior to the Union', and largely overlooked Henrietta Street's notorious tenement history.

Mitchell was not the only artist concerned with capturing the changing city of the 1960s, and comparison between her drawings and watercolours and the black and white photography of Elinor Wiltshire (1918–2017) offers an insight into the artists' differing perspectives.[72] At times the visual projects of artist and photographer overlap: for example, both captured the Brazen Head, Cathedral Lane, Charlemont House, Eccles Street, Moore Street, and several other locations around the city. Both were prodigious in their representation of Dublin, but Wiltshire's oeuvre suggests a greater willingness to engage with the people she met during her time in Dublin, and to actively document demolition works and, in some instances, the protests against the relocation of inner-city families for street clearance. For example, both women documented York Street, yet Wiltshire's photographs contrast strongly with Mitchell's drawing of the same street, showing several adults and children sitting on the pavement among rubble and warning signs. It is clear from Wiltshire's photographs that the dismantling of the houses was already well underway, and rather than showing net curtains and pot plants, most windows have already been removed. Both the photographs and the facts of the York Street case would suggest that Mitchell's representation of the street was based on observations made prior to the initial moving out of families in 1962.

Just as Barton benefits from being viewed within a growing circle of professional (if still elite) women at the *fin-de-siècle*, Mitchell is best understood as being part of a group of women, which included Wiltshire and the journalist Elizabeth Leslie, who recorded this important phase of Dublin's urban history.

The nostalgia for the Ascendency past, as expressed in the earlier generation, was giving way to a new type of urban nostalgia: that of working-class life in Dublin's inner city, threatened by suburbanisation and inner-city redevelopment. As Hanna notes, this new feeling of dislocation would be channelled into a significant movement in the 1960s – the Dublin Housing Action Committee.[73] It seems, however, that there has been a reticence to view Mitchell's Dublin drawings and watercolours as part of the historical record of this period. Her small interventions into the conservation debate were measured, but surely sensible: few could quibble with her call for the continued use of brick given its importance to the city's architectural history and character. A further measured intervention came in a letter to the editor of the *Irish Times*, when she asked what was to become of the material removed from the redeveloped historic sites, such as foundation stones, shop signs, original doors, and plasterwork: she wrote,

> All we can hope is that we shall be warned before the last nibbles at Crampton Court take place and the 200-year old doors vanish into thin air! – that we shall have the last opportunity to look our last on the enchanting house on Vance's Court, or visit the cottages of Paradise Court, with its shrine and communal mangle.[74]

Because of the artist's representational style, Mitchell's depictions of Dublin seem to provide a more reliable form of historical record than many of the artworks discussed in this book so far. The apparent technical nature of her line provides reassurance that she has made an accurate translation from eye to page. Her careful line-work stands in diametric opposition to the experimental abstract painting and sculpture emerging in 1960s Ireland, which has perhaps contributed to a lack of serious consideration of her artistic contribution to this period: reviewing her 1959 exhibition in the *Irish Times*, 'J. W.' noted that 'Miss Mitchell has absolutely no inhibitions about modern art or such irrelevancies', continuing that 'This is an exhibition of Old Dublin for lovers of Old Dublin. The style is not new, but the results are satisfying.'[75] Reviewing *Vanishing Dublin* for the *Irish Press*, T. P. O'Neill compared Mitchell's work to two earlier Dublin artists: James Malton and Samuel Frederick Brocas. Mitchell, O'Neill noted, completed something of a trio of painters of Georgian Dublin, with the twentieth-century artist succeeding in 'capturing beauty where many may have seen nothing but decay', continuing that book was 'a worthy successor to the prints of Malton and Brocas and is a fitting record of the final stage of much of the Georgian city which they recorded in its prime'.[76] A further review appeared in *The Dublin Magazine* (which, despite the shared title, was a different publication to that founded by O'Sullivan), and the author Gerard O'Flaherty proclaimed it to be 'one of the best pictorial records of Old Dublin ever to be published', and in which the artist 'caught the face and mood of the decaying centre of the city'.[77] Yet, in concluding his overview of the publication, O'Flaherty identifies an omission from it: 'something is missing,' he writes, 'it is the squalid wretchedness of many of the houses where whole families might live in a single room, and sanitary arrangements were of the most elementary type. Flora Mitchell glosses over this aspect and leaves us not with a Dublin we remember, but rather with Dublin exactly as we would like to remember it.'[78]

The appearance of Mitchell's publication in 1966 came at a key juncture in the representation of the city in visual and other media. Just as the *Darkest Dublin* photographs had been endowed with scientific credibility in the early twentieth century, in the 1960s, photography (such as the work of Elinor Wiltshire) was also seen to be more 'truthful' than an artist's impression. Moreover, in the 1960s, the voices of those living in the city's tenements were finally being heard: issues around displacement, the loss of community, and the other effects of moving inner-city populations to newly built suburbs were being published and recorded, spear-headed by groups such as the Dublin Housing Action Committee. While Mitchell's visual representations of the city recorded aspects of its built heritage before their destruction, the absence of proper contextual-isation in her text, of lived experience, and action for those living in the houses on York, Dominick, or Henrietta Street, reverts it to the realm of the 'ethical picturesque', which can only empathise, rather than act. Writing in the intro-duction to *Vanishing Dublin*, the Earl of Wicklow noted that Mitchell had 'an eye for the picturesque'; however, by 1966, it was more difficult to view the city's decay and decrepitude, and the social reality that entailed, in the same manner as those reading and viewing *Picturesque Dublin*.

Conclusion: 'Old' or 'Vanishing'?

In their depictions of Dublin, Solomons and Mitchell represented streets and landmarks that evoked associations with the city's past – for example, notable houses, places of birth, historic streets, or the set pieces of public Georgian architecture. Many of these locations had deteriorated into tenements or slum areas by the time each artist was depicting them, and this situation is either repeatedly ignored, or transfigured into something 'picturesque' or 'quaint'. This reading is supported by the descriptions and responses of contemporary critics, who considered these aesthetic qualities, along with the perceived his-torical importance of these representations of Dublin. When published, these images were further codified into the narrative of the city, projecting a specific reading of the urban environment to visitors and residents alike. Both the *Glamour of Dublin* and *Vanishing Dublin* participated in a type of city-on-paper that had its roots in nineteenth-century predecessors, such as *Picturesque Dublin: Old and New*. Returning to Michalski's description of guidebooks as being able to both 'shield' and 'reveal' aspects of the city, it is clear in these three publications that while the decay of Dublin was often revealed, the reader or viewer was generally shielded from the social reality that this entailed.

That said, while Barton, Solomons, and Mitchell shared an interest in the subject matter of 'old Dublin', the temporal shifts between the 1890s, 1920s, and 1960s altered how the term was understood. For example, Barton's water-colours (supported by Gerard's text) expressed a nostalgia for Dublin as a city of industrious and wealthy Protestant craftsmen and merchants; both artist and writer seemed to mourn the inevitable decline of the political union between Ireland and Britain. Theirs was a nostalgia for imperial Dublin, a state surely antithetical to the nationalist politics of Solomons. Rather, Solomons's interest in the courts and alleys of the city was driven more by aesthetics – whether those of the Etching Revival, or the aesthetic pleasure found by writers such as O'Sullivan in Dublin's eighteenth-century history. Solomons's representation of these spaces occurred concurrently with the destruction of many areas of the cityscape through warfare, which, other than the restrictions placed on her by the DORA regulations, did not impact on her view of Dublin. Mitchell's nostalgia for 'old Dublin' is different again; although it is suffused by a reverence for the city's aristocratic past and a continued use of the picturesque, her project was, in many ways, driven by the processes of urban development and change then taking place.

Notes

1 H. Allberry, 'Architects' Conference – Dublin, 1931', *Handbook for Delegates to the Annual Conference at Dublin, 17th to 20th June 1931* (London: Royal Institute of British Architects, 1931), p. xi.

2 'The Fault of Dublin', *Irish Times* (11 December 1934), p. 8.

3 D. L. Kelleher, *The Glamour of Dublin* (Dublin: The Talbot Press, 1928), n.p.

4 For more on Lynn and ffrench-Mullan, see S. Pašeta, *Irish Nationalist Women* (Cambridge: Cambridge University Press, 2016).

5 TCD, Ms 4529, Estella Frances Solomons Papers.

6 TCD, Ms 4526, Estella Frances Solomons Papers. See also H. Pyle, 'Notes from Estella', *Irish Arts Review* 25:1 (2008), 96–9.

7 This painting, and other early paintings by Solomons (including *Street Urchins and Bird Cage* and *Boy on a Roof Garden*) are illustrated in D. Britton and K. Reihill, *Estella Solomons HRHA (1882–1968)*, The Frederick Gallery (Dublin: The Frederick Gallery, 1999).

8 T. G. McMahon, *Grand Opportunity: The Gaelic Revival and Irish Society, 1893–1910* (Syracuse: Syracuse University Press, 2008), p. 114–15.

9 NLI, EPH E114, Inventory of gifts received to be sold at auction in Dublin in December 1916 for the benefit of the National Aid and Volunteer Dependents' Fund. Lavery wrote to Solomons that he was eager to assist in 'the alleviation of the distress in Dublin'. TCD, Ms 4631/374, Seumas O'Sullivan and Estella Frances Solomons Correspondence, letter from John Lavery to Estella Solomons, 21 August 1916.

10 TCD, Ms 4631/446, Seumus O'Sullivan and Estella Frances Solomons Correspondence, Cumann na mBan membership book for Estelle Nic Solomain [Estella Solomons], 15 November 1918. Records for the Cumann na mBan Ranelagh Branch are included in the Military Service Pensions Collection, Dublin City District Council, Military Archives Ireland, MA/MSPC/CMB/126.

11 NGI Yeats Archive, Y1/JY/24/1/6/213. The book is inscribed 'To Jack Yeats from Estella Solomons and Michael Scot'.

12 S. O'Sullivan, 'The Rose and Bottle', in S. O'Sullivan, *The Rose and Bottle and other Essays* (Dublin: The Talbot Press, 1946), p. 97.

13 See H. Pyle, *Estella Solomons: Portraits of Patriots* (Dublin: Allen Figgis and Company, 1966).

14 Ibid., p. 12.

15 O'Sullivan, 'The Rose and Bottle', p. 98.

16 See A. Griffith, 'Making their mark: Irish Painter-Etchers and the Etching Revival', in A. Griffith and A. Hodge (eds), *Making their Mark: Irish Painter-Etchers and the Etching Revival* (Dublin: National Gallery of Ireland, 2019), p. 29.

17 'Exhibition of Paintings, Etchings, and Sculpture', *Irish Times* (4 February 1914), p. 9.

18 'Exhibition of Paintings and Etchings', *Irish Times* (9 February 1914), p. 4.

19 TCD, Ms 4631/356 and Ms 4361/357, Seumus O'Sullivan and Estella Frances Solomons Correspondence, letter from Herbert Weil to Estella Solomons, 29 March 1916 and 31 March 1916.

20 TCD, Ms 4630/321, Seumus O'Sullivan and Estella Frances Solomons Correspondence, letter from Joseph Malachy Kavanagh to Royal Irish Constabulary, 21 June 1915.

21 TCD, Ms 4631/402a, Seumus O'Sullivan and Estella Frances Solomons Correspondence, letter from Provost Marshall, Dublin Castle, to Estella Solomons, 18 March 1917.

22 TCD, Ms 4631/402b, Seumus O'Sullivan and Estella Frances Solomons Correspondence, letter from Provost Marshall, Dublin Castle, to Estella Solomons, 19 March 1917.

23 'Exhibition of Etchings', *Irish Times* (3 March 1919), p. 6.

24 'Art in Dublin: Exhibition by Miss Solomons and Miss Duncan', *Freeman's Journal* (27 October 1919), p. 4.

25 'Irish Art: Two Interesting Exhibitions', *Freeman's Journal* (6 December 1920), p. 3.

26 'Art Exhibition: Miss Solomons' Paintings and Etchings', *Irish Times* (10 December 1921), p. 8.

27 'Miss Estella Solomons's Pictures: Exhibition in Dublin', *Irish Times* (6 December 1926), p. 9.

28 J. Carville, '"The glad smile of God's sunlight": photography and the imaginative geography of Darkest Dublin,' in Carville (ed.), *Visualizing Dublin*, p. 197.

29 Ibid., p. 199.

30 Ibid., p. 198.

31 Trinity College Dublin, Ms 4528, Estella Frances Solomons Papers.

32 Kelleher, *The Glamour of Dublin*, p. 11.

33 Ibid., p. 54.

34 Ibid., p. 59–60.

35 Walter Osborne, Sketch of the Leinster Market, Hawkins Street, undated, NGI. 2996; and NGI, Walter Osborne Archive, CSIA/OSB1/13 and CSIA/OSB1/14, undated photographs of the Leinster Market, D'Olier Street.

36 Griffith, 'Making their mark', p. 31.

37 TCD, Ms 4633/709a, Seumus O'Sullivan and Estella Frances Solomons Correspondence, letter from Sophie Solomons to Estella Solomons, 8 August 1926.

38 S. O'Sullivan, *Mud and Purple: Pages from the Diary of a Dublin Man* (Dublin: The Talbot Press; London: T. Fisher Unwin: 1918), p. 1.

39 For more O'Sullivan's interaction with the urban, see K. Milligan, 'Harry Clarke and *The Dublin Magazine*', in A. Griffith, M. Helmers, and R. Kennedy (eds), *Harry Clarke and Artistic Visions of the New Irish State* (Dublin: Irish Academic Press, 2018), pp. 181–201.

40 O'Sullivan, *Mud and Purple*, pp. 57–8.

41 Candida, 'An Irishwoman's Diary', *Irish Times* (9 May 1966), p. 9.

42 These are just two examples of this genre of illustrated book: R. W. Paul, *Vanishing London: A Series of Drawings, Illustrated Old Houses etc., in London and Westminster* (London: The Author, 1894); L. I. Wood, *Vanishing Edinburgh and Leith: Being a Pictorial Record Drawn by Wood* (Edinburgh: William J. Hay, 1903).

43 Joshua Allen, *Vanishing Dublin – A Handwritten Book with 30 Drawings*, 1888, ink on paper, NGI. 2724.

44 Snoddy, *Dictionary of Irish Artists: 20ᵗʰ Century*, p. 428.

45 NIVAL – National Irish Visual Arts Library, IE/NIVALCR/CR30/175; IE/NIVALCR/ CR33/205 and IE/NIVALCR/CR35/201. See also R. Minch, 'Mitchell, Flora Hippisley', in J. McGuire and J. Quinn (eds), *Dictionary of Irish Biography* (Cambridge: Cambridge University Press, 2009), http://dib.cambridge.org/viewReadPage.do?articleId=a9189 (accessed 21 April 2020).

46 Snoddy, *Dictionary of Irish Artists: 20ᵗʰ Century*, p. 428.

47 NLI, Ms 24, 554, 24–27 April 1916, Letter from Mrs Arthur C. Mitchell to Flora Mitchell.

48 These drawings are in a private collection, but were exhibited in 'James Stephens, the National Gallery of Ireland, and the 1916 Rising', 6 February–5 June 2016, National Gallery of Ireland.

49 Flora Mitchell, *Drawing of the Ruined Central Hall of the Four Courts, July 1922*, Dublin Civic Museum/Dublin City Archives, OBJ. 255; Flora Mitchell, *The Four Courts, July 1922*, Lot 611, James Adam and Sons, 18 April 2012.

50 See *Dublin Civic Week* (Dublin: Civic Week Council, 1927).

51 NLI, P6942, 20, an account by Flora Jameson of her life in England in the 1920s and 1930s, microfilm.

52 Ibid.

53 G. H. G., 'Fine Drawings', *Irish Times* (5 March 1955), p. 7.

54 Mitchell's London exhibition took place in August–September 1969 at the Upper Grosvenor Galleries, 19 Upper Grosvenor Street, W1.

55 'Candida', 'An Irishwoman's Diary', *Irish Times* (4 September 1959), p. 6.

56 P. St. John 'In the Rare Ould Times', composed for the Dublin City Ramblers in the 1970s: https://petestjohn.com/works/the-rare-ould-times/ (accessed 21 April 2020). Contemporary autobiographical accounts include: H. Tracey, '*Mind You, I've Said Nothing': Forays in the Irish Republic* (London: Methuen, 1953); O. Robertson, *Dublin Phoenix* (London: Jonathan Cape, 1957); C. P. Curran, *Under the Receding Wave* (Dublin: Gill and Macmillan, 1970); J. Ryan, *Remembering How We Stood* (Dublin: Gill and Macmillan, 1975); and A. Cronin, *Dead as Doornails: A Chronicle of Life* (Dublin: Dolmen Press; London: Calder and Boyars, 1976).

57 'National Gallery Purchases', *Irish Times* (6 October 1969), p. 8.

58 See J. Brady, *Dublin in the 1950s and 1960s: Cars, Shops and Suburbs* (Dublin: Four Courts Press, 2017), pp. 162–219.

59 F. H. Mitchell, *Vanishing Dublin* (Dublin: Allen Figgis, 1966), p. 1.

60 Ibid.

61 Ibid., p. 4 and p. 8.

62 See NGI. 7305.

63 See NGI. 7278.

64 See NGI. 7275.

65 Mitchell, *Vanishing Dublin*, p. 2.

66 E. Hanna, *Modern Dublin: Urban Change and the Irish Past, 1957–1973* (Oxford: Oxford University Press, 2013), p. 113.

67 Ibid., pp. 120–1. See also Rowley, *Housing, Architecture and the Edge Condition*, p. 227.

68 See NGI. 7302; NGI. 7277; NGI. 7274; NGI. 7279 and NGI. 7289.

69 Mitchell, *Vanishing Dublin*, p. 68.

70 Ibid.

71 Ibid.

72 Wiltshire's Dublin photographs have been digitised by the NLI and images from The Wiltshire Photographic Collection are available online through the library catalogue.

73 Hanna, *Modern Dublin*, p. 124.

74 F. H. Mitchell, 'The Light of Other Days: Letters to the Editor', *Irish Times* (21 November 1956), p. 5.

75 J. W., 'Drawings of Old Dublin', *Irish Times* (3 September 1959), p. 7.

76 T. P. O'Neill, 'New Record of Georgian Dublin', *Irish Press* (14 May 1966), p. 10.

77 G. O'Flaherty, 'Scene in Passing', *The Dublin Magazine* (Summer 1966), p. 24.

78 Ibid., p. 26.

Conclusion

Visual representations of Dublin have perhaps never been more numerous or prolific as they are in the present day. Social media and online resources have transformed the visual knowledge of the city and its history, through digitised photographic collections presented on institutional websites, to the many thousands of individual snaps that are shared on various social platforms. These images, encompassing urban landscapes, street art, protests, celebrations, public buildings, demolitions, and construction, among many other subjects, participate in a tradition of urban visualisation that has a long and varied history. While the medium may have changed, the impetus for doing so has not: the visualisation of the city still provides a means of locating oneself in time and space, of mapping our daily environment, and memorialising the passing scene. This, of course, is not limited to the visual arts: in a 2014 lecture on 'Writing the City', poet Peter Sirr noted that a 'relationship with a city is always a relationship with oneself, and with time', and that it (the city), 'functions as a map of emotional life, a set of marks in space and time that can be returned to and serve as emblems of self and society'.[1] In recent years, chapters of the Urban Sketchers – a global movement which brings together those who want to draw their cities – have been established in cities across Ireland, including Dublin, bringing a renewed focus to the visualisation of the city in a medium which Osborne, Barton, Yeats, Kernoff, Solomons, and Mitchell would be eminently familiar with. Many of the social issues facing the city might also be familiar – a housing crisis, commercial development, and a grappling between local and global identities – and can find many counterparts in the city's history.

The Introduction to this study opened with a description of Mahony's panoramic view of the city. Subsequent chapters have focused more closely on the different themes and figures connected with the representation of Dublin, exploring the lives of the streets through the different spectacles that played out there, through the eyes of artists who walked and rambled through them and who sought to capture a changing city and evoke its past. With the specificities of these different visions mapped out, we can return once more to the panoramic and begin to consider what these artists and artworks contribute to the portrait of the city, its history, and the story of Irish art. The ways in which artists in Ireland have approached the representation of the Dublin have varied in approach, technique, and subject. From Osborne to Mitchell, all these artists have demonstrated a commitment to representing the physical landscape of the city, including landmark bridges, buildings, parks, and streets to signify the location and environment of their paintings. Changing artistic styles and fashions are evident through the works of Osborne, Yeats, and Kernoff, while for Barton, Solomons, and Mitchell the human figure is secondary to the representation of the physical city. Through their portrayal of Dublin, these artists interact in different ways with the different modes and styles of painting found in other countries through this period, although there is less engagement with the dominant, or canonical, forms of non-representational modernism. Where Irish artists differ significantly from their international peers is in the fact that painters concerned with urban subjects did not form into a distinct group, as occurred, for example, with the Camden Town, Ashcan, East London, or Euston Road groups. This may be explained by the smaller number of artists working in Ireland, and within this the even smaller number of those who painted the city, along with the more limited art market in Ireland with artists of all persuasions struggling to make sales.

It is also evident that there are parallels with the depiction of the city in literature throughout the same period. This includes an interest in landmark public buildings and the physical situation of the city between the mountains and the sea, indicated in painting by frequent glimpses of these features through the maze of streets and buildings. Similarities in subject and form can be drawn between artists and writers working contemporaneously; for example, Osborne and Laffan, Barton and Moore, or Yeats and Joyce. While these counterparts are evident, by the nature of the medium, paintings cannot provide the expansive, in-depth narrative found in literary accounts of the city. For example, while painting can depict the city's citizens, it cannot express the 'constant verbal resourcefulness of the populace', or take the viewer inside the tenement buildings, as playwrights such as O'Casey did.[2] This, however, has more to do with the capabilities of the medium rather than a lack of interest in these aspects of Dublin life on the part of visual artists.

The literatures on representations of the city in nineteenth- and twentieth-century painting highlights the central presence of the *flâneur* or urban observer, who walks through the city streets immersing themselves, in different ways, in the life of the streets. Commenting on the widespread nature of walking in Dublin, Declan Kiberd has noted that in the early years of the twentieth century, 'everyone was a *flâneur*, a stroller in a city still felt to be cheerfully negotiable … People in Dublin … felt they owned the streets … and they spilled out on to the streets at every opportunity.'[3] As has been highlighted in the text, the urban observer takes many forms and is not limited to the definitive characterisation of the detached *flâneur*, and the variations found within this trope are reflected in the different approaches of the artists discussed in this book. What binds them together, however, is the constant attention paid to the acts of looking and seeing, before translating these experiences into painted scenes, whether the sights and sounds of the city were sketched *in situ*, photographed, or recalled from memory when the artist had returned to the studio.

Exploring the urban paintings and prints by artists in Ireland outside of the dominant theme of the discipline (nationalism and the formation of a national school) allows for a more open, interpretive, and alternative understanding of Irish art. By focusing on a broad theme, such as the 'urban' or 'the city', with its local and universal expressions and manifestations, the scope for comparison in a broad and inclusive context is revealed, even if this only serves to underline the singular or unique nature of the subject being examined. Alternatively, the opportunity to consider what might be described as canonical Irish artists – such as Osborne, Barton, and Yeats – in a new way, through a central theme, offers new and exciting insights into their lives and careers. Furthermore, to read the work of these 'major' figures alongside less well-known artists – such as Kernoff, Solomons, and Mitchell – expands the general knowledge of the art being produced in Ireland through this period, and the similarities, differences, and connections that existed between them.

The expression of national identity, ambition, and life through visual art undoubtedly forms an important part of Ireland's art history. While valid, the emphasis on the formation and celebration of a 'national school' of Irish art has precluded other voices and interpretations of artworks produced in Ireland, by artists from here or elsewhere. The marginal place of the city within the wider conversation around notions of 'Irishness' and national identity has contributed, until recently perhaps, to a lack of engagement with the themes and issues of urban or city life. Furthermore, as Dickson has identified, for a long time in histories of Dublin 'the idea of a past worth celebrating focused on the tiny medieval walled core, or at most on the Georgian city set within the canals'.[4] In combination, these facts have created a number of conventional histories; for example, that Irish art is mainly concerned with the depiction of the rural landscape and rural life, Irish identity is best represented through non-urban tropes, and Dublin's 'glory days' are located in 'old Dublin' and in the Georgian squares, houses, and wide streets. Recent research and writings have challenged the second and third of these shibboleths, and with the research presented here, it can be seen that among the multiple concerns of Irish artists was the representation of Dublin, the people of the city, and the individual experience of living and working there. Through the visions of these artists, we gain a new understanding of the changing city, and in turn, place our own experience of life in Ireland's capital into a rich and varied visual lineage.

Notes

1 P. Sirr, 'Writing the City,' UCD Scholarcast, Series 9 (Spring 2014), Dublin: One City, One Book Lectures 2014 (in association with Dublin City Public Libraries). Series Editor L. Collins, General Editor P. J. Matthews, 8. www.ucd.ie/scholarcast/transcripts/writing_the_city.pdf (accessed 21 April 2020).
2 J. Moynahan, 'The image of the City in nineteenth century Irish fiction', in M. Harmon (ed.), *The Irish Writer and the City* (Gerrards Cross: Colin Smythe; Totowa: Barnes and Noble, 1984), p. 16.
3 D. Kiberd, 'The city in Irish culture', in D. Kiberd (ed.), *The Irish Writer and the World* (Cambridge: Cambridge University Press, 2005), p. 294.
4 Dickson, 'The state of Dublin's history', 199.

Select bibliography

Archival Sources

Bureau of Military History
    Witness Statements
National Gallery of Ireland
    Harry Kernoff Archive
    Walter Osborne Archive
    Yeats Archive
National Library of Ireland
    Dermod O'Brien Papers
    Harry Kernoff Papers
Royal Hibernian Academy
    Minutes of the RHA General Assembly, 1900–24
Trinity College Dublin Manuscripts Collection
    Seumas O'Sullivan and Estella Frances Solomons Papers

Reports

Report by Committee of Inquiry into the work carried on by the Royal Hibernian Academy and the Metropolitan School of Art, Dublin. Dublin: Alexander Thom & Co, 1906.

Third Report of Her Majesty's commissioners for inquiring into the housing of the working classes in Ireland. London: Eyre and Spottiswoode, 1885.

M. Hayes, D. Hyde, and E. MacNeill, 'Report on the Irish Race Conference in Paris,' January 1922, Documents on Irish Foreign Policy, NAI DFA ES Box 11 File 77, www.difp.ie/docs/1922/Irish-Race-Convention-Paris/239.htm.

Printed Sources

Aalan, F. H. A. 'The working–class housing movement in Dublin, 1850–1920', in M. J. Bannon (ed.), *The Emergence of Irish Planning 1880–1920*. Dublin: Turoe Press, 1985, pp. 131–88.

Aalan, F. H. A. *The Iveagh Trust: The First Hundred Years, 1890–1900*. Dublin: Iveagh Trust, 1990.

Allen, Nicholas. 'Beckett's Dublin', in F. Croke (ed.), *Samuel Beckett: A Passion for Paintings*. Dublin: National Gallery of Ireland, 2006, pp. 44–51.

Allen, Nicholas. 'Cabaret, sex and independence: publishing in the early Free State', in M. Fanning and R. Gillespie (eds), *Print Culture and Intellectual Life in Ireland 1660–1941*. Dublin: The Woodfield Press, 2006, pp. 186–205.

Allen, Nicholas. *Modernism, Ireland and Civil War*. Cambridge: Cambridge University Press, 2009.

Allen, Nicholas. 'Ireland, Empire and the archipelago'. UCDScholarcast, Series 7 (Spring 2013) 'The literatures and cultures of the Irish Sea'. J. Brannigan and P. J. Matthews (eds), www.ucd.ie/scholarcast/scholarcast28.html.

Anderson, Ronald. 'Whistler in Dublin, 1884', *Irish Arts Review* 3:3 (1986), 45–51.

Andrews, Malcolm. 'The metropolitan picturesque', in S. Copley and P. Garside (eds), *The Politics of the Picturesque: Literature, Language and Aesthetics since 1770*. Cambridge: Cambridge University Press, 1994, pp. 282–98.

Armstrong, Gordon S. *Samuel Beckett, W.B. Yeats, and Jack Yeats*. Lewisberg: Bucknell University Press; London and Toronto: Associated University Presses, 1990.

Arnold, Bruce. *Jack Yeats*. New Haven: Yale University Press, 1998.

Arnold, Bruce. 'Jack Yeats: the need for reassessment', in Y. Scott (ed.), *Jack B. Yeats: Old and New Departures*. Dublin: Four Courts Press, 2008, pp. 47–56.

Arnold, Dana (ed.). *The Metropolis and its Image: Constructing Identities for London, c.1750–1950*. Oxford: Oxford University Press, 1999.

Arnold, Dana. 'Panoptic visions of London: possessing the metropolis', *Art History* 32:2 (2009), 333–50.

Arscott, Caroline. 'Victorian development and images of the past', in C. Shaw and M. Chase (eds), *The Imagined Past: History and Nostalgia*. Manchester: Manchester University Press, 1989, pp. 47–67.

Arscott, Caroline. 'The representation of the city in the visual arts', in M. Daunton (ed.) *The Cambridge Urban History of Britain, vol. III, 1840–1950*. Cambridge: Cambridge University Press, 2000, pp. 811–33.

Baigell, Matthew. *The American Scene: American Painting during the 1930s*. New York: Praeger, 1974.

Bairner, Alan. 'Urban walking and the pedagogies of the street', *Sport, Education and Society* 16:3 (2011), 371–84.

Baskind, Samantha. *Raphael Soyer and the Search for Modern Jewish Art*. Chapel Hill: University of North Carolina Press, 2004.

Baudelaire, Charles. 'The Painter of Modern Life', in *The Painter of Modern Life and Other Essays*. Trans. J. Mayne (ed.). London: Phaidon, 1995, pp. 1–41.

Beckett, Samuel. 'An Imaginative Work!', *The Dublin Magazine* (July–September 1936), pp. 80–1.

Bender, Thomas. 'New York City, 1910–1935, the politics and aesthetics of two modernities', in S. Spier (ed.), *Urban Visions: Experiencing and Envisioning the City*. Liverpool: Liverpool University Press, 2002, pp. 77–108.

Benjamin, Walter. *Charles Baudelaire: A Lyric Poet in the Era of High Capitalism*. London: NLB, 1973.

Benjamin, Walter. *The Arcades Project*. Trans. H. Eiland and K. McLaughlin. R. Tiedemann (ed.). Cambridge, MA: Belknap Press, 2002.

Bermingham, Ann. 'Urbanity and the spectacle of art', in J. Chandler and K. Gilmartin (eds), *Romantic Metropolis: The Urban Scene of British Culture, 1780–1840*. Cambridge: Cambridge University Press, 2005, pp. 151–76.

Berrey, Lester V. and Melvin van der Bark. *The American Thesaurus of Slang: A Complete Reference Book of Colloquial Slang*. London: Harrap, 1954.

Bhreathnach-Lynch, Síghle. 'Framing Ireland's history: art, politics and representation', in J. C. Steward (ed.), *When Time Began to Rant and Rage: Figurative Painting from Twentieth Century Ireland*. London: Merell Holberton, 1998, pp. 40–51.

Bielenberg, Andy. 'Late Victorian elite formation and philanthropy: the making of Edward Guinness', *Studia Hibernica* 32 (2002/2003), 133–54.

Bissell, William Cunningham. 'Engaging colonial nostalgia', *Cultural Anthropology* 40:2 (2005), 215–48.

Blackburn, Henry (ed.). *Academy Notes 1895, with Facsimiles of Sketches by the Artists*. London: Chatto and Windus, 1895.

Blumin, Stuart M. *The Encompassing City: Streetscapes in Early Modern Art and Culture*. Manchester: Manchester University Press, 2008.

Bodkin, Thomas. *Four Irish Landscape Painters*. Dublin: The Talbot Press, 1920.

Boland, Mary Jane. 'Visualizing the city: images of Ireland's urban world, c.1790–1820', in G. Laragy, O. Purdue, and J. J. Wright (eds), *Urban Spaces in Nineteenth-century Ireland*. Liverpool: Liverpool University Press, 2018, pp. 162–82.

Boran, Pat and Gerard Smith (eds). *If Ever You Go: A Map of Dublin in Poetry and Song*. Dublin: Dedalus Press, 2014.

Boskamp, Ulrike and S. Annette Kranen. 'Drawing the Dardanelles: art history and mobility studies', in A. A. Kjaerulff, S. Kesselring, P. Peters and K. Hannam (eds), *Envisioning Networked Urban Mobilities: Art, Performances, Impacts* (Routledge eBook, 2018), pp. 109–22.

Bourke, Marie. *The Story of Irish Museums, 1790–2000: Culture, Identity and Education*. Cork: Cork University Press, 2011.

Boutin, Aimée. 'Rethinking the flâneur: flânerie and the senses', *Dix–Neuf* 16:2, 124–32. DOI: 10.1179/dix.2012.16.2.01.

Boutros, Alexander and Will Straw. *Circulation and the City: Essays on Urban Culture*. Montreal: McGill-Queen's University Press, 2010.

Boym, Svetlana. *The Future of Nostalgia*. New York: Basic Books, 2001.

Brady, Joseph. *Dublin in the 1950s and 1960s: Cars, Shops and Suburbs*. Dublin: Four Courts Press, 2017.

Brady, Joseph and Anngret Simms (eds). *Dublin through Space and Time (c.900–1900)*. Dublin: Four Courts Press, 2001.

Brady Hampton, Jill. 'Ambivalent realism: May Laffan's "Flitters, Tatters, and the Counsellor"', *New Hibernia Review* 12:2 (2008), 127–41.

Bramen, Carrie Tirado. 'The urban picturesque and the spectacle of Americanization', *American Quarterly* 52:3 (2000), 444–77. www.jstor.org/stable/30041857.

Brazen, Robert. 'Sean O'Casey's Dublin trilogy and the "promise" of metropolitan modernity', *Studies in the Literary Imagination* 41:1 (2008), 21–46.

Brown, Rita. 'Painting the military–art into history, Ireland 1780–1930.' MPhil Diss., Trinity College Dublin, 2008.

Brown, Stephanie and Sara Dodd. 'The Society of Female Artists and the song of the sisterhood', in P. Barlow and C. Todd (eds), *Governing Cultures: Art Institutions in Victorian London*. Aldershot: Ashgate, 2000, pp. 86–96.

Brown, Terence. 'Dublin in twentieth–century writing: metaphor and subject', *Irish University Review* 8:1 (1978), 7–21.

Brown, Terence. 'The Edwardian condition of Ireland', in B. Cliff and N. Grene (eds), *Synge and Edwardian Ireland*. Oxford: Oxford University Press, 2013, pp. 9–19.

Bryan, Michael and George Charles Williamson. 'Osborne, Walter P' in *Bryan's Dictionary of Painters and Engravers*. New York: The Macmillan Company; London: George Hill and Sons, 1904. https://archive.org/details/bryansdiction04brya.

Bryant, Julius. *Kenwood: Paintings in the Iveagh Bequest*. Swindon: English Heritage, 2003.

Buckley, David. *From Bow to Biennale: Artists of the East London Group*. London: Francis Boutle Publishers, 2013.

Butler, Patricia. *The Brocas Collection: An Illustrated Selective Catalogue of Original Watercolours, Prints and Drawings in The National Library of Ireland*. Dublin: National Library of Ireland, 1997.

Butler, Patricia. *The Silent Companion: An Illustrated History of the Watercolour Society of Ireland*. Woodbridge: Antique Collectors' Club, 2010.

Calabrese, Omar. *Artists' Self-portraits*. Trans. Marguerite Shore. New York and London: Abbeville Press Publishers, 2006.

Campbell, Julian. 'Postcards from Brittany: Walter Osborne's wallet of photographs.' *Irish Arts Review Yearbook* 17 (2010), 150–5.

Cappock, Margarita. 'Dublin divided: September 1913', in L. Sisley and M. Cappock (eds), *Dublin Divided: September 1913*. Dublin: Dublin City Gallery the Hugh Lane, 2013, pp. 23–56

Carville, Justin. 'The city and the body in the archive: photography, history, and the representation of Dublin 1860–1922.' PhD Diss., Dublin City University, 2005.

Carville, Justin. 'Introduction: visual vulture and the making of modern Dublin', in J. Carville (ed.), *Visualizing Dublin: Visual Culture, Modernity and the Representation of Urban Space*. Bern and Oxford: Peter Lang, 2014, pp. 1–21.

Carville, Justin. 'The glad smile of God's sunlight': photography and the imaginative geography of Darkest Dublin', in J. Carville (ed.), *Visualizing Dublin: Visual Culture, Modernity and the Representation of Urban Space*. Bern and Oxford: Peter Lang, 2014, pp. 181–202.

Casey, Christine. *Dublin: The City within the Grand and Royal Canals and the Circular Road with the Phoenix Park*. New Haven: Yale University Press, 2005.

Clark, T. J. *The Painting of Modern Life: Paris in the Art of Manet and his Followers*. New Jersey: Princeton University Press, 1999.

Clark, T. J. 'Lowry's other England', in T. J. Clark and A. M. Wagner (eds), *Lowry and the Painting of Modern Life*. London: Tate Publishing, 2013, pp. 21–73.

Clayson, H. 'Painting the traffic in women', in V. R. Schwartz and J. M. Przblyski (eds), *The Nineteenth Century Visual Culture Reader*. Routledge: New York and London, 2004, pp. 299–312.

Cleary, Joe. 'Amongst empires: a short history of Ireland and empire studies in international context', *Éire–Ireland* 42:1&2 (2007), 11–57.

Codell, Julie F. 'Artists' professional societies: production, consumption, and aesthetics', in B. Allen (ed.), *Towards a Modern Art World*. New Haven: Yale University Press, 1995, pp. 169–88.

Conway, Hazel. *People's Parks: The Design and Development of Victorian Parks in Britain*. Cambridge: Cambridge University Press, 1991.

Cooper, Tarnya. *Paper Cities: Topography and Imagination in Urban Europe c.1490–1780*. London: UCL Art Collections, 2003.

Corlett, Christian. *Darkest Dublin*. Dublin: Royal Society of Antiquaries, 2008.

Cosgrave, Ephraim MacDowel. 'A contribution towards a catalogue of nineteenth-century engravings of Dublin', *The Journal of the Royal Society of Antiquaries* 5:36 (1906), 400–19.

Cosgrave, Ephraim MacDowel. 'A contribution towards a catalogue of nineteenth-century engravings of Dublin (continued)', *The Journal of the Royal Society of Antiquaries*, 5:37 (1907), 41–60.

Cosgrave, Ephraim MacDowel. 'Old Dublin, as represented in engravings', *Handbook to the City of Dublin and the Surrounding District, Prepared for the Meeting of the British Association*. Dublin: University Press, 1908.

Coughlin, Jack. 'The engravings of Estella Solomons', in L. Miller (ed.), *Retrospect: The Work of Seumas O'Sullivan 1879–1958 & Estella F. Solomons 1882–1968*. Dublin: Dolmen Editions, 1973, pp. 46–8.

Coulter, Riann. 'Irish exhibition of living art', in C. Marshall and P. Murray (eds), *Twentieth Century, Art and Architecture of Ireland*, vol. V. New Haven and Dublin: Yale University Press in association with the Royal Irish Academy, 2014, pp. 134–9.

Craig, Maurice. *Dublin 1660–1860*. London: Penguin, 1992.

Cresswell, Tim. *Place: A Short Introduction*. Oxford: Blackwell, 2004.

Cresswell, Tim. *On the Move: Mobility in the Modern Western World*. London: Routledge, 2006.

Crinson, Mark. 'Georgianism and the tenements, Dublin 1908–1926', *Art History* 29:4 (2006), 625–59. DOI 10.1111/j.1467-8365.2006.00518.x.

Crookshank, Anne and the Knight of Glin. *Ireland's Painters 1600–1940*. New Haven and London: Yale University Press from the Mellon Centre for Studies in British Art, 2002.

Crookshank, Anne and the Knight of Glin. *The Watercolours of Ireland: Works on Paper in Pencil, Pastel and Paint: c.1600–1914*. London: Barrie and Jenkins, 1994.

Crossman, Virginia. 'Cribbed, contained and confined? The care of children under the Irish Poor Law, 1850–1920', in M. Luddy and J. Smith (eds), *Children, Childhood and Irish Society, 1500– Present*. Dublin: Four Courts Press, 2014.

Cullen, Fintan. *Ireland on Show: Art, Union, and Nationhood*. Aldershot: Ashgate, 2012.

Cusack, Tricia. 'Crossing the Shannon: Ireland's "mighty stream"', *Visual Culture in Britain* 3:1 (2002), 77–97.

Cusack, Tricia. '"A living art": Jack Yeats, travelling west and the critique of modernity', in Y. Scott (ed.), *Jack B. Yeats: Old and New Departures*. Dublin: Four Courts Press, 2008, pp. 69–83.

Cusack, Tricia. *Riverscapes and National Identities*. Syracuse: Syracuse University Press, 2010.

Cusack, Tricia. 'Introduction: exploring the water's edge', in T. Cusack (ed.), *Art and Identity at the Water's Edge*. Aldershot: Ashgate, 2012, pp. 1–20

D'Souza, Aruna and Tom McDouough (eds). *The Invisible Flâneuse: Gender, Public Space* and *Visual Culture in Nineteenth Century Paris*. Manchester: Manchester University Press, 2006.

Daly, Mary. *The Deposed Capital: A Social and Economic History 1860–1914*. Cork: Cork University Press, 1984.

Daly, Mary. 'Housing conditions and the genesis of housing reform in Dublin, 1880–1920', in M. J. Bannon (ed.), *The Emergence of Irish Planning 1880–1920*. Dublin: Turoe Press, 1985, pp. 77–130.

Daly, Mary. 'An alien institution? Attitudes towards the city in nineteenth and twentieth century Irish Society', *Etudes Irlandaises* 10 (1985), 181–94.

Daly, Mary. 'Irish urban history: an agenda', *Urban History*, 13 (1986), 61–72.

Darwin, John. *The Empire Project: The Rise and Fall of the British World-System, 1830–1970*. Cambridge: Cambridge University Press, 2009.

Delaney, Enda. 'Directions in historiography: our island story? Towards a transnational history of late modern Ireland', *Irish Historical Studies* 37:148 (2011), 599–621.

Dennis, Richard. *Cities in Modernity: Representations and Productions of Metropolitan Space, 1840–1930*. Cambridge: Cambridge University Press, 2008.

Deutsch, R. 'Alienation in Berlin: Kirchner's street scenes', *Art in America* 71 (1983), 65–72.

Dickson, David. 'The state of Dublin's history', *Éire–Ireland* 45:1&2 (2010), 198–212. DOI 10.1353/eir.2010.0004.

Dickson, David. *Dublin: The Making of a Capital City*. London: Profile Books, 2014.

Dolan, Anne. 'Politics, economy and society in the Irish Free State, 1922–1939', in T. Bartlett (ed.), *Cambridge History of Ireland Vol. IV, 1880 – the Present*. Cambridge: Cambridge University Press, 2018, pp. 323–48.

Duffy, Shirely Armstrong. 'Late nineteenth century sketching clubs in Ireland.' BA Diss., Trinity College Dublin, 1984.

Eckett, Jane (ed.). *Art on the Move: Hidden Treasures from the CIÉ Art Collection*. Dublin: Córas Iompair Éireann, 2006.

Egerton, George. *The Wheel of Fortune*. New York and London: G. P. Putnam's Sons, 1898.

Elliott, David and Piotr Juszkiewicz. 'Socialist Realism', in *Grove Art Online. Oxford Art Online*. Oxford University Press. www.oxfordartonline.com/subscriber/article/grove/art/T079464.

Ellman, Richard. *James Joyce*. New York: Oxford University Press, 1959.

Elmes, Rosalind. *Catalogue of Irish Topographical Prints and Original Drawings*. Dublin: Malton Press from the National Library of Ireland Society, 1975

Emmons, Robert. *The Life and Opinions of Walter Sickert*. London: Faber and Faber, 1942.

Engle, Manfred. 'Erasing history – inscribing myth. The city in Joyce's *Portrait* and Woolf's *Mrs Dalloway*', in Y. Clavaron and B. Dieterle (eds), *La Mémoire de Villes/The Memory of Cities*. Saint-Étienne: Publications de l'Université de Saint-Étienne, 2003, pp. 367–78.

English, Bonnie. *A Cultural History of Fashion in the 20th Century*. Oxford and New York: Berg, 2007.

Evangelisti, Isabella. 'The nude in modern Irish art: Tradition and transgression.' PhD Diss., Trinity College Dublin, 2013.

Fallon, Brian. 'Estella Solomons, Painter', in L. Miller (ed.), *Retrospect: The Work of Seumas O'Sullivan 1879–1958 & Estella F. Solomons 1882–1968*. Dublin: Dolmen Editions, 1973, pp. 32–45.

Ferriter, Diarmaid. *Occasions of Sin: Sex and Society in Modern Ireland*. London: Profile, 2009.

Figgis, Nicola (ed.). *Painting 1600–1900, Art and Architecture of Ireland*, vol. II. New Haven and Dublin: Yale University Press in association with the Royal Irish Academy, 2014.

Figgis, Nicola. 'Barton, Rose Mary (1856–1929)', in N. Figgis (ed.), *Painting 1600–1900, Art and Architecture of Ireland*, vol. II. New Haven and Dublin: Yale University Press in association with the Royal Irish Academy, 2014, pp. 173–4.

Fitzpatrick, David. 'Ireland and the Empire', in Andrew Porter and Alaine Low (eds), *The Oxford History of the British Empire, Vol. III, The Nineteenth Century*. Oxford and New York: Oxford University Press, 1999, pp. 494–521.

Fitzpatrick Dean, Joan. 'Rewriting the past: historical pageantry in the Dublin civic weeks of 1927 and 1929', *New Hibernia Review*, 13:1 (2009), 20–41. DOI 10.1353/nhr.0.0053.

Fletcher, Pamela and Anne Helmreich (eds). *The Rise of the Modern Art Market in London, 1850–1939*. Manchester: Manchester University Press, 2011.

Forgione, Nancy. 'Everyday life in motion: the art of walking in late–nineteenth century Paris', *Art Bulletin*, 87 (2005), 664–87.

Foster, Roy. *Vivid Faces: The Revolutionary Generation in Ireland, 1890–1923*. London: Allen Lane, 2014.

Foster, Roy. ''The occupation of living': Jack B. Yeats and the Irish revolution', in B. Rooney (ed.), *Creating History: Stories of Ireland in Art*. Dublin: Irish Academic Press, 2016, pp. 251–73.

Frazier, Adrian. *George Moore, 1852–1933*. New Haven and London: Yale University Press, 2000.

Galavan, Susan. *Dublin's Bourgeois Homes: Building the Victorian Suburbs*. London: Routledge, 2017.

Gandal, Keith. *The Virtues of the Vicious: Jacob Riis, Stephen Crane, and the Spectacle of the Slum*. New York and Oxford: Oxford University Press, 1997.

Gillis, Liz. *The Fall of Dublin: 28 June to 5 July 1922*. Cork: Mercier Press, 2011.

Goodman, Susan T. *The Immigrant Generation: Jewish Artists in Britain, 1900–1945*. New York: Jewish Museum, 1983.

Gray, Donald J. 'Views and sketches of London in the nineteenth century', in I. B. Nadel and F. S. Schwarzbach (eds), *Victorian Artists and the City: A Collection of Critical Essays*. New York: Pergamon Press, 1980, pp. 43–58.

Gray, Peter and Olwen Purdue (eds). *The Irish Lord Lieutenancy, c.1541–1922*. Dublin: UCD Press, 2012.

Griffith, Angela. 'Impressions: Jack Yeats' approach to fine art printing', in Y. Scott (ed.), *Jack B Yeats: Old and New Departures*. Dublin: Four Courts Press, 2008, pp. 100–19.

Griffith, Angela. 'Making their mark: Irish Painter–Etchers and the Etching Revival', in A. Griffith and A. Hodge (eds), *Making their Mark: Irish Painter–Etchers and the Etching Revival*. Dublin: National Gallery of Ireland, 2019, pp. 14–31.

Gruetzner Robins, Anna (ed.). *Walter Sickert: The Complete Writings on Art*. Oxford: Oxford University Press, 2000.

Gwynn, Stephen. 'Walter Osborne and Ireland 1859–1903', *Studies: An Irish quarterly review*, 32:108 (1943), 463–6.

Hanna, Erika. *Modern Dublin: Urban Change and the Irish Past, 1957–1973*. Oxford: Oxford University Press, 2013.

Hanna, Erika and Richard Butler. 'Irish urban history: an agenda', *Urban History*, 1:8 (2018), 2–9.

Harmon, Maurice. 'Introduction', in M. Harmon (ed.), *The Irish Writer and the City*. Gerrards Cross: Colin Smythe; Totowa: Barnes and Noble Books, 1984, pp. vii–viii.

Haxthausen, Charles W. 'Kirchner's images of Berlin', in C. W. Haxthausen and H. Suhr (eds), *Berlin: Culture and Metropolis*. Minneapolis: University of Minnesota Press, 1990, pp. 58–94.

Hayden, Dolores. *The Power of Place: Urban Landscapes as Public History*. Cambridge MA: The MIT Press, 1996.

Hayes, Gearóid Arthur. 'The portraits of Walter Frederick Osborne (1859–1903): A critical analysis.' MPhil Diss., Trinity College Dublin, 2018.

Heller, Reinhold. '"The city is dark": conceptions of urban landscape and life in expressionist painting and architecture', in G. B. Pickar and K. E. Webb (eds), *Expressionism Reconsidered: Relationships and Affinities*. Munich: Wilhelm Fink Verlag, 1979, pp. 42–57.

Helmrich, Anne. 'Dynamic networks of circulation and exchange in Edwardian art', *Visual Culture in Britain*, 14:1 (2013), 36–54. DOI 10.1080/14714787.2013.750793.

Hemingway, Andrew. *Artists on the Left: American Artists and the Communist Movement 1926–1956*. New Haven: Yale University Press, 2002.

Hemingway, Andrew (ed.). *Marxism and the History of Art: From William Morris to the New Left*. London: Pluto Press, 2006.

Hill, Judith. *Irish Public Sculpture: A History*. Dublin: Four Courts Press, 1998.

Hills, Patricia. 'The socially concerned painters of the 1930s: an introduction', in *Social Concern and Urban Realism: American Painting in the 1930s*. Boston: Boston University Art Gallery, 1983, pp. 103–24.

Hobsbawm, Eric. 'Introduction: inventing tradition', in E. Hobsbawn and T. Ranger (eds), *The Invention of Tradition*. Cambridge: Cambridge University Press, 1983, pp. 1–14.

Hogan, David [*pseud.* F. Gallahger]. *Four Glorious Years*. Dublin: Irish Press, 1953.

Holt, Ysanne. 'The Camden Town Group: then and now', in H. Bonett, Y. Holt, and J. Mundy, *The Camden Town Group in Context*, Tate Online Research Publication, May 2012, www.tate.org.uk/art/research-publications/camden-town-group/ysanne-holt-the-camden-town-group-then-and-now- r1105679#f_1_37.

Horgan, Mervyn. 'Anti-urbanism as a way of life: disdain for Dublin in the nationalist imaginary', *The Canadian Journal of Irish Studies*, 30:2 (2004), 38–47.

House, John. 'The Impressionist vision of London', in I. B. Nadel and F. S. Schwarzbach (eds), *Victorian Artists and the City: A Collection of Critical Essays*. New York: Pergamon Press, 1980, pp. 78–90.

Humphrys, Gerard and Ciaran Craven. *Introduction to Military Law in Ireland*. Dublin: Round Hall, Sweet & Maxwell, 1997.

Hutton, Molly S. 'Walking in the city at the turn of the century: John Sloan's pedestrian aesthetics', in H. C. Coyle and J. K. Schiller (eds), *John Sloan's New York*. Delaware: Delaware Art Museum in association with Yale University Press, 2007, pp. 82–115.

Jackson, Alvin. 'Ireland, the Union, and the Empire, 1800–1960', in K. Kenny (ed.), *Ireland and the British Empire*. Oxford: Oxford University Press, 2004, pp. 123–81.

Jacobs, Jane M. *Edges of Empire: Postcolonialism and the City*. London: Routledge, 1996.

Johnson, E. D. H. 'Victorian artists and the urban milieu', in H. J. Dyos and M. Wolff (eds), *The Victorian City: Images and Realities*, vol. II. London: Routledge, 1973, pp. 449–74.

Joyce, James. *Ulysses*. London: Penguin, 2000.

Joyce, James. *A Portrait of the Artist as a Young Man*, ed. H. W. Gabler and W. Hettche. London: Vintage, 2012.

Joyce, James. *Dubliners*, ed. M. Norris. New York and London: W. W. Norton & Co., 2006.

Kahn, Andrea. 'Imaging New York: representations and perceptions of the city', in P. Masden and R. Plunz (eds), *The Urban Lifeworld: Formation, Perception and Representation*. London and New York: Routledge, 2002, pp. 237–51.

Kavanagh, Patrick. *Collected poems*, ed. Antoinette Quinn. London: Penguin, 2005.

Kearney, Hugh F. *Ireland: Contested Ideas of Nationalism and History*. Cork: Cork University Press, 2007.

Kearns, Kevin C. *Dublin Pub Life and Lore: An Oral History*. Dublin: Gill and Macmillan, 1996.

Kearns, Kevin C, ed. *Dublin Tenement Life: An Oral History*. Dublin: Gill and Macmillan, 2006.

Kennedy, Róisín. *Dublin Castle Art: The Historical and Contemporary Collection*. Dublin: Stationery Office, 1999.

Kennedy, Róisín. 'Divorcing Jack … from Irish politics', in Y. Scott (ed.), *Jack B. Yeats: Old and New Departures*. Dublin: Four Courts Press, 2008, pp. 33–46.

Kennedy, Róisín. 'Jack Yeats and Dublin', in D. J. Foley (ed.), *The Only Art of Jack B. Yeats: Letters and Essays*. Dublin: The Lilliput Press, 2009, pp. 150–8.

Kennedy, Róisín. 'Transmitting avant-garde art: post-impressionism in a Dublin context', *Visual Resources*, 31:1–2 (2015), 61–73. DOI 10.1080/01973762.2015.1004780.

Kennedy, Samuel Brian. *Irish Art and Modernism 1880–1950*. Belfast: Institute of Irish Studies, 1991.

Keogh, Dermot. *Jews in Twentieth-century Ireland: Refugees, Anti-Semitism and the Holocaust*. Cork: Cork University Press, 1998.

Kiberd, Declan. 'The city in Irish culture', in D. Kiberd (ed.), *The Irish Writer and the World*. Cambridge: Cambridge University Press, 2005, pp. 289–302.

Kissane, Bill. *The Politics of the Irish Civil War*. Oxford: Oxford University Press, 2005.

Kosk, Heinz. 'The image of Dublin in Anglo–Irish drama', in M. Harmon (ed.), *The Irish Writer and the City*. Gerrards Cross: Colin Smythe; Totowa: Barnes and Noble Books, 1984, pp. 18–36.

Krielkamp, Vera. '*Going to the levée* as ascendancy spectacle: alternative narratives in Irish painting', in A. Dalsimer (ed.), *Visualizing Ireland: National Identity and the Pictorial Tradition*. Boston and London: Faber and Faber, 1993, pp. 37–54.

Laffan, May. *Flitters, Tatters and the Counsellor and Other Sketches*. London: Macmillan and Co., 1881.

Laffan, William 'Buying, Selling and Exhibiting Art in Ireland, c.1700–c.1900', in N. Figgis (ed.), *Painting 1600–1900, Art and Architecture of Ireland*, vol. II. New Haven and Dublin: Yale University Press in association with the Royal Irish Academy, 2014, pp. 17–22.

Lane, Leeann. 'George Russell and James Stephens: class and cultural discourse, Dublin

1913', in F. Devine (ed.), *A Capital in Conflict: Dublin City and the 1913 Lockout.* Dublin: Dublin City Council, 2013, pp. 333–52.

Lanigan, Liam. 'The revival and the city in James Stephen's Dublin fiction', UCDScholarcast Series 12, in G. Bruna and C. Wilsdon (eds), *Modalities of Revival*, 2015. www.ucd.ie/scholarcast/transcripts/Revival_and_the_city.pdf.

Lanigan, Liam. *James Joyce, Urban Planning and Irish Modernism: Dublins of the Future.* London: Palgrave Macmillan, 2014.

Langa, Helen. *Radical Art: Printmaking and the Left in 1930s New York.* Berkeley: University of California Press, 2004.

Laughton, Bruce. *The Euston Road School: A Study in Objective Painting.* Aldershot: Scolar Press, 1986.

Loughery, John. 'John Sloan: the artist in modern life', in D. J. Foley (ed.), *The Only Art of Jack B. Yeats: Letters and Essays.* Dublin: The Lilliput Press, 2009, pp. 46–51.

Lucie-Smith, Edward. *American Realism.* London: Thames and Hudson, 2002.

Luddy, Maria. *Women and Philanthropy in Nineteenth Century Ireland.* Cambridge: Cambridge University Press, 1995.

Luddy, Maria. 'Sex and the single girl in 1920s and 1930s Ireland', *The Irish Review*, 35 (2007), 79–91.

Luddy, Maria. *Prostitution and Irish Society, 1800–1940.* Cambridge: Cambridge University Press, 2007.

Lynch, Brendan. *Parsons Bookshop: At the Heart of Bohemian Dublin 1949–1989.* Dublin: The Liffey Press, 2006.

MacColl, D. S. *The Administration of the Chantrey Bequest.* London: Grant Richards, 1904.

Mackenzie, John M. 'Empire and metropolitan cultures', in A. Porter and A. Low (eds), *The Oxford History of the British Empire, Vol. III, The Nineteenth Century.* Oxford and New York: Oxford University Press, 1999, pp. 270–93.

Maguire. M. *Precarious Childhood in Post-independence Ireland.* Manchester: Manchester University Press, 2009.

Mannion, Elizabeth. *The Urban Plays of the Early Abbey Theatre: Beyond O'Casey.* Syracuse: Syracuse University Press, 2014.

Mannion, Sean. 'Celtic arc light: the electric light in early twentieth century Dublin', in J. Carville (ed.), *Visualizing Dublin: Visual Culture, Modernity and the Representation of Urban Space.* Bern and Oxford: Peter Lang, 2014, pp. 111–31.

Marcus, Laura. *Dreams of Modernity: Psychoanalysis, Literature and Cinema.* Cambridge: Cambridge University Press, 2014.

Mark-Fitzgerald, Emily. *Commemorating the Irish Famine: Memory and the Monument.* Liverpool: Liverpool University Press, 2013.

Marshall, Nancy Rose. *City of Gold and Mud: Painting Victorian London.* New Haven and London: Published for the Paul Mellon Centre for Studies in British Art by Yale University Press, 2012.

Marstine, J. 'Eight, the (ii).' *Oxford Art Online. Grove Art Online.* Oxford University Press. www.oxfordartonline.com/subscriber/article/grove/art/T025690.

Mayne, Alan. *The Imagined Slum: Newspaper Representation in Three Cities, 1870–1914.* Leicester: Leicester University Press, 1993.

McAuley, Eve. 'The origins and early development of the Pembroke estate beyond the Grand Canal, 1860–1880.' PhD Diss., Trinity College Dublin, 2004.

McEvansoneya, Philip. 'Ireland on show: art, union, and nationhood', *Irish Studies Review*, 21:2 (2013), 231–3. DOI 10.1080/09670882.2013.777617.

McIntosh, Gillian. 'Children, street trading and the representation of public space in Edwardian Ireland', in M. Luddy and J. M. Smith (eds), *Children, Childhood and Irish Society, 1500 to the Present*. Dublin: Four Courts Press, 2014, pp. 46–64.

McMahon, Timothy G. *Grand Opportunity: The Gaelic Revival and Irish Society, 1893–1910*. Syracuse: Syracuse University Press, 2008.

McManus, Ruth. *Dublin 1910–1940: Shaping the City & Suburbs*. Dublin: Four Courts Press, 2002.

McManus, Ruth. *Such Happy Harmony: Early Twentieth Century Co–operation to Solve Dublin's Housing Problems*. Dublin: Dublin City Public Libraries, 2005.

Michalski, David. 'Portals to metropolis: 19th–century guidebooks and the assemblage of urban experience', *Tourist Studies* 4 (2004), 187–215.

Milligan, Kathryn. 'Edmond Delrenne: Witness to 1916', *Irish Arts Review* 32:4 (2015), 558–61.

Milligan, Kathryn. 'The Cultural Cost of 1916: The Property Losses (Ireland) Committee and the Royal Hibernian Academy', for Inspiring Ireland Project, Digital Repository of Ireland, May 2016: http://inspiring–ireland.ie/cultural-cost-of–1916–property-losses–ireland–committee–and–royal–hibernian–academy.

Milligan, Kathryn. 'Harry Clarke and *The Dublin Magazine*', in A. Griffith, M. Helmers, and R. Kennedy (eds), *Harry Clarke and Artistic Visions of the New Irish State*. Dublin: Irish Academic Press, 2018, pp. 180–200.

Milligan, Kathryn. 'Royal Visits to Dublin, 1821–1911: Pier, Procession, Presence Chamber', in M. Campbell and W. Derham (eds), *Making Majesty: The Throne Room at Dublin Castle, A Cultural History*. Dublin: Irish Academic Press, 2018, pp. 200–35.

Milne, Kenneth. *The Dublin Liberties, 1600–1850*. Dublin: Four Courts Press, 2009.

Moynahan, Julian. 'The image of the city in nineteenth century Irish fiction', in M. Harmon (ed.), *The Irish Writer and the City*. Gerrards Cross: Colin Smythe; Totowa: Barnes and Noble, 1984, pp. 1–17.

Murphy, D. J. (ed.). *Lady Gregory's Journals, Volume II, Books Thirty to Forty–four, 21 February 1925–9 May 1932*. Gerrards Cross: Colin Smythe, 1987.

Murphy, Paula. *Nineteenth Century Irish Sculpture: Native Genius Reaffirmed*. New Haven and London: Paul Mellon Centre for Studies in British Art and Yale University Press, 2010.

Murray, Paul. 'The Irish Race Congress, 21–28 January 1922', *History Ireland*, 9:4 (2001), 8–9.

Nead, Linda. *Victorian Babylon: People, Streets and Images in Nineteenth Century London*. New Haven: Yale University Press, 2005.

Newell, Christopher. *Victorian Watercolours*. London: Phaidon, 1987.

O'Brien, Gillian and Finola O'Kane. 'Portrait of the city: framing the significance of urban landscapes', in G. O'Brien and F. O'Kane (eds), *Portraits of the City: Dublin and the Wider World*. Dublin: Four Courts Press, 2012, pp. 17–21.

O'Brien, Joseph V. *Dear, Dirty Dublin: A City in Distress, 1899–1916*. Berkeley: University of California Press, 1982

O'Connor, Éimear. 'America called: the Helen Hackett Gallery and the Irish Art Rooms, 1924–1934', *New Hibernia Review* 15:4 (2011), 16–33.

O'Connor, Éimear. *Seán Keating: Art, Politics, and Building the Irish Nation*. Dublin: Irish Academic Press, 2013.

Ó Gráda, Cormac. *Jewish Ireland in the Age of Joyce: A Socioeconomic History*. Princeton: Princeton University Press, 2006.

Ó Gráda, Cormac. "Because she never let them in': Irish immigration a century ago and today', UCD Centre for Economic Research Working Paper Series: WP/13/19. www.ucd.ie/t4cms/WP13_19.pdf.

O'Neill, Ciaran and M. Yatani. Women, ambition, and the city, 1890–1910', in A. Pilz and W. Standlee (eds), *Irish Women's Writing, 1878–1922: Advancing the Cause of Liberty*. Manchester: Manchester University Press, 2016, pp. 100–20.

O'Sullivan, Seumas. *Mud and Purple: Pages from the Diary of a Dublin Man*. Dublin: The Talbot Press; London: T. Fisher Unwin: 1918.

O'Sullivan, Seumas. *The Rose and Bottle and Other Essays*. Dublin: The Talbot Press, 1946.

O'Toole, Fintan. 'Going west: the country versus the city in Irish writing', *The Crane Bag*, 9:2 (1985), 111–16.

Ó Tuathaigh, Gearóid. 'Ireland and Britain under the Union, 1800–1921', in P. J. Drudy (ed.), *Ireland and Britain Since 1922*. Cambridge: Cambridge University Press, 1986, pp. 1–20.

Ó Tuathaigh, Gearóid. 'Introduction: Ireland 1880–2016: Negotiating Sovereignty and Freedom', in T. Bartlett (ed.), *The Cambridge History of Ireland, Vol. IV, 1800 to the present*. Cambridge: Cambridge University Press, 2018, pp. 1–32.

Oehler, Sarah Kelly. *They Seek a City: Chicago and the Art of Migration 1910–1950*. Chicago: The Art Institute of Chicago, distributed by Yale University Press, New Haven and London, 2013.

Ollerenshaw, Philip. 'Neutrality and belligerence: Ireland, 1939–1945', in T. Bartlett (ed.), *Cambridge History of Ireland: Vol. IV, 1800–present*. Cambridge: Cambridge University Press, 2017, pp. 340–78.

Pašeta, Senia. *Irish Nationalist Women, 1900–1918*. Cambridge: Cambridge University Press, 2016.

Peters Corbett, David. 'Seeing in modernity: Walter Sickert's music hall scenes, c.1887–1907 and English modernism', *Modernism/Modernity*, 7:2 (2000), 285–306. DOI 10.1353/mod.2000.0043.

Peters Corbett, David. 'Camden Town and Ashcan: difference, similarity, and the "Anglo–American" in the work of Walter Sickert and John Sloan', in D. P. Corbett and S. Monks (eds), *Anglo–American: Artistic Exchange between Britain and the USA*. Chichester: Wiley Blackwell, 2012, pp. 152–73.

Peters Corbett, David. 'City visions: the urban scene in Camden Town Group painting', in H. Bonnet, Y. Holt, and J. Mundy, *The Camden Town Group in Context*. Tate Online Research Publication, May 2012. www.tate.org.uk/art/research-publications/camden-town-group/david-peters-corbett-city-visions-the-urban-scene-in-camden-town-group-and-ashcan-school-r1104351.

Peters Corbett, David and Lara Perry (eds), *English Art 1860–1914: Modern Artists and Identity*. Manchester: Manchester University Press, 2000.

Pickering, Michael and Emily Keightley. 'The modalities of nostalgia', *Current Sociology*, 54 (2006), 919–41. DOI 10.1177/0011392106068458.

Pollock, Griselda. *Vision and Difference: Feminism, Femininity and the Histories of Art*. London: Routledge, 2013.

Postle, Martin. 'Behind the screen: the studio model', in M. Postle and W. Vaughan (eds), *The Artist's Model from Etty to Spencer*. London: Merrell Holberton, 1999, pp. 55–64.

Potts, Alex. 'Picturing the modern metropolis: images of London in the nineteenth century', *History Workshop*, 26 (1988), 28–56.

Prunty, Jacinta. *Dublin Slums 1800–1925: A Study an Urban Geography*. Dublin: Irish Academic Press, 1998.

Prunty, Jacinta. 'Improving the urban environment: public health and housing in nineteenth century Dublin', in J. Brady and A. Simms (eds), *Dublin Through Space and Time*. Dublin: Four Courts Press, 2001, pp. 166–220.

Prunty, Jacinta. 'The townhouse as tenement in nineteenth–and early twentieth–century Dublin', in C. Casey (ed.), *The Eighteenth-century Dublin Town House: Form, Function, and Finance*. Dublin: Four Courts Press, 2010, pp. 149–73.

Pyle, Hilary. *Estella Solomons: Portraits of Patriots*. Dublin: Allen Figgis and Company, 1966.

Pyle, Hilary. *Jack B. Yeats: A Biography*. London: Routledge and Kegan Paul, 1989.

Pyle, Hilary. *Jack B. Yeats: A Catalogue Raisonné of the Oil Paintings*, vols. I–III. London: Deutsch, 1992.

Pyle, Hilary. 'Notes from Estella.' *Irish Arts Review*, 25:1 (2008), 96–9.

Pyne, Kathleen. 'Whistler and the politics of the urban picturesque', *American Art*, 8:3&4 (1994), 61–77.

Rains, Stephanie. *Commodity Culture and Social Class in Dublin 1850–1916*. Dublin: Irish Academic Press, 2010.

Rains, Stephanie. 'City streets and the city edition: newsboys and newspapers in early twentieth-century Ireland', *Irish Studies Review*, 24:2 (2016), 142–58. DOI 10.1080/09670882.2016.1153239.

Regan, John M. and Mike Cronin. 'Introduction: Ireland and the politics of independence 1922–49, new perspectives and re–considerations', in J. M. Regan and M. Cronin (eds), *Ireland: The Politics of Independence, 1922–49*. London: Macmillan, 2000, pp. 1–12.

Reznicek, Matthew. *The European Metropolis: Paris and Nineteenth-century Irish Women Novelists*. Clemson: Clemson University Press, 2017.

Rosenblatt, Stuart. *Alien Registration File 1914–1922 (A Police Record, Chancery Lane, Dublin, Ireland): Ada Shillman (Midwife) Birth Records, Dublin 1893–1908*. Dublin: The Jewish Genealogical Society, 2005.

Rouse, Paul. 'Popular culture in Ireland, 1880–2016', in T. Bartlett (ed.), *The Cambridge History of Ireland Vol. IV, 1800 to the Present*. Cambridge: Cambridge University Press, 2018, pp. 577–603.

Rowley, Ellen. *Housing, Architecture and the Edge Condition: Dublin is Building, 1935–1975*. London: Routledge, 2018.

Ryan, John. 'Harry Kernoff RHA', in *Harry Kernoff: A Selection of Dublin Paintings*, Dublin: Godolphin Gallery, 1974, n.p.

Ryan, John. *Remembering how we Stood: Bohemian Dublin at the Mid-century*. New York: Taplinger Publishing Co., 1975.

Ryan, Louise. 'Negotiating modernity and tradition: newspaper debates on the "modern girl" in the Irish Free State', *Journal of Gender Studies*, 7:2 (1998), 181–97. DOI 10.1080/09589236.1998.9960711.

Schiller, Joyce K. and Heather Campbell Coyle. 'John Sloan's urban encounters', in J. K.

Schiller and H. Campbell (eds), *John Sloan's New York*. Delaware: Delaware Art Museum in association with Yale University Press, 2007, pp. 22–81.

Schlör, Joachim. *Nights in the Big City: Paris, Berlin, London 1840–1930*. London: Reaktion, 1998.

Schönfeld, C. 'Streetwalking the metropolis: prostitutes in Expressionism', in C. Schönfeld (ed.), *Commodities of Desire: the Prostitute in Modern German Literature* (Woodbridge: Camden House, 2000), pp. 110–30.

Shapiro, Theda. 'The Metropolis in the visual arts: Paris, Berlin, New York, 1840– 1940', in A. Sutcliff (ed.), *Metropolis 1890–1940*. London: Mansell, 1984, pp. 95–128.

Sharpe, William Chapman. *New York Nocturne: The City after Dark in Literature, Painting, and Photography, 1850–1950*. Princeton: Princeton University Press, 2008.

Sheehy, Jeanne. 'Walter Osborne.' MLitt Diss., Trinity College Dublin, 1971.

Sheehy, Jeanne. 'The flight from South Kensington: British artists at the Antwerp Academy 1877–1885', *Art History*, 20:1 (1997), 124–53.

Shields, Rob. *Places on the Margin; Alternative Geographies of Modernity*. London: Routledge, 1991.

Simmons, Sherwin. 'Ernst Kirchner's streetwalkers: art, luxury, and immorality in Berlin, 1913–1916', *The Art Bulletin*, 82:1 (2000), 117–48.

Sisson, Elaine. 'Experimentalism and the Irish stage: theatre and German Expressionism in the 1920s', in L. King and E. Sisson (eds), *Ireland, Design and Visual Culture: Negotiating Modernity, 1922–1992*. Cork: Cork University Press, 2011, pp. 39–55.

Sisson, Elaine. 'Designing Modernism: Harry Kernoff, Russia, and Post-independence Ireland', *Éire-Ireland*, 52:3&4 (2017), 31–56.

Sisson, Elaine. 'Experiment and the Free State: Mrs Cogley's cabaret and the founding of the Gate Theatre, 1924–1920', in D. Clare, D. Lally and P. Lonergan (eds), *The Gate Theatre, Dublin: Inspiration and Craft*. Dublin: Carysfort Press, 2018.

Slattery, Peader. 'The uses of photography in Ireland, 1832–1900.' PhD Diss., Trinity College Dublin, 1992.

Smyth, Sara and W. D. Hogan. 'Shooting for the state? Photos of the civil war', *Field Day Review*, 2 (2006), 128–53.

Snoddy, Theo. *Dictionary of Irish Artists: 20th Century*, 2nd edn. Dublin: Merlin Publishing, 2006.

Snyder, Robert W. 'The Ashcan Artists: journalism, art and metropolitan life', in P. Masden and R. Plunz (eds), *The Urban Lifeworld: Formation, Perception and Representation*. London and New York: Routledge, 2002, pp. 279–92.

Somerville-Large, Peter. *1854–2004 The Story of the National Gallery of Ireland*. Dublin: National Gallery of Ireland, 2004.

Standlee, Whitney. 'George Egerton, James Joyce and the Irish *Küstlerroman*', *Irish Studies Review*, 18 (2010), 439–52.

Stewart, Ann M. *Royal Hibernian Academy of Arts: Index of Exhibitors, 1826–1979*, vols I–III. Dublin: Manton Publishing, 1987.

Stewart, Ann M. *Irish Art Loan Exhibitions, 1765–1927*, vols I–III. Dublin: Manton Publishing, 1990.

Stewart, Ann M. *Irish Art Societies and Sketching Clubs: Index of Exhibitors, 1870–1980*, vols I–II. Dublin: Four Courts Press, 1997.

Strickland, Walter. *A Dictionary of Irish Artists*, vols I and II. Dublin: Irish Academic Press, 1989.

Tallack, Douglas. *New York Sights: Visualizing Old and New New York*. New York: Berg, 2005.

Taylor, Dorceta E. 'Central park as a model for social control: urban parks, social class, and leisure behaviour in nineteenth century America', *Journal of Leisure Research*, 3:4 (1999), 420–77.

Thacker, Andrew. *Moving Through Modernity: Space and Geography in Modernism*. Manchester: Manchester University Press, 2009.

Thomas, Greg M. 'Women in public in the parks of Paris', in A. D'Souza and T. McDonough (eds), *The Invisible Flâneuse? Gender, Public Space, and Visual Culture in Nineteenth Century Paris*. Manchester: Manchester University Press, 2006, pp. 32–48.

Todd, James G. 'Social realism.' *Grove Art Online. Oxford Art Online*. Oxford University Press. www.oxfordartonline.com/subscriber/article/grove/art/T079466.

Tompson, Richard S. *The Atlantic Archipelago: A Political History of the British Isles*. Lewiston: Edwin Mellen Press, 1986.

Treuherz, Julian. *Hard Times: Social Realism in Victorian Art*. London: Lund Humphries, in association with Manchester City Art Galleries, 1987.

Turpin, John. 'The RHA schools 1826–1906', *Irish Arts Review Yearbook* (1991/1992), 198–209.

Turpin, John. *A School of Art in Dublin Since the Eighteenth Century*. Dublin: Gill & Macmillan, 1995.

Turpin, John. 'Dublin art institutions', in N. Figgis (ed.), *Painting, 1600–1900, Art and Architecture of Ireland*, vol. II. Dublin and New Haven: Royal Irish Academy and Yale University Press, 2014, pp. 28–31.

Turpin, John. *History of the Royal Hibernian Academy of Arts*, vols 1&2. Dublin: Lilliput Press, 2018.

Vaughan, Will. 'London topographers and urban change', in I. B. Nadel and F. S. Schwarzbach (eds), *Victorian Artists and the City: A Collection of Critical Essays*. New York: Pergamon, 1980, pp. 59–77.

Wallace, Ciarán. 'Local politics and government in Dublin city and suburbs 1899–1914.' PhD Diss., Trinity College Dublin, 2010.

Wallace, Ciarán. 'Fighting for unionist Home Rule: competing identities in Dublin 1880–1929', *Journal of Urban History*, 38:5 (2012), 932–49. DOI 10.1177/0096144212449144.

Wallace, Ciarán. 'A bridge to the future: Hugh Lane's Municipal Gallery of Modern Art, 1913', in F. Devine (ed.), *A capital in conflict: Dublin City and the 1913 Lockout*. Dublin: Dublin City Council, 2013, pp. 261–80.

Waller, Susan S. *The Invention of the Model: Artists and Models in Paris, 1830–1870*. Aldershot: Ashgate, 2006.

Weisberg, Gabriel P. *Beyond Impressionism: The Naturalist Impulse in European Art 1860–1905*. London: Thames and Hudson, 1992.

Whelan, Yvonne. *Reinventing Modern Dublin: Streetscape, Iconography and the Politics of Identity*. Dublin: University of Dublin Press, 2003.

Whitford, Frank. 'The city in painting', in E. Timms and D. Kelley (eds), *Unreal City: Urban Experience in Modern European Literature and Arts*. Manchester: Manchester University Press, 1985, pp. 46–56.

Wilde, 'The decay of lying: an observation', in G. Brandreth (ed.), *Beautiful and Impossible Things: Selected Essays of Oscar Wilde*. London: Notting Hill Editions, 2015, pp. 73–120.

Wilson, Elizabeth. 'Looking backward, nostalgia and the city', in S. Westwood and

J. Williams (eds), *Imagining Cities: Scripts, Signs, Memory*. London: Routledge, 1997, pp. 127–39.

Wood, Christopher. *Victorian Panorama: Paintings of Victorian Life*. London: Faber and Faber, 1990.

Wood, Paul. 'Realisms and Realities', in B. Fer, D. Batchelor, and P. Wood (eds), *Realism, Rationalism and Surrealism: Art Between the Wars*. New Haven and London: Yale University Press in association with the Open University, 1993, pp. 250–331.

Wrigley, Richard. 'Unreliable witness: the *flâneur* as artist and spectator of art in nineteenth century Paris', *Oxford Art Journal*, 39:2 (2016), 267–84.

Wye, Deborah. *Kirchner and the Berlin Street*. New York: Museum of Modern Art; London: Thames and Hudson, 2009.

Yeates, Pádraig. *A City in Wartime: Dublin 1914–1918*. Dublin: Gill and Macmillan, 2011.

Yeates, Pádraig. *A City in Turmoil: Dublin 1919–21*. Dublin: Gill and Macmillan, 2012.

Yeates, Pádraig. '1913 – a country and a city at the crossroads', in L. Sisley and M. Cappock (eds), *Dublin Divided: September 1913*. Dublin: Dublin City Gallery the Hugh Lane, 2013, pp. 11–22.

Yeats, Jack B. *Modern Aspects of Irish Art*. Dublin: Brown and Nolan for Cumann Léigheacht an Phobail, 1922.

Zurier, Rebecca. *Picturing the City: Urban Vision and the Ashcan School*. Berkeley: University of California Press, 2006.

Index